MW01079015

Recent Titles in
PSI Guides to Terrorists, Insurgents, and Armed Groups

The ETIM: China's Islamic Militants and the Global Terrorist Threat
J. Todd Reed and Diana Raschke

The Phinehas Priesthood: Violent Vanguard of the Christian Identity
Movement
Danny W. Davis

The Militant Kurds: A Dual Strategy for Freedom
Vera Eccarius-Kelly

The Palestine Liberation Organization: Terrorism and Prospects for Peace
in the Holy Land
Daniel Baracskay

Armed for Life: The Army of God and Anti-Abortion Terror in the United
States
Jennifer Jefferis

The IRA: The Irish Republican Army
James Dingley

The Khmer Rouge: Ideology, Militarism, and the Revolution That
Consumed a Generation
Boraden Nhem

The Lord's Resistance Army
Lawrence E. Cline

17N's Philosophy of Terror: An Analysis of the 17 November Revolutionary
Organization
Ioanna K. Lekea

THE TALIBAN

Afghanistan's Most Lethal Insurgents

Mark Silinsky

Foreword by Raymond Taras

PSI Guides to Terrorists, Insurgents, and Armed Groups
James J. F. Forest, Series Editor

PRAEGER

AN IMPRINT OF ABC-CLIO, LLC
Santa Barbara, California • Denver, Colorado • Oxford, England

Library of Congress Cataloging-in-Publication Data

Silinsky, Mark.
    The Taliban : Afghanistan's most lethal insurgents / Mark Silinsky ; foreword by
Raymond Taras.
        pages cm. — (PSI guides to terrorists, insurgents, and armed groups)
    Includes bibliographical references and index.
    ISBN 978–0–313–39897–1 (hardcopy : alk. paper) — ISBN 978–0–313–39898–8
(ebook) 1. Taliban. 2. Islamic fundamentalism—Afghanistan. 3. Afghanistan—Politics
and government—1989–2001. I. Title.
DS371.3.S56   2014
958.104′7—dc23   2013046869

ISBN: 978–0–313–39897–1
EISBN: 978–0–313–39898–8

18 17 16 15   2 3 4 5

This book is also available on the World Wide Web as an eBook.
Visit www.abc-clio.com for details.

Praeger
An Imprint of ABC-CLIO, LLC

ABC-CLIO, LLC
130 Cremona Drive, P.O. Box 1911
Santa Barbara, California 93116-1911

This book is printed on acid-free paper (∞)

Manufactured in the United States of America

This book is dedicated to my wife, Nadia.
*I stood by you, and you stood by me,
and now we stand together . . . always.*

Contents

Foreword by Raymond Taras   ix

Preface   xiii

Introduction   xvii

Abbreviations   xix

1. Afghanistan's Landscape, the People, and Islamism   1

2. Enter the Taliban   19

3. The Taliban in Power   29

4. The Taliban in Defeat   45

5. The Taliban's Recovery in Pakistan   81

6. The Taliban Improve Their Tactics and Firepower   101

7. Taliban Inc.   127

8. Affiliated Insurgent Groups and Foreign Connections   137

9. The Counterinsurgency in Afghanistan   157

Afterword: Salafist Dystopia   185

Appendix: Coalition Military Fatalities by Year   189

Notes   191

Bibliography   247

Index   253

Foreword

A book about the Taliban in Afghanistan, written in a detached and dispassionate way and striving to deliver an objective balanced account that brings different perspectives to bear, is not a commonplace event. Yet it may be the case that the most effective way to expose a rogue and regressive insurgency movement like the Taliban—not all insurgencies have necessarily been retrograde—is to separate facts from norms in the analysis. Among other achievements of Mark Silinsky's erudite and detailed study is how it raises important methodological questions about the use of the canons of historical and social science inquiry to soberly frame an odious politico-religious phenomenon, one that is all too often vilified rather than surgically dissected.

The author's professional background in the military and in academic life gives him a unique vantage point from which to examine the Taliban. He allows that, in a historical context, the Taliban are not uniquely cruel. Indeed, compared to National Socialism and communism—two other twentieth-century totalitarian ideologies—he admits that the Taliban have killed far fewer innocent people and have rarely been charged by even its most uncompromising adversaries of being hell-bent on genocide.

This book narrates how Afghan politics and society, like those in neighboring Pakistan, which it also examines, comprise many ethnolinguistic clans and subclans, as well as multiple ethnosectarian orientations. Wahhabism from Saudi Arabia now takes its place alongside Deobandi philosophy, which had emerged out of the nationalistic and religious fervor that followed the 1857 Sepoy revolt in mid-nineteenth-century India. This "Indian Mutiny," which engaged many Muslims as well, constituted a backlash against the British-organized Indian civil service, European tastes and mannerisms, and spreading secularism among the educated Indian elite. Silinsky skillfully draws on this sequence of events (otherwise rarely associated with contemporary Afghan politics) to convincingly argue that the Taliban are inheritors of an old cultural tradition opposed to nearly all aspects of modernity, Western lifestyles and thought, and democratic norms.

The Taliban: Afghanistan's Most Lethal Insurgents goes beyond historical and ideological claims to suggest that the Taliban's Islamism fuses the most puritanical elements of Islam with modern technocratic means of governance. The nuanced analysis points out that Osama bin Laden and Mullah Omar did not share identical views of Islam but did strive for a common goal: each wanted to establish a totalitarian Islamist state. Whether it represents a fascistic objective, as other writers have alleged, is open to debate. But Silinsky impresses on the reader that Islamism's hostility to the West is not. His extensive array of documentary sources accordingly cites the Taliban spokesman who asserted, "We want to re-create the time of the Prophet."

With a deep knowledge of the military aspects of the Afghan conflict, Silinsky's candid assessment is that the Taliban have demonstrated out-of-the-ordinary military innovation, resilience, and resolve. Taliban toughness and adaptability were already apparent in early combat operations in the fall of 2001, and this study documents how the general optimism of the initial post-Taliban period dissipated as the Taliban insurgency successfully regrouped, repositioned itself, and developed a complex network of strongholds across the country as well as in Pakistan. The author highlights the realism of the overwhelming majority of Afghans who today back the Karzai government's efforts to negotiate and reconcile with insurgent groups.

Silinsky's evenhandedness punctuates controversial policies and actions associated with the Taliban, ones sometimes evoking a one-sided or knee-jerk reaction in the West. For example, he quotes a British author, Yvonne Ridley, who cautions against rushing to judgment about non-Western values. There is also a Yale co-ed who opines, "As a white American feminist, I do not feel comfortable making statements or judgments about other cultures, especially statements that suggest one culture is more sexist and repressive than another." But invoking empirical data, Silinsky offers a scathing up-to-date indictment of the Taliban record of repression of women's rights. It is a bracing, thought-provoking dialogical approach.

A number of devices used throughout the book are particularly useful to the reader. There are many figures and tables that capture complex processes and relationships in a clear and vivid way. These extend from the nature of insurgencies to differing theoretical understandings of a failed state. Particularly illuminating is one figure identifying implications of the Taliban's goals for the daily life of Afghans.

Chapter summaries are the basis for undertaking more general reflections on political developments. Profiles of an array of individuals connected one way or another to the Taliban—as perpetrator, bystander, witness, victim—are a valuable textual device helping the reader to comprehend the scope of the insurgency experience.

This book offers not just a sure-footed account—based on declassified State Department cables, firsthand observation, archival and secondary source materials, interviews, and journalistic accounts—of an unparalleled force in international politics today. It is also engaging, accessible, knowledgeable, and well written, parsimonious, and fair—while pulling no punches.

Raymond Taras
Professor of Political Science
Tulane University

Preface

One day Mullah Nasruddin entered his favorite teahouse and said, "The moon is more useful than the sun." An old man asked, "Why mullah?" Nasruddin replied, "We need the light more during the night than during the day."[1]

—An old Afghan joke

Afghanistan is a drama in transition. There is no final act on the horizon. Much has changed there since I began to write this book, and probably much will change soon after this book's completion. This is a book about the Taliban, which is a multifaceted and ever-changing subject. More specifically, it is a book about the origin, evolution, philosophy, and general game plan of the Taliban. It is also about Coalition Forces' activities to extinguish the insurgency. This requires touching on military science, economics, regional politics, and some history. Above all, this is a book about people.

Afghanistan is a laboratory for the evolution of counterinsurgency tactics, as well as economic stratagems for development. Because the United States' involvement in insurgencies, brush fires, revolutions, or any other overseas contingency operation has no foreseeable or even imaginable end, the strategies and tactics directed against Afghan insurgents have broad global application elsewhere. The successes and failures of the insurgents provide lessons to be studied at military staff colleges, as well as universities.

The story of the Coalition Forces in Afghanistan is one of enduring hardships, courage, failure, and successes. It is also the stuff of colorful metaphor. There are "green-on-blue" attacks in which Afghans turn murderous and treasonous. Stealthily, the Taliban enemy looms in the rich maze of vines from which they ambush Coalition Forces. For soldiers of the Coalition, this is called "green hell." There is the "green-red," neo-romantic alliance of Islamists and European leftists; green is the color of Islam and red is the color of communism. American special operators, sometimes clad in dark clothing to fight Taliban at night, have been called "men in black." The British regiment "Black Watch" contains snipers. A new, if macabre, addition to the lexicon of the Afghan counterinsurgency describes the instantaneous disappearance of a soldier who stepped on a powerful land mine. In the split moment of the blast, that soldier, someone's best friend, becomes "pink mist." But his fellow soldiers carry on. And it was this author's privilege to have seen, from safe distances, Coalition Forces train and serve and soldier on in Afghanistan.

The book contains profiles of Afghans, Americans, a Ukrainian, a Canadian, Pakistanis, and other men and women and girls and boys. Some are victims, some are victimizers; some are passersby. There is the partnership of a British serviceman and his service dog, a springer spaniel who won a medal for valor. The courage and cowardice and the decency and depravation in this distant-but-enduring drama form the book's theme. The story of the Taliban is a story of people.

What is the future of this beleaguered country? There are no reasons apparent to the author of this book why the tribally oriented and technologically primitive Taliban will necessarily defeat the combined efforts of NATO-trained Afghan armed forces and the Afghan government. It is hardly possible for the Taliban, or the other insurgent groups, to develop military capabilities sufficient to defeat the U.S. Army in pitched battle. The Taliban understand this and have geared their efforts toward breaking the will of the contributing Coalition countries to continue combat operations. The Taliban understand that if Coalition countries quit the fight and if the Afghan government cannot fill the security vacuum, they will have won. In late 2013, the West's morale is flagging, and the Taliban are taking note. Only time will reveal if the hopes of the optimists will come to fruition or if the efforts of the Coalition will have failed and are tossed into the "graveyard of empires."

In the meantime, there is for sale, in a dusty shop on the outskirts of Kabul, a shoulder patch that creatively expresses the strategy of the current counterinsurgency efforts in Afghanistan. The patch prominently displays a peace symbol, a totem instantly recognizable to every American over 40, which is flanked by two flags: one American and one Afghan. And written below the peace symbol is a strategy "WIN HEART [*sic*] AND MINDS." That the creator of the patch neglected to pluralize "heart" matters very little, and adds to the artifact's charm. But the patch is more than clever. In this writer's opinion, it offers an understated wisdom that the goal in Afghanistan cannot be achieved if its strategy is flawed. That is, the goal of defeating the Taliban, expressed by the peace symbol, cannot be achieved unless the Afghans become stakeholders and custodians of their own security. The extent to which they are prepared will be tested in 2014.

There are many people who have supported my research and to whom I will always be grateful. In particular, Solveig of the National Intelligence University guided me and struggled through the labyrinth of my first drafts. Jim, Russell, and Bill were completely supportive of my administrative needs during my tenure at the university as a participant in the director of national intelligence's Exceptional Analyst Program. My supervisors Bud, Dan, Chasey, and Kerry were infinitely patient and generous with their time and the ACIC's strained resources. I am very grateful for the trust they placed in my labor, and I hope that they consider their optimism in this book's potential to have been rewarded. Some of my colleagues and friends at work—Bill; Tony; the "Mats," both big and little—from whom I learn about the Taliban and much more every working day, also slogged through a prepublication review. I hope to be able to repay them for their good counsel. The sketches of Marines wounded in Afghanistan are the artistry of veteran Marine Robert Bates, whose work can be viewed at http://rb-portraits.com/artist. Others who read the draft and made extensive and very necessary comments are Dr. Lester Grau, Shireen Burki, and Dr. James Forest. Thank you.

In Afghanistan, I was treated well by the members of the Defense Attaché Office, and at the Afghanistan Counterinsurgency Academy, Col. John Agoglia impressed me with his strong leadership skills, military bearing, and obvious competence. He was generous with his time and his resources, and I thank him. Employees at Skateistan reviewed Khorshid's story. Every day these young men and women from Australia, the United States, Germany, and other countries give Afghan children moments of happiness, excitement, and sunshine. I thank them, particularly, for that. I would like to thank Dr. Raymond Taras, of Tulane University, who waded through too many drafts and revisions of my graduate papers, some of which form the nucleus of this book.

I offer lifelong gratitude to Sir Michael Howard, who was my supervisor at Oxford University in the late 1970s and early 1980s. In the City of Dreaming Spires, in an age before personal computers and social media, Sir Michael taught me more than military facts; he taught me the importance of war. If my book has any value, it is drawn from the warm tutorials, on often-rainy Thursday afternoons, at All Souls College, during which Sir Michael underscored the human element in military conflict to this then-young American. Sir Michael is the wisest man I have ever known.

Above all, I thank my three beautiful daughters and wonderful wife who endured, usually without complaint, the countless hours when I was holed up in my man cave pounding on the keys and searching on the Internet for all things Taliban.

I need to stress that, although the director of national intelligence funded elements of this study, this is not to be construed, in any way, as an official view by any individual or agency of the U.S. government. The opinions and judgments contained in this study are mine and mine alone, as are any errors.

Kensington, Maryland, winter 2013

Introduction

When you're wounded and left on Afghanistan's plains,
And the women come out to cut up your remains,
Just roll on your rifle and blow out your brains,
And go to your Gad like a soldier.
—Rudyard Kipling

In some parts of the world, students are going to school every day. It's their nor-
mal life. But in other part of the world, we are starving for education . . . it's like
a precious gift. It's like a diamond.[1]
—Malala Yousafzai

For Westerners, Afghanistan has always been distant, exotic, and periodically threatening. In the Occident, the Afghan warrior tradition enjoys
well-earned respect. Many countries have invaded Afghanistan, but few have
controlled it for long. In the nineteenth century, the British conquered, then
were defeated, then conquered again, and then left Afghanistan. The Soviets
had an equally checkered relationship with Afghanistan and, like the British
before them, were defeated.

Afghans, too, suffered the wages of war. In the late twentieth century, the
Soviets carpet bombed villages and valleys, killing over 1 million Afghans
and dispersing many millions more into squalid, disease-ridden refugee
shanties. After the Soviet invasion, the always-fragile traditional economy
collapsed, plunging Afghans into destitution, fatalism, and despair.[2]

For more than 12 years, the United States has been at war in Afghanistan.
The counterinsurgency in Afghanistan is the United States' longest war and

is among its more complicated and draining. What had been a political and economic backwater in most of the twentieth century became the epicenter of U.S. military activity of the new millennium. Since 2001, Afghanistan has served as a grand laboratory of military and economic developmental polices. Lessons drawn from successes and failures would guide American policies in some of the most desperately poor nations of the world. This is a battle of wills.

The Taliban's goal of reestablishing Islamic law, or Sharia, is common to many Islamic organizations, both militant as well as those who proclaim themselves peaceful. The use of insurgency is one tactic to achieve the world domination of Islam. Militant Islam is expressed through different means and media. For this reason, it is a battle of ideas, as well as bullets. It is being waged through the Internet, in mosques, and in religious schools, or madrassas, as well as on the fields of battle in Afghanistan.

The Taliban offer an unrelenting dedication to conquer Afghanistan, an unconstrained use of terror, and solidarity with important fragments of global Islam. The Taliban leverage deeply engrained Afghan skepticism of Western promises for a better future. Foreign men have come and gone from Afghanistan, and, despite promises, only the poverty remains.[3] Taliban leaders boast that Afghans are armed with the religious fervor, honor, and resolve. "Such weapons are neither available in the arsenal of America nor in the warehouse of her allies."[4] In January 2013, the Taliban crowed, "No sooner will the foreigners quit than the Afghans will start living under the cover of an Islamic government and in the environment of Islamic brotherhood."

Perhaps, but progovernment forces also have centers of gravity.[5] Most Afghans fear the Taliban and remember the misery and brutality of their six-year tenure. The Taliban's world is a phantasmagoria of savagery. Women are stoned for promiscuity, and men are beheaded for trivial offenses. Boys are reared to blast themselves apart in bazaars, where other children and their mothers shop. There is no music or television in Taliban territory, and no kites soar above the orchards and towns. There is a poverty of empathy and compassion.

The American-led Coalition is determined to prevent the Taliban's triumph. Today's soldiers on both sides of the struggle have lived only in wartime. The sons of Taliban fighters, who were 10 when then the group was scattered into Pakistan, are now in their early 20s. Many are hardened fighters and will, undoubtedly, face the sons of the Northern Alliance.[6] The Taliban are tough, but so are many other Afghans.

Next year, U.S. forces are scheduled to leave, and the Taliban will certainly try to fill the security vacuum. Twelve years of building a civil service, army, police, and health and educational system will be put to the test. The extent to which Afghanistan's fortunes are intertwined with or independent of American military will be decided. Will the Taliban's power-sharing negotiations become a viper's embrace of the still-struggling Karzai regime? The stakes are survival for the new Afghan state.

Abbreviations

ACIC	Army Counterintelligence Center
ANA	Afghan National Army
ANP	Afghan National Police
ANSF	Afghan National Security Forces
ARSIC	Afghan Regional Security Command
ASPD	Antisocial Personality Disorder
CENTCOM	Central Command
CI	Counterintelligence
CIVMIL	Civil-military
CJCS	Chairman of the Joint Chiefs of Staff
CJTF	Combined Joint Task Force
CMA	Cooperative Medical Assistance
CORDS	Civil Operations and Rural Development System
CSTC-A	Combined Security Transition Command-Afghanistan
DoD	U.S. Department of Defense
DoS	U.S. Department of State
FATA	Federally Administered Tribal Areas
FTO	Foreign Terrorist Organization
HiG	Hizb-i-Islami

HTS	Human Terrain System
HTT	Human Terrain Team
HUMINT	Human Intelligence
ICRC	International Committee of the Red Cross
IED	Improvised Explosive Device
IO	Information Operations
IRGC	Islamic Revolutionary Guard Corps
ISAF	International Security Assistance Force
ISR	Intelligence, surveillance, and reconnaissance
KPP	Khyber Pakhtunkwa Province
LeT	Lashkar-e Taiba
MI	Military intelligence
MOD	Ministry of Defense
MOI	Ministry of Interior
MoPH	Afghan Ministry of Public Health
MSA	Muslim Students Association
NATO	North American Treaty Organization
NGO	Nongovernmental Organization Performance Assessment
NWFP	Northwest Frontiers Provinces
OMC-A	Office of Military Cooperation-Afghanistan
PETA	People for the Ethical Treatment of Animals
PRT	Provincial Reconstruction Team
PSYOP	Psychological Operations
PTSD	Posttraumatic stress disorder
RPG	Rocket-propelled grenade
RTC	Regional Training Center
TTP	Tactics, techniques, and procedures
TTP	Tehrik e-Taliban Pakistan
USAID	United States Agency for International Development
USFOR-A	United States Forces-Afghanistan
USJFCO	United States Joint Forces Command

1

Afghanistan's Landscape, the People, and Islamism

You can occupy it, you can put troops there and keep bombing, but you cannot win.

—Soviet Lt. Gen. Ruslan Aushev, who was decorated
for bravery during the Soviet 1979–89 war

THE LAND

Afghanistan is a remote and rugged land, which has been protected from modernity by a "mud curtain" of geographic and cultural isolation. Much like the people of Afghanistan, the country's terrain is tough. It is roughly the size of Texas and comprises over 250,000 square miles of diverse geography and climatic zones. Despite its relatively large size, only 12 percent of the land is arable. Vast tracts in southern and western Afghanistan are desert and have some geographic traits similar to the Southern Californian or New Mexican high desert. Other parts of Afghanistan are mountainous, and earthquakes are frequent there.[1]

As historical accounts of invading armies attest, Afghanistan is ideally suited for insurgency warfare. The unforgiving harshness of the land offers strong tactical advantage to insurgents, who can command the forbidding mountains and valleys with their intimate knowledge of the terrain. The deep gorges and valleys, craggy defiles, and primitive road network, which is generally aligned with watersheds, are ideal for ambushes and hit-and-run tactics. In the nineteenth century, the terrain wore down even the strongest British ponies, and in the twentieth century the dirty and rocky roads, mountain rock slides, and generally primitive infrastructure took a toll on sturdily built Soviet, and later American, all-terrain vehicles.[2] The myriad crevices that hid Afghan partisans in the nineteenth century gave sanctuary to late twentieth-century mujahedeen, and, now, it does so to their sons. Stinger-clutching mujahedeen instilled an often-paralyzing fear in the Soviet Army.

The famed Khyber Pass is draped in ancient, martial folklore.[3] Through its canyons passed the supply trains of Alexander's armies, which fought for their lives in 327 BCE. Centuries later, the marauding and plundering armies of Genghis Khan and later the Mughal warriors marched over this 33-mile pass through the Hindu Kush mountain range.[4] Beyond the Khyber Pass, Afghanistan's heartland and hinterland were battlegrounds of the Afghan wars. In these wars, British soldiers were at the mercy of Afghan marksmen, who with their jezails[5] effectively used the rugged terrain as shield and sanctuary. In the last century, as today, the well-hidden caves and heavily forested northern mountains provided shelter for both Afghan insurgents and the soldiers who pursued them. As with those of Alexander, the armies of the British, the Soviets, and the Americans would see their transport vehicles bogged down, their soldiers ambushed, and their morale challenged.

For many non-Afghans who have trespassed in north and northeastern Afghanistan, the Hindu Kush, or "killer of Hindus," has been true to its name. It is among the highest mountain ranges in the world, and Mount Nowshak, at 24,557 feet, approaches the mountain climbers' death zone.[6] It is 10,000 feet higher than the continental United States' highest peak, Mt. Whitney.[7] The bone-chilling cold of Afghan mountains, particularly in the higher elevations, has served as an ally for Afghan insurgents, just as "General Winter" ground down German forces in Moscow and Stalingrad. In sum, Afghanistan's landscape is Spartan. All these factors fuse to test the mettle, endurance, and military skills of both Afghan and non-Afghan progovernment forces (Figure 1.1).

A BRIEF HISTORY

The first Europeans to come en masse to Afghanistan were the armies of Alexander the Great. His tenure was fairly brief, but he imprinted a Hellenistic influence that endured for centuries.[8] His troops also gave a genetic bequest to the Afghan people, some of whom retain European racial features. Buddhism took root in the mid-sixth century BCE[9] and began to flourish alongside other religions, including Zoroastrianism.[10]

In 698 CE, Islam burst onto Afghanistan to stay, despite repeated challenges. Under successive caliphates, Afghans converted in large numbers to Sunni Islam, which became the dominant religion. Afghanistan was nearly decimated by the Mongols, who struck like lightening in the thirteenth

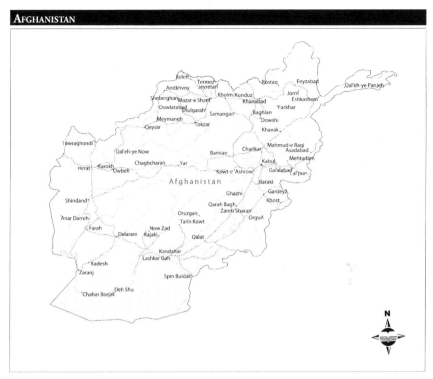

Figure 1.1   Afghanistan. (ABC-CLIO)

century. Not all of Afghanistan's cities were destroyed, but many were devastated never to be revived. Most towns west of the Helmand River moldered.

In a fragmented Central Asia, Timur, or Tamerlane, shaped a vast empire in the early fifteenth century. From his base in Samarkand, he also became a patron of the Islamic arts.[11] In the next century, Babur captured Kabul from the Mongols and founded the Mughal Empire in India.[12] The Mughals ruled until 1707.[13]

In the nineteenth century, European leaders wrestled for supremacy and empire in Central and South Asia. Afghanistan was torn between the ambitions of two expanding empires, the British and the Russian, in the "Great Game."[14] In this struggle, the Afghans proved themselves to be fierce fighters. In January 1842, Britain's Kabul garrison was forced to withdraw to its hard-pressed fort in Jalalabad. The retreating British-Indian units, some 16,000 soldiers and camp followers, were ambushed by Afghans and only a few, including a wounded doctor, survived to reach Jalalabad.[15] This death march crystalized in the European imagination. In art, Lady Butler's portrayal of the near-dead Dr. William Brydon, slouching in his saddle as he approached Jalalabad, became iconic. It brought to canvas the enervation and then annihilation of a once-proud British army.

In response, the British built an "Army of Retribution" in India, smashed its way through the Khyber Pass, recaptured Kabul, and set the ancient Great Bazaar aflame. But there were more British defeats to come. In July 1880, a British brigade led by Brig. George Burrows was overrun by forces led by the formidable Ayub Khan.[16] This time, however, there was not a public call for vengeance, and Parliament determined that retribution would not be worth the estimated expense. Britain was content to have Afghanistan serve as a buffer state during the Anglo-Russian rivalry.[17] In literature, Rudyard Kipling brought the Great Game to life in his novel *Kim*.[18]

In the late nineteenth and early twentieth centuries, Afghanistan lost some of its strategic importance to the West. Dominant European empires faded or dissolved after the First World War. A militarily fatigued Europe turned inward. Britain's world power waned in the twentieth century, and Tsarist Russia was reconstituted as the Soviet Union. As a result, neither country focused on Afghanistan. By the middle of the twentieth century, Britain, still the dominant though tired Western power in South Asia, was pessimistic about Afghanistan's ability govern itself. British diplomats seriously considered partitioning the state among the neighboring states of Pakistan and Iran.[19]

The great powers were not motivated to modernize Afghanistan, which suited Afghan leaders. National and tribal leaders were content to keep neutral in international struggles involving ideology and geopolitics. Afghanistan refused to ally itself in a formal pact with the United States in the 1950s, which was Washington's unprecedented period of alliance building in South Asia.[20] Instead, Afghanistan turned to the Soviet Union for military and economic aid and established a relationship based largely on barter.[21] This barter economy did little to end Afghanistan's isolation nor did it promote sustained human development.

Afghan prime minister Mohammed Daoud Khan, generally referred to as Daoud, who served from 1953 to 1963 and later in the mid- to late 1970s, was not ideologically wedded to any political or economic theory. He was a reformer who tried to court Washington and Moscow to integrate Afghanistan into southern and central Asian regional economies.[22]

Daoud gradually tried to end Afghanistan's isolation by courting international financing for developmental schemes. He had some success. But foreign aid slowed down in the 1970s, partly because of the declining geostrategic importance of Afghanistan to the West and to the Soviet Union. Afghanistan kept neutral.[23] A treaty of friendship between Afghanistan and the Soviet Union was promulgated in December 1978, which brought more Soviet aid and advisors to Kabul. The United States had given aid to Afghanistan since the 1950s, but most programs ended after the coup of April 1978.[24]

Standards of living began to increase in the 1960s and early 1970s. There was political stability and a belle epoch in Afghanistan under King

Mohammed Zahir Shah.[25] He was a well-liked and tough, but not dynamic, king. In a coup, King Shah was gently deposed by his cousin, the aforementioned Mohammed Daoud, and Shah went into exile.[26] He would return, if only briefly, after the Taliban were defeated in 2001.

ELEMENTS OF CONSTITUTIONAL LAW

Afghanistan was never a Jeffersonian democracy, but Afghans were afforded many human rights, most of which were revoked by the Taliban. The Afghan 1923 constitution abolished slavery[27] and gave protection to religions other than Islam, while still asserting that Afghanistan was an Islamic state.[28] It offered some measures of political freedom. The right to own private property was enshrined.[29] However, the constitution cannot be considered liberal by contemporary, Western standards. It asserted the supremacy of Sharia,[30] or Islamic law.[31]

Of enduring consequence in the 1923 constitution is a Loya Jirga.[32] The Jirga, a Pashtun tradition, is a loose assembly of village elders whose judgments and decisions impact national-level policy. For centuries it was the most important conflict-resolution mechanism that had democratic traits. The 1923 Constitution gave it unprecedented status, which shifted power to local levels. The Jirga would reemerge as an important component in Afghan law and policy making in the post-Taliban era.

In 1964, Afghanistan adopted a new constitution, which strengthened the role of the Shura, or Parliament, based on a bicameral legislature. Its references to "basic principles" of democratic rule were ambiguous,[33] its tolerance of religions other than Hanafi-Sunni Islam was suspect, and its civil and criminal protections for women were weak. Nonetheless, there was a progression toward adopting elements of universal human rights. This came to a halt when the Soviets invaded Afghanistan.

The promise of social change brought disquiet among the deeply religious. Not all of the young were attracted to the promises of the West. By the 1950s, the Egyptian Muslim Brotherhood had tenured scholars in Kabul University's Faculty of Islamic Studies. By the late 1960s, a Muslim Youth Organization of Afghanistan would include university students, such as Burhanuddi Rabbani and Gulbuddin Hekmatyar, as members. They became a bulwark against Western liberalism, and several of them became national leaders 20 years later.[34]

THE SOVIETS INVADE—THE "AFGHANISTANIS"

The tranquility of the 1970s was shattered in December 1979. The Soviet Union tried to shore up a moribund, secular-orientated Afghan government by deploying Soviet troops. What was planned as a quick intervention quickly stymied. In nearly 10 years of occupation, Soviet forces and their

Afghan communist allies reportedly killed 1.3 million Afghans, shattered the infrastructure in urban and rural areas of the country, and caused 5.5 million Afghans to flee to refugee camps in Iran and Pakistan. The melee in Afghanistan grew to an insurgency and, then, a civil war. Finally, it took on elements of a world war, as the United States entered into the fray.

The Soviet's muddle in Afghanistan afforded Washington an opportunity to inflict a slow-bleeding wound on Moscow. At a relatively low cost and without having to deploy any U.S. combat forces, the United States supplied mujahedeen with lethal ground-to-air Stinger missiles, in November 1986, against which Soviet aircraft were not adequately protected.[35] At the same time, Soviet dissidents made use of the disparaging war-related news. Informal information networks of mothers and fathers who lost their sons expanded. This war, compounded by the long-declining standard of living, ushered in the last days of the Soviet Union.

As the war progressed, more international players joined the fighting. Iranian support went largely to the Hazaras, who are Shia. The Saudis supported, in contrast, a Wahhabi network and a rival warlord, the brooding Gulbuddin Hekmatyar, who is still an active player. The Saudis also sponsored Wahhabi-guided madrassas to expand their influence in the country.[36]

The Soviet experience in Afghanistan illustrates failure in military pacification efforts. Stephen Pomper, a military analyst, notes that the Soviets saw early in the fight that they would have to train local forces and secure and maintain their sympathies, similar to the U.S. turn-of-the-twentieth-century counterinsurgency efforts in the Philippines,[37] or they would have to field an army of over 600,000 men.[38] This would have required a significant diversion of troops from Europe, a proposition certainly unacceptable after the inauguration of Ronald Reagan, or a vast increase in military personnel and expenditures.

Like the opponents they faced, the Soviets could be ruthless. A RAND Corporation study cited the devastation by napalm and fragmentation bombs and the wide use of antipersonnel mines, which maimed and killed indiscriminately. The study compared the tactics of Soviet pacification to those of the Nazis, a historic analogy that stirred American sympathy for the Afghans. Their use of booby-trapped toys and the execution of civilian hostages horrified many Americans.[39] A 1986 Amnesty International study agreed and charged that Afghan prisoners were routinely beaten and exercised, sometimes to death, in extreme cold or heat. Some spoke of electric shocks to sensitive parts of the body, and others were witness to the slaughter of fellow prisoners.[40]

The Soviets tried to soften their image but failed. Soviet information operators were, at best, marginally capable, unimaginative, and ill-equipped for the task of persuading a highly devoted, religious, and tribal society. The propaganda was largely guided to an Afghan population that could not process the largely secular messages. The Soviet-generated themes focused on class struggle and dialectic materialism but were heard by Afghans as muddled twaddle. Also, the quality of the transmission equipment was poor. Finally, the Soviet hubris assumed military superiority could trump the Afghans' primitive tactics.[41] They were wrong.

The Soviets refined their tactics as they expanded operations and tried to use honey. Moscow hoped to engage Afghans in international prestige projects, such as propelling an Afghan into space on a Soyuz spaceship. Hovering in the stratosphere, Afghan cosmonauts would perform scientific research.[42] Few Afghans were impressed. On earth, Moscow offered 15,000 Afghans free education in the Soviet Union and brought 50 professors from the Soviet Union and East Germany to the American-built Kabul University. It did not work. Frustrated Soviet workers grumbled, "It's all the Middle Ages . . . We just sink money in." This disenchantment was reciprocated by an Afghan who retorted that all the Russians have done was to create a "filthy, bloody mess of our country."[43]

Afghans agonized. In the spirit of the Mongols, the Soviet armies laid waste to vast stretches of Afghanistan.[44] The war ravaged the economy, throwing millions of Afghans, already living on the margins of human existence, into despair.[45] Corruption, always a problem in Afghanistan, thrived in the war years of the 1980s.[46] In the 1980s, households postponed long-term economic planning because of the future's uncertainty. Above all, most Afghans tried to survive, which was often difficult.

If the Soviet information operations were fruitless, the Taliban very effectively terrorized their Soviet enemy. Soviet prisoners were tortured and mutilated, and their corpses were photographed. This had a chilling and demoralizing effect on Soviets, many of whom became afraid to engage the enemy.[47] These morbid propaganda effects would be replicated by the Taliban years later and directed against Americans.

Historians refer to the war in Afghanistan as the Soviets' Vietnam. Though the analogy is inexact, it underscores the angst created within both the Soviet armed forces and civil-military relations. Things went poorly for the Soviets from the beginning, and there were drug problems. Some Soviets traded clothes, cigarettes, fur caps, even their weapons for hashish and heroin.[48] Abroad, anger at the Soviet Army's killing Muslims in Afghanistan also spurred Islamic fundamentalism in the Central Asian republics and in Chechnya.

Much like Americans in Vietnam a decade earlier, not all "Afghanistanis," often transliterated "Afghanistanys," the Soviet troops who fought in Afghanistan, could leave their battles behind. Years later, many exhibited signs of emotional distress associated with posttraumatic stress disorder (PTSD). Symptoms included alcohol and chemical dependency and high rates of suicide.[49]

Belatedly, the Soviet Army realized the inadequacy of its preparation. Soviet forces were ill-equipped for guerilla warfare and, initially, were poorly trained. Though the Soviets deployed advanced armored vehicles and attack rotary- and fixed-wing aircraft, they became highly vulnerable to U.S.-supplied ground-to-air missiles.[50] Almost anything that flew was subject to attack. The journalist Edward Girardet recounts the perhaps-apocryphal exchange between two mujahedeen in the fading days of the war. One observes that he has not seen any Siberian cranes flying over Kabul that year, which was unusual. "Have we even killed all the cranes?" replies the other.[51]

In February 1989, the Soviets left. The last Soviet soldier to leave after the nine-year intervention was Lt. Gen. Boris Gromov, who rode the last armored personnel carrier from the country, clutching a bouquet of flowers. Years later he would confess, without dreamy nostalgia, "I wasn't looking back."[52] But U.S. military planners, years later, would look back on the Soviet experience and would scrutinize all the major battles hoping to learn from their failures and successes.

Before they left, the Soviets handed over huge caches of weapons and ammunition to Najibullah's still-Soviet-friendly government forces. Moscow continued to provide materiel support for two years after the Soviets' departure, but their withdrawal essentially left the Kabul government to fend for itself. A civil war followed, resulting in the communist government stepping down in April 1992. Differences among the mujahedeen parties quickly revealed themselves. Each faction had a leader or warlord with aspirations of national power.

There was a global view that Soviets were defeated in Afghanistan.[53] The Soviet Union collapsed only several years later. The mujahedeen celebrated and savored their achievements as victory. Some Afghans were grateful to the United States for providing funding, logistical support, training, and the lethally effective Stinger missiles,[54] but other Afghans were not. And some mujahedeen and al Qaeda hoped to defeat the world's only remaining superpower, their former benefactor, the United States. Washington would be their next target.

Western leaders would examine the Soviets' tactics—both successful and unsuccessful. The use of overwhelming force and relatively sophisticated weapons were not necessarily adequate to defeat the enemy. Another lesson both the Americans and Soviets learned was the importance of domestic considerations and the necessity of popular resolve to fight a protracted, distant war.

Profile 1.1: Nekmuhammad: Afghanistani

Gennady Tsevam fought as an enlisted soldier in the Soviet Army in Afghanistan in the mid-1980s. A Ukrainian national, he was drafted into the army at 18, trained in Russia and Soviet Uzbekistan, and then deployed to Kunduz to fight the mujahedeen.[55] He did not last long.

His first night on sentry duty would be his last serving alongside his Red Army comrades. His outpost was attacked, and he was whisked away in a cloth sack as prisoner of the Taliban. Unlike other Soviet soldiers who were tortured and killed, Tsevam was given the option of becoming a Muslim or having his throat slit. He chose the former option, and Tsevam became Nekmuhammad, took a wife, and fathered three children.

When the Soviets left Afghanistan, he stayed behind with his wife and family. He may have felt the same dilemma other Soviet captives faced. How would he be greeted back home? Would the authorities and his Ukrainian family be sympathetic? There might be prison.[56] So he stayed in Afghanistan and worked odd jobs. After the Taliban were forced from the country, Nekmuhammad took a job as a driver for nongovernmental organizations (NGOs). In 2004 he was working for an Italian firm as a driver. Later, he would move his family to Kunduz.

But life was very difficult for him in Afghanistan, and he still suffered from a leg wound. His children were social outcasts because their dad was a "shuravi," or Soviet soldier.[57] Other children would not play with them. By 2003, both his parents had died in the Ukraine. They had not seen him since the day they saw him off from the Donetsk enlistment office 20 years earlier.

By the turn of the millennium, Nekmuhammad's world had changed many times.[58] The Soviet Union had not existed for years, and Ukraine became an independent state. He has a brother in Ukraine. But, Nekmuhammad confessed, "I am frightened that if I go and cannot come back, then who will feed my family and look after them?"[59] So Nekmuhammad would talk to his brother on the phone, and his children would notice their father's slow tears, as he spoke, with his voice cracking with emotion, in a strange-sounding language they did not understand.[60]

THE PEOPLE

A Pashtun is never at peace, except when he is at war.
—An old Pashtun saying

Living at the crossroads of ancient empires and migrating nations, the Afghans are living testimony to the racially diverse gene pool and the fusion of myriad ethnicities.[61] Over the centuries one ethnic group, the Pashtuns, came to dominate.[62] Today, they are the largest tribe, constituting approximately 42 percent of all Afghans.

The Taliban are overwhelmingly Pashtun, and this tribe holds regional prestige and power. The area in which Pashtun is the dominant ethnicity extends into much of Pakistan and is called the Pashtun belt. The Pashtuns are a tapestry of major clans, minor clans, and subclans of varying prestige and influence.[63] Deeply conservative, the Pashtun social code, or Pashtunwali, is a fusion of religious and clan supremacy.[64] When they held power, the Taliban imposed their Pashtun social codes on all those whom they conquered. The Taliban alienated many non-Pashtun Afghans when they were in power because many of the Taliban's laws and customs were based on Pashtunwali.[65] If some Pashtun recruits were attracted to the Taliban by bonds of tribal affinity, non-Pashtuns seethed with resentment, which would have repercussions in following years.[66]

Though the subtribes have some regional and clan differences, Pashtuns share a common social code. The home of Pashtunwali is a fiercely independent tribal region that straddles Afghanistan and Pakistan. Even by Afghan standards, this region is remote, barren, and inaccessible. The area is porous, and its resident clans often make their livings by smuggling. But Pashtunwali extends well beyond the Pashtun belt; it is imposed in all territory controlled by Pashtuns.

Pashtunwali rests on five principles: honor, revenge, hospitality, absolution, and protection. Honor, or nang, requires each Pashtun male to protect the honor of the family. Even small offenses, slights, and what Westerners would consider trivial, off-hand comments need to be resolved. Stemming from the first principle, nang, a Pashtun must exact revenge, or badal, if his family is shamed. Hospitality, or melmastia, the third principle, is a Pashtun trait that also has been acknowledged by many non-Pashtuns. A fourth principle is forgiveness, or nanawatay.

If a Pashtun wants to end a feud with a fellow Pashtun, he can approach his rival and ask for forgiveness. It is an alternative to revenge. The fifth Pashtun principle is allegiance with a stronger force, or hamsaya. This happens when a group or individuals give allegiance or switch sides to a stronger clan or subclan. In the current conflict, it became widely used as the Taliban were in retreat in 2001 and, once again, when they began to show muscle. As the United States prepares to withdraw most of its forces in 2014, the principle of hamsaya, could help determine the course of the insurgency (Table 1.1).

The tribal system in Afghanistan has been compared, if very loosely, to the clans of ancient Scotland or to the Hatfields and McCoys of American folklore. While exaggerated, this historical analogue holds some truth. Many Afghans will take their primary identity from their tribal affiliation and only secondarily see themselves as Afghan nationals. There are five dominant Afghan tribes.

The Durrani tribal confederation, mostly concentrated in southeast Afghanistan, has disproportionately produced Afghan leaders since Ahmad Shah Durrani, considered to be the founder of modern Afghanistan, founded a monarchy in 1747. The historic Pashtun rivals of the Durranis are the

Table 1.1   Pashtun Fundamentals and the Taliban

Pashtun Traits	Application to the Taliban
Nang: Honor	Serving as a warrior brings honor to family
Badal: Revenge	Revenge taken on those considered as betraying the tenets of Pashtunwali or collaborating with progovernment forces
Melmastia: Hospitality	Reason given to refuse extraditing bin Laden to the United States
Nanawatay: Absolution	Not the most important element in the counterinsurgency. The Taliban could require services of those who want to seek their forgiveness
Hamsaya: Protection	The Taliban rose to power quickly because they distinguished themselves as the strongest of all the tribes. If the Taliban appear weak to most Afghans, the Coalition appears to be the stronger tribe and will attract Afghans to its cause

Ghilzai tribal group, which is concentrated mostly in eastern Afghanistan. Some of the major Taliban leaders today are Ghilzais.[67]

The hoary rivalry between Pashtun bloodlines continues in twenty-first-century Afghanistan. Hamid Karzai, the current president of Afghanistan, is a Durrani, and Mullah Omar, the long-serving leader of the Taliban, is a Ghilzai. The Karlanris, or "hill tribes," are the third-largest group of Pashtuns.[68] Although geographically separated, two major groups make up the Sarbani.[69] The last major tribal group is the Ghurghusht, who live in and around Pakistan's Northwest Frontier Provinces.[70] Sometimes the subtribes coexist peacefully, and sometimes they do not.[71]

Two-thirds of the Pashtuns are Durrani or Ghilzai, and these two subtribes sparred and tangled on many issues over many centuries.[72] The Taliban continued to be led by Ghilzais, but by 2008–9 Durrani commanders had been given stronger leadership roles and positions of trust and responsibility (Table 1.2).

THE MIND OF THE TALIBAN

The mind of the Taliban is an amalgam of ethnic, geographic, historic, and religious elements. The Taliban's religious principles are framed by essentially three fundamentals: Salafism, Deobandism, and Sharia. These elements overlap and intertwine with each other. All three are expressions of puritanical and political Islam, which made resurgence in the late twentieth century, and today tests the grit of the Arab Spring throughout the Middle East.

Table 1.2   Pashtuns' Characteristics and Clans

	Location	Important Characteristics
Durranis	Southeast Afghanistan	Leader of Pashtun areas Ahmad Shah Durrani founded a monarchy in 1747
Gilzais	Eastern Afghanistan	Rival of the Durranis
Karanris	Pakistan and Afghanistan in Waziristan, Kurram, Peshawar, Khost, Paktia, and Paktika	Seen as hill tribes
Sarbanis	Located north of Peshwar, Pakistan, and Baluchistan	Includes tribes such as the Mohmands, Yusufzais, and Shinwaris, while the smaller segment consists of Sheranis and Tarins
Ghurghushts	Baluchistan and Northwest Frontiers Provinces	Includes tribes such as the Kakars, Mandokhels, Panars, and Musa Khel

Salafism is an Islamic revivalist philosophy intended to purify Islam from Western and modern contaminates.[73] To the extent the Taliban offered a coherent political philosophy during its 1996–2001 rule, it was based on a reactionary, fossilized, and absolutist belief system surrounding the world of Mohammed.[74] Salafists strive to re-create the world in which they imagined their Prophet lived.[75] This requires expurgating elements of modern society that, in the view of the Taliban, are superfluous, degenerate, or in any way contrary to the immutable teachings of the Koran.[76] Not all features of modernity are discarded. To spread their ideology, Salafists use state-of-the-art technology.[77]

In this spirit, the Taliban set out early to erase all non-Islamic influences in Afghanistan. They turned to Afghanistan's own internationally recognized art treasures and, with modern artillery, blasted the ancient Buddhas of Bamiyan from the hills into which they were carved. Though the world was stunned by the Taliban's demolition of the statutes, few Salafists openly objected. "We are not against culture, but we don't believe in these things [the statues]. They are against Islam," Taliban Foreign Minister Wakil Ahmed breezily declared.[78] Certainly, not all Muslims supported the Taliban's position. Muslims controlled Afghanistan for over 1,300 years and did not destroy the Buddhas until the Taliban.[79]

There were other examples of premeditated destruction. Uncertain that Afghanistan was sufficiently purged of non-Islamic cultural impurities, senior mullahs ordered a spree of destruction throughout Kabul's museum in March 2001. A pack of cudgel-wielding Taliban shattered antique limestone statues that had been excavated throughout the country, carefully restored, and acclaimed as universal artistic treasures.[80] The vandals were led by the Taliban's minister of culture.

The Taliban's outlook is also shaped by the Deobandi movement, which is a particular South Asian Salafist philosophy.[81] Deobandi refers to both an Islamic seminary and an Islamic philosophy, which reaches far beyond the northern Indian town of Deoband.[82] It is one of Sunni Islam's more influential Islamic schools in South and Central Asia and continues to produce edicts, or fatwas, based on Muslim law. It is an extreme and highly legalistic view of Islam that governs most of a Muslim's daily activities. Rules include what type of pet a Muslim can own, when and where he is allowed to fly a kite, how often he should bathe, what type of clothes he should wear, and myriad other daily activities. Life's conduct can be divided into two basic categories—permitted or prohibited. This Taliban theocracy fuses orthodox strains of Islam Wahhabism from Saudi Arabia and the Deobandi philosophy, which is taught in Pakistan and lavishly funded by Saudis.[83]

Deobandism also has paramilitary elements. The school in Deoband mandated military training to groom its seminary students to be warriors of Islam.[84] The seminary, Darul Uloom, or House of Knowledge, has been dubbed "Jihad University." Deobandi thinking was born of nationalistic and religiously reactionary fervor following the Sepoy revolt in the mid-nineteenth century, which is often called the Indian Mutiny.[85] It rejected the Indian civil service and the adoption of European tastes, mannerisms, and secularism among the Indian elite.[86] It remains decidedly opposed to all elements of modernity, Western life and thought, and democratic norms.[87]

The ideological foundation of the Taliban was built of Deobandi Islam. The architect and avatar was Mullah Omar. Although he had not finished his studies, the Taliban leader Mullah Omar was afforded an honorary degree by the seminary because, as one luminary noted, "he left to do jihad and to create a pristine Islamic government."[88]

The Deobandi philosophy is unique, but in many ways fits into the agenda of today's Muslim Brotherhood, which has strong Salafist underpinnings. Bin Laden was very attracted to Islamism, or political Islam, and promoted the teachings of its leaders. The term "Islamism" refers to a modern variant of Islam, which was developed and spread by the Muslim Brotherhood, or the Ikwan. From a nucleus of disaffected Egyptians led by a Sufi schoolteacher in the late 1920s, the Brotherhood tried to supplant secular society with Islamic rule. It became a global, dynamic, and expansionist force by the end of the twentieth century. The Brotherhood, which would inspire the leaders and core cadre of al Qaeda around the world, fused philosophical elements from other authoritarian movements of the twentieth century.[89] It thrives in the twenty-first century and challenges emerging democratic elements in the Arab Middle East.

The Egyptian Sayyid Qutb, whose writing heavily influenced bin Laden, was the Brotherhood's preeminent intellectual.[90] As Qutb explained, it was insufficient for individuals to reform themselves. Islamic mandates ordained that an Islamic heaven be created on earth. Only a completely "good" state, by which he meant a Sharia state, could produce good men.[91] He was executed in 1966 but is still celebrated throughout the Islamic world. Much like bin Laden, the often-quoted Qutb saw Islam as incompatible with modern pluralism. As a middle-aged exchange student in Colorado in the late 1940s, Qutb, soft-spoken and diffident, grew to see the new American superpower as Islam's greatest enemy.

In his extensive writings, Qutb expropriated terminology from the two radical socialist and utopian philosophies—National Socialism and communism—but rejected their atheism.[92] He held solidarity with Hitler's homicidal anti-Semitism. After the war, his main enemy became a soulless and capitalist United States. He derided American churches as brothels, jazz music as primitive, and American women as vixens. His portrayal of American culture as vacuous, aggressive, and bigoted would resonate with Muslims as well as leftists and would become reoccurring tropes in the propaganda of both.

This model of American aggression and degeneracy became more common in the 1950s among Islamists and European intellectuals. During the late 1960s and early 1970s, Islamist Arab nationalists made common cause with international leftists. Despite their strikingly opposing views on religion, women, and general politics, Islamists and leftists were strongly united in their hatred of the United States and Israel. Bin Laden, with his theatrical flights, would militarize this sentiment and bring it to Afghanistan.[93]

Bin Laden brought the ideas of the Brotherhood to the Taliban. Had he a rival for imparting Islamist ideologies in Afghanistan, that person would have been Sheikh Abdullah Azzam, a Palestinian ideologue and strategist who died young.

Azzam was born near Jenin in 1941 and graduated from the Sharia College at Damascus University in 1966, when Palestinian nationalism was becoming potent force. After the 1967 war, Azzam became active in several Palestinian terrorist groups in Gaza and the West Bank and embraced Salafism. He had a sharp mind and obtained graduate degrees from Al Azhar University. In 1979, he joined the first wave of Arab, anti-Soviet jihadis in Afghanistan. In Peshawar, Pakistan, he made his mark as an inspiring Islamist recruiter and rhapsodist.[94] The paladin's famous dictum was, "One hour of jihad in Allah's path is better than 60 years of praying."[95] With his two sons, he was killed in a massive car bombing in 1989 in Peshawar. His assassins are not publically known today.[96]

Both Azzam and bin Laden were members of the Muslim Brotherhood. Bin Laden's connection to the Muslim Brotherhood became clearer in September 2012, when his successor and longtime associate Ayman al-Zawahiri recalled a quote by bin Laden: "I was banished from my own organization. I used to belong to the Muslim Brotherhood, but they banished me." According to Zawahiri, bin Laden was too much of a maverick for the Brotherhood, whose leaders informed the Saudi, "You're banished." Bin Laden pithily responded, "Fine."[97]

FLORID CRUELTY "THAT SCREAMS WILL FRIGHTEN EVEN CROWS FROM THEIR NESTS"

Anyone can do beatings and starve people. I want your unit to find new ways of torture so terrible that if the person survives he will never again have a night's sleep.[98]

—Hafiz Sadiqulla Hassani, former Taliban torturer

The Taliban are not uniquely cruel. Compared to two totalitarian regimes of the twentieth century—the German National Socialists and Soviet communists[99]—the Taliban committed fewer murders and never refined genocide to an industrial science. However, much like the feared Gestapo of the Nazis and the KGB of the Soviets, the Taliban's secret police tortured and murdered enthusiastically and creatively. Prisoners were nailed to the wall and crucified; killed slowly by hanging upside down; and starved to death, while occasionally being forced to crawl and grabble for bread crumbs, to the amusement of guards.[100] One of the Taliban torturers explained, with some pangs of regret, "Maybe the worst thing I saw was a man beaten so much, such a pulp of skin and blood, that it was impossible to tell whether he had clothes on or not. Every time he fell unconscious, we rubbed salt into his wounds to make him scream."[101]

Taliban torture continues to make daily news. For nearly 19 years, 1994–2013, there has been a carnival-like atmosphere to public executions and amputations. In Taliban-controlled territory, whippings, beatings, shootings, face slashings, and occasional crucifixions take place in public squares. Even the dead are not spared desecration. The Taliban photograph their enemy dead as grim trophies. A village elder explained that when the Taliban killed a British soldier in July 2011, they, the Taliban, "kicked the body and threw it in the canal . . . then they [other Taliban] pulled him out of the canal and started trampling on him, stabbing him and even shot him [the corpse]."[102]

This cruelty first came to full light after the Taliban were rousted out of power in 2001. Books such as *The Kite Runner*, considered very well written by many critics, brought the full depravity of the Taliban to Western audiences.[103] Filled with scenes of murder and amputations, a 2003 movie, *Clouds*, was a romantic drama intended to expose the savagery of the Taliban and the misery of their era.[104] A critically acclaimed movie, *Osama*, highlighted the despair of beggars in the Taliban's Afghanistan and the plight of girls in the Sharia state.[105] Private screenings were held for then-first lady Laura Bush and senators Hillary Rodham Clinton and Kay

Bailey Hutchison.[106] *Escape from the Taliban* was an Indian-made movie that, like *Osama*, uncovered the depraved treatment of women.[107] Another movie, also critically admired, was *Kandahar*, which was filmed in Iran in 2002 and was a general indictment of the Taliban's rule.[108]

In the brief artistic spring of winter 2001, Afghan artists were optimistic. New plays were performed in the bombed-out theater of Kabul. The city's creative scene had promise. The theater's lead actor explained, "My dream is to have a proper theater with seats, a roof, and a stage . . . Maybe even a curtain."[109]

Profile 1.2: Marjan and Donatello

The Taliban's cruelty was not only directed at people; animals suffered too. The Taliban outlawed dog and pigeon fighting, popular male pastimes. But they did so because it was considered un-Islamic and involved gambling.[110] The Taliban do not like pets, but many Afghans enjoy them, particularly singing birds. Before the Taliban, Kabul residents delighted in visiting their zoo, which once housed 400 species of animals and an aquarium. Built in 1967, it became a point of civic pride. But zoos do not have a place in the Taliban's Salafist realm.

Taliban would beat and torture the zoo's animals, despite the pleas of the skeletal, largely unpaid staff for mercy. A particular target was a bear, Donatello, whose nose a Taliban cut off and whose festering wounds were poked by Taliban for fun. One of the zookeepers explained, "She is a poor little animal. She hasn't hurt anyone and yet, when the Taliban were here, they used to come in just to torment the animals."[111]

Marjan the lion was the prize of the zoo, where he had lived for 23 years. Like the human residents of Kabul, Marjan had a hard life and lived in cramped quarters. But he was cared for and fed regularly, until the Taliban came, because the zoo's staff loved him. When a bumptious Taliban jumped into the lion's cage to display his masculinity, Marjan bit off one of his legs. The following day, the recent amputee's brother threw a hand grenade at Marjan, blinding him in one eye.[112]

Marjan died in January 2002, and many Afghans grieved their loss. "This old, busted-up lion, with one eye, his jaw hanging down, was the symbol of the country. Old, ailing but proud, like Afghanistan," said John Walsh, of the World Society for the Protection of Animals, who was caring for Marjan in Kabul.[113] Marjan died at a moment when international aid was starting to restore the zoo and better the lives of its animals.[114] Donatello was nursed to health and given Marjan's pen, which was roomier. The animals at Kabul's zoo were accommodated better and fed healthier. They were treated with love again, and the Taliban were long gone.[115]

CHAPTER SUMMARY

The Afghan moniker "graveyard of empires" is well earned. Western and Eastern empires have invaded the country only to meet often stiff and sometimes insurmountable resistance. Among the invaders were the Greeks, Mongols, Arabs, British, and Soviets. Most Afghans saw Soviet developmental efforts as cosmetics to pretty up atheistic collectivism. The emergence of the Taliban could not have occurred without the collision of modernity with traditional Afghan society and the power vacuum left after the Soviet war.[116] Some of the Afghans and the Arabs who fought jihad against the Soviets would emerge as leaders in the Taliban, and one Arab, Osama bin Laden, would become the most wanted man in the world.

The fountainheads of the Taliban identity are Pashtun culture and Deobandi Islam. The Pashtuns are and have been the dominant tribe in Afghanistan. Pashtunwali is a code of conduct particular to the Pashtuns, and it characterizes many elements of the Taliban leadership and ranks. The cultural elements in Pashtun are honor, revenge, hospitality, requesting forgiveness, and serving a stronger tribe. The Deobandi School also made an imprint on the Taliban.

Islamism is a political variant of Islam that enshrines the most puritanical and primitive elements of the religion with modern political means of governance. The haughty bin Laden and the dour Mullah Omar did not share identical views of Islam, but held common goals. Both wanted to establish totalitarian, Islamist states. Whether or not Islamism, or modern political Islam, is fascistic is debatable. Its unrelenting hostility toward liberalism is not.

2

Enter the Taliban

Chapter 1 explored the geographic, cultural, religious, and ideological underpinnings of the Taliban. Chapter 2 focuses on the origins, victory, tenure, temporary destruction, and rejuvenation of the Taliban.

THE SETTING

The Taliban's ascent to power follows an ancient and often-practiced Afghan tradition of clan-tangled struggles for supremacy. In this perennial drama, ethnic and political factions vie to seize control of Kabul and to eliminate rivals.

The Taliban trace their origins from the mujahedeen of the Afghan-Soviet war. In the 1980s, Afghanistan was an inhospitable environment for ruling communist leaders and their sympathizers. There were some Afghans who supported the Communist Party, which promised to modernize and, to some extent, communize the country.[1] Soviets found some partners in Kabul's small, well-educated elites, who saw themselves as stakeholders in Afghanistan's development.

But Marxism-Leninism never resonated with Afghans. Soviet atheism and communist contempt for religion, no matter how well cosmeticized to an Afghan audience, became tropes of the anti-Soviet insurgency. Socialist, state-oriented planning panicked many Afghans, who feared the Soviet-led agenda as an attack on Islam.[2] As a result, a civil war erupted, the Soviets intervened, and the United States began to give the mujahedeen supplies. The Saudis, as well, gave aid to the mujahedeen.

Pakistani leaders had a strong role in training, equipping, provisioning, guiding, and leading the mujahedeen. The relationships forged during this period would be rekindled. A leading and flashy figure is the former Pakistani intelligence chief Hamid Gul (see Profile 8.3), who worked closely with several major mujahedeen fighters who today are battling U.S. troops and trying to topple the Afghan government. Some of Gul's former cohorts are insurgent leaders today. They include Gulbuddin Hekmatyar, who is not an associate of the Taliban, and Jalaluddin Haqqani, who is connected to them.[3]

The war against the Soviets was over, but there was not peace. In the 1990s Afghanistan continued to be a magnet for jihadis and zealots worldwide. It attracted Islamist ideologues, romantics, adventurers, and those trying to escape the routine and despair in the Middle East's failed states. Religious zealots who wanted to uproot corruption, secularism, and cronyism in the Middle East could not do so in the Middle Eastern states in which they lived. In many of the authoritarian states, such as Saudi Arabia and Egypt, the domestic intelligence and security services were very strong.

Islamic states, particularly Arab countries, began to take seriously the threat of the Brotherhood in the 1990s. In Arab countries, security and intelligence personnel purged the civil service, military, and, to the extent they could, seminaries of Islamists. There was an unwritten understanding that Islamism would be tolerated, as long as it was not focused on existing, local governments, such as the Saudi monarchy. For this reason, in the second half of the 1990s, many malcontents and Islamic dogmatists, often opulently funded by wealthy Arabs, moved to Afghanistan and Western states.[4] Liberal constitutions in Europe protected many doctrinaire Muslim preachers, and Afghanistan was wide-open country.

The foreign fighters in Afghanistan were drawn from many states including Chechnya, China, Indonesia, Pakistan, the Philippines, and Uzbekistan, and particularly the Arab Middle East. Some stayed in Afghanistan, took local wives, built families, and became known as "Arab Afghans." Over 2,000 Arab combatants, many apparently affiliated with and financed by bin Laden, were actively supporting the Taliban by 2001. Pakistanis living in and near the borders of Afghanistan had strong sympathies for the Taliban.

From the Taliban's earliest days, neighboring Pakistan played a strong role in Taliban affairs. The Jama 'a Islami party of Pakistan gave material and logistical support to the Taliban, in the early 1990s. Wealthy Saudis financed a vast network of madrassas, or religious schools, largely in Pakistan. These madrassas indoctrinated the young with a martial spirit.[5] With Saudi largess, the number of madrassas exploded from 245 in 1947 to 6,741 in 2007.[6]

The Taliban were developed, and to some extent nurtured, by the Pakistani Interservices Intelligence Directorate, the ISI, sometimes referred to as ISID. Afghanistan and Pakistan share a long border, and Pakistan views

Afghanistan's security concerns as its own.[7] Between 1997 and 1998, Pakistan provided the Taliban with an estimated $30 million. Bonds between Pakistani officials and the Taliban grew very strong. Some observers of the Pakistani scene said that the ISI officers had become "more Taliban than the Taliban."[8] The ISI introduced Osama bin Laden to the Taliban.[9]

THE TALIBAN BUILDS ROOTS

Afghanistan's government was never strong and usually tenuous during the reign of President Burhanuddin Rabbani, who held office from June 1992 until 1996.[10] He never had a durable base, lacked charisma, was not a Pashtun, and proved incapable of uniting Afghanistan.[11] Another civil war was on, and one year later the forces of Mullah Omar became combatants.

The reclusive leader of the Taliban, Mullah Mohammed Omar, led the Taliban to gain control of one-third of the country within two years, two-thirds of the country by three years, and nine-tenths of the country by five years. In the summer of 1994, Omar elbowed his small band of seminary students into the general Afghan fracas. He killed local warlords in Afghanistan's south who were connected to the rape of a girl.[12] During the next several years, he expanded his power base to control 90 percent of the country.[13]

The Taliban's leader was young, by the standards of a society that venerated age, associating it with wisdom, political acumen, and survival skills. Unlike some of his rivals who had university training, the canny Mullah Omar was largely self-educated. He rarely traveled outside of Kandahar. In keeping with Islamic tradition, he took several wives, some accounts say three, and fathered 13 children. He joined the jihad against the Soviet invasion of 1979, and lost one eye in an artillery battle.[14]

The fall of the Afghan capital Kabul to the Taliban militia in September 1996 marked a distinct break from the politics of the preceding decades. Both the communist regime and the Soviet-aligned government tried to modernize the country, within the confines of Afghan culture and the country's resources. But the Taliban had no such ambition. Instead, Taliban leaders were content to have their countrymen subsist in the margins of absolute poverty.

While the Taliban's victory ended a protracted civil war, it did not halt all the violence. The Taliban began to mete out their cruelty immediately after they took control in September 1996. They proclaimed Afghanistan to be the Islamic Emirate of Afghanistan and the law of the land to be Sharia. A first target of the Taliban was the former communist President Najibullah, whom the Taliban murdered and whose corpse, along with that of his brother, was horrifically displayed as war trophy (see Profile 3.2).[15]

In keeping with revenge, or badal, the Taliban settled tribal scores when they seized power. As an example, in the spring of 1997 the northern city of Mazar-i-Sharif jockeyed between Taliban and non-Pashtun Uzbek and Hazara civilians. When the Taliban controlled the city, they killed many Uzbeks and Hazaras. Later, when the Taliban lost control of the city, the ethnicities whom they persecuted took revenge on the now-weakened Taliban.[16] This reversal of fortune continued as towns and villages changed hands, and former victims became victimizers.

On their way to Kabul, the Taliban butchered Hazaras in well-planned and ruthless killing actions. Human Rights Watch, Asia division, wrote in 1998, "We are talking about the systematic execution of perhaps 2,000 civilians."[17] Often, Hazaras can be identified by a distinct Mongoloid appearance, and they often live in concentrated areas. According to verified reports, Taliban would go house to house dragging out the men, women, and children, shooting them in killing pits or along the roads. Survivors related, "The Taliban shot at anything that moved."[18]

By September 2000, the Taliban controlled 95 percent of the country and were fighting mainly against the Tajik Ahmed Shah Massoud, Prime Minister Rabbani's former defense minister, who defended parts of the north. This was the remaining part of the country not controlled by the Taliban.

Profile 2.1: Omar, "Commander of the Faithful," Consolidates His Power

From the beginning, Mullah Omar demonstrated political acumen and military savvy. His political charisma connected with his Pashtun constituency, and he drew and held people in even the most difficult times.[19] Omar developed a powerful hold on his followers, and his magnetism served as glue when the Taliban's fortunes were dire. He gave the poor of Kandahar a sense of value and of being a part of a great family of Muslims.[20] Initially, Omar lived frugally, in a mud-brick home. One journalist described him as a "simple man unaccustomed to the perks of power."[21] When the Taliban captured Kabul in September 1996, Omar remained in his Kandahar cocoon, along with a small coterie of Taliban leaders. He established a skeletal bureaucracy in Kabul.

Born in the mid- to late 1950s, Omar lived an impoverished childhood and learned early both self-reliance and leadership skills. As a young man, he showed an aptitude for religious study. After studying in a madrassa in Pakistan, he opened his own religious school and then fought in the anti-Soviet jihad from 1989 to 1992. On the battlefield and in the mosques, he delivered dulcet sermons, which resonated among the more pious. In the anti-Soviet fight, he lost an eye but gained tactical military skills and religious standing, which he would exploit several years later.

Omar made little attempt to converse with nonbelievers, in almost any circumstances.[22] Even among his closest congregants and political operatives, Omar was a recluse. He held extended conversations with no more than a handful of Westerners. His taciturn behavior is still seen as humble by many Afghans, which boosts his image.

His knowledge of the Koran, much of which was self-taught; fighting skills; soft-spoken self-confidence; and aptitude for bringing peace and rule of law, cemented his power. This autodidact became legendary when, in 1996, he donned a cloak reputed to have belonged to Mohammed and pronounced himself "commander of the faithful."[23] His followers in the audience began to swoon, weep, and faint.

Most men who could have deserted Omar during the nadir of the Taliban's fortunes in 2002 did not do so, despite grueling living conditions. Nor were there known, well-coordinated conspiracies to unseat Omar. Under Omar's leadership, the Taliban recruited, rebuilt, and quickly began to reengage the Coalition Forces in battle.

His charisma also had mesmerizing and twisted elements. Omar persuaded many Taliban to commit vicious crimes, such as mass murder, throwing acid in the face of girls, summary execution, and amputations for trivial offenses. Afghans have an image of being a tough people, but they do not have a reputation of being sadistic. The Taliban perpetrated unbounded cruelty far in excess of Afghan tradition. Nothing like that happened in the memory of modern Afghanistan.

Nonetheless, Mullah Omar attracted both Afghans and non-Afghans. It was not by coincidence that bin Laden was given refuge in the Taliban's Afghanistan. Saudi Arabia expelled bin Laden in 1991[24] and revoked his citizenship in 1994.[25] He declared war on the West in 1998.[26] In Afghanistan bin Laden, who was wanted by U.S. authorities,[27] continued his screeds against Americans, and Mullah Omar continued to offer him refuge.[28]

The Afghanistan of the Taliban was a natural refuge for bin Laden. Bin Laden and Mullah Omar shared charismatic traits that resonated in segments of the Islamic world. Both leaders distinguished their messages and agendas as being authentically Muslim, though from different legal schools of Sunni Islam. Both were ascetic and contemptuous of modern comforts. Bin Laden left the wealth and the fortune, to which he was heir, to toil among the Afghan poor. This helped cultivate an image of a stoic Muslim hero committed to austere self-discipline, which garnered international prestige. Mullah Omar expressed a more local and Pashtun-focused vision of Islam.

Today, years after Omar was pushed into exile, he holds the enduring loyalty of his still-smitten constituents. The devotion continues despite his absence. Few Taliban have seen him since he scurried on the back of a motorcycle from Kandahar in late 2001. Even when he was in power, he rarely made public appearances and ventured to Kabul only once from his home in Kandahar.[29]

There were two primary differences that distinguished Omar's and bin Laden's style of charisma. First, there was bin Laden's showiness. Bin Laden, despite his protestations to the contrary, reveled in celebrity status until the last few years of his life. He held court in his tent encampments, where he self-reverentially lectured Arab and some Western journalists about the impending wrath of his sword.[30] Bin Laden was very comfortable in front of a camera. During the anti-Soviet jihad, he commissioned a 50-minute video displaying him in manly pursuits, such as bareback riding on horses and firing weapons. Omar remains shy and retiring, preferring to be closeted with his staff.

Finally, their charisma appealed to distinctly different audiences. Bin Laden's audience was global, as were his ambitions, while Mullah Omar's continues to be markedly provincial and Afghan. Their leadership styles were dissimilar, but they shared a common goal of a global Islamic supremacy. They were also united in hatred of the United States.

THE TALIBAN AND THE GENERAL TEMPLATE OF INSURGENCY

Omar would lead his insurgency to victory. He would face many of the same strategic challenges leading the insurgency in exile after 2001. An insurgency is a type of small war that varies in intensity and time and levels of success and failure. Insurgencies attempt to undermine a government's legitimacy to force the insurgents' political agenda on the country. There are many definitions of insurgency, but most good ones have at least four elements:

- It is an organized movement with leadership, command, and control. A food riot or mob attack does not qualify as an insurgency.
- It intends to destroy the current government and replace it with a new and usually fundamentally different type of government. Insurgents are not reformers who intend to modify existing political conditions, such the civil rights marchers in the United States during the 1960s.
- It is a protracted struggle. There are few week- or month-long insurgencies.
- Tactics are directed at weakening the government's control and legitimacy. For this reason, propaganda is used extensively.

U.S. doctrine defines insurgency as "an organized movement aimed at the overthrow of a constituted government through the use of subversion and armed conflict."[31] This definition certainly applies to the insurgency in Afghanistan.

U.S. Army analysis of twentieth-century insurgencies determined that there were prerequisites for success. First, the population needed to be vulnerable to either the coercion or the soft power of the insurgents. If the insurgents effectively intimidated villages, as did the Viet Cong in Vietnam, the will of the villagers could be worn down. Sometimes, insurgents could successfully tap into common dissatisfaction with the government and widespread resentment of living conditions. In Afghanistan, there was certainly a vulnerable population segment. Because Afghanistan was only nominally a unitary state in the early 1990s, the Taliban could bully many villagers, and they did so. But they also controlled criminal syndicates and brigands.

Second, there needed to be competent insurgent leadership, and Omar was certainly capable. A third prerequisite was a lack of government control over substantial portions of the country. The greater control the government had, the less the chance of insurgent triumph. Afghanistan was largely in disarray in the early 1990s. From 1992 to 1996, the frailties of the Rabanni government were exploited by the Taliban's propaganda element.

THE PHASES OF AN INSURGENCY

The insurgency developed according to a well-established, historic pattern. Insurgencies evolve from a small nucleus and develop into a recognized and persistent threat to the government. Most insurgencies, including the current one in Afghanistan, follow a general chronological template. Mao, long considered the most successful practitioner of modern insurgency, developed his three-phase model in the 1930s. U.S. intelligence produced a template that is very similar to Mao's and integrates the elements of guerilla and conventional warfare.[32] There are three phases.

In the first phase, leadership emerges. Secret cells are created, supplies are gathered, propaganda is generated, but direct conflict is generally avoided. This is a building phase, which often focuses on developing, not destroying, infrastructure development.[33] Mao also articulated a set of principles to avoid alienating potential comrades. Violence is generally shunned and killings are highly selective and occur rarely. Insurgents speak in a vocabulary and cadence that draws the confidence of villagers.

In their first surge to power, in the mid-1990s, the Taliban won the confidence of local Afghans. They came to attention when they interceded to protect a young woman who was sexually violated. They built legitimacy among clerics, who in turn legitimized the Taliban. Clerics praised the Taliban in their sermons. Support of clerics to justify violence is essential.[34]

In this first phase of the Afghan insurgency, as in the second, Arabs came en masse to swell the Taliban's ranks. By the time the Taliban consolidated power, Arab jihadis were noticeable in key cities. Arabs, particularly those affiliated with al Qaeda, brought enthusiasm, financing, and technical expertise. But there is no evidence that any major Taliban victories were determined exclusively by the fighting Arabs. The Taliban displayed military acumen and uncanny intelligence capabilities, which continue to this day. They cultivated a vast network of informants and sympathizers and bought off enemies with foreign-supplied money. They also learned from mistakes and innovated.

The Taliban understood, perhaps as well as any Afghan political cohort, the significance of the mullah in South Asian culture. Becoming a mullah gives an Afghan social mobility; he is no longer constrained to the occupation of his father.[35] Mullahs can travel freely across Afghanistan and are treated respectfully and hospitably by village commoners and grandees. They can also establish their own madrassas.[36] In Afghan culture, only a mullah can declare jihad with any credibility.[37] Omar understood that building ties with mullahs would enable the Taliban to move to the second phase of their insurgency.

In the second phase of an insurgency, the insurgents take military action to dislodge the government. This can include attacks, assassinations, sabotage, or subversive activities. This is the "organizational phase" in which the group builds its infrastructure, recruits and trains cadre, and acquires supplies.[38] The Taliban pursued this from 1994 to 1996 when they fought rival groups of different ethnicities, sometimes in pitched battle.[39] They also settled scores with rivaling ethnicities and clans.

The third and final phase of insurgent warfare is conventional warfare. In the last phase of the war in Vietnam, it was armor, artillery, and massive infantry power that conquered Saigon.[40] If the transition is properly timed, the government has been weakened sufficiently to succumb to assault by an onslaught of insurgent forces.[41] Many insurgencies never reach this stage. The Taliban reached this point during their final drive to Kabul in 1996.

Many killings in all three evolutionary stages were driven by military necessity. Some of the Taliban's brutality, however, was driven by revenge or gratuitous sadism. For example, in 1998 in Mazar-i-Sharif, after wreaking bloody vengeance on the civilians, the Taliban rounded up 11 Iranian diplomats and shot them dead. In Mazar, the Taliban's mass suffocations, executions, and torture stunned UN observers, who calculated that between 4,000 and 5,000 people were slaughtered.[42]

The Taliban continued to hound men and dislodge children and women after 1996. As late as 1999, the Taliban swept across the Shomali Plains north of Kabul and arrested, killed, and drove away women and children in buses to remote destinations. There, they would suffer and some would die

Table 2.1   Three Phases of Warfare and the Taliban

	Phase 1: Preinsurgency	Phase 2: Guerilla Warfare	Phase 3: Mobile Warfare
Defining Elements	Developing secret cells, gathering supplies, building bases of operations, expanding credibility, disseminating propaganda	Initiate attacks against enemy targets, recruit and train cadre, and eliminate opposition forces. Use terror, if necessary, to subdue hostile elements in society	War of movement, infantry, supported by artillery and armor. Engages government forces in pitched battle
Application to Afghanistan	The Taliban were engaged in this stage in the very early 1990s when Mullah Omar was consolidating power. When the Taliban were forced from Afghanistan in 2001, they returned to this phase in the borderlands by consolidating their power and regrouping	As of winter 2013, the Taliban are currently in this stage. They target progovernment forces and terrorize those they suspect of working against their cause	The Taliban reached this stage in 1994–1996 prior to their ascension to power in 1996

from privation. The United Nations estimated that up to 20,000 women and children were evicted from their homes and forcibly relocated.[43]

Killing was common, and many Afghans did not see the Taliban as liberators. After the Taliban concluded the third phase of the insurgency, they blocked aid to starving villagers swept up in a war they could not escape and hoped only to survive. One example took place in Hazarajat, located in the mountainous regions of central Afghanistan, in 1998, when 1.5 million people began to starve after the Taliban blocked supply routes. Afghans died of starvation, measles, and diseases brought on by degraded immune systems. Blockades are common in war, but this one was directed at the Hazaras, whom the Taliban loathe for religious and racial reasons.[44]

Table 2.1 lists the three phases of Mao's model and their applications to Afghanistan.

CHAPTER SUMMARY

The Taliban's ascent to power followed a general template of insurgencies. The first phase is one of building and organizing. The second phase initiated violent attacks; the third is one of maneuver and pitched battle. Mullah Omar and Osama bin Laden shared a Salafist view of Islam and had contempt for the West. The prickly Omar revealed a soft-spoken charisma, and bin Laden exhibited more sizzle and braggadocio. The Taliban took power in a standard three-stage insurgency pattern. The Taliban promised to create a self-contained Islamic state. They certainly tried to do just that, under a suffocating theocracy, which is the subject of the third chapter.

3

The Taliban in Power

Jihad in the path of Allah is greater than any individual or organization.
—Ayman al-Zawahiri[1]

Chapter 2 traced the Taliban's ascent to power. It discussed the ideological bond of a preening bin Laden and reclusive Mullah Omar and the general template of insurgencies. It offered a three-stage model for insurgencies and analyzed the Taliban's rise to power in its context. Chapter 3 will discuss the Taliban's agenda and policies when they held power from 1996 to 2001.

THE TALIBAN BUILDS ITS BASE

During their sweep to power, the Taliban looked to boys and young men to fill their periodically depleted ranks. Recruits were largely drawn from slums located near refugee camps in Afghanistan and adjacent areas in Pakistan. They were often chronically unemployed, with low levels of education and weak skill sets. Many were drifters, dead-enders, or were very young, alone, and in search of parental figures. Some were religious zealots searching for a community. Religious schools in Afghanistan and Pakistan continued to serve as pools from which the Taliban's leadership drew foot soldiers.[2]

The Taliban determined to beat out any hint of humanity in their boys. Boys and young men were indoctrinated and hardened to ensure that they would kill their enemy without mercy or hesitation. A brutal example was captured on video, as a preadolescent boy slit the throat of a blindfolded man. The victim was accused of being an American spy. As the child hoisted the severed head in the air, he cried, "God is great!"[3] Boys who resisted this hardening were whipped or sometimes killed. Those suspected of disloyalty would be hanged with dollar bills shoved in their mouths.[4] This indoctrination would continue in the Taliban's exile. The Taliban tapped into the boys' innate aggression and unrelieved sexual frustration. Celestial harems of nubile virgins, or houris, await Muslim men who fall in battle for Islam.[5]

Beyond their malice, the Taliban were totalitarian. Bin Laden and the Arabs and other international fighters fused the Islamism of Qutb and Azzam with the Deobandi philosophy of Afghan elites. All human activity was to be channeled toward replicating the time of their Prophet. In this spirit, music, dancing, kite flying, and chess playing were all banned.[6] Soccer matches were permitted, but spectators could only legally cheer "Allahu Akbar" to rally their teams.[7] The games themselves had sadistic elements of Caligula's Rome, as those convicted of crimes were publicly whipped, clubbed, and killed. Limbs were amputated, as Taliban leaders exhorted the audience to shout approval. The cruelty was vast, frequent, cavalier, and often morbid. As a result, morale plummeted among the educated and relatively secular, and those who had the ability to flee often did so.

How people behaved and thought, raised their children, spoke to their spouse, engaged in civil society, and practiced religion were monitored by Taliban agents. Fear was pervasive. There was a communally shared responsibility to expose those who did not conform to political/economic orthodoxy and to eliminate any contagion of deviationism. Villagers would notify the secret police about neighbors' transgressions. Often, the accused would be hauled to prison.

Life was difficult for Muslims in Afghanistan and even more so for the relatively few non-Muslims. The Taliban demanded that non-Muslims subordinate themselves to Muslims. Life was particularly onerous for Hindus, who, during the Taliban's tenure, were required to carry badges identifying themselves as non-Muslims.

BACK TO THE PROPHET

Mullah Omar's spokesman explained, "We want to re-create the time of the Prophet." It would have been more accurate to state that the Taliban intended to regress to an era in Arabia that was imagined by the Taliban. The life and customs of Mohammed's world have long been obscured by hagiography, legend, and literary embellishments. There are no extant and accurate accounts of the life of Mohammed.[8] But the Taliban believe that living in the world of the first-generation Muslims requires purging elements of modern society that are contrary to the Koran.

The worldview of the Taliban was also shaped by the interplay of isolation and poverty. The Taliban were cloistered from modernity and wanted to keep Afghanistan safe from globalization. To tighten further this insulation, Mullah Omar tried to ban the Internet, a task made easy by the county's

Table 3.1   Traits of the Taliban

	Taliban's Goals	Implications for Daily Life Today
Salafism	To re-create the political, social, and economic world of the early seventh century. To rid Afghanistan of all modern and corruptive influences	Antithetical to all modern norms of economic and social development. Undercuts all economic and financial innovations of the last 1,300 years
Isolation and Poverty	To keep Afghanistan separate from globalization. The Taliban prize the geographic isolation as a barrier against Western contamination	Wireless communications made strides in linking Afghans to their villages and their country to the outside world. But the Taliban threaten to reduce these gains
Totalitarian	To monitor the behavior of all Afghans by re-creating and expanding informant networks. Any deviation of Islamic law is punished	States that become heavily regulated reduce entrepreneurial creativity and risk taking. The quality of life deteriorates and people become fatalistic

primitive communication systems. What few international organizations remained in Afghanistan were heavily monitored, censored, and muzzled.[9]

In July 1998, the Taliban gave Afghan families 15 days to rid themselves of television sets, videocassette recorders, and satellite dishes.[10] For many Afghans, the decision was irrelevant because there was no television available. Many villages also had no access to electricity. The electrical grids in much of the country had long ceased to function. Afghans did not need electricity to sing folk songs. But the Taliban banned them too. Unless the songs promoted Islam, they were not to be sung. An enforced silence would give more Muslims more time to pray.

Table 3.1 shows the Taliban's goals and the implications for the Taliban's agenda on the daily life of Afghans, should the Taliban take power again.

A NEW DARK AGE—LIFE UNDER THE TALIBAN

The Economy Declines

The Taliban's conquest of Kabul brought a new, if reactionary, era to Afghanistan. By almost all standards of living, the quality of life for Afghans, poor as it was, deteriorated. It is unlikely that any influential Taliban leader had a sophisticated understanding of contemporary, market-based economic theories.[11] Several modern Islamic countries, particularly Malaysia and Turkey, have enjoyed sustained economic development in recent years without significant petroleum exports. But the Afghan economy withered because the Taliban did not promote sustained economic growth. They subordinated economic growth to cloying religiosity in all of Afghanistan.[12]

By any set of credible economic standards, Afghanistan was a failed state.[13] Failed states have several defining characteristics, including the inability to control the physical territory of the state; provide basic social services, such as electricity, potable water, emergency services, and police services; collect adequate tax revenue or combat corruption; sustain adequate levels of economic growth, employment, and job creation; mitigate the effects of social and sexual discrimination and group-based inequality; and prevent the erosion of the environment.[14] Afghanistan in the Taliban's time failed on all counts.

In 1998 and 1999 agricultural production increased; livestock herds sharply rose in numbers, taking advantage of grazing lands that had not been used in years; and horticulture improved with the expansion of orchards and vineyards. But this economic uptick was misleading. The economic recovery was concentrated in areas of the country conquered relatively early by the Taliban. Economic growth occurred because the peace prompted Afghans to invest. When the investment stopped, the economy began to crater.

The Taliban impoverished more than the lives of Afghan citizens from 1996 to 2001. The effects of their botched programs seeped into the larger South and Central Asian neighborhood.[15] The consequences of political, economic, and social instability of the failed Afghan state had spillover effects on neighboring countries. Among those effects were vast problems with refugees, public health, and sanitation.

In Table 3.2, the traits of the failed states are shown.

In their governance, the Taliban preferred small government to expansive administration.[16] This inattention to large-scale infrastructure development soon degraded the quality of public service. Soon, the deterioration in basic social services—public administration, health, communications, and education—took root and was aggravated by the Taliban's inchoate policies, which largely excluded women from work and girls from employment and education. The already shambolic Afghan civil service was largely collapsed by the Taliban rule. While a primary goal of most civil services is to provide essential services, the Taliban's priority was to prevent moral corruption. Religious police sometimes beat those who did not conform to the Taliban's norms. This resulted in a hemorrhage of educated talent in many public bureaucracies.

Communications and education that did not promote the expansion of Islam were neglected or prohibited. In a country with very limited print, radio, and electronic communications, it became very difficult for men and women to communicate at all, other than between immediate family members. Females could not leave the home without a male guardian. The Taliban heavily regulated content on the radio and television. The one

Table 3.2   Failed States and Afghanistan 1996–2001

Traits of a Failed or Failing State	Application to Afghanistan
Inability to control the physical territory	The Taliban controlled most of Afghanistan, but never all of it. Control of much of the country was shared by narco-traffickers
Inability to provide basic services	Lack of capacity, corruption, and disorganization militate against effective public administration. Delivery of basic services is improving significantly in cities and slowly in villages
Inability to sustain adequate levels of economic growth, employment, and job creation	Initial, slight increase in economic growth, followed by stagnation
Inability to mitigate the effects of social and sexual discrimination and group-based inequality	There was vast inequality between the sexes, as well as tribal inequities

European pop singer who was regularly broadcast was the Greek-Anglo crooner-turned-Salafist Yusuf Islam, or Cat Stevens.[17] Other Western pop and movie stars were declared menacing to Afghan values. The movie *Titanic* and its theme song were banned, as was the then-fashionable Leonardo DiCaprio floppy haircut, which was declared foppish and sacrilegious.[18] By January 2001, the Taliban imprisoned 22 barbers for offering this hairstyle under the puzzling reasoning that the long bangs impede the ability to bow and pray.[19]

The country's health care, poor as it was, decayed. As in all other sectors of human development, girls and women suffered disproportionately under the welter of Taliban restraints. The Taliban drastically limited access to medical services.[20] The State Department's 1998 *Human Rights Report* described "the Taliban's devastating disregard for the physical and psychological health of women and girls." Women and girls who were starving were not allowed to beg. The depravations of girls and women were publicized in the United States by celebrities.[21] First Lady Hillary Clinton publically protested.

The melancholy and despondency endured by Afghans in the Taliban era was revealed in a 2002 study conducted by the U.S. Centers for Disease Control and Prevention. It found, unsurprisingly, that approximately 70 percent of Afghan people showed signs of clinical depression and anxiety. The rates were even higher for women and the disabled. After the Taliban were ejected, the collective mental health of the Afghan people, particularly females, improved, though unevenly and not everywhere.

As with the Afghan people, the economy of Afghanistan was made sick by the Taliban's farrago of religious edicts. Despite opportunities for foreign investment in the post–civil war peace, few investors, domestic or foreign, were eager to risk capital that could be easily expropriated at the whim of a mullah. Commercial transactions that did not conform to Taliban's standards of virtue could be nullified by civil servants on the basis that they promoted vice and evil. Also, international lending agencies were kept at bay, as were many NGOs.

If there is any human development sector in which the Taliban's tenure was not an unmitigated catastrophe, it is the security sector. The Taliban's victory ended the civil war in 1996. In this sense, they increased the level of security in Afghanistan. The mass, unregulated killings were stopped.[22] But this came at a cost of a fear-induced social paralysis. The Taliban offered only the eerie and sullen calm of effective autarchy.

Despite the misery and forced conformity, the Taliban made the streets safer.[23] Ironically, the Taliban brought the promise of stability, reform, and economic recovery in the initial days of their rule. In what proved to be wildly optimistic accounts of the Taliban's early days in Kandahar, the Taliban's bellwether, some Western journalists described the Taliban as moderate reformers.[24] This seems shocking in retrospect, but the Taliban restored a sense of order. Fun was outlawed in Afghanistan, but crime was low.

The Taliban's rule of law was characterized by a wide-ranging set of draconian measures that insinuated themselves into all elements of daily life. They criminalized all activity that led men to neglect religious study. The legal system segregated women, who were banned from schools and most workplaces and were virtually imprisoned in their homes. Taliban authorities struck men suspected of trimming their beards, and men who had difficulty growing the required four inches of facial hair sometimes sported false beards to avoid harassment. Those accused or convicted of crimes were at the mercy of Islamic courts. Amnesty International claimed that 1,000 people were arrested within a month of the takeover and that many disappeared.[25]

Particularly notorious were the legally sanctioned and internationally broadcast public revenge killings and amputations. As in Saudi Arabia, Afghan Sharia courts administered Koran-mandated single and double amputations, which were often held publically. In the Kabul Sports Stadium, sedated criminals, usually punished for stealing small amounts, had their right hands amputated by Taliban physicians as a prequel to the main attraction of shooting more serious offenders. Often women would be vigorously whipped before the crowd. One woman was flogged 100 times for being with a man to whom she was not related. Women in the stadium wept as she was lashed.[26] After the killing and torture, a soccer game, often modified with Islamic rules, would be played. As one Afghan said in 1998, "In America, you have television and movies—the cinema. Here, we can only have this."[27]

Profile 3.1: Zarmina's Hammer

Zarmina should never have been killed. She had a hard life. She was not educated. She wasn't aware of Islamic law. All she knew was that her husband beat her.
                    —Rana Sayeed, Afghan policewoman and detective[28]

Some pictures of Afghan women have become iconic: the 1984 *National Geographic* picture of Gula, the rattily clad girl with the haunting green eyes;[29] *Time's* cover photograph of Bibi Aisha, whose husband slashed her face and cut off her nose;[30] and the killing of Zarmina, the woman without a face.

Unlike those of Gula and Bibi Aisha, Zarmina's face was obscured to the world by her burka, which she wore to her death. Accused of killing her husband, the mother of seven children was transported in the back of a Toyota pickup, dragged to Kabul's Olympic Stadium, forced to kneel between the goalposts of the soccer field, and shot in the head by a Taliban.[31]

Raised in northern Kabul and described as pretty and feisty, Zarmina was wed at 16 to a Pashtun, Khwazak, who was a policeman and part-time proprietor of a small general store. Khwazak's personality began to sour as the Taliban solidified power. Some neighbors speculated that the trauma of the killings, rapes, and bombings warped his mind and turned him into a brute. Others saw his descent into cruelty as being in line with his solidarity with the Taliban.

Khwazak beat Zarmina and their children regularly. He became a policeman for the Taliban and pestered and tormented girls and women. His moods were unpredictable, and neither Zarmina nor her children could anticipate what would send him into a ruthless rage. Zarmina decided to kill Khwazak. She may have drugged him by lacing his food with opiates and then clubbing him with a 10-pound mason's hammer. It may have been an elder daughter who delivered the lethal blow and then staged a scene of a burglary that became violent.[32]

The Taliban police were suspicious immediately, and Zarmina and her two youngest children were imprisoned for three years. Zarmina confessed to the murder, claiming she acted alone. She was kept alive in prison by the compassion of fellow inmates, who gave her bits of food and a blanket.[33] Zarmina's elder children were placed in the custody of her Taliban brother-in-law, who told Zarmina, two months before she was executed, that he sold her two elder daughters into prostitution. According to an investigator, the brother-in-law told Zarmina the price he received for each of her daughters. It is not unusual to sell unwanted girls and women. Prices typically go between $530 and $3,200 for the more nubile and attractive.[34]

On November 15, 1999, the Taliban told Zarmina that she would be killed in two days. The Toyota, in which Zarmina was captive, circled the soccer field twice, which is caught on video and posted on YouTube. She was forced to kneel between the goalposts, and Zarmina prepared herself. But men and women in the stadium began to jump and shout, and begged the Taliban to show Zarmina mercy. "Let her live," many cried. This startled but did not deter the Taliban. Bracing herself, Zarmina raised both arms and pleaded for somebody to hold them, to help her steady herself.[35] The Taliban then shot her in the head.[36]

Her body lay unclaimed for weeks because nobody wanted it. Her mother avowed, "She brought shame. She deserved what she got. She is not even a memory to me."[37] She is buried in an unmarked, pauper's grave, and several of her children were living as beggars in 2002. The whereabouts of her other children are not known. A police-woman who investigated Zarmina's death in 2002 said with a sigh, "At last Zarmina's story can be told. It is the story of one woman. But it is also the story of Afghan women under the Taliban ... brutes who turned our country into a zoo and our women into dogs."[38]

Resistance

There was defiance, though usually subtle and nonphysical. As in other repressed totalitarian regimes, intellectuals and free spirits found expression in quiet humor. Away from eyes of backwater bureaucrats, boys, being boys, would play makeshift games. Villagers would ridicule the pettiness of the mullah disciplinarians behind their backs, and the more daring might pull a prank. The desire to learn could not be entirely sapped from the more-clever and curious children. In village shadows, women taught girls elementary subjects, with child sentries posted to watch for Taliban or informers.[39] One girl pretended to be a boy. She fooled the Taliban, studied hard, and won a scholarship to Middlebury College. Years later, she would return to Kabul to build her own school.

But many could not escape the Taliban's gaze or their often-capricious poundings. Old men accustomed to respectful treatment were often publically humiliated. Boys caught playing games in violation of local rules could have their bones broken. Punishment, including lapidation, was delivered in wild disproportion to offenses. For example, when an irascible mullah overheard two men snicker at him in a car, he took all the passengers and incarcerated them in a dark room where he pummeled and burned them. One of the victims said, "I have always been a laughing man, but they broke my heart."[40]

Those who sought temporary escape from the tedium of Taliban life through narcotics prayed that they would not be caught.[41] Hashish was strictly prohibited. The Taliban's treatment was unlike anything substance abusers would enjoy in a California rehabilitation clinic. First, the convict was tortured until he identified the seller. He was then given an automatic jail sentence of usually one year in a lice-infested, cramped cell. To break his addiction, he was repeatedly dunked in ice water for up to three hours each day. Sometimes it worked. "When they put me it that cold water, I forgot about hashish," said one drug abuser in 1997.[42]

There was little occasion for creative artistic expression in the Taliban's world. In Muslims' holy writings, stringed instruments and flutes are considered pagan. One saying warns that on the day of resurrection, "Allah will pour molten lead into the ears of whomever sits listening to a songstress."[43]

But art that promotes Islamic virtue, though heavily censored, was and is allowed. Taliban have composed darkly lyrical poetry. In an anthology of Taliban poetry complied by two European researchers, the personal dimension to Taliban cadre emerges. Some poems refer to youthful longings for home: "I know the black, black mountains / My home is the mountains."[44] There are also satirical barbs at an imaginary love affair between President Karzai and President Bush.

But most comedians were straightjacketed by prohibitive speech codes. Taliban are not known for their sense of humor. A popular Pakistani jokester was kidnapped and threatened with death by the Taliban if he made Islamic audiences laugh. After he was roughed up and released in Peshawar in 2009, the funnyman explained to his fans, "I'm retiring from showbiz."[45]

Other entertainers have not been as lucky. In early 2009 a regionally famous Pakistani dancer, Shabana, pleading for her life, was thrown into the middle of a town square in Swat Valley, where she promised, " 'I quit, I won't sing again, leave me for God's sake, I am a Muslim, I am fasting. Don't behead me.' Weeping over her beaten and fallen daughter, Shabana's mother promised, 'We will leave this city and we never return.' "[46] But the Taliban riddled Shabana with bullets and tossed bank notes, CDs of her dance performances, and pictures of her smiling and dancing on her lifeless body.[47] Then, they strung the 25-year-old's corpse from a telegraph pole to frighten other girls and women from dancing. They continued to kill. Elsewhere in Pakistan singers at a wedding festival were assaulted and the harmonium player was killed. As one skittish singer in the Northwest Frontier Province confessed, "I'm scared to leave my home."[48]

But an 11-year-old girl who lived in Shabana's village of Mingora resolved to chronicle the killings and inform the world. "They cannot stop me. I will get my education if it is my home, school or any place. This is our request to all the world. Save our schools. Save our world. Save our Pakistan. Save our Swat."[49] She was Malala Yousafzai and, under the guidance and protection of her father, she became an online diarist recording a child's life under the Taliban.

Taliban Rules

The Taliban, like other insurgent groups or governments, have a set of defined political and social codes. The Taliban's rules were and are governed by different sources. There were the dictates of Mullah Omar and those of the Council of Advisors. A permanent source of Taliban law is its Constitution. Should the Taliban return to power, it is likely that many of these rules will be imposed throughout Afghanistan.

There were explicit and implicit rules. Almost all of these rules were defined in terms of Sharia or other canonical Islamic texts. If there is one document that could be considered a constitution or statement of principles, it would be the Taliban's Book of Rules. In the words of its authors, "This Book of Rules is intended for the Mujahideen who dedicate their lives to Islam and the almighty Allah."[50] These rules were issued during a high-level Taliban meeting in fall 2002 and can be divided into three categories.

The first rule set, comprising 20 rules, primarily lays out the conventions by which Taliban members must abide. There are specific prohibitions on smoking, financially profiting from connections to the Taliban, misusing Taliban equipment, working for or in any way helping NGOs without explicit permission from Taliban authorities, moving to another district without the permission of a regional commander, harming fellow Taliban, or harming "innocent" people, whose innocence is determined by provisional Taliban leaders.[51]

In addition, regional Taliban group leaders may not recruit from other Taliban regional groups without written permission from high-level authorities, which would occur under only special circumstances. These circumstances include a dearth of fighters in a particular group. A Taliban may not search houses or confiscate property without the express permission of his leader.

There are also guidelines for the distribution of booty. Taliban must distribute weapons and other confiscated items fairly among their cadre. Taliban who violate the rules and are expelled from Taliban groups may not affiliate themselves with any other Taliban groups. If a violator is contrite to the satisfaction of a group leader, he may be provisionally readmitted to the group from which he was expelled.

A second set of rules guide the recruitment of new cadre. A recruit has to be old enough to have facial hair, and those who have acted "dishonorably" in their private lives may not be candidates. A new recruit who is deemed disloyal will be considered a traitor and will be punished, perhaps killed.[52]

A third set of rules pertain to the behavior of non-Taliban. Taliban will not target those civil authorities whom they deem loyal to the Taliban's cause. However, those who cooperate with "infidels" face retribution. In the rules, teachers are singled out. Teachers are forbidden from working with "the current puppet regime" because it strengthens the government and weakens the rule of Islam. If a teacher promotes any material that breaks fidelity with the Koran, he should be warned once to stop. If he continues, he should be beaten. If this does not dissuade him, he should be killed. Schools that do not comply must be burned.[53]

Some of the Constitution's articles are very clear. For example, in the General Principles chapter, Islam is declared the state religion, the Hanafi school of law is supreme, Sharia is the only source of law in the country, all Afghan daily life and commercial activity must conform to Islam, and the calendar is based on their Prophet's pilgrimage. Other constitutional requirements are ambiguous or have been disregarded. For example, prohibitions on torture, arbitrary arrest, compulsory confessions, presumption of innocence, and unauthorized home searches were routinely ignored in the Taliban era.[54]

During the Taliban's era, rules were created, revised, and abrogated at will. A journalist noted that under the Department of Prevention of Vice and Promotion of Virtue in the late 1990s, playing chess was punishable by one month in jail, watching pornography gave the offender three months, and listening to music was two weeks. For boys convicted of teasing girls, there was a three-month sentence, and selling girls ice cream or French fries would land the convict two weeks in prison.[55]

Profile 3.2: Ali Safi and the Young Afghan Intellectuals

An intellectual, Ali Safi and his nine collaborators made a spectacular escape from Afghanistan. On trial at London's Old Bailey, Safi explained his motives for hijacking a plane with 187 passengers, in February 2000. The conspirators needed to leave Afghanistan and wanted to force the world's attention to the "living nightmare" of Afghan life.[56] Safi was arrested for playing chess in 1997 and was battered with an electric cable for seven days. The former university professor joined a group called the Young Intellectuals of Afghanistan to subvert Taliban rule, after his son died from a respiratory ailment. According to Safi, his boy's condition could have been treated at a Kabul hospital, but his wife could not take the small boy without a male escort, and none were available.[57]

In London, Safi testified about the Taliban's lurid rampages. He was horrified by Kabul's circus of slaughter, to which he bore witness. Apparitions of President Najibullah's body hanging with his brother's from a traffic light haunted his dreams. "I couldn't believe my eyes. He [Najibullah] had been hit in the head by bullets, and there were cigarette butts in his nostrils."[58] Standing before the bar, Safi described the stoning of a woman whose eight-year-old child begged for Taliban mercy, as well as the amputated limbs festooned on trees as macabre ornaments. In Mazar-i-Sharif, in August 1998, he saw Taliban storm a hospital and shoot nurses and patients.[59] Safi put his wife and children on the plane he hijacked. He was desperate and calculated that, although he would serve time in prison, his family might not be deported. Perhaps they could live in the West while he sat in a British prison.

In the event, the hijackers were jailed for between 27 and 30 months, and most were released soon after the sentence was passed. But Safi and two other men, who are brothers, were sentenced to five years each for organizing the hijack.[60] However, their convictions were overturned in 2004.[61] There was public sympathy for the hijackers, particularly after the Taliban's atrocities had been broadcast after September 2001. Richard Ferguson, QC, defending Safi, told the jury, "This was a desperate gamble taken by desperate men—flight or death. The choice was stark and simple—either you get out or you die."[62] Safi and his compatriots resolved not to stay and die. They got their families out, and they lived.

TOWARD WAR

The Taliban, Foreign Relations, and the United States 1996–2001

The Taliban's domestic plans floundered and most failed, and their foreign relations were no more successful. They had warm relations with *elements* of Pakistan and the Pakistani intelligence. But they did not enjoy close relations with other neighbors. The governments of Iran and Afghanistan were often at odds and sometimes came near blows during the Taliban's reign. Part of this is explained by sectarian differences—the Taliban are Sunni and the Iranians are Shia. But the frosty diplomatic relations cannot be understood by religious division alone.

The 1998 killing of Iranian diplomats was followed by the Taliban's accusation that Iran was funding its enemies.[63] Early in the Taliban's rule, the mullahs made enemies with principals in Teheran. Iranian leaders criticized the destruction of the Buddhist statues as barbaric. Several times, Iran and the Taliban came close to war. The Taliban army threatened to deploy medium-range missiles, which may not have been serviceable, to any Iranian attack. The Taliban also accused Iran of harboring Shia enemies.

After the September 2001 attacks, Afghanistan's foreign relations suffered a significant blow when its two Arab links severed diplomatic relations. Saudi Arabia and the United Arab Emirates cut their relations shortly after the attack. Pakistan, the only other nation recognizing the Taliban government, withdrew all staff from its Kabul embassy. After Pakistan cut its relations in November 2001, Afghanistan became completely diplomatically isolated.

Well before September 2001, the Taliban had a significant image problem that could not be easily prettied up. It would be challenging to create a government whose political philosophy, statecraft, and social mores were more antithetical to U.S. values than those of the Taliban. U.S. Secretary of State Madeleine Albright spoke for many elites with her full-throated attack of the Taliban's treatment of women and children as "despicable." This was important in Democratic Party-led Washington, where women's issues were loudly trumpeted.[64]

Hollywood stars, led by Meryl Streep, Geena Davis, and Sidney Poitier, joined the Feminist Majority to lobby the White House and the State Department to torque up sanctions on the Taliban and cut off aid to countries that recognized and traded with them. They also entreated Washington to increase humanitarian assistance to Afghan women refugees.[65] In a "Dear Abby" column, Mavis Leno claimed partial victory by quoting a woman in Kabul who whispered, "Let me call you the angels of mercy. Your love is our hope."[66]

Ms. Leno scored successes. The Department of State admitted more Afghan refugee women to the United States.[67] American conservatives and liberals saluted the prowoman, anti-Taliban agenda of Ms. Leno. She was applauded by the popular television host Bill O'Reilly as being a "patriot."[68] Nonetheless, there is no evidence that the Taliban were concerned with, or even took note of, Hollywood's efforts.[69]

Washington's smart set saw Taliban leaders as primitive, patriarchal, heartless, and vulgar. To the extent to which he was known, Mullah Omar was loathed by political leaders and opinion makers in the nation's capital. First Lady Hillary Clinton denounced the servitude in which all Afghan females subsisted.[70] Any positive image of the Afghan fighting spirit against the Soviets was largely forgotten. Washington's embrace of the zealous and self-sacrificial anti-Soviet Afghan mujahedeen of the 1980s had long waned by the mid-1990s.

Western media became incredulous as the Taliban revived the darkest imagery of the Nazi era. Statesmen and journalists registered disgust and alarm at the Taliban's plans to force all Hindus in the country to wear identity tags.[71] In turn, the Taliban were openly contemptuous of the United States. A reclusive Omar did not show interest in warming relations with the United States, and his only verified direct contact with U.S. officials took place in August 1998, two days after President Clinton ordered a missile strike to blast bin Laden's training camps.[72] In response to the attack and fear of more strikes, Omar tried to assure State Department officials that bin Laden was leashed. But Omar refused to extradite him.[73]

The Taliban explained that mandates of Afghan culture, particularly the requirement to give guests protection, or melmastia, precluded yielding bin Laden, who was their honored guest. The Taliban leadership claimed that they could not relinquish him to the United States without weakening the Taliban's global prestige.[74]

However, the U.S. State Department was not swayed by the force of this argument. Senior leaders proffered evidence that bin Laden was directly tied to many terrorist activities and plots. Diplomatic cables revealed bin Laden's imprimatur in other high-profile plots, including a plan to blow up U.S. airliners in the Pacific.[75] In response, the Taliban underscored that they "have always and always will condemn terrorism, including hijacking."[76]

Though the August 20, 1998, missile strike quieted, if only temporarily, Mullah Omar, it had no such effect on his most infamous guest. Ever loquacious, bin Laden continued to inveigh against Americans, Jews, Christians, and other non-Muslims. He became particularly vocal after the missile strike, reiterating his fatwa (religious ruling) urging Muslims to kill American, British, and Israeli citizens, and reserving the right to use weapons of mass destruction.[77]

According to declassified State Department cables, Mullah Omar hoped to open a dialogue with State Department officials in August 1998. In October 1999, the Taliban suggested a trial by a panel of Islamic scholars by the Organization of Islamic Conference[78] or the United Nations.[79] The White House was not persuaded.

Sanctions and Hostilities

Imposing sanctions on the Taliban was an intermediate response between rhetoric and war. International organizations and individual states applied financial and military sanctions of Afghanistan. Many governments restricted travel by Taliban officials and downgraded their diplomatic missions abroad.[80]

Either through miscalculation or with the unexplained intention of being provocative, the Taliban unchained bin Laden, allowing him to be interviewed by Western journalists. Once again, he claimed the right to use large-scale weapons against Western targets. After he did so in September 2001, he became the most wanted man in the world by American authorities.

American leaders demanded his extradition, but the Taliban balked, offering rococo explanations of Islamic mandates and Afghan customs. Gratuitously, the Taliban's foreign minister boasted that the Taliban would never deport bin Laden. "We will not hand him to an infidel nation."[81] True to their word, the Taliban never did yield him, continuing to cavil and balk. But U.S. authorities were determined to kill or capture him.

President Bush and Secretary of Defense Donald Rumsfeld swore to destroy the Taliban unless they surrendered bin Laden immediately.[82]

In stormy discussions, U.S. Ambassador Wendy Chamberlin bluntly expressed to Pakistani President Musharraf "that the September 11 attacks had ended the debate about the Taliban, who were now considered an enemy of the US."[83] Secretary of State Colin Powell cautioned the Taliban end their torpor and "think properly."[84] Pakistan was cooperating with the United States, and the Central Asian states were offering Washington staging grounds. The Iranians were quiet on the issue. Only Iraq "didn't find what happened to us a tragedy."[85] President Bush offered to spare the Taliban war if they extradited bin Laden.[86] They declined, scuppering the talks.

CHAPTER SUMMARY

The Taliban took advantage of a late twentieth-century power vacuum in Afghanistan to expand their areas of influence quickly. The Taliban have four, basic, defining characteristics. They are Salafists, which refers to their illiberal view of Islam; they are Pashtuns, which refers to their ethnicity and social code; they are isolated, which helps to explain their philosophy, ethnic supremacy, and xenophobia; and they are totalitarian, intending to monitor all aspects of human behavior.

Taliban's domestic policies from 1996 to 2001 would likely be replicated should Omar seize power again. The rule of the Taliban threw the Afghanistan into a miasma of mullah-imposed viciousness. The few economic and social gains of the 1970s, which were sincerely pursued by a relatively progressive head of state, were eliminated. The status of women declined; there was economic entropy; the civil service was stripped of all elements of professionalism; fewer Afghans could move or communicate; and standards in education and health plummeted. Much of life was dreary, and Afghans were dispirited. Nonetheless, most of the country was secure, and the mass killings ended with the cessation of the civil war.

The attacks of September 2001 galvanized the United States, but the Taliban continued to be nonchalant under American threats. An obliging host, Mullah Omar refused to surrender Osama bin Laden. In consequence, President Bush prepared the United States for war.

4

---∞---

The Taliban in Defeat

Chapter 3 was a brief portrait of Afghanistan during the Taliban rule of 1996–2001. Chapter 4 will cover the Taliban after their expulsion from Afghanistan, when the group became revivified, armed, and, once again, lethal.

THE UNITED STATES PREPARES TO ATTACK

The Taliban expected the United States to retaliate for their hosting bin Laden, but were optimistic about their prospects. As mujahedeen, many of the Taliban's senior leaders had engaged the Soviet armor and artillery in the 1980s, and some would storm through Afghan cities as Taliban leaders in the 1990s. In autumn 2001, the Taliban were emboldened by religious zeal and nationalistic hubris and challenged the United States to deploy to Afghanistan. U.S. Special Forces would soon oblige them. Al Zawahiri, al Qaeda's second in command, disparaged the fighting qualities of American men. He airily asserted, "The American soldier is not fit for combat. The Hollywood promotion will not succeed on the real battlefield."[1] Other Muslims shared this disdain because the United States left Somalia and Lebanon in defeat. Islamist élan defeated Washington and could do so again.

Jingoism, religious fervor, and the prestige associated with battle drew young Afghan and Pakistani men to swell the ranks of the Taliban, literally by the busload. Trickling, then pouring through the open borders, Pakistani volunteers came to Afghanistan to fight the United States in a holy war. Caravans of buses, cars, motorcycles, and harlequin-colored jingle trucks ferried aspiring fighters from the Pakistani town of Quetta and the

Chaman crossing to points north into Afghanistan.[2] Much of "Pashtun-istan"[3] held solidarity with the insurgents, as the United States prepared to invade Afghanistan in 2001.[4]

In Pakistan, public opinion, particularly among the clergy and intelligentsia, was loudly opposed to U.S. military action against Afghanistan. The streets of Pakistan's cities teemed with placard-wielding protesters railing against American intervention.[5] Many screamed for battle.[6] An al Qaeda leader clarified, "The mujahedeen gathered from all countries . . . to fight this new global Crusader alliance and their hypocritical lackeys, mercenaries, and highway bandits . . . The proud Afghan people fights for its [sic] faith."[7]

Some were clamoring for battle, but not all Afghans had an appetite for war. Many were drained, war weary, and remembered well the devastating effects of the Soviet and civil wars. Middle-aged men and women recalled the privations they endured as youngsters and, a generation later, now feared for the safety of their own children. Some were mystified as they braced for an American invasion in response to attacks perpetrated by unwanted Arab guests who had long overstayed their welcome.

Further, some Afghans detested the Arabs they knew. The Arab-speaking cadre who came to Afghanistan to fight the Soviets often did not learn the local customs or language, made little effort to socialize, and seemed overweening and patronizing towards indigenous Afghans.[8]

As in Afghanistan, there was divided opinion in the United States about hastening to war. Muslim and left-oriented university student groups deprecated what they considered President Bush's chauvinism. At a venue long associated with utopian pacifism and multiculturalism, the University of California–Berkeley's campus, more than 2,500 demonstrators cautioned against a military response. As an example, one student pleaded, "You don't want the hand of the United States killing innocent civilians. Send them food rather than bombs."[9] Afghans would get both.

There were echoes of the 1960s in the media, intellectual circles, and academia, as many opinion makers counseled against war. But there was little smash-mouthed, anti-Americanism of the earlier, radical era. The rhetoric was more dispassionate. Gary Sick, who advised President Carter on the National Security Council, recommended stringent sanctions to force the Taliban's hand, and Steven Zunes warned that military attacks would enrage and embolden Muslims around the world.[10] Richard Falk of Princeton put the onus of the Bush administration to comply with the Taliban's demands to provide evidence that bin Laden was culpable for the attack.[11] People for the Ethical Treatment of Animals (PETA) took out magazine ads decrying U.S. military action in Afghanistan.[12]

Critics in Congress voiced early concerns. Representative Cynthia A. McKinney accused the U.S. media of disseminating only "white noise." She said in late October 2001, "I don't think anybody is supporting the Taliban, except maybe some elements of the State Department and the CIA," while, in her view, the military was contaminating the nation's moral hygiene with its push to war.[13] She also accused the Bush administration of having received advance warning of the September attack and intentionally failing to act.[14]

But most Americans were resigned to, and many were eagerly anticipating, meting out punishment against for those culpable for attacking the United States. And they were convinced that this would be a just war. When the fighting started, the United States did send food, as well as clothing, medicine, and basic provisions, to the Afghan noncombatants. But the U.S. Air Force also dropped bombs to kill Taliban who would not surrender.

At this time, President Bush pledged to eradicate the terrorist networks in Afghanistan and elsewhere. He famously declared, "Either you are with us, or you are with the terrorists."[15] And he underscored that these demands were not negotiable[16] and that individuals and groups that collaborated with al Qaeda were subject to attack.[17]

As this was happening, the Pentagon organized for war. Veteran B-52 bombers, a workhorse in the South East Asian war, were prepped for action in Afghanistan. Soldiers, sailors, and airmen were readied, as war planners looked to history for lessons on how to fight in Afghanistan. Defense Secretary Donald H. Rumsfeld was determined not to repeat the mistakes of other invaders of Afghanistan. He pledged to use the full spectrum of the military, but it was unclear precisely whom the United States would be fighting. Not all of bin Laden's forces and training camps were colocated with Afghanistan's military rulers. The United States needed more intelligence.

Two weeks after the attack on the U.S. heartland, the United States deployed a small team, called Jawbreaker, under the direction of Gary Schroen, to rebuild the capabilities of the Northern Alliance. They succeeded. Schroen, a seasoned operative with vast experience in South Asia and who knew many of the leading Alliance personalities, bypassed the Pakistanis and established bases for American special operations forces. From these bases, he and his men guided the Alliance with advanced technology.[18] In 2012, Schroen would claim, "CIA station chief Cofer Black told me, 'find Bin Laden, kill him and cut off his head, put it on dry ice and ship it back to me, and I'm going to take it down to show the President.'"[19]

The celebrated U.S. Green Berets, lauded in military folklore and popular culture, were deployed to Afghanistan.[20] Some had trained in Pakistan and knew the languages, culture, and terrain. They studied the mujahedeen's tactics on the Soviets in detail.[21] They were ready.

Opposing U.S. forces were the Taliban, whose precise numbers and military capabilities were not clearly known. Many estimates were about 50,000 troops and foreign volunteers. Many Taliban were armed with AK assault rifles, some of which were locally fabricated, and some heavier individual weapons, such as rocket-propelled grenades (RPGs).

The basic Taliban fighting unit consisted of 8–10 men who were transported in the back of pickup trucks. Of the estimated 50,000 Taliban force, about 8,000–12,000 were foreign. In September and October 2001, most of the units were ad hoc and weakly organized. However, they were augmented by elements from the Islamic Movement of Uzbekistan (IMU) and Pakistan's Islamist organizations. The Taliban had about 650 armored vehicles, mostly Soviet-era scout cars and armored personnel carriers.[22] Their air force consisted of a few old Soviet fighters, used almost exclusively as bombers. There were about 10 transport planes of dubious reliability and quality.[23]

THE FIGHTING STARTS

When Mullah Omar would not surrender bin Laden, the United States initiated hostilities. Initially, elite teams of U.S. and British soldiers were deployed to target key Taliban command-and-control centers. Small teams of 4 to 12 men were infiltrated to pinpoint command posts, supply depots, and training headquarters for air- and sea-launched munitions that began to devastate Taliban positions in early October 2001.[24] Targets included air defenses, military communications sites, and training camps inside Afghanistan.

American and British military and political leaders debated which set of tactics would be more suitable to ferret out and destroy al Qaeda and the Taliban. They determined that American and British forces should have a light ground presence and should support indigenous anti-Taliban forces, particularly from the Northern Alliance. These Afghan soldiers were rugged, eager, and well positioned to kill Taliban. Uzbekistan became a main forward base for allied forces. Tajikistan and Kazakhstan were supportive.[25] In addition to ground fighting, U.S. bombers pulverized Taliban targets from the air.[26]

The devastating effects became cinematic, as thermo-baric plasma bombs ignited the air in tunnels and cave complexes. The Taliban had shown ingenuity building quarters in caves with brick or cement floors and steel doors. Some of these quarters were powered by generators and had a perimeter of antiaircraft guns and rocket launchers. Many were equipped with computers and modern communications.[27] But this offered little protection against the blast power of U.S. advanced munitions, such as the 5,000-pound "bunker-buster," or "big blue," the 15,000-pound relic of the Vietnam era. Also called the "daisy cutter," the BLU-82 killed anything within a radius of 600 yards.

In what was described as a "blowtorch effect," many Taliban who, like their Afghan forbearers, took refuge in tunnels and caves were cremated alive. When channeled to underground tunnels, blast pressure and heat crushed and incinerated almost anything inside.[28] From a distance, video coverage captured small mountains collapsing under the blast of these and other U.S. munitions. The vice chairman of the Joint Chiefs of Staff, General Peter Pace, said, "As you would expect, they make a heck of a bang when they go off and they intent is to kill people."[29] Later in the counterinsurgency, the United States would share the Afghan airspace with its British ally. The famed 617 Squadron, know to history as the "Dambusters," would unleash its Tornado GR4s over the warzone.[30] Several of the navigators were women.[31]

It was hard for Taliban and al Qaeda to escape the allied juggernaut, though bin Laden and some of his compatriots famously and sometimes inexplicably did so. U.S. aerial surveillance craft prevented large deployments of Taliban from taking effective shelter, which was often a death sentence. Some of the munitions were guided, and others were unguided. This war initiated the widespread use of Global Hawk unmanned spy planes and Predator-launched drone warfare. Another advantage for the United States was the ability to deploy and resupply hundreds of assault troops by helicopter onto a mountain target.

Not all the warfare was gory, and there were moments for the human touch in battle. After U.S. Army Rangers stormed the compounds of in-flight Taliban, they left American mementos. In mid-October, soldiers left the famous photograph of American firefighters hoisting the U.S. flag in the rubble of the World Trade Center on September 11, 2001. The Rangers also left some American graffiti on the walls of a Kandahar building, which read "Freedom Endures."[32]

Across the Asian continent, Europeans were largely sympathetic to Washington's efforts. Britain and the Netherlands polled as the Europeans with the highest levels of support.[33] Queen Elizabeth II expressed "disbelief and total shock" at the September attacks, at St Paul's Cathedral.[34] Polls revealed that half of all Europeans championed what President Bush called the "War on Terrorism." Parisians, often very reluctant to praise American foreign policy, were very responsive to President Bush's decision to fight. About two-thirds of the French backed the American war on the Taliban in October 2001.[35] Many European intellectuals recognized the attacks as a threat to the core tenets of international order and law. For there to be peace in the world, there needed to be war on the Taliban.

As the Taliban became an international news item, European journalists looked for new angles to cover the war. Over the course of the insurgency, several would be abducted and some killed. British journalist, Yvonne Ridley, infiltrated herself in the Taliban's lair in late September 2001 and was caught immediately.[36] In Taliban captivity, she became a sensation on Fleet Street and, after she was released 10 days later, took a new job for Al Jazeera.[37] She then became a Muslim.

But others saw her, as well as some other headline-grabbing journalists, as narcissistic and irresponsible. During the ordeal, her nine-year-old daughter, Daisy, begged for her mother's life on television.[38] After the mother was released, a pouting Daisy confided on an open microphone, "I wish you were a normal mummy ... No one else's mummy has been caught by the Taliban."[39]

THE TALIBAN IN RETREAT

Initially, the Taliban responded to the United States' war making by calling for jihad and inviting the United States to share the blood-spattered fate as the Soviets of a generation earlier.[40] This bravado quickly subsided as a rain of munitions on Taliban strongholds sapped their morale and military capabilities. The Taliban's hold on northern Afghanistan began to collapse in the second week of October 2001. The Taliban also met their match in the skilled mountain fighters of the Northern Alliance, made up largely of Uzbek, Tajik, and Hazara tribes.[41]

Raised in the mountains and spurred by revenge, soldiers of the Northern Alliance pursued the fleeing Taliban with much gusto and scant mercy. One leader bragged, "Everywhere they go, we hit them. They can't go anywhere because of the American planes that bomb them."[42] By early November, many Taliban who could not escape into Pakistan were hungry, cold, despondent, and defeated. At night, packs of Taliban were betrayed by the campfires they lit to keep from freezing. Other Taliban taking refuge in the mountains, hills, and crevices were middle-aged or elderly mullahs and bureaucrats who were ill-prepared for such hard living conditions. Some froze and starved. Over the many weeks, some near-skeletal figures straggled from the mountains in pairs or triples to surrender.[43] Still others, raddled and weary, blended into local villages.

Though many Afghans were glad to have their country rid of the Taliban, Pakistanis in the Baluchi capital of Quetta began burning offices of the United Nations in solidarity with the Taliban. After the first week of October, 1 person was killed and 26 injured in a spontaneous and massive outburst of violence.[44] The UN Office for Refugees in Quetta, whose only purpose was to help alleviate the destitution of displaced families and the despair of children, was showered with stones and was torched. The provisional head of the religious party Jamiat Ulema-e Islam in Quetta decreed, "To all Muslims around the world: prepare yourselves for Jihad."[45] And many did.

Pakistani tribesmen developed their own roughly hewn army to march to the aid of beleaguered Islamist comrades. Armed with a potpourri of individual weapons, from hand axes and swords to rocket launchers, Pakistanis rallied to the holy war. A 70-year-old man clutching an 80-year-old rifle proclaimed, "I am an old man. I consider myself lucky to go and face death as a martyr." A man young enough to be his grandson left his fiancée for battle in Afghanistan explaining, "Whether I come back dead or alive, I'll be fortunate because I am fighting in the cause of Islam."[46]

Some Afghan villagers had very little grasp of the political or strategic dynamics of the U.S.-Afghan conflict. They were aware only that bombs were falling near their homes, killings some of their neighbors, and threatening their families' safety. By late October 2001, the United Nations estimated that 50,000 Afghan refugees entered Pakistan. Lines, miles long, snaked from Kandahar to Chaman, Pakistan. But without connections, families were ill-equipped to make the trek to their common destination—Quetta.[47]

THE MARCH OF THE NORTHERN ALLIANCE

If the Taliban were in despair, fortune had smiled on the Northern Alliance, who now had the full support and military backing of the United States. The Northern Alliance, a shotgun marriage of non-Pashtun ethnicities, was eager to settle scores with the Taliban and al Qaeda and often did so. The Alliance's greatest commander, who would become lionized as a dauntless national hero, Ahmed Shah Massoud, was murdered by a team of al Qaeda suicide bombers on September 9, 2001. The slain Lion of the Pansjir was a Tajik, and many Northern Alliance fighters were eager for retribution.

The Northern Alliance's intoxicating success and their impulsive killing of the Taliban remnants still trapped in the mountains alarmed human rights activists who feared expanded retaliation for the mid-1990s slaughter. Leaders of Amnesty International and other human rights groups pleaded with the U.S.-backed Alliance leaders to leash their vengeance seekers. The full scope of the 1990s-era Taliban atrocities, in which many parties participated, would be publicized through excavations of corpse-strewn murder pits.[48] Some of those implicated denied the accusations or claimed they were exaggerated or biased. But one former mujahedeen commander sniffed, "One cannot make war with rosewater."[49] In 2001, there were fewer illegal killings, but bloody battles continued. There was little rosewater.

The most famous battle was Operation Anaconda, which, like its reptilian namesake, intended to encircle and squeeze the Taliban from a 60-square-mile belt around Tora Bora.[50] In a joint operation of the Northern Alliance and U.S. Special Forces, 2,000 Coalition personnel, half of whom were Afghan, decimated the Taliban.

The quick victories of the Northern Alliance and the implosion of the Taliban's fighting infrastructure did not surprise a seasoned veteran of the Soviet war in Afghanistan. Retired Soviet Maj. Georgi Derluguian opined, in mid-October 2001, that the Taliban would disintegrate or switch sides quickly. He cautioned about loose Stinger missiles, the effects of which he saw firsthand many years earlier.[51] There were very few U.S. casualties, and the much-feared Stinger missiles were never used against Coalition Forces. But the second phase of combat operations would prove the greater challenge. This would be hunting down and killing the small pockets of Taliban. This would be the start of the counterinsurgency.

There were quick successes for American forces but also bloody failures and mistakes. The Pentagon targeted roads; supply depots; oil, petroleum, and lubricant facilities; and barracks. But bombs went astray, and in late

October cluster bombs accidentally killed villagers. In Herat, a 1000-pound bomb demolished a senior citizens' home, and two 500-pound bombs hit a residential neighborhood in Kabul.[52] The UN mine removal spokesman explained the danger of unexploded bombs, particularly the cluster bombs: "If they don't explode on impact, they remain primed for months."[53]

Details and causes of other incidents were hotly disputed by both Coalition Forces and Afghans. It is likely that in the confusing, impassioned first few weeks of the war, Afghans unconnected to the Taliban were mistakenly targeted. Special Forces interdicted and destroyed supplies of fuel that U.S. intelligence determined was to be used by Taliban. When suspicious trucks were intercepted, they were sometimes blasted by U.S. warplanes, and the drivers were whisked away in plastic ties for interrogation. Some of the drivers protested their innocence and demanded compensation, which was sometimes granted if the drivers had a compelling case for innocence.

But many were Taliban or their agents, and they understood immediately that they were facing a new type of soldier. The Special Forces, with night-vision goggles, bulletproof chest plates, and helmet-mounted radios and video cameras, had dazzling equipment unlike anything the Taliban could imagine. Word began to spread within the Taliban's ranks that American soldiers were not the feckless Hollywood imagery Zawahiri promised. American soldiers were not cowardly and effete; they could fight. And so could the British.

The United States hurriedly provided basic assistance to the Afghan populace. Washington did not want to alienate large segments of Afghan society nor did it want imagines of starving Afghans to populate the Internet. The provision of food and medical supplies would reduce illness and hunger. It would also bring stability.[54] This responsiveness, in turn, would fortify the image of the yet-to-be-established government in Kabul and undercut support for the Taliban. This logic—stability by ensuring sustained human development—became the main piston powering the Coalition's counter-insurgency strategy and would often be tested.

Some of the Taliban remained loyal to Omar; some left and returned to their villages; others were captured and imprisoned. According to the International Red Cross, captured Taliban were weak, gaunt, malnourished, lice ridden, and ill. Many suffered from tuberculosis, severe diarrhea, and other medical afflictions. However, many of the Taliban prisoners were in dreadful physical condition when they were taken prisoners. Their caloric intake and the quality of their health care increased, usually substantially, in Coalition custody. Finally, U.S. prisons were infinitely healthier than those run by the Northern Alliance. When Taliban in the Northern Alliance-controlled Shibergan prison, located 75 miles west of Mazar-i-Sharif, saw Red Cross inspectors they pleaded, while clutching the prison bars, "We want to go to an American prison."[55]

Occasionally, the Taliban would do the work of the Coalition Forces by executing their own commanders. In late October 2001, they slaughtered five fellow Taliban on charges of collaborating with the United States in Mazar-i-Sharif.[56] The victims may or may not have been cooperating with the United States. Some Afghans who were victims of summary firing squads were former leaders in the anti-Soviet jihad, such as Abdul Haq. The burly hero and former police chief of Kabul was nabbed and killed as he tried to rally Afghans to the cause of the returning former king.[57]

ALL FALL DOWN

By the end of November 2001, most Taliban-held cities had fallen to Northern Alliance-led forces. Air Force Gen. Richard Myers, the chairman of the Joint Chiefs of Staff, said that the Taliban air defenses and transportation and communications lines were severed.[58] General Myers underscored that this would be a drawn-out campaign and that more U.S. special operators would be deployed to help the Northern Alliance fighters.

On November 11, 2001, a cavalcade of Northern Alliance troops, led by Atta Mohammed, drove through the streets of Mazar-i-Sharif and were warmly greeted and gently pelted with candy and flowers. The Taliban's green, white, and black flag was yanked to the ground, and Mohammed announced from the Blue Mosque, one of the holiest places in Northern Afghanistan, "This is a great moment for us and the people of Mazar."[59] The Taliban's defense minister conceded the defeat: "Mazar is gone. The city and the airport are with the opposition."[60]

Capturing Mazar-i-Sharif opened communication lines and a corridor to relieve starving Afghans and gave the Coalition a potential military staging ground. It is less than 20 miles from Uzbekistan. Prime Minister Tony Blair broadcasted, "I don't think there's any doubt that the military momentum is now moving against the Taliban."[61] After weeks of U.S. blitzing of Taliban positions, a Northern Alliance advance cleared the Taliban from the north and stormed Kabul, the capital, in mid-November. Then, with the surrender of Kunduz, only one major city was left in Taliban hands. This was their home city—Kandahar.

Captured Taliban were housed in austere, makeshift, U.S.-controlled detention centers. But these were luxurious compared to the prisons that had been run by the Taliban for six years. Starving and freezing in Taliban prisons, Northern Alliance soldiers and political prisoners[62] were soon to be liberated by Coalition Forces. Stories began to circulate quickly about the anguish in Sar-e-Poza[63] prison in Kandahar, where prisoners were forced to live on bread and fetid water and tea, sometimes for years.[64]

Characteristic of the Taliban, sadism was rampant. One of the guards was nicknamed Mullah "Cable" because of his penchant for pummeling men with a steel cable.[65] One prisoner suspected of spying for the Northern

Alliance was frequently tortured. In Kandahar, he was paraded in front of villagers, and the Taliban encouraged children to throw stones at him. He recollected, "I was screaming 'Oh God, don't kill me. They [the Taliban] told me, "Even God cannot help you." ' "[66] But the Northern Alliance did help him. He and other nearly dead prisoners were liberated in mid-December.

The Northern Alliance's march to Kandahar continued almost unchecked. Many of the anti-Taliban leaders were grizzled veterans, but not all. Mohammed Humayun was 15 years old when he led an army of 300 soldiers, with tanks and rocket launchers, against the Taliban enemy. He inherited his position after his father, a Northern Alliance leader, was killed in August 2001. As an adolescent himself, Humayun recruited other boys who would be of U.S. middle school or early-high school age. He explained, "Children make great soldiers. In the West, you have the wrong idea about this. Children are strong and fast and they are brave."[67] The Taliban concurred and would soon use children to plant roadside bombs and conduct suicide attacks, many of which killed other children.

Not all the fighting went painlessly for Coalition Forces. Even some of the most battle-hardened and expert Special Forces were stunned by the ferocity of the Taliban, particularly those who were guarding Mullah Omar's compound and his coterie. In October 2001, there was a near disaster as U.S. Special Forces stormed Omar's compound near Kandahar. In the words of one U.S. soldier, the intensity of resistance by Taliban and al Qaeda "scared the crap out of everyone."[68] There was an unsuccessful breakout from temporary prison during which an intelligence operative was murdered. The prisoners were mainly foreigners from Uzbekistan, Pakistan, Yemen, Chechnya, and elsewhere. There was one American who would become known "Taliban" John Walker or "Jihad Johnny."[69]

In the United States some Americans, still smarting from the September attacks on the homeland, could now lampoon those who hosted their Afghanistan-based enemy. Not all the jokes were clever, and many smacked of a conqueror's hubris. Jokes such as, "That's as fast as a Taliban switching sides," showed a sardonic delight in the crumbling status of the Taliban. Despite the Christmas holiday warmth, the American public was not spared gelid humor. "What is the difference between Osama bin Laden and the cave dwellers of Mesa Verde in Colorado? The cave dwellers survived."[70] But many al Qaeda did survive, and U.S. forces determined to hunt them down and kill them.

Some snags, disappointments, and reverses were expected, given the sturdiness of the Taliban enemy. Many U.S. special operators found exactly what they anticipated in Taliban and al Qaeda fighters—men and boys fanatically dedicated to their cause and comrades. In early December, an American major said, "I thought Kandahar would fall in about a week and it hasn't. I lost a lot of beers on that."[71] But the momentum was irreversibly with the United States and its allies. One U.S. gunship pilot and part-time graphic artist, Capt. Alex "Sketch" Fulford, conceded that the Taliban "still had teeth" but retorted that Americans "have pliers."[72]

U.S. troops were particularly eager to capture or kill bin Laden, who slipped from their grip into Pakistan. But they did find his computers, hard drives, and diaries, as well as myriad documents confirming the Omar-bin Laden relationship. Central Command (CENTCOM) Commander Gen. Tommy Franks vowed prophetically, "The world is not a large enough place for him to hide."[73]

There were other reasons for American confidence. When it became clear that the Taliban were being thrashed, many Afghans switched allegiance to the victorious Americans and Northern Alliance leaders. General Franks took delight in the village elders' keenness to lead their tribal councils, or Shuras, toward peaceful terms with U.S. forces. More than a few Taliban leaders flipped sides by late 2001. Often, there is no shame among Afghans in switching sides, as long as it does not happen too frequently. In other countries what would be considered treasonous is, in Afghanistan, seen as political chess. One Taliban commander stated in January 2002, "This is a normal thing in Afghanistan, because everyone loves their lives and wants to stay alive. We switch sides all the time."[74] This is hamsaya.

Profile 4.1: Sayed Rahmatullah Hashemi: God and Taliban at Yale

The late 2001 sudden diaspora of the Taliban forced its leadership into distant places. Most sought refuge in Pakistan; some straggled to Iran; others were cuffed and crated to Guantanamo. One enrolled at Yale. Sayed Rahmatullah Hashemi, the former Taliban spokesman and ambassador at large, though with only four years of standardized education, was given special student status at Yale. At 27, he was much older than the average Yale freshman.[75] This special student was special indeed.

Hashemi grew up in the border areas of Afghanistan and Pakistan. He attended school until he was 13, and most of his English instruction came from an American charity group.[76] In the wake of the Soviet defeat, he hitched his star to the Taliban in 1995. And, his fortunes soared. He became a spokesman and general diplomat for the Taliban government at an age when Ivy League men are usually chasing coeds.[77] But like his meteoric ascent, his failing fortunes mirrored those of other Taliban leaders. In 2002 he was broke and unemployed with few prospects.

But he knew something of the United States, which he had visited a year earlier. As a roving ambassador, in March 2001 he spoke to students at the University of Southern California.[78] In the shadow of Tommy Trojan, Hashemi cast Afghanistan as a victim and denied the destruction of the Buddhas. They had been worn by rain. Also,

Afghanistan was tolerant of other religions. The Taliban did not hate or harm women. The only thing the Taliban hated was the old king of Afghanistan, whom he deprecated as "a rotten old, knucklehead."[79] Afghans were hungry and poor, and it was largely the fault of Western policy and the current sanctions.

But not all in the audience were charmed. A woman approached him slowly, tore off her burka, and shouted solidarity with Afghan women and scorn for the Taliban. Bridling himself, the diplomat responded, "I'm really sorry for your husband. He might have a very difficult time with you."

Hashemi made important connections as an ambassador. One proved to be his booster and got him into Yale after the Taliban were crushed. A famous political science professor, John Gaddis, wrote, "I think it's great. It seems to me that's exactly what we ought to be doing. I'm happy he is here."[80] Even some ardent Yale feminists gave support, though cautious and convoluted. A co-ed explained, "As a white American feminist, I do not feel comfortable making statements or judgments about other cultures, especially statements that suggest one culture is more sexist and repressive than another. American feminism is often linked to and manipulated by the state in order to further its own imperialist ends."[81]

But many Yale alumni were not so supportive. A gay Yalie was not keen on bunking with a dorm mate who "not only discriminated against gays, but actually stoned them to death."[82] U.S. Army Captain Flagg Youngblood protested, "That my alma mater would embrace an ambassador from one of America's declared and defeated enemies and in the same breath keep ROTC and military recruiters off campus shows where Yale's allegiance falls. Yale's actions show that they consider the U.S. military more evil than the Taliban.[83]

David Bookstabber added to the brouhaha by instigating a campaign to mail plastic fingernails to Yale's administration. The fingernails were symbolic of the Taliban's practice of yanking out the fingernails of women who wore nail polish in the time of the Taliban.[84] An administrator in the law school's development office barked incredulously at Mr. Bookstabber, "What is wrong with you? Are you retarded?"[85] In response to the "Nail Yale" hullabaloo, the dean of admissions at Yale explained that if Yale did not admit the Taliban, he would have "enrolled at Harvard."

Hashemi did not make the final cut for regular admissions. Whether or not the plastic-nail mail-in protests were effective or if Hashemi did not pass the Ivy League academic muster, the candidate was not accepted to George Bush's alma matter. Some chuckled that he was "Talibanned."

AN AL QAEDA STRATEGIST ANALYZES THE EARLY FIGHT

Soon after the initial American victories and the Taliban defeats, al Qaeda leaders began to write lessons from the war. One student and practitioner of war was Said al-Adel (see Profile 8.1), a former Egyptian special forces officer and later an al Qaeda military operations commander. Al-Adel wrote a series of articles of lessons learned in Afghanistan for his Islamist compatriots in Iraq. Through these articles, he evaluated the war in Afghanistan and offered suggestions about how Muslims could defeat Americans.[86]

According to al-Adel, the Taliban were very inventive in provisioning and billeting soldiers and their families. Hot meals were provided to fighting men, often during long battles. Administrative affairs were decentralized, and each staging ground for battle had a mobile kitchen. Al-Adel and others were impressed by the ability to keep Taliban fighters clothed, fed, and sometimes upbeat during battle.

In Kandahar, the Taliban used a zone defense to fend off American attacks. They reformulated the pre–September 2001 defensive tactics to concentrate on protecting sectors. They created three sectors: Airport and Camp Operations Sector, City Operations Sector, and Emergency Force Sector. The Emergency Force, unlike the Airport and Camp units, was mobile. It was well equipped with modern trucks to deploy rapidly in the greater Kandahar area. It had antiarmor and antiaircraft and howitzers, and contained the best fighters. These zone defenses delayed but could not possibly prevent the conquest by the fortified Northern Alliance fighters, who were supported by U.S. air power.

For offensive operations, the Taliban would divide into groups of 10, which would work independently during the day and more closely coordinate in night operations. They preferred operating in units of 10 men to avoid concentrating forces en masse, which would give the Coalition Forces opportunity to attack with air forces.[87]

Veteran Taliban would lead these groups of 10 men and engage Coalition Forces in ambushes and direct firefights. Less-experienced Taliban forces would serve in secondary positions to gain experience and ready themselves as a reserve force. Taliban used sewers as avenues of approach.[88] The Taliban also could evict women and children from parts of a city to local villages very quickly in anticipation of hostilities. The noncombatants could be sheltered or removed from the combat zone when the fighting began. When Taliban soldiers were injured, they were often transported to hospitals or field units in Pakistan. Casualties were generally not left in Afghan hospitals.[89] This impressed non-Taliban military observers.

Maintaining effective communications was a constant challenge for the Taliban because of the advanced U.S. electronic capabilities and the Taliban's relatively primitive systems. Even here, the Taliban showed inventiveness by sending multiple couriers and using different routes in battle time. These lessons would impact future operations.

THE FIGHTING FINISHES—TEMPORARILY

Unlike other wars, there were few named battles in the Coalition's destruction of the Taliban in 2001. There were several, quasi-suicidal attacks similar to Japanese banzai attacks of the dying days of the War in the Pacific. Fighters, presumed to be Chechens, became suicide bombers, strapping explosives to their bodies and pretending to surrender before blowing themselves when captured by Northern Alliance soldiers.[90] By most accounts, the Taliban and their allies fought bravely. In Kunduz, a key city that straddles the only main road to Kabul and the south, American B-52 and F-18 bombers were called in to support the Northern Alliance after pleading for air support. North of Kunduz, Chechen and Arab fighters staged a last stand in the village of Dasht-e-Archi, near Afghanistan's border with Tajikistan.[91] The Taliban lost the engagements but impressed their opponents with their steady determination. The Taliban were not through fighting.

For the first time in five years, the warlords of the Afghan north celebrated strategic victory. Gen. Mohammed Qasim Fahim, the middle-aged leader of the Northern Alliance, succeeded the recently murdered and still-treasured Ahmed Shah Masood. Like Masood, Fahim was a Tajik and built his reputation battling the Soviets.

Gen. Abdul Rashid Dostum, an eccentric, often garrulous, and large man, had vast experience as a soldier and politician. An Uzbek Muslim, not at all wedded to the puritanical demands of Sharia, Dostum enjoyed whiskey.[92] He left school at 14 and developed political acumen and street cunning during his rise to power among Uzbeks and other northern Afghans.[93] In the civil war of the 1990s, he remained holed up in a stronghold, called the Fort of War, and ran territory in Northern Afghanistan as a personal fiefdom. The former communist became a capitalist when it became clear the Soviet-leaning government in Kabul was moribund.

By Afghan standards, Dostum has a liberal outlook, which is partially explained by his street-wise pragmatism and bargaining with secular leaders in the pre-Taliban, relatively progressive circles. Under Dostum's quasi-dictatorial, if idiosyncratic, rule in the north, girls and women attended school and worked.[94] However, Dostum was hardly a gentle heart. He would be accused of imprisoning Taliban in shipping containers, in which they slowly died of suffocation and heat exhaustion in 2001.[95]

General Ismail Khan, the "Lion of Herat," a Tajik, was supported by the Iranians. Though known for his corruption, he, like Dostum, was far less misogynistic than the Taliban and gave women some opportunities, though limited. He developed administrative experience as governor in Herat after the Russians left.[96] Khan's relations with the United States were troubling for many years because of his often-opaque connections to Iran. The Bush administration accused him of allowing Iran to infiltrate weapons, supplies, and operatives into Herat Province. Administration spokesmen claimed that Iranian intelligence and military advisors were active in Herat, to which Khan responded in 2002, "I've got plenty of military experience. I don't need foreign advisers."[97] There were other Northern Alliance leaders who would assume different positions of influence.

Profile 4.2: Zardad and Shah: The Pashtun Master and His Human Dog

Non-Taliban warlords could be every bit as bestial as the Taliban. One such case was that of small-time warlord and his prisoner-accomplice. Faryadi Sarwar Zardad, who was motivated by greed and viciousness, not religion or ethnicity, maintained his private house of horrors in a small area outside of Kabul, called Sarobi.[98] Between 1992 and 1996, Zardad controlled a small militia who patrolled roads near Sarobi, on which travelers would pass to visit Kabul or other areas.[99] Zardad would arrest travelers, including international aid workers, and imprison them in his self-made prison. He would beat them until they yielded their money and valuables. Even then, he would often shoot or mutilate some.

As a boy, Zardad gained skill killing and torturing victims. He joined the mujahedeen when he was 17 and rose to command 2,000 men against the Soviets.[100] He explained his involvement in the anti-Soviet jihad, "Of course we killed many people, but we never harmed the civilian population."[101]

But civilians who trespassed in Zardad's zone of operations in the mid-1990s could certainly be harmed in unimaginably monstrous ways. Zardad liked to hurt people. Among his many tortures was his use of a captive "man-dog," Abdullah Shah, who attacked prisoners like a wild dog, biting off and swallowing their testicles and chewing and gnawing their flesh.[102] There are different accounts about the relationship between Zardad and Shah. Some witnesses said that Zardad kept Shah, literally, in chains, which Zardad would remove in front of a captive. He would then sic Shah on the hapless and certainly confused prey and watch the spirited performance. Shah was then, once again, enchained and returned to his living pit through a hole in the floor.[103] Others observed a more collegial relationship. It was less of a master-dog relationship than one of a morbid partnership.

Zardad escaped the Taliban's advance toward Kabul in 1998 and fled to London, where he worked delivering pizza.[104] There are no reports that he tried to harm or bite anyone. But the 41-year-old

Pashtun was arrested and tried in the Old Bailey under international war crimes laws in 2005 and sentenced to 20 years in prison.[105] His old partner, Mr. Shah, did not fare as well. In Kabul, he was the first person to receive a death sentence since the fall of the Taliban. Shah's trial was secretly filmed by Afghan documentarians who made the movie *Zardad's Dog*.[106] In 2002, for the enormity of his crimes of killing 20 people including his wife, whom he burned alive, he was shot in the back of the head in Kabul's Pul-e-Charkhi prison, with the approval of Hamid Karzai.[107]

DANCING IN THE STREETS

When the Taliban fled the Northern Alliance's march to Kabul in mid-November 2001, uncontained joy poured into the streets. Young men who, under the Taliban, were forbidden from laughing and dancing and talking to unrelated girls and women kicked in the doors of the Ministry for the Prevention of Vice and the Promotion of Virtue and trashed it.[108] Routed in defeat, rapacious Taliban plundered shops and absconded what they could to exile. Some of those who could not escape lay dead in the streets, as their once-cowering countrymen spit on their corpses.[109]

Quickly, entrepreneurs tried to match the demand for once-forbidden items. TVs, cassettes, and videotapes poured in from Iran and India, and those that were secreted during the Taliban era were restocked for rental.[110] One shopkeeper had hidden over 500 videocassettes. After half a decade, the boarded-up cinemas of Kabul sprang to life again, as lines formed around blocks. Guards searched the moviegoers for weapons. Young men admitted to the theater were compelled to hand over "brass knuckles, switchblades, radios" and to leave their AK-47s at the door.[111]

Then, there was *Titanic*. No movie approached the status of this long-banned and nationally revered movie. *Titanic* became a subculture. Creative vendors, long shackled by mullahs in the marketplace, sold a wide variety of *Titanic*-themed products. *Titanic* poisons to repel insects and perfumes to attract lovers were piled on merchants' tables, in Kabul's central market, for all to buy. The lethality of "Titanic Mosquito Killer" could not be verified and neither could the alluring power of "Titanic Making Love Ecstasy Perfume Body Spray," which would certainly have roiled the mullahs.[112]

In Kandahar, merchants could, once again, offer songbirds for sale. Earlier, their caged chirpings were declared un-Islamic by the Taliban.[113] Turbans, one of the many despised emblems of the Taliban rule, were discarded into the trash.

In an interview, Diane Sawyer revealed to Kate Winslet that her portrayal of the movie's heroine, Rose, helped Afghan women endure the darkest hours of Taliban times. A young Afghan said, "Films were banned under the Taliban. But now we can watch brilliant films like this whenever we want."[114]

Postadolescent men shorn their beards and rejoiced and, like the younger generation, sang long-forbidden songs. Women and girls could walk the streets of the nation's capital without fear of being pummeled with leather whips. Some women continued to wear the burka, just as many men kept their full, if trimmed, beards. But for the first time in five years they had a choice. Sufi Muslims, despised by the Taliban, emerged from the shadows and celebrated their Islamic sect through song and dance and laughter.[115]

When Northern Alliance forces poured into the city, they were greeted with roses, and cheery children climbed on the armored vehicles.[116] Gone were the rubber truncheons of the Taliban and their yawn-producing, puritanical sermons. Songs declared outré by the Taliban now blasted from cars and stores in Kandahar. Lyrics serenaded, "I'm waiting for you here, alone. Please come to me. Let's run away and get married." Women could indulge their femininity. An American woman, Debbie Rodriguez, established a beauty school in Kabul.[117] A young Afghan woman said, "I can come here regularly now to make myself beautiful. Before, it was illegal."[118]

Men played chess again, a game they traditionally cherished. The dangers of arrest were gone but so were many of the old chess sets, some of which were buried as hidden treasure and became lost forever in the soil. Though it was winter, kites were soaring in the skies of Afghanistan. In late fall 2001 and early 2002, the pall of national depression had been lifted, and, once again, many Afghans had hope.

The full extent of Afghanistan's Generation X's cultural isolation from the West was revealed in December 2001 when an MTV-associated journalist popped "man-in-the-street" questions to Afghan youth. Most of the questions dealt with popular culture, and few of the still-shell-shocked Afghan tweens, teens, and twenty-somethings could identify any of the Spice Girls or Backstreet Boys. Nonetheless, one teenage girl, who was wearing a *Titanic* head scarf, plaintively asked the roaming former MTV video jockey if it were true that Leonardo DiCaprio died on September 11, 2001. When assured that he was very much alive, the girl was visibly relieved.[119]

Humor was back in style. Laughing was officially reviled as silly, superfluous, and girlish by the Taliban's mullahs. But there continued to circulate an underground stock of Afghan jokes, of varying degrees of quality and cleanliness. Some of the jokes made a public comeback when comedy, including political jokes, was once again legalized.

Often the jokes had a universal quality, with a parochial twist. For example, a standard American yarn might begin, "So, a New Yorker, a Texan, and a Californian go into a bar and ..." In the same comedic spirit, an Afghan gagman began his routine with, "There are five brothers, a Hazara, a Charikari, a Panshiri, a Shiberghani, and a Kandahari," and he then indulged in regional and ethnic stereotypes that sent his audience into side-splitting laughter.[120] Other routines included a popular male comic impersonating a belly dancer.

Yesterday's wooly-minded mullahs and their martinets were today's fair game for parody. The now-crushed Taliban became a favored target of acidic humor, and the master of caricature was Mubariz Bidar. Dressed in a long black turban and toting a toy AK-47, the Mubariz Show parodied mullahs howling at boys to shave their *Titanic* haircuts. In restaurants, on radio and television, and in shops and homes, Afghans were laughing. Some of it was sweet revenge.[121]

Buzkashi, a game that is often chaotic, naturally brutal, and always popular in Afghanistan, galloped back to popularity after the Taliban retreated. Two horse-mounted and whip-clutching teams vie for possession of a headless goat carcass, which they carry around a flagpole to earn one point. Players thrash the horses of their opponents.[122] One enthusiast explained, "We haven't seen this game played in more than five years. It's part of our culture, and we're very happy to have it back again."[123] An Englishman described Buzkashi as a game "quite like rugby on four legs."[124]

Beyond laughter, songs, and games, there was time for Afghans to ruminate about the religious state of their country and to call to mind an Islam practiced earlier and differently. Islam rested at the very soul of Afghanistan. Islam had withstood a surge of Buddhist enthusiasm in the 900s, the animism and paganism of the Mongols, and the atheism of the Soviets.[125] Most Afghans were still strongly connected to their religion. Islam was in Afghanistan to stay. But many had become cynical, and in the early post-Taliban months many mosques were often vacant.

A lachrymose mullah, who served in Kabul for 32 years, opined, "When the Taliban came, they defamed the name of Islam. They beat everyone; they forced people to pray. People became disillusioned in [*sic*] Islam because of the Taliban."[126] The more optimistic Afghans looked forward to greater religious freedom. As one mullah said, "At the time of the Taliban, most people's prayers weren't heartfelt because people were forced to pray. Now, I think people pray for real, because God released them from the Taliban."[127]

Profile 4.3: Rapping Sosan: "We Were Kings and Queen in Our Own Land"

Listen to my story! Listen to my pain and suffering!
—Rap lyrics of Sosan Firooz[128]

Perhaps it is the Taliban's abhorrence of popular singing, as well as their scorn for free-spirited women that explains the popularity of

Afghanistan's first notable female rapper, Sosan Firooz.[129] Anyone so detested by Taliban mullahs would draw an audience among the Afghan young. It might be the artistic genre itself, rap music, which is intoned in clubs and city streets around the world. Perhaps the cross-cultural lyrics of her songs bridge Pashtun, Tajik, Uzbek, Hazara, and myriad other ethnic and clan lines. Finally, it might be the 23-year-old, pretty and plucky singer herself that explains her lure. Young men and adolescent boys think she is sexy, and girls want to look and sing like her.

Like many Afghans, Sosan is a child of poverty and her lyrics echo the despair of her early youth. She lived as an exile in Iran, where her family fled to escape the Taliban in 1996, and hated it there. As paupers, washing dishes in restaurants and sweeping streets, her family scrounged for food and, according to her songs, endured the taunts and snickering of Iranians. These are the lyrics of her song "Our Neighbors"

> We were kings and queens in our own land
> But here, we are waiters and dish washers[130]

There is a patriotic appeal to some of Sosan's works, which also explains her popularity. Like other rappers, Sosan is angry, and her art laments the despair of the Afghan diaspora. But many of her verses shine with hope for Afghanistan's tomorrow.

Sosan has her Internet video fans. But she also has detractors, including family members. Her uncle no longer speaks to her family because he considers Sosan to be flirty and frisky. But her father is her biggest fan and left his civil service job to serve as her bodyguard, chauffer, and secretary.

There are those in the West who admire her sassy creativity, even if they cannot understand the lyrics, which are in Dari. Sosan's words plead that Afghan girls and women be treated with equality and dignity. She also condemns narcotics as a national tragedy. Accompanying her songs on a website are pictures of the young ingénue in rap poses and Western grab. Blog commentary on popular Western sites, such as the Huffington Post, wishes her the best, but fears for the worst. One comment from Ramshackle, a blogger, anticipates, "There will be a sad and predictable update to this story."[131]

WINTER SETS IN

Though many Afghans were euphoric, yesterday's Taliban were tremulous and dispossessed. The Taliban and their supporters had every reason to fear quick vengeance from the armed ethnicities, Tajik, Uzbek, and, particularly, Hazara, whom they harangued and demeaned for five years; from the Americans whom they outraged; and from the myriad villagers whose lives they made miserable and mundane. Armed with few skills and having made themselves pariahs in their home villages, many Taliban left for Pakistan. Most had no clear agenda, employment prospects, or precise destination. But they needed to leave Afghanistan immediately.

Some former Taliban trimmed their beards and bought Western-style clothes because they felt free to sever their Taliban ties. But others, still true believers, did so to disguise their Taliban connections. Taliban who could not slither back into their tribe or into the masses of refugees needed to wear Western dress to evade detection as former Taliban.[132] Some of these secretly remained loyal to the Taliban's cause but many seethed with resentment at the Arabs and al Qaeda. Many were confused and started to make their way to Quetta, Pakistan.

The vacuum left in the wake of the Taliban's ever-present, moral watchfulness gave rise to vice, by Salafist standards, and some social license. Dog fighting was back. Afghans would bet on muscular dogs, who, with savage bark and bite, chewed each other, sometimes to the death.[133] One of the best dog-fighting arenas also offered panoramic beauty atop a local hill. Dogs battled in long-drained Bib Mahru swimming pool, overlooking Kabul. When the Taliban were in power they would use the diving platforms as execution planks for their victims.[134]

In Kabul, sex-starved young men could have access to prostitutes, many of whom were war widows. Despairing and pathetic, these women were abandoned, homeless, and desperate to feed their children.[135] Gambling dens, forbidden in Taliban times, opened in the cities. But like prostitution, the ready availability of alcohol presented moral dilemmas for more conservative Afghans, fearful of a growing national prurience.

Afghan villages were free of Taliban, but many villagers were uncertain about their families' future. The situation was often far worse for those Afghans who lived in remote villages. For some, their existence became subsistence. The end of the Taliban did nothing to bring them food immediately. The United States delivered food to many villages, but not everybody was eating. Many Afghan were still hungry and cold and the oncoming winter brought panic and desperation.

Western aid organizations made determined and unorthodox efforts to provide relief. PETA, which in October remonstrated against the military action, implored Americans to surrender their fur coats, particularly mink coats, to the freezing Afghans in January 2001.[136] PETA partnered with the American Friends Committee who helped pay for shipping the furs. Soon, a load of worn minks and ermines was mailed to drape Afghans, who were shivering in the midwinter frost.[137]

Some of the hungry and cold Afghans began to starve in remote Afghan areas, before food could be sent. In a village near Mazar-i-Sharif, people began to eat bread made from grass. Symptoms of starvation developed, accompanied by the lethargy it produces. As one villager said, "We are waiting to die. If food does not come we will eat dirt. We will die."[138]

Still-imprisoned Taliban and al Qaeda were also concerned about their future. The United States was not freeing all of the captives. Arabs, Pakistanis, and other foreign fighters loyal to Osama bin Laden were caged in camps until U.S.-led coalition amnestied, locally imprisoned, or transported them to U.S. facilities, such as the Guantanamo military prison, for interrogation and incarceration. The United States insisted that suspected al Qaeda members not be allowed to go free.[139] Some were taken directly to U.S. military prisons.[140]

The killing was over and the United States and other nations determined to meet and coordinate on stabilization operations in Afghanistan. A new Afghan dawn was made brighter by the return from Europe of the respected, if geriatric, 87-year-old former king, Mohammed Zahir Shah. Washington saw Shah as force to unite the many Afghan ethnicities.[141] Charities, large and small, were reinvigorating their efforts. Some became creative, such as the mountain-climbing Greg Mortenson, who built schools in the region and would write about his accounts, if embellished, in *Three Cups of Tea*.[142] As for heads of state, the victors agreed to unite their efforts and to meet in Bonn to begin the rebuilding process in Afghanistan.

AN AGREEMENT GROWS IN BONN

Food started to flow to hungry Afghans in November, if in limited supply. In December more than 115,000 tons of food, enough to feed 6 million refugees for two months, arrived in Afghanistan. This was the largest amount of food delivered to any country since the 1980s and one of the largest since the Berlin Airlift.[143] The pounding poverty and tribal feuding continued. But by late January the Afghans were no longer starving, as aircraft brought food, dry clothing, medicine, and provisions. President Bush declared that feeding the displaced people of Afghanistan would be his top priority in Afghanistan. It was.

The victors in the Afghan war inherited a thoroughly failed state, which they determined to rebuild to keep the Taliban at bay. The most important of the early, post-Taliban, international documents was the Bonn Agreement, which created and legitimized the Afghan government; the basic legal structure, particularly the Constitution; the Supreme Court; and the economy.[144] Agreements were hammered out in Bonn in November 2001 among four main Afghan factions.[145] Signed in December 2001, it created the Afghan Interim Authority (AIA) whose chairman, Hamid Karzai, took office December 22, 2001.

It also pledged to hold elections and reorganize the armed forces and security and intelligence organizations and to legitimize the role of the

United Nations and the International Security Assistance Force (ISAF), as administrators of security and humanitarian and reconstruction aid in Afghanistan.[146] An Interim Authority would rule for six months when a Loya Jirga, deliberative body of elders, would converge to elect national-level representatives.[147]

The Bonn delegates chose Hamid Karzai because he was trusted by the American delegation, was a Pashtun, and had political and administrative experience serving as a clan chief for the Polpolzai-Durrani clan, which produced Afghan kings for 200 years.[148] Karzai had strong family connections to the United States. He was studying political science in India when the Soviets invaded Afghanistan. His family fled to major U.S. cities and opened Afghan restaurants.[149] During the anti-Soviet war, Karzai soon moved to Pakistan to support the mujahedeen.

In Bonn, Karzai's main rival, the veteran statesman Burhanuddin Rabbani, was not found suitable by the American and German governments.[150] The Bonn Agreement did not satisfy all signatories nor resolve all the nettling issues. But it did provide a basic peace agreement and a blueprint for building the then-tenuous peace into an enduring one.[151] The donors would craft a blueprint for development in general sectors—generating economic growth; building an army, civil service, police services, and communication, education, and health systems. The Taliban could challenge all these goals.

To Build an Economy

Economists at the World Bank determined that merely ballasting the economy was insufficient for Afghanistan's long-term prospects. That would keep the country at relatively primitive levels of human development. An impoverished Afghanistan would be hostage to the Taliban's resurgence. But developing Afghanistan would produce stakeholders and stability. There would be a trickle-down effect to the other sectors: the quality of civil service would improve if civil servants were paid higher wages and were trained better; security would grow as the number of stakeholders in economic stability increased; there would be a greater capacity for health care and secular-oriented education. This reasoning is the foundation of contemporary human development theory, as well as counterintelligence doctrine.

Bringing young men into the workforce would give them status and allow them enough money to afford to marry. A married man would be less likely to join an insurgency because had he family obligations.[152] In the 1960s and 1970s, Afghanistan's economic growth spurred other human development sectors. It could happen again in an Afghanistan rid of the Taliban.

Some economists were guardedly optimistic, providing sufficient seed money was allocated to begin reconstruction and development projects in earnest. Afghanistan had a prewar success, by Third World standards, of developing some key infrastructure projects, such as electric power and gas pipelines.[153] The new government needed to repatriate the educated and talented who fled the country in the Taliban period. The return of human capital in the post-Taliban era, particularly engineers, businessmen, and computer technicians, was seen as essential for sustained economic development. But they needed to be protected against the Taliban.[154]

Building in the Villages and in the Provinces

In 2001 and 2002, progovernment donors to Afghanistan's future were overwhelmed with the reconstruction and development demands. They determined to move quickly to outflank the incipient Taliban threat through building sustained, broad-sector economic growth. Beginning with handfuls of developmental specialists with a formidable military bodyguard, the provincial reconstruction team (PRT) became the engine of local economic growth and village stability.

PRTs were natural instruments to maintain a light military "footprint" to guard against the Taliban, while providing protection for developmental experts.[155] The first phases of the conflict removed the Taliban and al Qaeda from power; the next phase concentrated on stabilizing the Karzai regime and developing the country.[156] By early 2002, the U.S. Army deployed the PRT's precursor, the Coalition Humanitarian Liaison Cells, as small outposts to determine reconstruction and developmental needs.[157] They were soon nicknamed "Chiclets," a creative if not precise acronym, and comprised 10–15 soldiers, generally with civil affairs backgrounds. Soldiers worked with NGOs in the field.

Local Afghans had been contemptuous of many civilian aid workers in the early post-Taliban period, whom they saw as mollycoddled, excessively bureaucratic, and often lackadaisical. Many also stayed closeted in safe compounds. In contrast, many Afghans in the Bamiyan Province respected the risk-taking Chiclet-5, whose members were actively and personally engaged with the Afghans and who could deliver promises to protect them from the Taliban.[158] The title of these teams was, once again, changed in November 2002.

The first of the newly named PRTs was deployed to Gardez in November 2002. The province was considered to be a permissive environment for developmental activities.[159] They included staff from several U.S. agencies with equities in developing Afghanistan and security peace there. The U.S. Agency for International Development (AID) was a major player. Its developmental specialists served in the front lines of Afghanistan's developmental efforts. A dean at the United States Institute for Peace (USIP) underscored the need to serve in dangerous and contested territory in Afghanistan: "That [the developmental danger zone] is where the reality is. The Ronald Reagan Building [the headquarters of the AID] is Brigadoon."[160]

PRTs were also intended to be temporary tools to provide stability and economic optimism. After the developmental and stabilization fundamentals were achieved, the PRT would be dismantled to allow traditional, indigenous development efforts. According to plan, PRTs would coordinate the reconstruction process, identify and prioritize local projects, conduct village assessments, and coordinate with regional commanders.[161] The Taliban grew to hate the PRTs, which signaled to Kabul that the PRTs were winning.

To Build an Army

In 2002, Afghanistan did not have a professional army, and one had to be built to keep order and to prevent the Taliban's return. The army's facilities had been shattered during the incessant wars of the previous two decades. The military's leadership was sapped, and most of the weapons were antiquated and not serviceable. The last military entity that could reasonably be classified as an army crumpled with Dr. Mohammad Najibullah's Soviet-supported regime in 1992.[162]

What was left was a large pool of guerilla fighters who were tied to regional militias or, later, to the Taliban. There was no standardized training, career advancement, nationwide billeting program, unified ranking system, or other indicators of a modern, professional army. Developing the Afghan National Security Forces (ANSF), which includes the Afghan National Army (ANA), became a top priority for Western donors to Afghanistan, particularly for the United States.[163]

An important, early security-related task for the new army was disarming many of the Afghans, particularly the Taliban. That would be difficult because of the important place firearms have in Afghan culture.[164] There could be not effective, unified, and credible armed forces until local militias and former Taliban surrendered most of their weapons, particularly crew-served weapons.[165] A strong security apparatus—robust military capabilities, effective paramilitary forces, strong civil-military relations—would shore up the government. It would also underscore the government's monopoly on the legitimate use of force.

Many Afghans, particularly those who lived in areas contiguous to Pakistan, vacillated between periods of optimism, pessimism, confusion, and fatigue, as they tried to gage the staying power of government forces in contested areas. The Afghan government determined that reintegrating militias into a unified, ethnically balanced, well-armed and well-trained military force would win the confidence of the doubting Afghans.

In building the Afghan Army, there were knotty problems from the beginning, such as high levels of desertion, drug use, illiteracy, and national confusion. The early record of building the army was mixed. It was commanded by maladroit leaders, offered meager pay, provided uncomfortable billeting and foul food, and made little effort to retain the services of young men who were away from home for the first time.[166] The high rates of desertion declined by 2009, but still remained high.[167] The lower rate of desertion was attributed to a presidential decree that criminalized taking leave without authorization, a media campaign to discourage this activity, and higher unemployment. It is also an indication that employment in the army became more attractive to many soldiers.[168] But in summer and fall 2012, the army was plagued with a desertion rate somewhere between 14 and 20 percent per year, which is staggering.

To Build a Police Force

I need 20 good police officers, and could use 100. Good people—not any hashish smokers. And I need sleeping bags and mattresses and a generator for power.
—Lieutenant Colonel Amanuddin, Afghan police supervisor, early 2008

Some of the conferees in Bonn in 2001 understood the importance of a strong national police. They looked to history. In the early twentieth century, then-Capt. John Pershing built a constabulary force in the Philippines, which became a model for future counterinsurgency operations. Strong policing helped to establish zones of security. As the French counterinsurgency theoretician David Galula pointed out, police help to identify insurgents and their supporters. Today's U.S. Army counterinsurgency field manual states that the police, not the military, are the frontline forces in a counterinsurgency.

This applies to Afghanistan. In rural Afghanistan the police are responsible for maintaining security, addressing community problems, and brokering disputes. Police interact with the population daily, forging ongoing relations with key members of the community. Through these daily interactions and relationships, police develop intimate knowledge of the physical and human terrain.[169] It is for these reasons that the Taliban made police primary targets for death and intimidation.

Some of the Afghan National Police (ANP) and Interior Ministry Forces have become effective at patrolling.[170] However, there is an overwhelming consensus that the overall training program for the ANP has been weak. The poor quality of the police was, and remains, a large problem for the public administration and security sectors of human development. The police force was rampant with tribalism and favoritism, which has played into the hands of the Taliban.[171]

Profile 4.4: The "Gangster" Policewoman of Kandahar

You have long mustaches, but you have no bravery.
—Officer Malalai Kakar to fellow police officers who ran from the
Taliban in a gun fight[172]

Like her father and her brothers before her, Malalai Kakar determined to become a police officer. She entered the police academy at age 15 and became an officer in 1982. "I'm very famous as a dangerous person in Kandahar. People fear me."[173] The five-foot dynamo earned this local fear, as well as nationwide respect, by standing tall when men fled in the face of the Taliban. She also grappled, literally, with street-thug violence. She explained that her arms bore scars created by teeth marks of a suspect whom she wrestled to the ground and arrested. She called herself "part gangster." But women in Kandahar loved her and trusted her and came to her pleading for protection from abusive husbands.

Tales of her bravery resonated as a recruiting tool at a time when many Afghan city police forces, certainly Kandahar, sought out more women recruits. In 2006, 10 men reported to her in the field. "She is higher-ranked than me," explained a young male subordinate. "So she has to give orders, and I have to obey."[174] She had long shed her burka and began to wear a man's loose-fitting police uniform and visibly carry sidearms when she became Kandahar's first woman investigator.[175] In her office, she adjudicated problems with an emphasis on domestic abuse. Malalai became the touchstone for Afghan police officers.

In the Taliban era, while living in Pakistan, she married a Western-oriented employee of the United Nations and by 2008 had five children. She would prepare breakfast each morning, usually green-onion pancakes. On September 30, 2008, while she was leaving for work with one of her sons, Taliban shot her in the head, killing her at the scene.[176] Later, at the ribbon-cutting ceremony of the Malalai Kakar Women's Police Corps Training Center, which opened in December 2009, Malalai's father said, "Malalai was proud to serve her country. I thank the United States for making this possible."[177]

To Build a Civil Service

A quality civil service has been a key goal in developing Afghanistan.[178] In 2001, the victors in Bonn found a hollow civil service. There was a lack of capacity and weak communications between Kabul and outlying provinces. Under the Taliban, public administrators were poorly and infrequently paid; unprofessional, in that they were directed by theocrats; and marginally trained in public administration skills. They were also cowed by the mullahs who controlled important decision making and who could end their careers and even their lives very quickly. It not surprising that post-Taliban donors to Afghanistan were alarmed at the lack of experience, talent, ambition, and general competence in the civil service.[179]

An effective Afghan civil service would spur all other developmental sectors and increase stability. In the larger cities, civil servants would issue construction permits; maintain basic infrastructure, including roads, power stations, water facilities, sanitation, and communications; and perform other duties associated with the civil service. This, in turn, would increase the level of health, education, communications, rule of law, and security. According to plan, the credibility of the government would be boosted if vital services improved, and citizens would become greater stakeholders in reconstruction and development issues. This would weaken the attractiveness of the Taliban, and the Taliban knew it.

To Build Communications

Economists in Bonn concluded that improvements in communications would spur growth in all developmental sectors. The Afghan economy would grow if costs, expenses, and levels of demand were communicated broadly. Civil servants in Kabul needed to communicate with counterparts in the provinces for administrative purposes, and the education and health sectors were dependent on harnessing the power of the internet to modernize. Increased security required soldiers to communicate at all levels, particularly for close-support combat operations, and for the rule of law.

In a country that is isolated, illiterate, and unstable, the side that can better communicate its agenda and can coordinate civil and military operations has a distinct advantage. In addition to telephonic communications, radio communications are particularly important in Afghanistan because of the extraordinarily high level of illiteracy. In some areas, female illiteracy rate is nearly 99 percent. Radio is the only way the government can communicate their programs for democratization, advise farmers on agricultural issues and family on health issues, and warn of security threats by the Taliban.[180] Strong communications allow villagers to contact the ANA, ANP, or ISAF operators. For this reason, the insurgents have placed a high premium on destroying radio towers and have stepped up their use of radio technology to communicate their political agenda. This battle for the "information space" in Afghanistan continues.

Profile 4.5: Zakia Zaki and Her Voice of Peace

Atop a hill in lush landscape 70 kilometers north of Kabul, Zakia Zaki and her husband broadcasted to 200,000 listeners four hours each day. A pioneer woman in Afghan broadcasting, her "Voice of Peace" was initially funded by the French in a Tajik locale, in the Panjshir Valley. Its warm voice resonated as an alternative to the Taliban's cold message of absolute obedience. Her hero was Ahmed Shah Massoud, who helped win the financial support necessary to keep the old equipment running and the staff paid.[181]

When the Coalition invaded in 2001, the United States continued funding the station to broadcast local news, issues of women's concerns, music, children's shows, and household and educational shows.[182] The dark-complexioned, 35-year-old Zakia explained in 2004, "This is the only place where they [women] dare to speak out."[183] She received warm letters from all over Parwan, Kapisa, and Kabul provinces. An inviting sign on the studio's door had "Voice of Peace" written above a picture of a flying dove and a pretty, smiling woman.[184] But inside the broadcasting facility there was an ambient dread of Taliban attacks. The night letters came and so did verbal threats. This did not deter Zakia, who was also a teacher, loved by her students.

In June 2007 as Zakia lay sleeping, with her 20-month infant in her arms, in her Kabul home, two Taliban entered and shot her seven times in the head, and half of her face was blown off. Her eight-year-old son was in the room too. Immediately, Taliban called other women journalists, chuckling, boasting, and threatening, "At least people can recognize her from one side of her face. We will shoot your face, and nobody will recognize you."[185] Another threat came soon: "Daughter of America! We will kill you like we killed her."

Zaki was neither the first nor last female broadcaster killed. In 2005 Shaim Rezayee, an Afghan video jockey who spun popular tunes and dressed in jeans, was shot and killed. After Zaki was shot, another newscaster was murdered in her home.[186] Police apprehended six suspects for killing Zaki, but they were all released.[187] Authorities judged that there was not enough evidence to win a conviction.

To Educate a People

Before the Taliban, education was expanding, modernizing, and becoming more secular and accessible, particularly to girls.[188] Elements of Afghanistan's higher education system were points of pride for Afghan Western-oriented intellectuals.[189] One-half of Afghanistan's children had access to primary education in the 1960s and early 1970s, and Kabul University attracted the country's top intellectual talent.

By 2002, less than 40 percent of primary-school-age children attended school, and only 3 percent of girls did so. Secondary school attendance was 10 percent, and only 2 percent of the girls attended schools. Almost 80 percent of school buildings had been destroyed. Many teachers and administrators either had fled the country or had been killed. Those who remained had not been paid for six months. Other than religious indoctrination, the Taliban cared nothing about education.

The Bonn donors determined that literacy was a vital component of human capital. States with low levels of literacy are at a striking competitive disadvantage. Education would build the human capital necessary to expand the sectors in Afghanistan's economy, empower women, create physical infrastructure, build competent administration, promote job creation, and foster a sense of national purpose.[190] Vocational education was particularly important because skilled workmen are vital to build, service, and repair communications, health, education, and security-related facilities.

Literacy has strong security benefits because education boosts military capabilities to fight the Taliban.[191] Illiterate Afghan recruits could not be easily taught how to function as a soldier. One soldier explained, "I face difficulties. If someone calls me and tells me to go somewhere, I can't read the street signs."[192] But literate soldiers could serve as mechanics, medics, logisticians, and artillery specialists. There are also intangibles that boost morale in the army. Literacy brings prestige, commands respect, and confers status and credibility.[193] It brings dignity.

There are secular, after-school activities. The new regime in Kabul brought boy and girl scouting back to Afghanistan, to supplement after-school education and to instill values of consensual rule. First introduced in Afghanistan in 1931, scouting flourished in the 1960s and 1970s.[194] Afghan Boy and Girl Scouts share the moral code of scouts worldwide. But there are unique elements. In Afghanistan a boy can earn a merit badge for "identifying land mines and roadside bombs."[195]

To Treat and Heal a People

Donors in Bonn, 2001, understood that Afghanistan is a phenomenally unhealthy country. In the twentieth century, Afghanistan's dismal health situation proved to be an ally for Afghans in their wars against foreign invaders from the British through the Soviets. In the 1980s, sickness took a heavy toll on Soviet forces in Afghanistan.[196] Among the diseases that Soviet forces suffered were hepatitis A, typhoid fever, malaria, dysentery, and even plague.[197]

For this reason, the victors in late 2001 made health care a top priority, and U.S. military personnel and other counterinsurgency operators were well equipped to make contributions. A key counterinsurgency-related health care goal was developing and implementing a basic health care plan that had broad application and could bring quick results.[198] Taliban tactics proved effective in forcing out and keeping out foreign health practitioners. In August 2004, Doctors Without Borders closed medical programs after 24 years in Afghanistan.[199]

Profile 4.6: Khorshid: Sunshine and Happiness

If you are scared you end up doing nothing and without doing you cannot achieve anything. But if you do things, all that can happen is you succeed or fail.

—Khorshid[200]

Those who try to boost the mental health of Afghans face the ever-present sense of impending death. But this did not stop Australian skateboarder Oliver Percovich, who became a Kabul sensation in 2007 when he showed children how to ride his skateboard. The children loved it. So, Percovich built a skateboard school called Skateistan. He did this to give children happiness and allow them to escape, if only for a few moments, the drudgery of their daily lives.

On seeing Percovich coming with skateboards, children would yell, "Ollie! Ollie!" The pitted and dirty streets of Kabul teemed with rocketing and beaming kids. They cruised and swooshed and collided and jumped in Afghanistan's first skate park and school built by Skateistan.[201] Ollie explained, "The boards are just our carrots. They're a way to connect with the kids and build trust."[202]

Khorshid was a 14-year-old girl, born in the late Taliban era and into desperate poverty. She had her own skateboard, earned by volunteering as a skateboarding teacher for girls at Skateistan. She shared it with her eight-year-old sister. Khorshid had to persuade her mother to give her time away from hawking goods. But her mother agreed because Khorshid lit a smile as she zipped on her board, and other girls looked up to her. If boys could skate, so could girls. The name Khorshid means "radiant sun," as well as "happy."[203]

People remarked how radiant she was, particularly for a girl who lived in a home with no electricity and occasionally went hungry. She was also a tough girl who supervised other girls and taught them to skate and stand up to boys. One of her students said, "She was very brave and gave courage to all of us girls. She was always telling us to be brave like the boys and then no one would dare to touch us."[204] Khorshid was a natural leader.

But this leader's courage did not save her or her eight-year-old sister; or two other young up-and-coming skaters. They were selling trinkets in a park in mid-September 2012 when they were all killed by a boy the same age as Khorshid, about 14 years old, who set off a suicide bomb. The street was located directly outside of NATO facilities, which was the target.[205] Had they left five minutes earlier or had the child suicide bomber changed his mind or had the bomb failed to detonate,

Khorshid might be skating today. She might still be teaching other girls to skate and be strong and to stand up to boys. Perhaps, this natural leader would have become a national leader. But as a Skateistan official wrote, "She was in the wrong place at the wrong time."[206]

CLASHING VALUES AND CIVILIZATIONS

Many Coalition Forces found that Afghans are quick to take offense. For this reason, Coalition Forces have become increasingly schooled in the peculiarities of Pashtunwali to avoid cultural mishaps.[207] But if many Afghans were skeptical of the Coalition's intentions and practices, many Westerners had problems with quirks, foibles, and sexual predations in Afghan society. First, Afghans have proven difficult to train in military skills. U.S. trainers have expressed their skull-crashing frustration at developing basic-unit tactics and even basic marksmanship in a country renowned for its love of firearms. There were also difficulties in maintaining equipment.

Many Westerners have been appalled at the churlishness in elements of Afghan society. U.S. soldiers reported many cases of child abuse. For example, bacha bazi, translated as "boy play," is the sexual exploitation of small boys.[208] There are also boys who dance in drag to the delight of middle-aged and elderly men, who toss them meager sums of money.[209] In the view of many Coalition Forces, Afghan children were generally neglected and girls and women were subjected to virtual serfdom.[210]

Coalition Forces were stymied by the high level of drug abuse, particularly opium and cannabis. A Coalition officer commented, "They would smoke drugs so they couldn't walk straight, and these are people with our weapons." As an American physician explained, "There is a culture that smoking of opium or cannabis is, to them, like to us the smoking of cigarettes."[211] By the time an Afghan recruit begins training, he may have consumed opiates for years.[212]

The full cultural chasm exploded when U.S. soldiers burned Korans. These books were taken from the Parwan Detention Facility, after guards found that prisoners used them to exchange messages.[213] When an Afghan found the charred pages of the Korans, word reached Afghan clerics who rebuked it as "an evil act" that required physical punishment. Protests took momentum.

In February 2012, an Afghan soldier killed two U.S. soldiers as a personal, lethal protest.[214] Top U.S. leaders, including Gen. John Allen and President Barack Obama, apologized. Nonetheless, thousands of tires were set ablaze.[215] Some Afghans who were passive in combat against the insurgents appeared eager to die in violent protest against the Koran burning.

Profile 4.7: Hasan and al-Awlaki: Ticking Time Bombs and Soldiers of Allah

Jihad is becoming as American as apple pie and as British as afternoon tea.

—Anwar al-Awlaki[216]

Nidal Malik Hasan and Anwar al-Awlaki, often spelled al-Aulaqi, were American-born, highly accomplished, and widely respected Jihadists who made war on the United States. One was a physician, who became increasingly devout in early adulthood and then homicidal in early middle age; the other was a sheik, or preacher, who was born in New Mexico, mastered, with eloquence, Islam's sacred scripts, and chased prostitutes in the California night. Both held solidarity with al Qaeda and the Taliban. Both hated the United States.

Nidal Hasan is a Virginian. His parents were born near Jerusalem and identified as Palestinians. He joined the army out of college, served in the enlisted ranks, then attended Virginia Tech and, later, earned a medical degree from the military's medical school at Walter Reed Army Medical Center. He became a psychiatrist.

Hasan's loyalty to the United States had been dubious for years. On forms requesting his nationality, he began listing himself as a Palestinian rather than American. More than a few times, he penned vitriolic comments against the United States on Internet forums, and he was flamboyant about his contempt for American foreign policy. Further, he injected politics into issues, social gatherings, and professional meetings where such topics would not be naturally found. For example, while a resident at Walter Reed, the young physician was required to give a lecture on a psychiatric issue and instead used his podium to pontificate against anti-Muslim sentiment in the United States and justify suicide bombings. The presentation "freaked a lot of doctors out."[217]

His behavior did not go unnoticed by other coworkers, some of whom became suspicious and nervous. His fellow soldiers and physicians did not know what to make of his behavior or how to deal with it. The army had stressed religious inclusion and tolerance, and officers accused of insensitivity could be penalized on their annual evaluations. On Hasan's business card he had "SoA" printed on it, which meant "Soldier of Allah." Army officials at his last assignment, Fort Hood, referred to him as a "ticking time bomb."[218]

On November 5, 2009, this time bomb exploded at Fort Hood's Soldier Readiness Center. Major Hasan shot at anything that moved, killing 13 people and wounding two dozen others. His fellow soldiers were preparing to deploy to Afghanistan. Al Qaeda's Adam Gahdahn (see Profile 8.1) bloviated,[219] "Nidal Hasan is a hero . . . In fact, the only way a Muslim could justify serving as a soldier in the U.S. army is if his intention is to follow the footsteps of men like Nidal."[220]

Initially, Maj. Nidal Hasan's lawyer said that his client was not sane when he killed. Counsel pressed Hasan to keep this strategy, given the premeditation, calculation, and apparent enthusiasm with which the defendant slaughtered so many "soft targets." But Hasan fired his lawyer, defended himself, was convicted of murder, and sentenced to death. The lead prosecutor explained he would not die as a martyr. "He is not giving his life, we are taking his life!" But Hasan never wavered in his defense; he was engaged in combat against the American enemy. He was simply serving as a soldier of Allah, just as he wrote on his U.S. Army business card and freely distributed to anyone interested.

Hasan Meets al Awlaki

Nidal Hasan crossed paths with Anwar al-Awlaki, sometimes referred to as the "bin Laden of the Internet," at the Dar al-Hijrah mosque in Falls Church, Virginia. They became e-mail pen pals. Like Hasan, Awlaki's parents were Arab. His father was a Fulbright Scholar from Yemen. Anwar was born in New Mexico, but lived much of his early life in Yemen. He returned to the United States to attend university. He may have traveled to Afghanistan in the mid-1990s, probably before the Taliban rose to power.

Awlaki loved political Islam, particularly the writings of Qutb (see chapter 1) as well as those of Azzam (see chapter 6).[221] He became president of the Colorado Muslim Students Association. Around 1995, he began preaching in a mosque in San Diego, where he carped about American degeneracy. He was then arrested in that city for soliciting prostitutes.[222] The sheik then moved to Virginia to become the spiritual leader of the Dar al-Hijrah mosque. Among the congregants were Nawaf al-Hamzi and Hani Hanjour, two of the September 11, 2001, hijackers.[223] Hasan met the sheik there in 2001.

Fearing that the U.S. law was closing in on him, Awlaki fled to Yemen and began to boast of his fugitive status. He crowed in 2010, "I move freely in Yemen. There is a support among my tribesmen."[224] But his tribesman's support could not save him from a Hellfire missile fired from a U.S. drone, which decimated him and his Denver-born son in October 2011.[225] Some civil libertarians decried the killing as imposing a death penalty without trial. One man claimed Awlaki was innocent and that the United States made a homicidal error. The American security establishment had it all wrong. Nasser al-Awlaki explained that his son was simply an "all-American boy" (Table 4.1).[226]

Table 4.1   Hasan and al-Awlaki

	Nidal Hasan	**Anwar al-Awlaki**
Born	Virginia, United States, to Palestinian parents	New Mexico, United States, to Yemeni parents
Background	Enlisted soldier; university and medical student; U.S. Army officer; psychiatrist	Raised mostly in Yemen; attended university in Colorado, engineering, and George Washington University, management systems
Connection to Islam	Turned to Salafist and militant Islam in his 20s	Was taught in Koranic Arabic in Yemen and self-taught in Islamism
Foibles and Oddities	Repeatedly made threats to non-Muslims; gave indications that he was unpatriotic and hated the United States and Jews	Arrested in California for soliciting prostitution
Connection to and View of Afghanistan	Decried what he considered to be the illegal and immoral war in Afghanistan; killed U.S. soldiers who were preparing to deploy to Afghanistan	Spent some summer months in Afghanistan in the early 1990s; rhetorically supported the Taliban and advocated killing their opponents, particularly Americans

CHAPTER SUMMARY

After the Taliban were removed, economists and policy decision makers were concerned with three major perceived obstacles: the high financial cost for reconstruction and development; the lack of indigenous capacity; and the provincial outlook of Afghan and foreign decision makers. The National Development Plan set the reconstruction and development process in motion. At the same time, the Taliban became revitalized.

The victors determined to build the economy, army, police force, civil service, education, and a health service. This strengthened stability, increased national optimism, and weakened support of the Taliban. In the early post-Taliban era, there was a sense of national relief. Boys could wear "*Titanic* haircuts" without fear of being forcibly shorn, and girls could hum the movie's theme romantic song, "My Heart Will Go On."[227] But bitterness between the Afghans and the Coalition Forces had grown. Coalition Forces became disgusted by the pedophilia to which they were witness, the misogyny still rampant, and the malignant neglect of children and pets. Some Afghans saw Coalition soldiers as their parents saw the Soviets—infidel invaders of their homeland.

5

The Taliban's Recovery in Pakistan

Chapter 4 discussed the Taliban's downfall and the security and developmental priorities for the conquering nations, which met in Bonn. Chapter 5 will analyze the specific target sets, tactics, and their effects on the counterinsurgency with greater granularity. This is a chapter on how the Taliban fight.

THE TALIBAN'S DIASPORA

Before its ejection in late 2001, the Taliban's governmental structure was similar to those other impoverished Third World, one-party states. The Taliban had a monopoly on the use of force and law enforcement. There were chains of command and a clearly stated, if not always followed, hierarchy of control from Mullah Omar to the regional bureaucrats. But communications were poor and effective decision making was often decentralized outside of Kabul and Kandahar.

The Taliban had nothing that resembled a professional civil service. However, there was a rank order of decision making in the Taliban. Most important decisions were made by Mullah Omar and religious clerics on the basis of their interpretation of religious law. Hiring and promotion were based on performance but also on cronyism and patronage. Within the government, there were rivaling factions, ambitious bureaucrats, petty arguments, and other characteristics universal to large organizations. When the Taliban became outcasts, they took this system of governance, with all its assets and idiosyncrasies, and adopted it to the circumstances and environment of their exile.

Leaving Afghanistan, the Taliban looted what remained of the Afghan treasury. In early 2002, the Taliban traded in barter and began to expand its criminal operations. By 2011 the Taliban would raise nearly $400 million per year. This money would come from taxes, donations, and criminal enterprises, to be discussed in chapter 7.[1]

The Taliban needed sanctuary. Mao Tse Tung, recalling his long march to escape Nationalist Chinese forces, defined sanctuary as an area that is strategically located in which insurgents can train and build their forces.[2] The area should provide limited freedom of movement but not for conventional maneuver. In sanctuaries, insurgents can supply and refit and regroup free of significant enemy interference. The ideal local population would welcome the insurgents. In early 2002, the Taliban certainly found sanctuary in Waziristan.[3] Waziristan is an autonomous tribal zone contiguous to Afghanistan. Stretching 1,500 miles from Baluchistan to the Hindu Kush, it is largely Pashtun, deeply religious, and, for the Taliban, friendly.

When they were scattered into Pakistan in 2001 and 2002, they were fortunate to have preexisting logistical networks and madrassas and charities that served as billeting facilities and, later, bases of operations. As in their earlier climb to power, or phase 1 in the government's insurgency model, the Taliban forged amiable relations with local mullahs.[4] In FATA and Northwest Frontier Provinces (NWFP), renamed Khyber Pakhtunkhwa, Mullah Omar pooled his resources and lent his prestige to local chieftains, some of whom would emerge as important allies.[5]

The Taliban warmed relations with Baitullah Mehsud, who forged his local Taliban organization, the TTP, in 2007, to be discussed in chapter 8. The bond between Mehsud and Omar was strong but sometimes ambiguous. Mehsud performed as the subordinate member of this Taliban team from the beginning, even though he was playing host to the fugitive Omar. Even before the TTP was formalized, Mehsud required his forces to prove fealty to Omar as their leader.[6]

The local Taliban under Mehsud, in conjunction with the Omar's exiled Taliban, brought an order to the territories that had eluded the government forces of Pakistan. They punished criminals swiftly and severely. They also suppressed or eliminated village elders who defied them. They enforced Sharia.[7] The Taliban recuperated in Waziristan, and then many dispersed in different regions of the Pakistan-Afghanistan, Pashtun-belt area. Mullah Omar went south to Baluchistan and so did many other Taliban.

The Taliban received a warm reception from Quetta's devout and elderly in the hardscrabble Baluchi capital.[8] But not everybody welcomed them, and Quetta's small middle class, particularly its women, detested them. The flood of unemployable and penurious Taliban youth put pressure on the already-fragile economy.[9] Tourism, even then weak, declined, and owners of the few cyber cafes faced uncertain prospects.

˙ Within one year, clerics openly preached hatred for the United States and recruited in the cities' madrassas and mosques. In the bazaars, Taliban hawked the paraphernalia of jihad—taped speeches of bin Laden and bumper stickers advocating martyrdom.[10] Quetta became no place for the liberal minded.

The Shura appointed four committees—military, political, cultural, and economic—to regulate all relevant matters. Other committees would be established.[11] As of late 2013, Mullah Omar leads the Quetta Shura and the other three. He is presumed to live in Quetta. He is assisted by a staff with military and organizational responsibilities. Some of these leaders have overlapping regional responsibilities. The Afghan Taliban have regional military Shuras for four major geographical areas of operations. The eponymous Shuras are named after the areas in which they are based—Quetta, Peshawar, Miramshah, and Gerdi Jangal.

THE SHURAS

The shura principle is rooted in the Koran, as noted in chapter 1. It is the activity of consultation via a council that deliberates and passes judgment on social and political issues that involve the Islamic community, or ummah. Mullah Omar is, by far, the most important decision maker, but he does not rule like a dictator. The Taliban Supreme Shura, heavily guided by Omar, carries out strategic planning, issues directives to regional commanders, and disseminates the directives to village cells as fatwas, or diktats. The village cell acts in a semi-independent manner with minimum control from higher echelons. Sometimes the orders from the Supreme Shura are precise; often they take the form of broad guidance.

Quetta Regional Military Shura—Life in the Pakistani Badlands

The term "Quetta Shura" originated from Mullah Omar's relocation of the Taliban organization to Quetta, Baluchistan, after spending some time in Waziristan. In Quetta, Mullah Omar's Taliban refer to themselves as the Islamic Emirate of Afghanistan.[12] The Quetta Regional Military Shura directs activities in southern and western Afghanistan.

Balochistan is impoverished, even by the standards of Pakistan, and seethes with resentment of federal governance. Some of the ethnic prejudices of Afghanistan pour into the Baloch territory. As in Afghanistan, the Hazaras, who are set apart from many other South Asians by their distinct East Asiatic appearance, are relegated to menial work as a lower caste.[13] In June 2012, a university bus filled with Hazaras was blown up, killing four. According to the Hazara Democratic Party, over 700 Hazaras were murdered since 2002 in sectarian violence.[14] Also, the Baloch feel exploited by the Punjabis, the dominant ethnicity of Pakistan's 180 million. The police patrol just 5 percent of Balochistan. The rest is manned by tribal bands and 50,000 Pakistani troops.

Today Quetta, like the fabled outlaw territory of the American old west, is a vast danger zone, and its inhabitants are often inclined to sling weapons. Many individuals, groups, and political cohorts live outside of the law. In the 1980s, the city served as a sanctuary for anti-Soviet fighters and as a transit route, or "jihad trail," for their supplies. By the 1990s, there were criminal enterprises, weapons smugglers, camps of Islamist and separatists, adventurers, and desperados. Bin Laden was popular in Balochistan, and his smiling image was ubiquitous in shops and coffeehouses by the late 1990s.

For over 30 years, Afghans and Arabs intermarried with local women and many have obtained Pakistani identification documents. Today, the blend of cultural and national backgrounds makes it difficult to distinguish between some of the indigenous and Afghan residents. Reliable information about Quetta is scarce because so many journalists are killed, particularly those who are critical of powerful men.

Death is common in Quetta. A woman professor of communications was shot dead in a rickshaw traveling to a radio station.[15] It was probably related to her politics. A former Olympian boxer was shot by unknown assailants for reasons unknown.[16] The body of a boy, approximately 10 years old, was found in Quetta. He was strangled and his body dumped by the road.[17] In a tribal clash, three people were shot to death, including a woman. The assailants escaped.[18] A much-respected Baloch scholar, writer, and poet, Professor Saba Dahtyari authored 24 books on Balochi literature. He loved his Balochistan, and many of his country's intellectuals loved him. But in June 2011 he was shot and killed.[19] Sometimes the sick and dying cannot be treated in Quetta. There are periodic strikes when doctors protest a number of issues, such as privatizing hospitals and low wages. These homicidal anecdotes represent the constant death that is daily life in Balochistan today.

Life has become progressively worse for women. By 2009, most restaurants stopped serving women. At the behest of Taliban and their ideological cohorts, owners placed signs stating, "For gentlemen only. Women not allowed."[20] Of Pakistan's four provinces, Balochistan has the fewest per capita number of female health care workers.[21] The Taliban are largely responsible for that.

From early in the insurgency, some U.S. military and political leaders fulminated that Pakistan had turned a blind eye to the presence of the Taliban. Some drew analogies to Vietnam and the sanctuary in Cambodia that communists enjoyed.[22] In 2006, British Col. Chris Vernon, chief of staff for southern Afghanistan, identified Quetta as the key center of operations. He also accused the Pakistani military of training and arming Taliban in Quetta.[23]

For years, Coalition generals and diplomats have advocated a hard-hitting response. Lt. Gen. David Barno, former commander of U.S. forces in Afghanistan, said, "The Quetta Shura is extremely important. They are the intellectual and ideological underpinning of the Taliban insurgency."[24] Gen. Stanley McChrystal, former U.S. commander in Afghanistan, claimed that the Taliban leadership was there, and in 2009 Gen. David Petraeus and Lt. Gen. Douglas E. Lute, a White House official on Afghanistan, recommended that drone operations be extended to Quetta.[25]

The Taliban's Leadership in Quetta

Much like the political landscape of Baluchistan, the inner workings of the Quetta Shura are surrounded in secrets. The Taliban's leadership provides tactical direction and guidance to its fighters and commanders in the field. Senior commanders resident in Afghanistan travel to Quetta to confer on strategy, obtain supplies, provide intelligence, and receive instruction from the shura.[26]

The Quetta leadership typically sets goals at the beginning of the spring fighting year. The operational orders typically appear in the form of a planned offensive, subject to revision and adaption.[27] The Quetta Shura also provides tactical direction and guidance to its fighters and commanders in the field.[28] The Shura is composed of indigenous and foreign fighters.[29] This is the nerve center for all of the Taliban's operations. Its leaders direct military strategy, craft policy and political and military strategy, appoint field commanders, and manage a shadow government.[30] Fearing U.S. drone attacks, a large number of Taliban leaders have shifted from Quetta to Karachi, Peshawar, and other cities.[31]

Profile 5.1: Saad Haroon: Pakistani Funnyman and His Burka Woman

Burka woman I love you still; come on and give me a thrill.
—From Saad Haroon's "Burka Woman" to the tune of Roy Orbison's
"Pretty Woman," on YouTube[32]

If anyone can find humor in the Taliban's mounting menace in Pakistan and the generalized misery, he is the U.S.-educated Saad Haroon. With his friend, the young humorist hosts a unique website from their Karachi-based home. He mocks the Taliban and the dreary life they seek to impose on his country. Armed with an indestructible sense of humor, Haroon determined to fight the Taliban with jokes after he witnessed a terrorist attack in Karachi that killed 140 people.[33]

Some topics are off limits for comedic barbs. Jokes about the Pakistani Army or major political parties would not be a laughing matter to Pakistani authorities. Clowning about Islam could become gallows humor. But Haroon rips into burkas with satirical song. A popular parody of Roy Orbison's "Pretty Woman" is "Burka Woman." In this routine, which is posted on YouTube, a young Pakistani man fanaticizes about the female flesh hidden behind the burka. "My love for you it grows, every time I see your toes. Nail polish, Rrrrrr," goes one line. "With your eyes, my mystery prize."[34] One of his most popular jokes is, literally, toilet humor. He snickers that Pakistani public toilets are the dream of terrorists; they are biological warfare themselves.[35] His routine brings chuckles to the South Asia diaspora. He has performed in New York, London, and other cities where there are large Pakistani communities.

Not everybody thinks he is funny, and some Pakistani elders are concerned that he is part of an Indian conspiracy to corrupt the morals of Pakistan's youth. Others simply find his comedy stale. Yet others salute his efforts to find anything thing funny about Pakistan or the Taliban. As a blogger wrote, "In general, Pakistan is just not funny these days. Bless this comic nevertheless; he has his work cut out for him."[36]

The Leaders

Mullah Muhammad Omar is the current leader of the Taliban, and he was profiled in chapter 2. He is the Afghan Taliban's supreme leader, believed to be hiding in Pakistan. The other leaders are:

Mullah Abdul Ghani Baradar: Generally considered to have been the second-most important leader in the Taliban, Mullah Baradar is an intimate of Mullah Omar who was captured by the ISI. He is of the same clan and subclan as Hamid Karzai, a Populzai Durrani Pashtun.[37] His was captured and imprisoned by the ISI.[38] In late September 2013 he was released, under the provision that he remain in Pakistan.[39]

Muhammad Hassan Rahmani: A strategist and leader, he was a governor of Kandahar and may be the shadow governor today.[40]

Mullah Abdul Qayoum Zakir: He is a commander of operations for southern Afghanistan. Captured in 2001 and held in Guantanamo until 2007, he was transferred to Kabul and freed in 2008. He is assumed active today organizing attacks against Coalition Forces in the south.[41] Zakir has charisma and experience, and, should Mullah Omar be killed, he is a candidate to replace him.[42]

Maulavi Abdul Kabir (captured): Commander of forces in eastern Afghanistan, Kabir was a member of the Quetta Shura.[43]

Mullah Abdul Razzak: Chief propagandist for the Taliban from 1996 to 2001, Mullah Razzak was arrested by Pakistan in 2003. He was released and rejoined the group where he serves today as a strategist.[44]

Amir Khan Muttaqi: He currently heads propaganda efforts.[45]

Sayyid Tayyab Agha: He is the Taliban's chief diplomat.[46]

Peshawar Regional Military Shura

The Peshawar Shura directs activities in eastern and northeastern Afghanistan. In many places, Peshawar resembles Quetta, with sprawling back alleys, bazaars, haunts, and slums. There is a similar atmosphere of anxiety in Peshawar's streets because of the summary justice meted out by factions and tribes competing for control and power. The Taliban's control of Peshawar ebbs and flows. The Taliban have enough control to enforce their puritanical Islamic code. There is a conflict with well-placed residents and old families who will not easily surrender their status or influence to the Taliban, whom they consider uninvited and unwanted guests.[47]

In the Khyber Pakhtunkhwa region, formerly known as the Northwest Frontier Province, Peshawar is the capital. Here, Taliban have committed 1,962 acts of terror since 2008, killed 6,200 persons, and injured more than 9,000 others.[48]

Miramshah Regional Military Shura and the Haqqani Connection

North Waziristan, the Miramshah Regional Military Shura, directs activities in southeastern Afghanistan, including the provinces of Paktika, Paktia, Khost, Logar, and Wardak. Jalaluddin Haqqani and his son Sirajuddin command an element of the Taliban that has far more independence than any others.[49] The Haqqani network has been described, incorrectly, as an entirely autonomous terrorist-narcotic gang.[50] The Haqqanis have sworn fealty to Mullah Omar, though this arm of the Taliban has greater license for conducting independent operations. At times they operate autonomously, but also in conjunction with other militant groups, including other Taliban elements. In mid-November 2012, the father-son duo Jalaluddin and Sirajuddin Haqqani indicated that they would participate in peace talks with ISAF negotiators if the Taliban agree.[51] In mid-November 2013, Nasiruddin Haqqani, the younger brother of Sirajuddin and the chief fund-raiser of the Haqqani network, was killed, as assassins on motorcycles sprayed him and his vehicle with gunfire.[52]

The network is tribally diverse and comprises Uzbeks, Chechens, Kashmiris, Pakistanis, as well as Afghans who live in FATA. Its areas of influence extend from North and South Waziristan to Parachinar and Kurram agencies, all in Pakistan. From these bases, the Haqqanis conduct attacks on the border areas of Paktika, Khowst, and Paktia provinces. The Haqqanis also had a strong connection to bin Laden.

Gerdi Jangal Regional Military Shura

Based in the Baluchistan, this regional military Shura focuses exclusively on Helmand Province and, perhaps, Nimroz Province.

THE STRUCTURE OF THE TALIBAN

The Taliban is organized hierarchically from the supreme leader, Mullah Omar, to the foot soldiers. At the top, the Supreme Leadership, in conjunction with the Shura Council, gives guidance. The cadre is composed of dedicated mid- to senior-level operatives. Foot soldiers are the rank and file of the Taliban. Finally, mercenaries are fair-weather Taliban whose devotion to the ideology is tenuous and who serve for lack of better employment opportunities.

Rings of Support

The Taliban's structure is hierarchical, from the Supreme Shura, through the foot soldiers, to the pool of mercenaries. But levels of support can also be seen in terms of concentric rings. As with other insurgent and terrorist groups, such as the defunct German Red Army Faction, the Taliban have expanding rings of progressively weakened support. There is a nucleus of hardened fighters and key decision makers at the Taliban's core. The rings beyond this nucleus are increasingly less senior, though still important.

The ring beyond the inner nucleus is that of the active fighters. This nucleus is built of the most dedicated and hardened and, usually, veteran support. Moving centrifugally, there is second ring of active key cadre who serve as leaders and trainers. They, too, are veteran fighters but do not have the high-leadership position of the first-ring cadre.

Beyond this ring is a third ring of active noncombatants. They are active in the political, fund-raising, and information activities of the group. They sometimes conduct intelligence and surveillance activities, and provide safe haven, shelter, financial contributions, medical aid, and transit assistance. They are particularly instrumental in madrassas, where they recruit and groom future foot soldiers and leaders.

The fourth ring is one of passive supporters and sympathizers. They may not be aware of their precise relation to the terrorist group. Sympathizers can be useful for political activities, fund-raising, and intelligence gathering and other nonviolent activities.[53]

Table 5.1   The Committee of Ten Council[1]

Committees	Functions
Ulema, or Religious Council	Builds and maintains Sharia courts; vets, appoints, promotes, and cashiers judges; approves death sentences
Finance	Raises funds and distributes money to provincial leaders. Budgets money and pays for operations.
Political Affairs	Serves as diplomats and fund-raisers. Maintains contacts with Gulf states patrons
Culture and Information	Propaganda arm of the Taliban. Serves as a media arm for information operations; distributes videos; maintains Taliban websites; prints large-circulation material, including books and pamphlets
Military Council	Maintains military capabilities; directs operations; trains recruits; equips insurgents
Prisoners and Refugees/ Martyrs	Provides financial assistance to families of Taliban killed or captured
Education	Organizes, recruits, and partially funds madrassas under Taliban control
Recruitment	Recruits for the Taliban
Repatriation	Mission not clear
Interior Affairs	Likely that has an intelligence and counterintelligence function

[1]Waheed Mozhda, Afghan daily Hasht-e Sobh, May 18, 2008.

The Committees

Along with the four regional commands, the Afghan Taliban have 10 functional committees that address specific issues. Some of the members of the committees are also members of the Quetta Shura. The committees are: Ulema Council, or Religious Council; Finance; Political Affairs; Culture and Information; Military Council; Prisoners and Refugees; Education; Recruitment; Repatriation; and Interior Affairs.[54] Table 5.1 shows the committees and their functions.

Funding

In addition to trading in commodities, trafficking in narcotics, and running extortion rackets, the Taliban operate the informal money transfer system commonly known as hawala. In this system, money is transferred between two parties informally. There is little paperwork kept. These formal and informal value transfers enable the Taliban to sustain the organization.

According to the Afghanistan Centre for Research and Policy Studies director Haroun Mir, there is a vast network of charities that solicit funds for the Taliban. Much funding comes through rich donors in the petrol-exporting Gulf states. The funds are flowing through ghost charities. "Nobody has an idea where this money goes as it is being used by extremist groups to purchase weapons or recruit suicide bombers."[55]

Intelligence, Security Functions, and Interrogation

Intelligence plays a vital role in the Taliban's operations. The Taliban cannot match the military capabilities of the Coalition Forces, so they try to erode the will of the enemy through unconventional tactics. Without strong intelligence, the Taliban would not be able to commit effective suicide bombings nor could they infiltrate effectively the Afghan military, intelligence, and police. Without effective intelligence, the "green-on-blue" attacks, Afghan soldiers turning their weapons on fellow soldiers and Western soldiers, would be very difficult.

The Taliban's offensive intelligence operations rely on human intelligence. These operations include preoperation surveillance for attacks. They plant disinformation about the Coalition Forces, gather intelligence-related data that can be used in green-on-blue attacks, monitor the behavior of villagers, conduct surveillance of places and persons of interest, and engage in a wide variety of intelligence operations.

The Taliban have experience in collection activity. During their rule, they had developed a quasi-totalitarian security apparatus to cement their Sharia-based theocracy.[56] Today, the Taliban have personnel who exclusively focus on intelligence and counterintelligence.[57] They are deployed to the regional and provincial levels to help facilitate the flow of information and run informant networks.[58] At least one Western official has stated that the Afghan Taliban have a de facto head of intelligence, although the identity of this individual remains unclear.[59]

Well-dressed Taliban, often young men, perform preoperational surveillance. They photograph areas with digital cameras, obtain GPS coordinates, and watch people and places. Operatives will spend many hours observing who walks into buildings connected to intelligence or military services. Some of the operators bring an array of sophisticated tracking devices and webcams and are careful not to bring weapons. In Kabul, Kandahar, and Mazar-I-Sharif, Taliban also reconnoiter cities from motor vehicles. There are also countermeasures in case they are apprehended. Files on Taliban computers are disguised under file names such as "poetry" or "jokes."

The Taliban are skilled at counterintelligence. They are capable at unmasking penetrations or double agents who are cooperating with

Table 5.2   Taliban Offensive and Counterintelligence and Target Sets

Target Set	Offensive Intelligence Operations	Counterintelligence Operations
Afghan Government Forces	Infiltrate government services to obtain military capabilities material and to conduct paramilitary and green-on-blue attacks. Lower morale through subversion. Conduct espionage	Infiltrate government to uncover agents and efforts to infiltrate the Taliban
Coalition Forces	Prepare green-on-blue attacks. Lower morale through subversion. Conduct espionage	Infiltrate Coalition Forces to uncover agents and efforts to infiltrate the Taliban
Afghan Noncombatants	Conduct village-level operations to determine who is sympathetic to the Taliban's agenda and who is hostile. Understand tribal and extended-family dynamics and power players	Determine who is cooperating with the Karzai government and Coalition Forces
Foreign Noncombatants	Target foreign contractors and understand their circle of acquaintances and family. Understand vulnerabilities	Who among foreign noncombatants are trying to infiltrate Taliban? Particular focus on non-Pashtuns

Coalition Forces because the Taliban have extensive knowledge of the leading families, tribal elders, and widows in the Pashtun areas of Afghanistan. As in former communist states, they channel much of their limited resources toward spying. This fits into the strategy of terror.[60] Taliban intelligence targets include Afghan government forces, Coalition Forces, military personnel, noncombatants, and foreign noncombatants.[61]

The mind of the Taliban is well suited for intelligence, particularly counterintelligence. The mentality of the Taliban is one of suspicion and hostility to nonconformity. Its view holds that lying is acceptable and sometimes required in defense of Islam.[62] The Taliban have broad license to extract information by even the most grim interrogation techniques.[63] Taliban suspected of collaborating with Coalition Forces can be executed without appeal or pity, and their severed heads could be exposed on Taliban-run media.[64] Taliban mullahs justify the torturous interrogation by references in the Koran (Table 5.2).[65]

THE TALIBAN'S FOUR STRATEGIES

The term "strategy" is central to the language of war. It is a broad course of action to achieve victory. The Taliban's strategies are to cripple Afghanistan's economy, terrorize the enemy, increase their support base, and destroy the national will of states that support the current government. These four strategies remain central. Chapter 6 will explain the specific tactics in greater detail.

A foremost Taliban strategy is to *cripple the economy*. Insurgents target the economy because an economically prosperous Afghanistan will shore up the credibility of the government; attract greater international investment, particularly in extractive resources; encourage domestic savings and investment; and develop human capital. Afghans would become stakeholders in the economy, if the returns on their investment appeared promising.

In turn, young Afghans would be more attracted to vocationally based education and technological, engineering, and scientific subjects that are likely to bring financial reward. Afghanistan's intellectually talented would be less likely to devote their energies toward memorizing the Koran had they the option of pursuing education that would increase their standard of living. This is why the donors in Bonn gave economic growth such importance, and this is why the Taliban find it threatening.

A second Taliban strategy is to *terrorize* the Afghan and non-Afghan enemy. Fear successfully paralyzed incipient dissent during their 1996–2001 rule. The insurgents have a long list of enemies, including all those involved in modernizing the country. The insurgents have targeted teachers, health care practitioners, public administrators, all those involved in the armed forces and intelligence and security services, many NGO workers, as well as others under the category of collaborator.

A third strategy is to *expand the Taliban's bases of support*. These include financial support, access to weapons, and recruitment capabilities from all over the Islamic world. Pakistan provided millions of dollars, arms, and adolescents to the Taliban in the 1990s. The Pakistani connection to the Taliban continues.[66] Pakistan also supported other insurgent groups, to be discussed in chapter 8. In addition to domestic and Pakistani support, the Taliban received significant aid from Arabs. They still do.

The fourth strategic goal is to *destroy the will of the government's international patrons*. The Taliban have scored significant success in incrementally eroding the once-solid will of Western societies to continue their military presence in Afghanistan, as indicated by polls.[67] Five years into the counterinsurgency, President Bush became concerned that American steadfastness would wane as U.S. soldiers were killed.[68]

THE TALIBAN'S BASIC SETS OF TACTICS AND TARGETS

The term "strategy" refers to the Taliban's bedrock military and political agenda. The means by which the strategy is implemented is through "tactics." The Taliban have successfully adopted their tactics to suit the environment and circumstances. There are three main groupings of tactics: violent attacks, nonviolent intimidation, and information operations. The basic sets are discussed below and the specific tactics will be discussed in the next chapter.

Violent Tactics

The first tactic is the use of brute violence. The mujahedeen tortured and mutilated the corpses of Soviet soldiers, and some of these insurgents would continue their brutal tactics in their next war fighting as Taliban.[69] In their second charge to conquest, from 2001 until today, Taliban have killed and maimed their enemies. Assassination and indiscriminate murder is a proven, cost-effective weapon in an insurgency because of the fear it induces. The insurgents have reviewed terrorist trends from Iraq and Israel and have calculated the human and roadside bombs are very effective.[70] There are many targets for the Taliban. Several of the more important target sets are education, communications, the civil service, and police and security forces, listed in the following subsections.

Target Set: Economic and Entrepreneurial Enterprises

One target set of the Taliban centers on businesses or businessmen who cater to affluent Afghans, foreigners, or progovernment personnel. Upscale hotels and restaurants are prime targets for several reasons. The Taliban and the Haqqani insurgents see swanky hotels as pretentious and view the proprietors and wait staff as collaborators serving a foreign, conquering force. These venues also attract the rich and powerful of Afghanistan. The Taliban also attack cafes, markets, and shopping centers.

The Taliban also terrorize the entrepreneurial poor. Trying to support families by peddling secondhand goods, toiletries, and DVDs and cosmetics, poor hawkers set themselves at the mercy of Taliban's often-dotty and always-thuggish moral code. The Taliban morality police beat those who listen to music, wear Western clothes, watch television, and engage in all but the most Islamic and primitive forms of recreation. They also punish, often with great severity, entrepreneurs who sell the proscribed clothing, DVDs, and television sets.[71] By doing so, the Taliban restrict even further the ability of Afghans to earn a living.

Target: Education

Education is the factory that turns animals into human beings.
—Ghulam Hazrat Tanha, Herat's director of education[72]

From the beginning, the Taliban persistently and aggressively targeted education. During their five-year rule they shuttered schools, completely segregated the sexes, and purged the texts for what they considered un-Islamic elements. Today, out of power, the Taliban fear the power of education in building national capacity, empowering women, creating physical infrastructure, assuring competent administration, promoting job creation, and fostering a sense of national purpose.

They attack a broad set of educational targets: students, teachers, parents, facilities. Tactics include stand-off attacks, assassinations, murders, and morbid, disfiguring attacks, such as throwing acid into the faces of school-children. One of the countless attacks occurred in August and September 2003. Taliban burned several buildings at an elementary school near Kabul and, as their standard modus operandi, left leaflets threatening to kill teachers, parents, and children should they pursue education. After the attack, nearly 200 of the 400 boys and girls stayed away for some time.[73] The Taliban's intimidation worked and often still does.

But outgunned Afghans sometimes fight the Taliban. The Afghan villagers have organized broadly and often effectively against Taliban attacks on educational facilities, educators, and students. By summer 2012, there were more coordinated, village-level self-defense efforts to save the schools. Sometimes, with or without government help, villagers took up arms to protect their schools.[74] According to a report, a school principal organized 500 students to fight against the Taliban attempts to shut down the schools in August 2012.[75]

In addition, villagers have defied the Taliban through nonphysical resistance. Fully aware of the dangers should they be uncovered, schoolteachers and administrators have kept schools open, if cautiously and surreptitiously. They have secreted themselves in guesthouses teaching in small groups to reduce the possibility of detection. In eastern Afghanistan, an underground education system has arisen.[76] In some cases government forces have kept Afghanistan's schools open; in other cases they compromised with the Taliban on school content and attendance. In other cases the Taliban closed schools down entirely.

Target: Communications

The Taliban also target communications systems and their operators. The Taliban regularly attack radio programing and the transmission towers. Cell phones have helped to leapfrog over more primitive communications.

Counterinsurgency operators use transmissions to fight the insurgents. The Taliban attack towers and threaten to kill operators and technicians who service them. When these threats are credible, service stops during the night and sometimes during the day. The Taliban believe informants use cell phones to alert U.S. troops after dark. In neighboring Pakistan, operators of the Voice of America acceded to the demands of the local insurgents to cease broadcasting.

Target: Civil Servants and Police

Taliban kill Afghans who work for the Kabul government and Coalition Forces. From the beginning of the counterinsurgency, there was a limited pool of well-educated Afghans who had in-demand skills. They are referred to as the "second civil service." These skills include English language skills; technical skills, particularly information systems; and accounting skills.[77] Taliban need to kill them or dissuade them from helping the government.

Of the branches of the civil service, the Afghan police have been the most targeted. The U.S. Army's counterinsurgency manual states clearly that the police, not the military, are the frontline soldiers in a counterinsurgency. As David Galula points out, the police are the government's most effective and efficient organization for eradicating insurgent political agents from the population. For Coalition Forces to hold and build an area, there needs to be a credible police force. Through daily interactions and relationships, police develop intimate knowledge of the physical and human terrain. The police gather intelligence from local villagers involving the presence and identity of Taliban. Finally, there is also the criminal incentive to killing police officers. The Taliban are involved in criminal enterprises, which puts them at odds with the police who have not been corrupted.

The Taliban use different means to kill and maim police. Many are killed by explosives, particularly mines placed in roads. Sometimes police officials, such as chiefs, are targeted. For example, in August 2012 the Taliban tracked the routes of a police chief. When he passed a set route in Badghis Province, a roadside bomb was detonated, wounding him and killing others.[78] Some attacks use Taliban impersonating police officers.[79] In the first recorded attack of its kind, an Afghan policewoman killed a U.S. police contractor in late December 2012.

Taliban terror infects the Pakistani police force also. In Peshawar, the home of one of the four Shuras, the Taliban often outgun the police opponents and fight with a terrifying ferocity. The police inspector remarked in December 2012 that the militants' wildness against security forces has sapped morale at many local stations and checkpoints, forcing them to suspend night duty.[80]

Target: Health Care Providers

The Taliban target health care providers, particularly those connected to NGOs. Sometimes they kill these providers randomly, and sometimes they target specific health care professionals. Superstitions sometimes drive kill orders. For example Taliban, and some other Afghans, believed that efforts to eradicate polio, a disease long conquered in most of the West, were un-Islamic and part of American plots.[81] In late December 2012, Western medical personnel were killed administering polio vaccines.

For this reason, some NGOs have withdrawn their presence from Afghanistan. Medicins Sans Fontieres (MSF) withdrew from Afghanistan early in the insurgency, June 2004, because of their inability to protect their employees. MSF had worked in Afghanistan for nearly 25 years. Other NGOs, such as the International Committee for the Red Cross (ICRC), became skittish.

Nonviolent Intimidation Tactics

The Taliban use *fear* of impending violence. A common tactic to accomplish this is the shabnamah, or "night letter," which is a communiqué to a target that he or she is subject to punishment. The recipient is notified that unless he or she behaves as the insurgents demand, the punishment will be swift and severe.

This is a common theme. One example is a letter distributed to residents of Khost, in 2008. It warned that tribal elders must not cooperate with government forces or "they will regret it." Those employed by the Karzai or regional governments were instructed to quit their jobs immediately or "they will see something that they have never seen in their lives." The fate of those who abet government forces during a firefight would "be the same as the U.S. puppets."[82] They too would die.

INFORMATION OPERATIONS

> *The Taliban are lying through their teeth.*
> —Secretary of Defense Donald Rumsfeld in response to very early Taliban charges involving alleged U.S. atrocities, 2001[83]

The insurgents, particularly the Taliban, use the media to generate propaganda. There are several dominant themes. First, they portray the government as corrupt, illegitimate, inept, and controlled by outside, Western powers. Second, they state that Afghanistan is a front in an international crusade against Islam led by the United States. Third, Islam is a solution to the problems that confront Afghans. This last theme is dominant in the Islamist reformist world.

The Taliban tap into a national anxiety and failed expectations. Disillusionment of the government began to spread early in the insurgency, as the gap between popular expectations and the delivery of services grew. Many Afghans did not understand why civilians suffered casualties, though inadvertent, from the Coalition Forces. This made fodder for the Taliban who used unintentional killings as false evidence of American murderous designs.

Today's Taliban use print and electronic media. The print publication *Azam*, which means tenacity in Pashtu, was closed in 2003.[84] *Al Somood* and several other publications continue to operate in both Afghanistan and largely Pakistan. *Al Somood* is the flagship paper of the Taliban. Replete with glossy prints, statistics, and in-depth interviews, it is issued by the Taliban's media center, probably located in Quetta.[85]

Taliban DVDs have recitations of poetry; some contain interviews with leaders, such as Jalaluddin Haqqani, who extoll the virtues and rectitude of Islam; and some air decapitations of suspected enemies.[86] The contents of these DVDs, even the more gruesome, are placed on the Taliban's website El Emarah. Common topics are Pashtun nationalism, Afghan patriotism, and anti-Americanism.[87] Guantanamo, often likened to Devil's Island, is a frequent target.[88]

Some of the information operations have been effective. In February 2006, then U.S. Secretary of Defense Donald Rumsfeld expressed concern that the United States was "losing the media war to Al-Qaeda." Other leaders agreed. At times, stories need very little spin. In January 2012, U.S. Marines video-taped themselves urinating on Taliban corpses. A Pentagon spokesman verified the authenticity of the film, adding, "It turned my stomach." The following year, U.S. soldiers posed with the bomb-blasted remains of suicide bombers.

The Taliban have generally been unsuccessful in persuading Western journalists to write flattering accounts of them. One exception is Yvonne Ridley, who wrote in *In the Hands of the Taliban* that the Taliban had treated her with courtesy and respect. She was thankful to the Taliban for acquainting her with Islam and, in her view, the freedom and respect that Islam gives women.[89] "My heart has been stolen by Afghanistan."[90]

But even the most sympathetic journalists take risks covering the Taliban. Joanie De Rijke, a Dutch journalist, asked to interview a Taliban commander, identified as Ghazi Gul, in 2009. She got her interview. But after a brief conversation and some photo taking, Gul proceeded to rape her, holding her captive for six days and then ransoming her to her Dutch magazine for an unspecified sum. Upon release, she was surprisingly accepting of the sexual violence to which she was victim, speculating that Gul "could not control his testosterone … He knew it was wrong … He treated me respectfully … as well as generously." [91] Gul offered Ms. De Rijke one of his three wives for a sexual threesome, which she declined, as well as tea and biscuits, which she accepted.

Listed in Table 5.3 are the three broad categories of the Taliban's tactics and the purpose, type, and examples.

Table 5.3   The Purpose, Type, and Examples of the Taliban's Tactics

	Violent Tactics	Nonviolent Intimidation Tactics	Information Operations
Purpose	To kill opposition; to set examples to others; to drive out foreigners; to cause enough sensational violence that the will of foreign states will collapse. To project image that the Taliban are everywhere and are all powerful and merciless	To stop or to prevent unwanted behavior. A target is given a warning that he or she or his or her family would be harmed unless target complies with Taliban. To create climate of fear	To reach large audiences. To respond to and to preempt government broadcasts. To threaten individuals or groups. To send messages to the government and to lower morale of their supporters
Type	Bombings in public places, targeted assassinations, morbid violence to include tape-recorded beheading	"Night letters" delivered to target or target's family. Verbal warning	Broadcasts from Taliban-controlled and Taliban-directed stations and presses. Cooperation with international, Jihadist-sympathizes, such as Al Jazeera
Examples	A bombing at a Kabul hotel frequented by foreigners, many of whom are participants in reconstruction and development. A school teacher is beheaded in front on pupils. After surveillance, a Taliban operative will place a roadside IED and wait until a thin-skinned ISAF vehicle passes by. Then the bomb is detonated	A man returns home after work to find a letter placed under his door, which his wife received. The letter demands that he stop working on a construction project or his children will be killed. Children are approached by a stranger who tells them that their fathers will be killed if they continue to attend a secular school	Taliban broadcast accused Coalition Forces of intentionally killing children and poisoning water systems

CHAPTER SUMMARY

In 2001, the Western and Afghan anti-Taliban elements achieved impressive military successes in routing the Taliban from Afghanistan. The United States had broad international and domestic support.[92] But the Taliban regrouped and organized into four Shuras, the most important of which is in Quetta, Pakistan. The structure of the Taliban is hierarchical from the Supreme Leadership, the Shura Council, the cadre, the foot soldiers, and the mercenaries.

The Taliban found sanctuary in parts of Afghanistan and Pakistan and are, once again, ascendant and eager to impose a new totalitarianism on Afghanistan. The Taliban are one of several insurgent groups aspiring to create a Salafist Afghanistan. The others are al Qaeda, the Haqqani network, and Hekmatyar Gulbuddin's Hizb-i-Islami.[93] The insurgents intend to cripple the economy, terrorize their enemies, expand their support base, solidify their external base, and collapse the will of nations, particularly the United States.

6

─∞∞∞─

The Taliban Improve Their Tactics and Firepower

Chapter 5 examined the fall of the Taliban. It touched on the blueprint crafted in Bonn to build sustained development and military and political stability in Afghanistan. It discussed the Taliban's strategy, tactics, targets, and general rebuilding efforts. Chapter 6 will investigate the tactics with more specificity. This is a chapter on how the Taliban fight and kill.

From the beginning, the Taliban adopted a strategy of hide-and-wait tactics.[1] Jallaluddin Haqqani, the seasoned anti-Soviet fighter and tightly affiliated with Mullah Omar, opined that, like the Soviets, whom he helped defeat, the Americans could not endure a long war. By October 2001, the Taliban dispersed much of its remaining tanks and artillery and hid them from marauding U.S. aircraft.[2] Taliban soldiers fanned out in different directions.[3]

TOUGH FIGHTERS AND FOUR-LEGGED WARFARE

Since recorded memory, the Afghans have been skilled and determined fighters. Though long dominant in Afghanistan, Pashtuns have not been the only renowned Afghan warriors. Other Afghan ethnicities—Hazaras, Tajiks, Uzbeks—have proven their mettle on the battlefield. In the early stages of the present war in Afghanistan, the Northern Alliance of Tajiks and Uzbeks tested their mountain fighting skills against the Taliban's military capabilities. The Northern Alliance, which enjoyed U.S. tactical air support as well as military hardware, performed well, particularly in the mountainous north, as discussed in chapter 4. Like their Taliban counterparts, many climbed mountains in sandals and slept in the open, wrapped in their blankets.[4]

But the Taliban are particularly strong-minded and clever fighters. From the very beginning, the Taliban demonstrated military innovation, resilience, and resolve. This toughness and adaptability shone early in the post–September 2001 fight, which concerned U.S. war planners. The confidence of the early post-Taliban period began to wane, as the Taliban successfully regrouped, repositioned itself, and built strongholds.[5] While still militarily disoriented in early 2002, the Taliban were content to harass Coalition Forces by attacking in cells and planning for the future.[6]

Taliban elements not decimated in November and December 2001 partnered effectively with al Qaeda forces in 2002 and 2003 to expand and improve their set of tactics.[7] Al Qaeda had expertise, and its operatives were trained in unconventional tactics. Al Qaeda studied war intently, and some of its leaders were literate and university trained. Several were professional soldiers. Al-Adel, the al Qaeda military commander and insurgent theoretician, strongly recommended that his fellow mujahedeen follow several key principles to counter U.S. military superiority.[8] First, convert large military units to small bands of fighters led by men with strong administrative and leadership skills.[9] Al Qaeda found that administering large numbers was more difficult and less productive than controlling bands of 10–15. It was also easier to avoid detection by aerial surveillance in smaller units.

The second al Qaeda recommendation was that insurgents build defensive fortifications, which al-Adel referred to as "trenches."[10] These were temporary dirt shelters, which the Taliban colocated with homes in Kandahar. Building shelters close to homes was preferable to building these structures in open fields.[11] The Coalition Forces might not bomb them, for fear of killing civilians.

Third, al Qaeda suggested practicing reconnaissance, traps, and raiding operations, rather than large-scale operations. They also recommended acquiring antiair weapons because air warfare gives the Coalition Forces significant advantage.[12] Fourth, like other insurgent and terrorist forces, al Qaeda highlighted the use of political rhetoric.

From the beginning there were tensions between the Taliban and al Qaeda. The Arabs appeared patronizing, offering unwanted advice and giving orders they were not authorized to issue in Afghanistan.[13] But many Taliban leaders understood the advantages that al Qaeda brought in terms of bin Laden's funding, expertise, and dedicated cadre.

Profile 6.1: Mohammad Ashan: Home Alone

The Taliban are known for their ingenuity and battlefield prowess. But many are not very sophisticated. This was demonstrated by the get-rich-quick motives of Mohammad Ashan, a mid-level Taliban in Paktika province, who perfunctorily identified a Taliban on an Afghanistan most-wanted poster to a Coalition soldier. Extending an open hand with palm up, he requested the finder's fee of $100. This is months' income in parts of Afghanistan. Curiously, the picture in the wanted poster bore an uncanny likeness to the man demanding the reward. "A U.S. soldier asked him, 'Is this you?' To which Mohammad Ashan energetically responded, 'Yes, yes, that's me! Can I get my award now?'"[14] Ashan was arrested, and it is not known if he was able to collect the promised $100. "This guy is the Taliban equivalent of the 'Home Alone' burglars,' one U.S. official said. Another U.S. official scoffed in agreement, 'Clearly, the man is an imbecile.'"[15]

WEAPONS

An Afghan man will kiss his rifle before he kisses his wife.

—An old Afghan saying[16]

Many of the Taliban carried their weapons with them to Pakistan. But they left larger individual, as well as crew-served weapons behind. Particularly concerning to Coalition Forces was the number of weapons caches and the unexplained reluctance of Afghans to surrender them. The Taliban used donkeys to transport shells manufactured in innumerable small Pakistani villages in the tribal belt along the Afghan border. Accomplished horsemen, many Taliban used their mounts regularly and in many environments. In some cases, horses outperformed four-wheel-drive vehicles.[17]

It was common for Afghans to possess several weapons. It is part of Afghan culture. But this did not explain why so many undeclared storages of weapons were hidden in barns, basements, and attics. In fact, rather than help the Coalition Forces, many villagers placed obstacles in the way of Coalition efforts to locate weapons stockpiles. It was the policy of the Coalition Forces to leave one AK-47 per family. But this was not satisfactory to many Afghan men who, like many American men, had a keen interest in firearms. More difficult to justify was the private possession of rocket-propelled grenades and components of homemade bombs for home protection.[18]

Early in the counterinsurgency, U.S. military personnel knew that disarming Afghanistan of large-caliber, crew-served weapons and preventing the fabrication of explosives would be difficult. There were still weapons left from the Soviet Union.[19] But increasingly, U.S. soldiers had to go home to home in Taliban-sympathizing areas, like Kandahar, to find weapons and components. Sometimes, homes would be demolished for fear of booby traps. The military used armored bulldozers, explosives, and air strikes.[20] Many Afghans were not nearly as cooperative as Coalition Forces anticipated or hoped. Some became hostile and, in turn, many Coalition Forces became suspicious.

Individual Weapons

Like many other insurgents, Taliban stressed mobility over firepower. The Taliban's standard individual weapon is the Kalashnikov—the AK-47 and its modern variants the AK-47M or AK-74. This is the most widely produced individual weapon in service today.[21] The quality, durability, and to some extent the military lore associated the AK- 47 have made it the global assault weapon of choice.[22] Because it is relatively uncomplicated, it can be repaired with scrap metal in backstreet workshops by the many talented Afghan gunsmiths.

The affinity for the AK-47 was shared by combatants on both sides in the early fighting. Easy to carry and clean, the weapon's qualities that shone in the humid, swampy terrain of Southeast Asia did so again in Afghanistan.[23] In the early stages of the Afghanistan war, many of the exclusive British SAS troops armed themselves with the weapons to blend in more easily and forage for ammunition.

Today, the typical Taliban carries a knife, a pistol, and, possibly, a shoulder-held RPG-7 Soviet rocket launcher. Some men have grenades. Much like the Vietnamese insurgents, the Taliban will have a distinct and local appearance, rather than a military uniform. In Vietnam, the cone-shaped "Viet Cong" headdress became iconic. So, too, has the Afghan "lunge," which looks like a turban and is often worn by the Taliban. He might wear a woven hat called a pakol. Often, he will have long-sleeved chapan jacket and trousers. The soles of his sandals will often be made of tires, and he will carry his own blanket.

Much like the AK-47, the RPG-7 is simple, rugged, and deadly. Like the Kalashnikov, the RPG-7 is the stuff of guerilla legend. It is an improved version of the German tank-busting "Panzerfaust," which wreaked havoc on Allied armor, particularly in World War II's final year. Most Taliban fighters can carry two of these 14-pound weapons. The RPG can blast a hole through more than six inches of armor, which makes U.S. helicopters vulnerable.[24] These weapons were, in the view of al-Adel, very effective.[25]

There are many sources of weapons. For years, Afghanistan was awash in weapons left by the Soviets. The Taliban had ready access to weapons through smuggling routes. As one smuggler said, "I have my customers in Kandahar. I make good profit. I can buy an AK-47 for $200 in the north and sell it for $400 in the south."[26] Profit, as much as ideological solidarity, drove the weapons trade in the early postwar period. There were also external sources of weapons, particularly from Iran and China. Defense Secretary Robert Gates commented several times on Chinese and Iranian arms that were used against Coalition Forces.[27]

Quickly, the Coalition Forces began to fear the Taliban's ability to innovate with explosives. They were increasingly challenged by Taliban's skills and ingenuity in crafting weapons and upgrading the lethality of weapons. One of many examples of a Taliban's improved weapon is an RPG packed with ball bearings that could kill persons in a 30-feet radius with its impact. As a British soldier said, "This is a worrying twist as their weaponry becomes more and more sophisticated. Who knows how many of these rockets are out there?"[28]

TACTICS

From Timid Tactics to Blitzkrieg Warfare

Some of the early tactics, particularly during their first ascent to power in the mid-1990s, included unconventional, often daring tactics, referred to as "Mad Max style." They were effective, if primitive. Also called "blitzkreig" combat, some early Taliban tactics included plunging heavily armed men, supported by armored pickup trucks, into enemy positions. These tactics were developed by the mujahedeen in the 1980s. They stripped downed Soviet MI-8 and MI-24 gunships of their weapons and fashioned them onto pickup trucks. They were initially used against the Northern Alliance and later against the Coalition. They would designate these armed trucks of the makeshift cavalry as "ahu," or deer.[29]

In the tactic, these pickup trucks armed with crew-served weapons stormed at full speed and sprayed fire as they charged to disorient the targets. In some charges, as many as 50 trucks took part in shooting, terrorizing, and scattering the enemy. Some of these attacks were effective.[30]

Many of the Taliban's vehicles were well suited for the environment. The al Qaeda leader and theoretician al-Adel, in his observation of early battles, toasted the durability and adaptability of the "Corolla vehicles." Though not all of the Taliban's trucks were Toyotas, al-Adel joked that "if the Japanese had seen the vehicles in action, they would have used them in advertisements."[31] Motorcycles, referred to as "iron horses"—as well as living, four-legged horses—were quick, agile, and well suited to the mountainous terrain. Horses often took the place of trucks in transporting leaders to well-hidden caves and encampments. Like other insurgents, the Taliban tended to travel lightly, with far less reliance on the road network or logistic resupply. But the Taliban own their environment and have mastered desert-like terrain.

By 2003, the Taliban began to husband some of their larger-caliber munitions. According to al-Adel, the Taliban and al Qaeda stopped firing on Coalition aircraft because their antiaircraft guns were not accurate enough to bring them down. Also, firing these weapons disclosed their location and invited counterfire from Coalition Forces.[32]

Profile 6.2: Aafia Sadiqui: Brandeis's Lady Al Qaeda

In some ways, Dr. Aafia Sadiqui (sometimes spelled Saddiqui or Siddiqui) fits the standard profile of many American-educated Islamists. Like several other al Qaeda compatriots who studied in the West, the Pakistan-born, Texas-raised, MIT-educated neuroscientist was heavily involved in Islamic activities during her university days in Boston. She was active in the MSA.[33] She earned advanced degrees in science. What certainly sets her apart from of other al Qaeda cadre is her receipt of a PhD in brain science from Brandeis University, an unlikely venue for promoting Islamic supremacy.

In Boston, where she lived in the late 1990s, she became very involved in the Muslim community, particularly the more devout sub-culture. She involved herself in the workings of the Islamic Society of Boston, where the Tsarnaev brothers would later attend services. She became enamored of the works of Abullah Azzam. She married a Pakistani, had three children, got divorced, and then left the United States for Pakistan on Christmas Day 2002. She wedded the nephew of Kahled Sheik Mohammed or KSM, the planner of the September 2001 attacks and who is also a cousin of Ramzi Yousef, a man convicted of the 1993 World Trade Center bombing. People joked that she married into al Qaeda royalty. What happened during the next five years is mysterious.

She was arrested at a border crossing into Afghanistan and she was remanded to U.S. authorities. She possessed information on chemical and biological weapons and other documents found on a disk that were connected to terrorist operations.[34] She also possessed sodium cyanide, and could not explain why she was carrying it into Afghanistan. Earlier, her name had been coughed up by KSM. He accused her of being complicit in al Qaeda fund-raising operations.[35]

While in U.S. detention, Sadiqui obtained an assault rifle and, while screaming profanities, shot at a U.S. soldier. She missed, but the soldier returned fire, hitting her in the abdomen. She survived and was brought back to the United States to stand trial.[36]

At trial, her lawyer claimed that Sadiqui's identity was stolen by a woman who might have worked with KSM. In court, Lady al Qaeda, who had become a sensation in her native Pakistan, began to act brusquely.[37] Despite her ties to Brandeis, Aafia demanded that no Jews sit on her jury.[38] She shouted at Judge Berman, "The next question will be on anti-Semitism, Israel was behind 9/11. That's not anti-Semitic!"[39] She yelled at an army officer, "I was never planning a bombing! You're lying!"[40] Her facial contortions, simpering, and outbursts did not help her case. In September 2010, the tirade-prone 37-year-old was sentenced to 86 years in a federal prison for attempted murder, armed assault, and other charges.

Her case was taken up by Yvonne Ridley in Britain.[41] Former congresswoman Cynthia McKinney dubbed the sentence "political" and proclaimed in Lahore, "I am here for Sidiqui [sic]. I decided to stand by her when I heard of her."[42] The sentence was upheld on appeal in November 2012. But the whole affair was confusing for some of Sadiqui's old Boston acquaintances. They remember a shy, studious, and exotic young woman who spent a lot of time at the local mosque. "She was just nice and soft-spoken . . . and not terribly assertive."[43]

Suicide Attacks

Children are tools to achieve God's will. And whatever comes your way, you sacrifice it.
—Taliban commander to Western journalist[44]

The first Taliban suicide attack came in 2004, and they continue. Volunteers to perform suicide attacks are sometimes mentally ill or retarded, sometimes addicted to and high on narcotics, and sometimes too young to make their own decision. Others aspire to martyrdom. Yet other incentives include monies paid to the families of suicide bombers, often from foreign patrons, and the temptation of an Islamic paradise filled with sexually enthusiastic virgins.[45] Finally, there is the praise boys receive from insurgent leaders, who often serve as father figures.

But many boys and young men conscripted for suicide attacks are neither naïve nor slow-witted. They are simply captive. Often, boys are delivered from their families to the care of a madrassa in which they are educated, housed, and fed at no cost to the family.[46] In turn, they are then expected to kill themselves and others when directed to do so. Many madrassas do not associate themselves with indiscriminate violence, but many do.[47] There are an estimated 10,000–20,000 madrassas in Pakistan.[48]

To prepare for suicide attacks, boys are isolated from their families. This process is similar to that used by cults in Western societies to break their ties to the past. In the madrassa process, boys are gradually and gently groomed to kill and die. If they hesitate, they are shamed, mocked, and likened to girls. When they show cruelty with gusto, the boys are applauded. The boys are also inculcated to hate Westerners, Jews, and Americans with a special zeal. There may be an underground, informal trade in abandoned children. Some American journalists have claimed that there is a trade in future-suicide-bombing children with some children commanding the price of $14,000 per child.[49]

One example of attempted child suicide bombing was the arrest of two 10-year-old boys who were fastened with suicide vests in southern Afghanistan. They were apprehended and, given their age, pardoned. One of the boys, Azizulah, explained that the Taliban who assured him that when "the Americans fire at you [they] cannot hit you." "They taught me how to blow my vest; the showed me how to press the button in my hand." They ordered him to sit by the road and wait for foreign forces to come. But police arrested him. Back in school as of early 2012, Azizulah does not want to repeat the experience. "I ask all my madrassa teachers not to teach kids to become suicide bombers."[50]

Almost anyone in Afghanistan can be a victim of a suicide attack. Many of the victims are noncombatants, completely unconnected to the insurgency. Suicide bombings are often directed at broad targets of opportunity. Hotels that cater to foreign workers, such as Kabul's Serena, are target-rich environments. The Taliban calculate that because all non-Muslim foreigners are the enemy, all are subject to violent attacks.

The Taliban receive a penalty in public opinion. Suicide bombing alienates some Afghans who might otherwise support the Taliban. This is because many Afghans view impressing captive, deranged, or brain-washed young men and schoolchildren, sometimes referred to as "Omar's missiles," as distinctly un-Islamic and an unacceptable form of warfare. Until the advent of the Taliban, suicide attacks in Afghanistan were virtually unknown. Some of the tactics would become morbid, such as booby-trapping bodies and withholding the bodies of killed Coalition soldiers to be swapped for munitions or money.

Attacks in bazaars and marketplaces are indiscriminate. It is often difficult to understand why the Taliban target public gatherings that are not likely to attract a government or foreign workers. Children, adults, brides, grooms, widows, and widowers are possible targets. At a funeral of a former provincial governor, a suicide bomber disguising himself as a mourner killed those paying last respects to the governor as he was laid to rest.[51]

While many attacks are indiscriminate, others are well planned and narrowly targeted. As an example, an attack in the Defense Ministry in 2011 was sophisticated and combined several tactics of the Taliban. It involved at least four elements of planning. First, there was preoperational surveillance. The Taliban have strong human intelligence capabilities. Second, there was the infiltration of the ministry to gain access and information. Third, there was an attempt to impersonate Afghan government personnel, and, finally, there was the suicide blast. The attacker, who was not an employee of ministry, gained access to the first several barriers. This was one of the more heavily guarded and checkpointed facilities in Afghanistan.[52]

Some of the suicide bombings are both narrowly targeted and indiscriminate in their killing. They intend to kill a specific target and, in addition, kill persons inadvertently. For example, a suicide attack at a wedding in Samangan Province slew top bureaucrats—a provincial member of Parliament and a provincial director of the security. But it also slaughtered up to 15 others in attendance, most of whom had no political role in the province.[53] Among those killed were the bride and her father.[54]

Not all attacks go as planned. Some children are lucky and never hurt themselves or others. This was the case with a nine-year-old schoolgirl who was plucked off the streets, drugged, outfitted with a suicide vest, and escaped. In an abduction technique that was replicated many times, helpless children are kidnapped by adults whom they have never seen before.[55] But as with boys, most girls are not abducted, but are developed to be a suicide bomber. Those girls are guided by those whom they love and trust, which makes them easier to manipulate and kill.[56]

The motives for some attacks are not clear. An example is the suicide bombing conducted by a woman in Kabul in mid-September 2012. Hekmatyar's Hezb-e-Islami explained that a car bombing that killed 12 people was the response to a low-budget and amateurish movie, the *Innocence of the Muslims*.[57] The bomber, identified as Fatima, blew herself up in a car parked near a wedding hall. Many of the killed were foreigners, which may explain the targeting.

Suicide bombings also take place in Pakistan. A large suicide attack occurred in the Punjab Regiment Centre in northwest Pakistan. A young teenager impersonating a cadet in a new blue uniform slipped past several security checkpoints, probably with the help of Taliban operatives. He flung himself into an assembled crowd and killed 31 army cadets, boys and young men, and wounded over 40 others.[58] This was the deadliest attack in Pakistan since a Christmas Day 2010 suicide attack when a woman killed 43 people at a UN food distribution points in the tribal district of Bajaur.[59]

Profile 6.3: Juma and Sameena: A Boy and a Girl

He said he was four, but he was probably about six or seven years old. He was too tall for a four-year-old. Like the other boys in Ghazni Province with whom he played, rag-clad and hair-mussed Juma Gul collected scraps of metal to help his family eat.[60] Juma enjoyed watching soccer. In June 2007, the Taliban grabbed the boy off the streets and placed a suicide vest on him. They told him to hurl himself against U.S. soldiers and pull a magic cord.

But Juma thought the better of it and decided to deliver himself to Afghan soldiers, saving his life and probably several Afghan and U.S. troops. "When they first put the vest on my body I didn't know what to think, but then I felt the bomb. After I figured out it was a bomb, I went to the Afghan soldiers for help."[61]

The Taliban denied the story, adding that they did not involve small children in suicide operations.[62] They did not, however, explain how a suicide belt managed to fasten itself to the torso of a six-year-old boy. Juma did not walk away empty-handed from his decision not to explode himself among American soldiers. U.S. forces in the area passed the hat for Juma, and the boy was given ample money to feed his family without having collect scrap metal for months. He had plenty of time to watch soccer.

Sameena was 13 in 2008 when she and another schoolgirl were ensnared in a suicide-bombing development program run by teachers in a madrassa in North Waziristan. When she went missing, her mother contacted local police who began a search for her.[63] In the program, Sameena was indoctrinated into the jihadist cause. "We saw thousands of video clips in which the atrocities of the U.S. forces against Muslims in Iraq, Afghanistan and Guantanamo Bay had been shown. We were ready to act as suicide bombers, kill pro-US forces, and win the blessings of God."[64] She was rescued by police, one of whom said, "The situation is extremely bad. We have saved the two girls from becoming suicide bombers, but indications are that the trend of women training as suicide bombers has gained currency."[65]

Ambush Attacks—"Green Hell" and "Omar's Bed"

The suicide bombs are dreaded because they are unexpected and lethal. So are ambushes, a common tactic of the Taliban. Ambushes depend on stealth, preparation, and coordination. They are intended to outmaneuver the superior military capabilities of the Afghan and Coalition Forces.[66]

The Taliban will attack government patrols in teams, often firing volleys of two or three RPGs from multiple firing positions, followed by light and heavy machine-gun fire. Sometimes, this operation is reversed, with bursts of machine-gun fire preceding attacks by RPGs and mortars. The Taliban often attack from mutually supporting fields of fire.

The Taliban will often fire from trenches that adjoin the roads. In both Afghanistan and Pakistan, they will hide in the near mountains, open fire, and then retreat into the mountains. One U.S. soldier said, "This is what they do. They come out of their hideouts and fire at the troops and then disappear."[67] The Taliban also taunt patrolling soldiers by wrapping white ribbons to trees, which demonstrates their ability to attack at will. One U.S. soldier explained that the Taliban signal that "we're here and we're watching you." This causes anxiety among U.S. forces because "it's the way the Taliban operate that makes the war so terrifying and so difficult. You can't even see the enemy before they open fire."[68]

Ambush is a daily fear for soldiers and Marines, and bullets and munitions appear from nowhere and everywhere. In 2010, Marine Lt. Cpl. Kyle Carpenter, shown in Figure 6.1, saw a hand grenade tossed from a rooftop during the battle of Marjah. It landed near a fellow Marine, and Carpenter

Figure 6.1   Sketch of Marine Lance Cpl. Kyle Carpenter, who shielded a fellow Marine from the blast. The writing on the sketch reads, "Wounded by an enemy hand grenade while engaged with Taliban forces, Marjan, Afghanistan, 2010." (© Robert William Bates. Used by permission.)

shielded the Marine, absorbing much of the blast and shrapnel.[69] As a result, he lost an eye and the use of an arm. His face was permanently and severely scarred, as sketched by Marine combat artist Robert Bates in Figure 6.1. Carpenter has been nominated for the Congressional Medal of Honor.

Throughout the year, the Taliban ambush government and Coalition Forces. But springtime gives strong tactical advantage to the Taliban because parts of Afghanistan become draped with thick vegetation. As with the foliage and canopy exploited by insurgents in the Philippines, Vietnam, and Central America, Afghanistan's green belts give the Taliban concealment. Snipers have become adept at using foliage to screen their movements and to lure Afghan patrols.[70] One American officer explained, "They've watched us all winter, seeing how we work."

The green grasses and balmy nights of springtime draw fighters from Waziristan and Swat, in Pakistan, as well as Afghan provinces to sleep outdoors. One tribal elder referred to the masses of Taliban sleeping under the stars as "Mullah Omar's beds."

The green vegetation of springtime makes it easier to conceal and plant roadside bombs. As one American soldier explained, "Everywhere we walk out there could be our last step. Guys are very meticulous about what they do. They're scared, I hate to use that term, but they're just very aware of what they're doing."

Taliban have improvised and shifted their tactics. Their military capabilities continue to improve. In 2007, a group of 75 Taliban tried to overrun a U.S.-led Coalition base in southern Afghanistan in a rare frontal assault. They attacked from three sides, firing their weapons and supported by mortar fire and 107 mm rockets.[71] The capability of these large-scale, coordinated attacks increased. By summer 2010, some Taliban fighters used tactics similar to Coalition Forces.[72] The Taliban have also adapted to city surveillance and sniping.

Murder Holes and Snipers

Ambushes in Afghanistan occur inside and outside the "green hell" of the countryside. A senior NATO official likened the tactics to those of Hezbollah in Lebanon. In the cities, Taliban disguise themselves in many outfits, including women's garb. "This kind of strategy is very, very difficult not only for NATO in Afghanistan but also in other parts of the world."[73] The city Taliban have created their own hell for Coalition and Afghan security forces in cities. Cleverly hidden Taliban snipers fire from inside of buildings, often with impressive precision. In towns and cities, Taliban gunmen bore holes in the homes of sympathizers or hostages that give a sniper a direct field of fire up to 400 meters. The Taliban use camouflage and keep the hole too small to notice at a distance.[74]

The quality of the Taliban's marksmanship has improved. Though U.S. trainers have struggled to boost the overall precision of ANA marksmen, the Taliban have produced excellent sharpshooters. The Taliban's use of camouflage, effective stalking, high-powered optics, and coordinated engagement has made them formidable shooters.

One Taliban sniper was particularly lethal. In 2009, there began an ensuing drama that was reminiscent of the famous sniper dual in Stalingrad, in which the finest of the Red Army's and Wehrmacht's snipers were pitted against each other in a death match. A British officer determined to ferret out and kill the Taliban's top shooter.[75] By April 2010, the Taliban killer shot dead seven British troops in a five-month period. The youngest of his quarry was 19. "Their sniper is giving us real problems and we've not yet worked out how to take him out," said a British officer. Three of the sniper's victims were British sharpshooters. Coalition leaders are convinced that Taliban snipers are being trained outside of Afghanistan.[76]

The snipers kill and wound noncombatants. One was a middle-aged, part-time postman in England, who earlier served in elite British units such as the SAS.[77] An official combat artist deployed to Afghanistan, Graeme Lothian was photographing military operations when a Taliban sniper shot him in his left hand in late June 2013. "The tragic thing is that he was a fine artist—his painting is his life and he is left-handed," said his physician girlfriend.

There is one case of a Taliban sniper killing two British soldiers with one bullet. These victims had the mission of finding and killing Taliban snipers, but it was they who became prey.[78] Taliban snipers are effective in cities where they can hide more easily.[79] Sometimes, Taliban snipers reveal their positions, which prove lethal mistakes. A British lieutenant explained that Taliban place wet leaves around their murder hole so dust does not emerge. But sometimes it does not work. "One of these guys [Taliban] used a murder hole to shoot one of my guys, so we used a guided missile to take him out."[80]

But Coalition snipers are often the match of their Taliban counterparts. Like the best of the Taliban snipers, Coalition snipers often hit their mark at long distances and often lie in wait days to kill their prey. In 2009, British Cpl. Christopher Reynolds killed his 33rd suspected Taliban. Firing from a tiny hole at a target over 2,000 yards away, "Crackshot Christopher" shot a man who was carrying an AK-47 and who collapsed in the arms of the Taliban behind him. "Crackshot" guffawed that he had delivered a "lead sleeping pill." "I was quite proud of that—it is the longest record kill in Afghanistan. I am going to use that fact as a chat-up line in the pub when I get back home."[81] He did, and it scored him a girlfriend.

Roadside Bombs and "Pink Mist"

Roadside bombs continue to terrorize government soldiers and to hamper movement. Like the ambushes hidden in the greenery of the Afghan spring, roadside bombs have a devastating psychological impact on Coalition Forces. About 70 percent of the attacks on Coalition Forces come from roadside bombs, and their sophistication has increased in the past 11 years. Many of the bombs are still not very sophisticated but are nonetheless powerful, deadly, and hard to detect.

Afghanistan was filled with mines during the war against the Soviets. In croplands, footpaths, and roads, land mines killed and maimed Afghans for a generation.[82] Innocuously named the "butterfly bomb," the weapon, planted copiously in areas suspected of harboring mujahedeen, was designed to maim insurgents. These munitions could not distinguish between combatants and noncombatants and were triggered by the weight of an average man. Hundreds of thousands of these bombs were scattered by helicopters. As they glided to earth, their small wings would flutter, giving them their sweet-sounding moniker.

The dread of land mines became a dramatic theme for journalists and dramatists. In David Edgar's play *Black Tulips*, Soviet soldiers are briefed by a sapper on the profusion and lethality of their own land mines, which were retrieved by the mujahedeen and used against Soviet armor resourcefully. The mujahedeen would place an antipersonnel mine on top of other mines, and the blast power would destroy armor. The Taliban used this tactic effectively against ISAF forces.[83] The tactic still works.

The Soviets left stockpiles of munitions for Afghans, but there are many other sources of weapons. Today, bombs and bomb components pour into Afghanistan from other countries, namely Pakistan, Iran, and China. British diplomats claimed that advanced antiaircraft missiles, components for armor-piercing roadside bombs, and land mines were discovered and traced back to Chinese factories.[84]

But Pakistan is, by far, the major source of munitions and chemical elements needed to fabricate improvised bombs. Particularly threatening has been the stream ammonium nitrate.[85] Sen. Richard Blumenthal has demanded, "The Pakistanis need to prove that they are stopping and stemming the flow of fertilizer."[86] His is not a lone voice.

Much of the ammonium nitrate is imported from Pakistan, but most of the bombs are fabricated in Afghanistan. In one raid in 2009, Coalition Forces uncovered 225,000 kilograms, or half a million pounds, of ammonium nitrate. This single haul could have powered thousands of bombs. A typical improvised bomb weighs less than 30 kilograms.[87] Seizures of ammonium-nitrate fertilizer in Afghanistan doubled in the first seven months of 2012 compared to the same period in 2011. According to a senior U.S. advisor, "We are sweeping ammonium nitrate fertilizer off the battlefield at historic rates. But the bombs are going up at historic rates too, and it is directly related. It is a supply issue."[88]

Roadside bombs are very difficult to detect. For this reason, Coalition Forces have experimented with both offensive and defensive tactics and

CPL MATHEW BOWMAN OF BLT 3/8
TAKES A BREAK FROM PHYSICAL
THERAPY. HIS FATHER, KEN BOWMAN,
GIVES HIM A SIP OF WATER
BEFORE GOING BACK TO DOING
EXERCISES.
30 MARCH 2011
1348

RBATES

Figure 6.2   Marine Cpl. Mathew Bowman being helped by his father during rehabilitation. The sketch reads, "CPL Mathew Bowman of BLT 3/8 takes a break from physical therapy. His father, Ken Bowman, gives him a sip of water before going back to doing exercises. 30 March 2011." (© Robert William Bates. Used by permission.)

vehicles. Transportation vehicles have become more rugged. Mine-protected troop carriers have been developed to withstand direct hits from roadside bombs, with personnel escaping with relatively minor injuries.[89] Mini-flails have become much more effective than the traditional flails, attached in front of armored antimine vehicles.[90]

But there is the constant dread by soldiers and Marines on patrol. U.S. Marine Cpl. Matt Bowman explained, "We were on patrol. We ran into an IED. I was the one that got hit by it." The high school wrestler from Indiana lost both legs above the knee and most of his left hand.[91] He is shown in Figure 6.2, as sketched by Robert Bates.

Profile 6.4: Best Friends and Broken Hearts in the Afghan Hurt Locker

Two Britons, Liam and Theo, were partners in a particularly dangerous assignment. They were counter-IED specialists whose mission it was to ferret out hidden IEDs planted by the Taliban. This requires steady nerves and precision. The two had undergone rigorous and specialized training before serving as partners. Though they had much in common beyond undaunted courage, they were also clearly physically different. Lance Cpl. Liam Tasker was a Scottish-born soldier in the Royal Army Veterinary Corps, and Theo was a springer spaniel. They were also best friends.

The two were inseparable, searching for roadside bombs in Helmand province. Once, Theo discovered a Taliban underground facility in which IEDs were likely made.[92] Together, they set a record for finding the most weapons and bombs in Afghanistan.[93] And they loved each other. Tasker's father recalled, "Theo would sleep at the bottom of his [Tasker's] bed but he would wait until he thought Liam was asleep and then get in beside him."[94] They slept together, lived together, worked together, and they both died on the same day in Afghanistan.

The Ministry of Defence of the United Kingdom issued the following communication: "On 1 March 2011, LCpl Tasker was taking part in a patrol with his dog, Theo, when they were engaged by small arms fire, during which LCpl Tasker was struck and died from the injuries he sustained. Sadly on return to Camp Bastion, Theo suffered a seizure and died."[95]

Earlier, Liam had nominated his partner for a special medal of valor for combat animals. Liam's mother said, "Liam was so proud of Theo. He was his world. I treasure the letter he wrote recommending him for the medal."[96] The remains of Liam and Theo returned to Britain together on the same flight. Theo's ashes were handed to Liam's girlfriend, Leah.[97] Both Liam and Theo were remembered with love and respect by soldiers in their unit. One soldier said, "Theo and LCpl Tasker did a brave job together in Afghanistan and . . . saved a lot of lives." British Defence Secretary Dr. Liam Fox added that Britain will be "eternally grateful."[98] And Liam's mother is openly indebted for the love that Theo gave her son. But she is not entirely convinced that her boy's best friend died of a seizure. "He and Theo had a very special bond. They worked together and died together."[99] Tasker's mother is convinced that Theo "died of broken heart."[100]

Unlike Theo (profiled above), most of the dogs deployed into combat in Afghanistan come home safely. Courageous canines, like the men who serve with them, are acknowledged for valor in Britain. Treo, not to be confused with Theo the springer spaniel in Profile 6.4, is an eight-year-old black Labrador retriever who received the animal equivalent of the Victoria Cross for his valor in Afghanistan on February 25, 2010. Her Royal Highness Princess Alexandra presented Treo with the medal at the Imperial War Museum.[101] The citation praised Treo "for his gallantry in saving countless human lives. He continued with his duties irrespective of the dangers that faced him and, in the process, saved many, many lives."[102] The dog became the subject of a biography penned by his master.

Since 2012, American and British forces have increased the use of dogs in sniffing out explosives.[103] As one handler said, "If something is not supposed to be in the ground, a dog will find it."[104] The U.S. Army uses dogs in Afghanistan too. The "Houn Dawg," 203rd Engineer Battalion, Missouri National Guard's explosive detection experts, have cleared about 75 percent of the IEDs in their area of responsibility in Afghanistan.[105] They receive K9 support, but this is not the norm. The missions use route clearance equipment and soldiers on the ground.[106]

Profile 6.5: Collin J. Bowen: "He Went to Afghanistan to Protect the Land"[107]

Its been 3 yrs Bud . . . you will never be forgotten.
—Spc. 1st Class Carl Olney

Had he not been in his vehicle on Khost road on January 2, 2008, he probably would have been home, unharmed, two weeks later. His wife and children were excited about his homecoming. His home was in Maryland, and the 38-year-old Staff Sgt. Collin J. Bowen had received his degree in computer science and hunted and fished and raised his family there.[108] He loved the army, and the duty he treasured most was teaching computer basics to enthusiastic Afghan soldiers. A natural teacher and a warmhearted man, he completed his first combat assignment and signed up for another. Very popular with children, Collin loved handing out candy and pencils and trinkets to street kids, who smiled and scampered along with their presents.[109]

He completed his last mission and was six miles from base when his vehicle was blasted by a roadside bomb. He had burns over 50 percent of his body, but he was expected to live. A breathing tube placed in his throat, he was sent home. After the attack he could not talk, but on good days he could lift his fingers to signal his family and friends that he understood some words.[110] But the injuries were too severe and the multiple infections too lethal. He died after 13 surgeries in March 2008 and was buried in Arlington Cemetery. Posthumously, he was promoted to E7.[111]

Figure 6.3   Gabriella Bowen holds a doll of her daddy in Arlington National Cemetery. (© Ursula B. Palmer. Used by permission.)

His sacrifice was saluted by the People's Burn Foundation, as he was posthumously bestowed the True Blue Award for loyalty. They quoted the ancient Greeks, "All men have fears ... but the brave put down their fears and go forward ... sometimes to death ... but always to victory." (Figure 6.3)[112]

Poison

The Taliban use poison to disable, to kill, and to terrorize the enemy. The Taliban have not used poisons extensively against military targets, but do so occasionally. In mid-October 2012, during the rash of green-on-blue and green-on-green insider killings, an Afghan police officer and cook poisoned fellow officers. The incapacitated police were easy prey for Taliban, who fired fatal shots.[113] The killers escaped by motorcycle.

Schoolgirls are the targets of choice for Taliban poisoners. Al Qaeda brought their expertise to Afghanistan and had written about poisonings in their manuals. In a chapter on sabotage, various poisons are discussed.[114] Detailed instruction is given on poisonous plants, how to make poison gas, and tactics on applying poison with lethal effect.[115]

Chemical poisons most often used in Afghanistan are arsenic, cyanide, mercury compounds, and thallium to poison food and beverages.[116] There have been many reports of poisoning en masse, particularly against school-children and police. In one case, Taliban were suspected of giving girls poisoned biscuits Khost Province in May 2004.[117] In Konduz, the head of the Department of Education claimed that the Taliban poisoned girls, causing illness. The poison was administered by aerosol, while the girls were enjoying a break from classes. Other poisons in Konduz contaminated food and beverages.[118] In April 2010, three girls were poisoned in the same Afghan province, Konduz. Symptoms included vomiting, dizziness, and nausea. In April 2012, 150 schoolgirls were suspected of being poisoned after drinking contaminated water in Takhar Province.[119]

Many cases of poisoning go unreported. Some of the poisonings are ineffective or marginally effective. Also, the effects of poisoning may be long term, and the low level of medical technology cannot detect some poisoning.

Infiltration, Impersonation, and Betrayal

I have never heard of anything in Vietnam comparable to what we have recently experienced in Afghanistan.
— James McAllister, a political science professor at Williams College in Massachusetts in reference to the green-on-blue killings[120]

In the summer and fall of 2012, incidents of Afghan soldiers killing Coalition Forces captured world headlines. Journalists, war planners, military operatives, and others grappled to make sense of this apparent fratricide among allies. From May 2007 through January 2012, there were approximately 70 NATO soldiers killed in 42 attacks.[121] In all of 2011, 35 NATO forces were killed in green-on-blue attacks in 21 incidents.[122] In the first nine months of 2012, 35 NATO soldiers were killed in 29 attacks. This would become a deadly trend.

Part of this may reflect enhanced Taliban infiltration techniques, and part may reflect the greater participation of NATO forces with the Afghan military and police as part of the mentoring programs. Coalition Forces have trained 300 counterintelligence specialists and ordered increased security review for 150,000 Afghan soldiers.

Gen. John Allen, U.S. and NATO commander, determined that these green-on-blue attacks involved the Taliban only 50 percent of the time. Many of the attackers were, in the general's words, "self-radicalized" and did not carry out the attack at the behest of the Taliban or other insurgent groups.[123] The Pentagon's statistics provide a complex picture of motives and opportunities. If any one incident is heavily correlated with an uptick in these attacks in 2011, it was a Koran-burning incident discussed in chapter 4.

In late August 2012, General Allen attributed the spike in targeting American troops to the psychological and physiological effects of fasting during Ramadan.[124] Other observers downplay the role of fasting or emotional aberrations, noting that some have been meticulously planned and coordinated.[125]

These green-on-blue attacks fuse many Taliban tactics. In a sense, they are "multitactical attacks." They require infiltrating the ranks of the ANA or ANP and placing agents in those ranks. Sometimes, the Taliban infiltrate their agents directly as recruits. Some ANA and ANP are intimidated into coercion through information operations. Taliban threaten them or their families. This is made possible through the Taliban's skills at intelligence collecting and operations. They are able to gain physical proximity to senior leaders, and possession of uniforms and identification. Pentagon officials have blamed some of the green-on-blue attacks on insurgents who gained access to army uniforms.[126]

Some of the green-on-blue attacks are suicide attacks that appear not to have been planned well in advance. They were conducted when the opportunity arose. Other attacks were meticulously planned, allowing the perpetrator to escape.

There are many attacks that are difficult to defeat. As an example, in Herat Province in April 2007, Taliban fighters, dressed in fabricated ANP uniforms, established an illegal checkpoint, then attempted to ambush the combined ANA and Coalition patrol as they approached their makeshift checkpoint. Afghans and Coalition Army forces confiscated over 100 fabricated ANP uniforms and recovered more than a dozen false personnel identification documents in Herat Province in one raid alone.[127] The Taliban may have acted alone. Or they could have received the uniforms and identification from insiders.

Another example of a well-planned, multiple-tactic attack was conducted against the Defense Ministry in Kabul in 2011. The attacker obtained a special pass that gave him entry to the compound. Once inside, a man in an army uniform jumped from the car and burst into the main office building, gunning down two soldiers before he was killed.[128] This attack required pre-operational surveillance; learning the security system and the schedule of personnel in the office; anticipating when the target, a high-level ministry official, would be present; gaining the required passes; probably securing agents in the ministry; and training at least two operatives to embark on what was almost certainly a suicide attack. The Taliban may have had operatives on the inside.

The police are heavily targeted by infiltrators.[129] The trend toward infiltration has moved steadily upward since 2006. By 2010, the infiltration prompted concern that there was an attack planned to kill British Prime Minister David Cameron during his visit.[130] Since then, infiltration tactics have had become more sophisticated and pervasive.[131]

A chilling illustration of this is revealed in a November 2013 photograph snapped in the very last moments of the young lives of two British soldiers and an Afghan police candidate. In the photo, a smiling, muscular British soldier, Cpl. Brent McCarthy, towers beside a diminutive Afghan, whom he had trained in police tactics. Behind the two is a relaxed Welsh Guardsman who had just kidded McCarthy that the Afghan had wet his pants. The photograph indicates the outline of a urine pattern in the Afghan's crotch area, perhaps portending what would happen next. The Guardsman ribbed, "Look, he's pissed himself, he's scared of you." These were the last words he would ever speak. Seconds later, the Afghan and an accomplice shot the two Britons dead.[132]

One of the most notorious infiltration operations was the murder of President Karzai's brother in July 2011. An influential politician, he was assassinated by a bodyguard who was a longtime family friend. The bodyguard asked to speak to Karzai on a personal matter and then shot him. The Taliban claimed responsibility, and it is likely that they had a hand in the operation, which was almost certainly a suicide operation. The bodyguard was killed very quickly and did not reveal his motives.[133]

Successful Taliban infiltration has also enabled the Taliban to conduct large-scale, theatrical escapes. Much like in the movie depicting World War II's most celebrated escape, the June 2008 "Great Escape" from Kandahar released 480 inmates from jail. The escapees tunneled for over five months building a 1,050-foot tunnel to the main prison in southern Afghanistan, bypassing government checkpoints, watchtowers, and concrete barriers topped with razor wire.[134]

In August 2011, the United States announced that it would remain in control of Afghanistan's high-profile prison indefinitely and certainly until 2014. Reasons cited were the questionable level of the rule of law in Afghanistan.[135]

Profile 6.6: Three Bullets and One Leg: The Life and Death of the Taliban's "Al-Zarqawi": Mullah Dadullah Akhund

A Pashtun born in Kandahar Province, Dadullah Akhund, referred to as Mullah Dadullah, was educated in a madrassa in Balochistan. Mullah Dadullah fought against the Soviets and lost a leg when he stepped on a land mine. Far from hobbling into retirement, he persevered to fight against the Soviets, the Northern Alliance, and then the Karzai government and Coalition Forces. Using contacts with Pakistani leaders, he helped the Taliban protect convoys of supplies from Turkmenistan to Pakistan that traveled through the Herat area of Afghanistan.[136] He made his mark.

He fought against the Northern Alliance in the late 1990s and helped capture Mazar-i-Sharif. Dadullah was taken prisoner by the forces of Abdul Rashid Dostum, but his loss of a leg did not prevent him from escaping. He became a hero, particularly among his fellow tribesmen.[137] By most accounts, Dadullah had a copious amount of blood on his hands.[138] More than any other Taliban leader, he was associated with the atrocities against the Hazara.

He became a leading field commander for Mullah Omar after 2001 but was detested by intimates because of his kidnappings, beheadings, egotism, and unpredictable spasms of ghoulish sadism.[139] In the last few years of his life, he earned the moniker the "al-Zarqawi" of Afghanistan because of his blood-drunk zeal to decapitate hostages. He is also credited with building the "kamikaze tactic," discussed earlier in this chapter.[140] Feared by both his opponents and his comrades, he churned out ghastly propaganda snuff films. In one film, he and his colleagues slit the throats of six men accused of spying for the Americans.[141]

Dadullah was most active in FATA, where he was credited with building the Taliban to about 20,000, with the help of Pakistani services.[142] In 2005, a Pakistan court sentenced him to life in prison for trying to kill a Pakistani politician, but he continued to move freely in Quetta. When he was killed in May 2007, he was 39 years old. His corpse, with one leg and three bullet holes, was exhibited to journalists, lest anyone would claim that he, once again, dodged the Coalition Forces. The prodigious killer had been on the Coalition's most-wanted list for years.[143] He was taken off that list. Now, inert on stainless-steel table, Dadullah lay visibly dead, to kill no more.

Profile 6.7: Jihad "Johnny" Lind Walker and Adam Gahdahn

The Taliban are largely Afghan, but there are exceptions.[144] In October 2001, there were an estimated 150 British-born Muslims fighting alongside the Taliban. James McLinton had the moniker the Tartan Taliban because the Scottish-born, Catholic-raised Briton moved to Pakistan and became enmeshed in the insurgency.[145] The British Tipton Taliban, or Tipton Five, were captured on Afghan battlefields. Raised in the English Midlands and committed to jihad in Afghanistan, they were shipped to Guantanamo and interrogated.[146] There were other Westerners, but there was only one Jihad Johnny.

Intelligent and self-directed, the California boy, John Phillip Walker Lindh, became a Muslim at age 16, after being moved by the *Autobiography of Malcolm X*.[147] The upper-middle-class product of self-described progressive parents who divorced when he was young, he wanted to be able to speak and read Koranic Arabic. This was unusual for a boy raised in the leafy suburbs of Washington, DC.[148] Few who knew Walker when he was a teenager would have anticipated his joining any pugnacious organization. His father said, "John is a very sweet kid, devoted, and religious."[149]

Walker moved to Pakistan, enrolled in a madrassa, and immersed himself in Urdu and Pashto, and Islamic religious studies. He made himself valuable to Islamist organizations because he could leverage his knowledge of American customs, ceremonies, and sensitivities, and his transparent dedication to Salafist Islam impressed fellow Muslims. His mother related to *Newsweek* that his son was not "totally streetwise." In sweeping understatement, his father conceded that his boy "made a bad decision going to Afghanistan," but added "we love him unconditionally."[150]

Few Americans were sympathetic to him when he was caught, wet, simpering, and hiding in a cave. A December 2001 poll showed that 70 percent of respondents thought Walker should be jailed or executed. He was sentenced to 20 years in prison, where he remains today.[151]

While John Walker is introspective and intellectual, his fellow Californian, Adam Gadahn, exhibits a chuckleheaded persona. Like Walker, he converted to Islam to find spirituality lacking in his countercultural lifestyle. His early religious background was eclectic and confusing. His grandfather was Jewish who married a Presbyterian, and his father is a self-described atheist. His mother is nominally Roman Catholic.[152] Adam spent some of his boyhood living with family on a California goat farm. Unfulfilled with farm life, he looked for employment online and found Islam instead. He embraced Islam after seeing videotapes of Muslims killing Americans and others.

He joined al Qaeda and serves as a propagandist of questionable quality.[153] For his many incitements to kill Americans, Adam Gadahn is wanted for treason.[154] But he is largely seen as an embarrassment for al Qaeda. Few non-Muslim Americans see his jihadist bombast as anything more than worn prattle. But not all analysts of Al Qaeda view him as foolish. One political scientist came to respect many elements of his information operations after analyzing documents captured from bin Laden's home Abbotabad.[155] Table 6.1 is a quick, comparative analysis of the two former Californians.

Table 6.1   California Boys

	John Lindh Walker	**Adam Gahdahn**
Alias	"Jihad Johnny," "Taliban Johnny," and others	Azzam al-Amriki or "Azzam the American"; other names
Islamist Organization	Taliban and al Qaeda	al Qaeda
Background	Upper-middle-class suburbanite, California and Kensington, Maryland; strong school performance and active intellect	Middle-class suburbanite, California; also lived on a California goat farm
Reason for Conversion to Salafist Islam	Was impressed with *The Autobiography of Malcolm X*; searched for a pure, early strain of Islam	Explained he felt lost in American society. "Islam fit my personal theology and intellect as well as basic human logic"
Responsibility	Specific role was not clear. He was certainly a foot soldier and may have been aspiring cadre; too young and inexperienced to have played a major role in decision making	Chief propagandist for al Qaeda's Western-oriented publicity
Actions Directed against United States	Unclear. Gave advice to Taliban and al Qaeda leaders; was apprehended in a combat situation and participated in a failed prison breakout during which an American citizen was murdered	Publically advocated violence against the United States and U.S. citizens and, particularly, soldiers; applauded the death of Americans
Dubious Distinction	First American known to be Taliban operative	First person charged with treason since World War II.[1]
Current Status	Sentenced to 20 years in prison. Petitioning the courts, with the help of civil libertarians, to be able to pray in a group	Has a $1 million bounty on his head; considered armed and extremely dangerous by the FBI

[1]He is the first American charged with treason since Tomoya Kawakita, a Japanese-American who was convicted in 1952 after abusing U.S. prisoners during World War II.

CHAPTER SUMMARY

The Taliban's fighting capabilities have improved considerably. They use infiltration, ambushes, hit-and-run tactics, sniper tactics, roadside bombs, and other tactics. Espousing a blinkered and militaristic ideology, they are well organized and often ruthless. The Taliban's tactics and capabilities have steadily increased since 2001, when many observers of international relations were certain that it was crushed.

The Taliban's more effective tactics include assassinations, roadside bombs, infiltration and impersonation, and suicide attacks. The Taliban are also proficient at offensive intelligence and counterintelligence operations. Two of the more colorful, if unbalanced, characters connected to the Taliban and al Qaeda-supported insurgency are the Californians John "Taliban Johnny" Walker and Adam "Azzam the American" Gahdahn.

7

─-⚉⚉⚉-─

Taliban Inc.

*The Taliban are a group of thieves. If it [my property] were God's, they'd steal
from him, too.*

—A Karachi businessman

Chapters 5 and 6 discussed the target sets and tactics of the Taliban. Chapter
7 will examine the Taliban from a criminal perspective.

Taliban behavior can be as piratical as it is puritanical. Like U.S. criminal
syndicates made infamous on screen and in print, the Taliban's criminal
activities include narcotics trafficking, extortion, shakedown operations,
murder for hire, money laundering, theft, and, occasionally, bank robbery
and kidnapping. Both the Taliban and the U.S. Mafia operate within a frame-
work of established social norms, an acknowledged chain of command and
responsibility, and quick and decisive justice.

When in power, the Taliban effectively controlled the level of crime in
Afghanistan with morally primitive, if effective, justice. In a significant
role reversal the Taliban, who were enforcers of law when they ruled
Afghanistan, became criminals when they were removed from power. To
obtain the revenue necessary to continue operations and to sustain a force
in the field, the Taliban turned to crime including extortion, kidnapping,
bank robbery, murder, and narcotics trafficking.

When the Taliban fled to Pakistan, they brought their infantry weapons
with them. The Taliban moved into several border areas in later 2001 and
2002, and they expanded their bases of insurgent and criminal operations.
By 2009 Karachi, the large Pakistani city of 18 million, as well as other cities,
became a leading sanctuary of the Taliban. They could melt into the social

fabric because they shared customs and ceremonies. They also brought with them discipline and a vast knowledge of firearms.[1]

Despite its persistent poverty rate, there is lot to steal in Afghanistan. Afghanistan's roads carry about 3,000 tons of supplies destined for Coalition-related activities daily to sustain the counterinsurgency.[2] They are vulnerable to the Taliban. Supplies include food, water, fuel and ammunition, which are trucked in Afghanistan, usually through Pakistan.[3] These goods come overland through Pakistan or Central Asia to distribution hubs at 200 points, including Bagram Air Force base north of Kabul and a similar base outside Kandahar.[4] Most of the trucks are owned and operated by Afghans.[5] Many of the roads are largely controlled by warlords and insurgent groups, particularly the Taliban.[6] They are a source of revenue.

HIGHWAY ROBBERY

From the earliest days of the current counterinsurgency, Coalition Forces faced an ethical and logistical dilemma. This was the same predicament the Moghul and British forces faced when they sought to ensure safe transport of their goods and personnel into Afghanistan. In what is often called sarcastically a "pay-to-play" operation, Coalition Forces periodically pay individuals and organizations to protect trucks, which often travel in convoy. As with the turf wars of Chicago and New York in the 1930s, different insurgent and criminal enterprises sometimes battle each other for territory. For this reason, it is difficult to know whom to pay or who controls the area into which Coalition goods and services need to be delivered.[7]

Some of the more experienced U.S. Army logisticians charged with delivering goods to remote Afghan destinations through hostile terrain found that the Afghan security services were more inept and corrupt than their counterparts in Iraq.[8] Military logisticians faced the ethical dilemma of paying off regional warlords or having their supplies interrupted.[9] The logisticians also dealt with Coalition-imposed restrictions and prohibitions that made safe passage more difficult. For example, one handicap was prohibiting companies that ship U.S. goods across Afghanistan from arming their security personnel or drivers with weapons heavier than an assault rifle. This rule prevented private security companies from devolving into private militias, but it rendered truck drivers ill-prepared to combat criminals and insurgents armed with RPGs.

The warlords became stronger through the payoffs when the logisticians paid them to protect their goods.[10] Further, some of the money filtered its way to the Taliban. This not only weakens the rule of law and promotes extortion, it helps to fund the insurgent enemy, whom the Coalition Forces are trying to destroy or suppress.[11] U.S. congressional inquiries,[12] in July 2010, confirmed the labyrinthine and morally questionable practice of paying for protection when some of that money was channeled to the Taliban enemy.[13]

Extortion through Taxation

From its earliest days in power, the Taliban began use zakat, or required Islamic taxes. Not all zakat is extortionist, and many Muslims give alms out of a sense of strong Islamic obligation. But the Taliban forced a tax on those under their rule, and there was nothing voluntary about compliance. During its 1996–2001 tenure, the Taliban required narcotic cultivators and traffickers to pay them a specified amount of their revenue. Several years into their rule, the Taliban controlled 96 percent of Afghanistan's poppy-growing regions and taxed the poppy growers and those who refine poppies into opium. Despite denials to the contrary, the Taliban were heavily engaged and still are engaged in the narcotics trade.[14] This "narco-terrorism" is a symbiosis in which both sides profit; the narco-traffickers have their products protected, and the terrorist groups, such as Sendero Luminoso in Peru, obtain necessary funding. The Pakistani Taliban, to be discussed in chapter 8, has a flexible taxation. Sometimes the wheat farmers can pay in fuel or agriculture.

There is community and individual profiling, particularly of successful businessmen who are candidates for kidnapping or extortion. The more refined procedures take place in Pakistan. Pakistan intelligence noted that in Taliban-ridden areas, wealthier persons agree to pay protection money or bhatta to avoid being kidnapped.[15] The process is very similar to methods of Mafioso. First, the Taliban call the target and suggest that he pay a specified sum, which is usually large and which is referred to as a donation to a holy cause. If the target responds he does not have and cannot acquire that money, his home or car is attacked.[16] Later, he might be killed.

Robberies

Insurgents and revolutionaries, such as the determined Joseph Stalin or the disoriented American Patty Hearst, have robbed banks. The Taliban showed an early enthusiasm for robbing banks. What began as amateurish and comical, if brutal, heists evolved into relatively sophisticated and well-rehearsed operations. When the Taliban found themselves cut off from traditional sources of money, they turned to bank robbery to supplement their meager and sporadic income flows. Many of the attacks are brazen, with little attempt by the culprits to disguise their identities. Some of the robbers have a distinctive look, with swarthy complexions, and long, black beards, and AK-47s. They tend to kill the bank guards. Robberies have become paramilitary operations, sometimes executing the operations with impressive precision.[17]

Many of the Taliban's bank robberies take place in Pakistan, which has more wealth than Afghanistan. It is not unusual for bank robbers to move quickly and with more precision than is generally associated with amateurs. For example, a successful robbery in 2009, according to police, took only three minutes in broad daylight.[18]

The Taliban rob banks largely to steal money, and any other benefits are secondary. But some operations cause social disruptions and divert the capabilities of police forces. This becomes particularly important at high-profile events that are designed to strengthen the legitimacy of the government.[19] As an example, government forces, already strapped of well-trained, uncorrupted security personnel, were diverted when military and paramilitary forces were needed to protect polling stations during elections in 2009.[20] The threat of bank robberies diverts security personnel from protecting government buildings and protecting government figures.

Many security personnel are vulnerable to bribes or threats by the Taliban. Because of systemic corruption and vast poverty in Pakistan and Afghanistan, robbers can coordinate with security personnel to facilitate the heists. Taliban offer both positive and negative inducements. Some targets are bought off with bribes and others are intimidated by threats. Pakistani newspapers have commented about the lack of resistance to the Taliban heists.[21]

Kidnapping

The Taliban kidnap high-value targets because ransoms have paid very well. Kidnapping is not uncommon in Latin America and other areas of the world where there are desperately poor groups of criminals or terrorists and a tier of rich and vulnerable targets. Kidnapping is a significant source of the Taliban's overall income.[22] The high-profile targets bring the Taliban revenue of nearly $10 million each year, but this figure may be low. Some payoffs go unreported. Foreigners, high-profile political or administrative figures, and businessmen are prime targets and are likely to remain so as long as ransoms are paid for their release.

Pakistani counterterrorism officials say they believe that kidnapping for ransom may have been the single largest revenue source for the Pakistani Taliban's Baitullah Mehsud, before he was killed. In 2008, Mr. Mehsud's network may have held as many as 70 hostages. Though just 10 percent of kidnappings are connected to the Taliban, according to the police, the ransoms they generate—some as high as $60,000 to $250,000 each—collect more money than all the other cases combined.[23]

There have been spectacular kidnappings of large groups or high-profile personalities. One example was the wholesale kidnapping of dozens of students and staff members from a Pakistani army preparatory school in North Waziristan, Pakistan, in 2009. Most were rescued by the Pakistani

Army.[24] There was also the 2007 kidnapping of 23 Korean Christian aid workers who were abducted while traveling in a bus. Two were killed and the rest were released after six weeks of negotiation. In addition to paying what has been speculated to be significant money, perhaps $20 million, South Korea pledged to withdraw its 200 troops from Afghanistan, as previously planned, and agreed to prohibit Christian evangelizing in Afghanistan.[25] The kidnapping was successful in two ways: it garnered money and forced South Korea from military participation. The threat of kidnapping also gives foreigners, whose governments and corporations have paid ransom in the past, pause for fear of being kidnapped themselves.

Kidnapped prisoners are a human exchange currency. American Bowe Bergdahl is the only known U.S. prisoner of war. The United Nations' al Qaeda and Taliban Monitoring Team has speculated that the Taliban might exchange Bergdahl for leading Taliban prisoners.[26]

An Italian journalist, Danielle Mastrogiacomo of the Rome-based *La Republica* newspaper, was captured by the Taliban and held for ransom with his Afghan translator/fixer. He was held for 15 days and then released in a prisoner swap with the Taliban.[27] But the driver and then the translator were decapitated.[28] The man who is suspected of ordering their killing was the one-legged and deceased Mullah Dadullah (see chapter 6).[29]

Profile 7.1: Beverly Giesbrecht, Who Became Khadija Qahaar

Sometimes the motives, or even the authenticity of a kidnapping, are confusing or dubious. This is the case of Beverly Giesbrecht, a former magazine publisher and Canadian convert to Islam who became reborn as Khadija Qahaar, also known as Khadija Abudl Qahaarand, and who broadcasted her allegiance to the international jihadist movement.

Sometime in the late twentieth century, Giesbrecht, while in her early or mid-50s, had declared herself a born-again Christian. She wanted to return to her spiritual roots after some wild times. But after the September 2001 attacks, she converted to Islam and established a website called Jihad Unspun. She worked as a freelance journalist for Al Jazeera and tried to advance the cause of militant Islam. But things did not work out as she had planned after she flew to Pakistan to join a jihadist group.[30]

Despite her enthusiasm about promoting the Afghan jihad, she was *allegedly* kidnapped by insurgents in April 2008 and held for a ransom that neither her family nor the Canadian government was prepared to pay. Unconfirmed reporting in November 2011 indicated that she died, succumbing to hepatitis. But her kidnapping, as well as her spiritual path from materialism and hard drinking to Islamic zeal, is surrounded by speculation. Was she really kidnapped, or was this a ruse to extort money for the Taliban? If this were the case, she may have been a party to a ploy from the beginning. In fact, she might still be alive, though there is no evidence to support this.[31]

Not everybody commiserated with Khadija's plight. She never revealed the details of a game plan beyond flying to Pakistan, traveling to Waziristan, and hoping to team with jihadis. In an acerbic, but probably widely shared, analysis of the situation, a Western blogger sniggered, "People like that remind me of that film about the man who went to live out in the woods and make friends with the grizzly bears . . . He got eaten."[32]

Murder

The Taliban murder for several reasons. As discussed earlier, they kill to advance their political goal of ridding Afghanistan of a foreign military presence, to remove the current government, and to eliminate criminal rivals. They also kill for a fusion of reasons, including savagery, revenge, and spontaneous behavior. As with Mafioso psychopaths, some Taliban enjoy killing and do it when they have the chance.[33]

First, they kill to pursue their political agenda, as discussed in earlier chapters. When the Taliban were in power they killed political rivals, and today, when they are out of power, they continue to kill the enemies. Their enemies list is very long. Accomplished women are threats to the Taliban and are targeted. Prominent female police officers in Afghanistan have been murdered because they worked for the government, held a higher social and work-related position than many men, and tried to rescue women and girls from fundamentalists.[34] Ministers are also routinely targeted. For example, Abdul Rahman, Afghanistan's civil aviation and tourism minister, was murdered despite his record as a hero of the war against the Soviets in late 1980s.[35] In recent years, the Taliban began to murder lower-level, less-protected officials, some of whom have only the slimmest connections to the authorities.[36]

Journalists critical of insurgents or Sharia have a high place on the Taliban's death list. The Pakistani Taliban have claimed responsibility for the killing of a senior journalist, Misri Khan Orakzai, because, in the words of the Taliban spokesman, "he twisted facts whenever we gave him a report. He [had] a leaning towards the army in his reports."[37] Western journalists who are sympathetic to the insurgency, such as Yvonne Ridley, or who work for Al Jazeera are in less danger of being harmed because of their propaganda value.

Religious figures who disagree with the Taliban are often labeled apostates. The penalty for apostasy in Islam is death. This is taken seriously, and those working for the government, including religious figures, are often labeled apostates. A Taliban note affixed to the corpse in Kunar read, "This will be the punishment of those who offer prayers for [dead] apostates."[38] According to the BBC, the Taliban killed more than 800 religious scholars over theological disputes and perceived threats to their power.[39] Some of the murdered religious figures were obscure, but others had local celebrity. The Taliban claimed responsibility for the killing of renowned religious scholar and psychiatrist Farooq Khan, who helped troubled youth. The 56-year-old Khan, who was trained in Vienna, ran a school to help deprogram Taliban-indoctrinated youth and offer a gentler Islam. Similarly, in August 2010 Dr. Karen Woo, a British surgeon, was robbed, lined up against a wall, and shot with nine other health care workers in Afghanistan. One member of the health care team escaped death by reciting verses from the Koran and pleading, "I am a Muslim. Don't kill me."[40] But the Taliban accused Dr. Woo of spreading Christianity and killed her.

The tactics of the Taliban differ in the provinces. For example, the Taliban use more high-profile attacks and tend to focus more on government leaders and commercial buildings in Kabul. In contrast, the Taliban use more speed and stealth and focus on lower-level officials, such as beat cops, aid workers, and opposition tribal officials elsewhere.[41] If there is any region is a murder capital, it is Kandahar.

Sometimes, they kill for no apparent reason. It is sometimes difficult to separate criminal from political intent. For example, if a local Taliban commander orders a specific policeman killed, the decision could have sprung from a number of reasons. The policeman may have been seen as a political enemy or an impediment to narcotics trafficking, or was targeted because the killer had a sudden impulse to kill someone.[42]

An example is a killing in August 2012 that makes little apparent sense to anyone but the perpetrators and, perhaps, the victims. On an ordinary Saturday in summer 2012, Taliban murdered six miners in a chromite mine in Parwan Province.[43] But there were no clearly stated reasons for killing the miners, none of whom were known to be associated with security forces. Nor was there evidence that these victims were individually targeted. They could have been randomly killed. The Taliban claimed that they killed policemen, which was a lie (Table 7.1).

Blowback from Crime

The Taliban have paid a penalty in Afghan public opinion. Now that the Taliban are out of power and are themselves the criminals, they continue the cruelty and compound it with extortion, kidnapping, murder, and narcotics trafficking. There is an ambient fear of being harmed or threatened

Table 7.1 The Taliban's Crime Matrix

	Standard Criminal Motives	Taliban's Motives	Taliban's Successful Practices	Taliban's Unsuccessful Practices
Extortion	Obtain money; sustain territory for prestige	Obtain money; prove the government has no control; assert power over individuals	Keep the level of extortion sustainable; negotiate level of zakat	Demand a level of taxation that victims cannot afford; Taliban's cruelty angers many Afghans
Kidnapping	Obtain money; not common practice in the United States	Obtain money; terrify foreigners residing in Afghanistan	Targeting victims whose families or employers can pay	Targeting victims who are ill and are likely to die in Taliban custody
Bank Robbery	Obtain money	Obtain money; divert government security resources	Professional and well-rehearsed operations that limit killings	Clumsy and brutal attacks with unnecessary killing
Murder	Enforce criminal order; revenge; money contract	Tactic to terrorize the enemy; prevent collaboration with the government	Highly selective targeting	Target children and persons not connected to the insurgency
Narcotics Trafficking	Obtain money	Obtain money	Preventing a surplus of narcotics, which lowers prices; partnering with cultivators	Demanding excessive payments from cultivators and traffickers

by the Taliban. Part of this stems from an element of unpredictability to Taliban's criminal behavior, and this causes confusion and alienation. Sometimes the Taliban do not communicate with each other, and villagers do not know when to expect murders or shakedowns.

CHAPTER SUMMARY

The Taliban are violent criminals. They commit a variety of crimes including extortion, kidnapping, bank robbery, murder, and narcotics trafficking. They have established networks for their criminal enterprises and are adept at intimidating and extorting large populations of villagers in Afghanistan and in Pakistan who feel vulnerable. They are often tolerated because villagers are powerless to repel them. But there is growing resistance.

8

—◦◦◦—

Affiliated Insurgent Groups and Foreign Connections

Earlier chapters primarily focused on the Taliban. Chapter 8 discusses four other insurgent organizations of varying types. These groups are al Qaeda, the Haqqani network, Gulbuddin Hekmatyar's Hizb-i-Islami, often spelled Hizb-i-Islami, and the Pakistani Taliban or Tehrik-i-Taliban (TTP). There are other, smaller insurgent groups with varying agendas and other largely criminal groups. It will also discuss Pakistani and Iranian aid.

AFFILIATED GROUPS

Al Qaeda

Afghanistan is the epicenter of violent extremism practiced by al Qaeda.
—President Barack Obama[1]

The death of bin Laden reverberated in the ranks of the Taliban but did not shatter its capabilities or morale. While al Qaeda and the Taliban embrace similar Salafist philosophies and partner in operations, they are distinct organizations, composed of different ethnicities and cultures, and maintain separate leadership structure and chains of command.[2]

The Taliban is fundamentally an Afghan organization with a local agenda, and al Qaeda is primarily an Arab association with global ambitions. Tensions escalated between the Taliban and bin Laden when the

2001 fighting started. Some Taliban began snickering at the Arab bin Laden, whom they increasingly saw egotistical. "I think our brother [bin Laden] has caught the disease of screens, flashes, fans, and applause," said one disapproving Taliban.[3] Bin Laden sometimes spoke of himself in the third person and referred to himself often in public and private forums. This was not the style of the Taliban.[4] This narcissistic tone grated on many Taliban ears.

Bin Laden's death could have significant implications for the counterinsurgency. In December 2009, President Obama told cadets at West Point that Afghanistan is al Qaeda's core operating base.[5] With the death of bin Laden, arguments surrounding Afghanistan's strategic importance lessened to some in the Obama administration. Many U.S. leaders, both Democrats and Republicans, were openly talking about an exit strategy.[6] Other observers were quick to downplay the importance of bin Laden's death. They argued that bin Laden's death was largely symbolic. There was no indication that the Taliban would fight any less ferociously or effectively because bin Laden was dead.

Leaders

Osama bin Laden was the leader of al Qaeda until his death in May 2011.

Dr. Ayman al-Zawahiri is currently the leader. A surgeon from Cairo University and the former leader of the Islamic Jihad (IJ) group in Afghanistan in the 1980s, he became bin Laden's deputy after the IJ merged with al Qaeda in 1998.[7] A skilled infighter and tactician, Zawahiri has, according to many sources, weak interpersonal skills. As one expert remarked, "Everybody is quick to comment on how Zawahiri is a polarizing figure, uncharismatic, disagreeable—people can't stand him."[8] Nonetheless, he has strong survival skills. He is also a hero to Islamists around the world.[9]

Abu Yahya al-Libi was the second-most important al Qaeda leader and was from Libya. He headed the Sharia and Political Committee, probably in Quetta, until he was killed in a drone attack in June 2012. Like bin Laden, he was a charismatic leader and connected with the younger and more aggressive members.[10] Congresswoman Barbara Lee of Texas congratulated President Obama for having him killed.[11] In September 2012, the Taliban and Arabs in the Middle East cited his assassination as one of many reasons for the unrest and murder of U.S. diplomatic personnel in Libya. Al-Libi had a $1 million bounty on his head at the time of his death.[12]

Saif al-Adel, "Sword of Justice," is a former Egyptian Army commando and was temporarily designated as the al Qaeda "caretaker" after bin Laden was assassinated.[13] He is a strategist and trainer and is regarded as intelligent and competent (see Profile 8.1).

Profile 8.1: Saif al-Adel: Al Qaeda's Caretaker

In mid-May 2011, the Egyptian Saif al-Adel, the Egyptian ex-Special Forces officer, became a caretaker of the world's most notorious Islamic terrorist group.[14] Al-Adel is the nom de guerre of Col. Muhammad Ibrahim Makkawi. With vast militant experience beginning in the 1980s, al-Adel helped mastermind the 1998 bombings of U.S. embassies in Africa. He was probably involved with the Black Hawk Down battle in Somalia. Now in his mid-50s, he remains the FBI's most-wanted terrorist with a $5 million bounty.[15]

He has a five-part strategy for fighting the United States, which he calls the "ponderous American elephant." First, draw the United States into fighting Muslims in distant lands. This has been in place since 1998. The second stage is to awake the "Islamic elephant," and the third is to expand the conflict throughout the Islamic world.[16] The fourth stage is developing al Qaeda franchises throughout the world. In the fifth stage, the United States will collapse under the financial and military strain of fighting multiple wars on many fronts.[17]

There have been many accounts of al-Adel's residence in Iran.[18] Iran is a friendly venue for al Qaeda because Coalition Forces are less likely to conduct U.S. commando raid or drone strikes.[19] He has a wife and several children in Iran. Other reports as of spring 2011 have placed Al-Adel in North Waziristan.[20]

Adam Gadahn, portly and ineloquent, is an American convert and propaganda specialist. He targets Americans but, as with Tokyo Rose in Japan, he is seen as more comic than convincing (see Profile 6.7).[21]

Strength

As of 2012, there are approximately several hundred operatives in the Afghanistan/Pakistan.

Operational Base

Al Qaeda's operational base is in Pakistan's tribal areas, primarily North Waziristan. It has operatives in many parts of the world, and the Afghanistan/Pakistan theater of operations is currently less important than Middle Eastern or African states where al Qaeda is building momentum.

Agenda

The ultimate goal is to achieve Islam's global domination. Long-term goals include subduing the United States and overthrowing all Muslim governments that, in the view of al Qaeda, are insufficiently Salafist. More immediate objectives include rejuvenating and rebuilding leadership; training and inspiring other militants; and attacking U.S. and NATO forces in eastern Afghanistan and Pakistan. After bin Laden's death, al Qaeda switched its geographic focus to Somalia and Yemen.

Status

The death of bin Laden signaled what may become the moribund status of al Qaeda in Afghanistan. The apogee of al Qaeda's power was early September 2001, when bin Laden assassinated his and Mullah Omar's last remaining significant rival in the Afghan power play. This was followed by the multiple and devastating attacks on the U.S. homeland. Like his host, Mullah Omar, bin Laden was forced from Afghanistan and took refuge in Pakistan. By virtue of his prestige, bin Laden drew recruits and financial support from many parts of the Islamic world.

Al Qaeda is more fragmented, and has more difficulty communicating and maintaining organizational control.[22] In January 2012 James Clapper, director of national intelligence, commented that al Qaeda was so ineffective that it was becoming of "largely symbolic importance."[23] This view became increasingly disputed by summer 2013. In August of that year the president shuttered U.S embassies throughout the Middle East in response to al Qaeda threats.

Haqqani Network

He [Jalaluddin Haqqani] is goodness personified.
—Texas congressman Charlie Wilson[24]

Jalaluddin Haqqani and his son Sirajuddin are leaders of their own quasi-independent insurgent band. One of Jalaluddin's sons, Badruddin, was killed in a drone strike in August 2012.[25] The Haqqanis operate as an element of the Afghan Taliban, sometimes autonomously, and also in conjunction with other militant groups such as Hizb-i-Islami-Gulbuddin (HiG).[26] It is also tied to traditionally Kashmir-focused groups. It is more tribally diverse than is the Taliban and is comprised of Uzbecks, Chechens, Kashmiris, and Pakistanis who live in FATA. Its areas of influence extend from North and South Waziristan to Parachinar and Kurram agencies. From these bases, the Haqqanis conduct attacks on the border areas of Paktika, Khowst, and Paktia provinces.

Like the Taliban, the Haqqanis tap deep into Pashtun chauvinism. The leaders are from the Pashtun Zadran subtribe, which is generously represented in Khost, Paktika, and Paktia provinces. The deployment of international forces to this area in 2001 stirred unease there. There are also many Zadrans in Pakistan's Miram Shah, which is also the seat of a Taliban Shura.

There is also a strong bin Laden connection. Steven Coll explained that Jalaluddin Haqqani has very long and intimate roots with bin Laden. Bin Laden lived in Haqqani territory and built his first important training camp there.[27]

Jalaluddin charmed U.S. politicians during the jihad against the Soviets. Former U.S. Congressman Charlie Wilson famously called Jalaluddin "goodness personified," and he received a disproportionate share of U.S. money.[28] The Haqqanis are long favorites of Arab patrons, in part because of his effectiveness against the Soviets. He was also admired because he promoted a newly established bin Laden.

The Haqqanis attracted some European jihadis, indicating a connection, however tenuous, to European recruiters.[29] Unlike the Taliban, which had had few known Western operatives, except one American superstar, the Haqqanis are more eager to use foreigners and to cooperate with international jihadists.[30] A German-Turk, who was likely operating under the command of the Haqqanis, detonated himself at a U.S. military base in Khost in 2008.[31] In Germany, the Sauerland Cell is composed of Turks and ethnic German coverts who conspire to attack sites in Europe, particularly in Germany (see Profile 8.2). This group is reported to have connections with the Haqqanis.[32]

The multinational element distinguishes it from the Taliban. The relative sophistication of their suicide attacks has been another distinction. Until recent years, the Haqqanis have generally outperformed the Taliban in their ability to inflict mass murder on secure targets through suicide bombing.[33] Their attacks are relatively sophisticated and occur in steps. First, a suicide bomber will detonate himself at a bazaar, and when first responders attend the injured, another bomber detonates himself. There might then be a third wave of attacks from small-arms fire.

Among the more notorious attacks attributed to and claimed by the Haqqanis was the July 7, 2008, bombing of the Indian Embassy in Kabul, which killed 54 people. The group is alleged to be behind many high-profile assaults, including a raid on a luxury hotel in Kabul in January 2008.[34]

The Haqqanis learned military technology from al Qaeda operatives, who were operating in Iraq. The successful Iraqi operations were studied and replicated in Afghanistan. Analysts and Afghan government officials have accused Pakistan of protecting the Haqqani network as allies.[35] In November 2011, Sirajuddin Haqqani publically reaffirmed his allegiance and subordination to Mullah Omar. He also stressed that he would not negotiate with Americans independently.

The Haqqanis also affect relationships between the United States and Pakistan. U.S. officials and commanders have derided the ISI as providing passive and sometimes active support to the Haqqanis.[36] There is evidence that retired Pakistani Army and security personnel have advised that the Pakistani government not sever its ties to the Haqqanis.[37]

Leaders

The leaders of the Haqqani network are Jalaluddin Haqqani and his son Sirajuddin.

Strength

The strength of the network is unknown.

Operational Base

The leadership, according to U.S. and Afghan sources, is based near Miramshah, North Waziristan, in the Pakistani tribal areas.[38]

Agenda

It has some independence but is largely subordinated to the Afghan Taliban. Like the Taliban, it attacks Coalition Forces and intends to replace the current regime in Kabul with an anti-Western, Salafist government. Among other tactics, it uses suicide bombings effectively. In 2008 it blew up the Senera Hotel, the only five-star hotel in Afghanistan; in the same year, it came close to killing President Karzai; and in 2008, it launched a multistage suicide wave attack at Camp Salerno.[39] The first known female suicide bomber was probably a Haqqani operator.[40] Their agenda is almost identical to that of the Taliban, but there is more of an anti-Indian element.

Status

If there is a "first family" of Pashtun insurgents, Jalaluddin Haqqani and his son Sirajuddin would hold that moniker. Both they and other family members have cobbled together a patchwork of Salafists and disenfranchised groups in the Quetta Shura. The Haqqanis have cooperated with the ISI to attack Indian targets.[41]

Profile 8.2: German Taliban and the Curious Case of Thomas U

There is a twentieth-century German connection to militant Islam. By the late 1930s, Hitler liked what he saw among the pro-Axis, antiliberal Islamic clerics and nationalists in the Arab Middle East. The Grand Mufti of Jerusalem was a passionate admirer of Adolf Hitler. He was feted with a villa near Berlin, dined with Nazi luminaries, and collaborated with architects of genocide, particularly Adolf Eichmann, whom he considered a friend.[42] But German cultural and academic interest in the Muslim world preceded the arrival of the Nazis, and it continued well after the destruction of the Third Reich. During the 1950s, the Islamic Brotherhood developed deep roots in Germany cities.[43] By 2010 there were approximately 20 million Muslims in Europe.

Today, there are European Islamist groups, and perhaps several hundred Europeans, who serve alongside the Taliban or other insurgent groups in the Afghanistan/Pakistan area. The German Taliban is among these groups and its origins and disposition are obscure. If it still exists, it may operate under the name of the Saarland Cell, or an outgrowth of elements within the Islamic Jihad Union. In October 2008, a group of German Islamists claiming to live in Pakistan mailed the German press a video called *A Call from Hindu Kush*. In it, the German jihadis threaten to kill those supporting the United States in Afghanistan.[44]

What is certain is that the 20-something, Saarland-raised Eric Breininger led fellow Germans to attack NATO positions in Afghanistan.[45] But his luck ran out in October 2010 when he and seven other German mujahedeen became shaheeds, or martyrs. They were killed by U.S. missiles in Pakistan, near the Afghan border.[46] They were training other militants for future Taliban-directed or Taliban-associated attacks.

Along the path to jihad in the Afghan border regions, many German Taliban became disheartened and cynical. Some of their European friends who fought alongside them in Afghanistan/Pakistan were killed and others deserted the jihad. Others fell into poor health or were arrested.

The case of Thomas U, whose last name was withheld by German authorities, illustrates the declined fortunes of the German Taliban. In 2009 Thomas, then in his early 20s, had infiltrated himself into Waziristan for weapons training and combat. He had been a neo-Nazi sympathizer and then converted to Islam. Thomas expected to kill nonbelievers, particularly Americans. But things did not work out as he hoped in Pakistan. Thomas and his wife escaped to Turkey in

August 2012, where he was arrested and remanded to German custody.[47]

Under interrogation, he revealed his disgust with the living conditions, which he described as not fit for human habitation. "It was a terrible experience. I was shocked at the lack of hygiene, people were spitting and vomiting. My wife was very unhappy because traditionally women are treated badly."[48] Thomas was relieved when he made his way to Turkey. "Finally I could hold hands with my wife in public."

But more than any other factor, it was the gruesome deaths of his German friends in a firefight with Pakistani soldiers that forced him from the fight. "The sight of their terribly mangled bodies moved me. From then on, I no longer wanted to take part in violence. I had been completely wrong." The overly masculine attitudes and the rampant drug consumption of the Taliban were also getting on his nerves. "Waziristan was not what I had been looking for."[49]

Hezb-i-Islami

I hate Hekmatyar because he buried my brother alive, and now my brother's children have no father. They are forced to be beggars.
        —A victim of Hekmatyar, 2002[50]

Another group, Hezb-i-Islami, is led by Hekmatyar Gulbuddin, two-time former prime minster of Afghanistan, veteran politician, and long-term antagonist of the Karzai government. Gulbuddin Hekmatyar is a vicious, brutal, and devious warlord. Hekmatyar and his group were among those most active against the Soviets and most well funded by the United States. Hekmatyar is a Sunni Muslim, ethnic Pashtun who speaks excellent English. He gained a reputation for extreme violence while leading militant attacks during the 1979–89 Soviet occupation, and repeatedly shifted his support between different Afghan groups during more than 20 years of conflict in this landlocked Central Asian nation. Bin Laden and Hekmatyar forged their relationship during the mujahedeen campaign against the Soviets. For years, Pakistan backed Hekmatyar as the leader of a united Afghanistan, switching to the Taliban when it seemed he was a loser.

During the 1992–96 civil war Hekmatyar, as a prime minister, turned his militant forces against those of President Burhanuddin Rabbani, an ethnic Tajik, and pummeled Kabul with artillery. In June 1996, Hekmatyar resumed the office of prime minister. But his participation in the government polarized public opinion. He became also sworn enemy of the Taliban.[51] He fled to Iran and returned to fight with the Taliban after the September 2001 attacks. Hekmatyar praised attacks on U.S. and international forces.[52]

His home base has been Peshawar, which served off and on since the late 1980s as a base of operations. In what might be apocryphal, in the late 1990s Peshawar's residents speculated that floating corpses in canals near Hekmatyar's compound were victims of his summary justice, paranoia, boredom, or bad moods. In May 2002, a U.S. drone fired a Hellfire missile and came close to killing him.

By any standard of humanity, Hekmatyar is sadistic and could be a psychopath. In Afghanistan, he emerges as a cold-blooded figure whose sadism cannot be explained by any political, religious, or strategic imperative.

Leaders

The leader of Hezb-i-Islami is Gulbuddin Hekmatyar, a former prime minister and probable psychopath.[53]

Strength

Hezb-i-Islami's strength is unknown, but it is the weakest of the three primary Taliban factions in Afghanistan.

Operational Base

Its operational base is Peshawar, Pakistan; Kunar, Nangarhar, in Afghanistan; and Afghan refugee camps near these areas.

Agenda

Hezb-i-Islami's agenda is attacks on U.S., NATO, and Afghan targets in Afghanistan.

Status

Hezb-i-Islami has long been linked to al Qaeda and the Taliban in Afghanistan but is also considered the group most likely to reconcile with the Afghan government.

Tehrik i-Taliban Pakistan (TTP)

In December 2007, Baitullah Mehsud, a Pashtun, Salafist, and a Pakistani, stitched together as many as 40 groups, some of which were very small, into an organization outside the direct command structure of the Afghan Taliban.[54] Mullah Omar may have helped form the TTP.[55] Mehsud recruited for Mullah Omar, established training facilities, conducted operations against Pakistani government facilities, and punished criminals. He also brought Sharia.[56] Hakimullah Mehsud, who succeeded Baitullah after he was killed, pledged loyalty to Mullah Omar.[57] In November 2013, he was killed in a drone strike against his relatively opulent villa near Miranshah.[58]

The TTP is the most important insurgent force in Pakistan that threatens the sovereignty of the government. Pakistani political and administrative figures conceded that the TTP held great sway in in the Khyber Agency, North Waziristan, South Waziristan, and FATA. These militants have been resisting and sometimes defeating the Pakistan Army.[59] They have termed their efforts against Pakistan as a "defensive Jihad."[60]

Similar in many ways to the Afghan Taliban, the TTP is guided by a Shura of about 40 elders and is governed along subtribal lines. Like the Afghan Taliban, it is organized by committees. There are law enforcement and administrative functions, including intelligence and revenue collection, law and order preservation, and other functions.[61] Some of the constituent members of the TTP Coalition have nuanced, but rarely divergent, aims. The organization has a public relations cell that serves as its propaganda branch, which busily claims credit for attacks on Pakistan military targets and denies killing former Prime Minister Benazir Bhutto.[62] The TTP launched a December 2009 suicide attack on a U.S. military base in Khowst, Afghanistan, which killed seven U.S. citizens, and an April 2010 suicide bombing against the U.S. Consulate in Peshawar, Pakistan, which killed six Pakistani citizens.

While the Pakistani Taliban hold a political philosophy similar to their Afghan counterparts, they are far more focused on attacking forces of the Pakistan government. Like the Afghan Taliban, the TTP do not accept the Durrand Line separating the two countries. There is cooperation between the TTP and the Afghan Taliban and the Lashkar-e-Tabya (LET), a small but vicious anti-Western, anti-Indian group, and ISI-connected group.[63]

On September 1, 2010, the U.S. Department of State designated the TTP as a Foreign Terrorist Organization (FTO), and declared Hakimullah Mehsud, the emir of TTP, and his deputy Waliur Rehman as Specially Designated Global Terrorists. A reward of $5 million each was placed on the two terrorist commanders.

Like the Taliban in Afghanistan, the TTP conduct criminal operations. They are bank robbers and kidnappers and finance their operations through these and other criminal operations. They also practice extortion and smuggle timber and emeralds.[64]

Leaders

Mullah Fazlullah, the Radio Mullah or Weeping Mullah, succeeded Hakimullah Mehsud, who was killed in a drone strike, in November 2013.

Strength

There are between 10,000 and 35,000 allied fighters[65] in the TTP.

Operational Base

The TTP's operation base is North and South Waziristan and Orakzai.

Agenda

The TTP's agenda is to mount attacks on U.S. and NATO forces in Afghanistan and on the Pakistani Army.

Status

An umbrella group of local militant organizations that joined together in December 2007 under the late Baitullah Mehsud, TTP has provided suicide bombers to the Haqqanis and the Quetta Shura. They probably killed Benazir Bhutto.

The TTP has been hurt by the U.S. drone attacks, and Pakistani offensives are forcing the group underground and creating fractures. In October 2013, Latif Mehsud, a senior TTP commander, was captured by U.S. forces. Close links between homegrown terrorists in Western countries and the TTP pose threats to the United States and European states (Table 8.1).[66] Maulana Fazlullah, Meshud's successor, issued a fatwa in November 2013 promoting an all-species jihad against Americans. He emphasized, "Even a dog killed by the U.S. is a martyr."[67]

Borders between states are often not clearly defined and the rule of law often depends upon the decrees and sometimes the caprice of local warlords. But two of Afghanistan's neighbors, Pakistan and Iran, have long aided insurgents in Afghanistan undermine the rule of law there.

PAKISTAN

I categorically deny the presence of Osama bin Laden, his deputy Ayman al-Zawahiri, and even Mullah Omar in any part of Pakistan.
—Pakistan's Interior Minister Rehman Malik, 2005[68]

Pakistan has long been an important player in South Asia and certainly in Afghanistan's internal affairs. It was created as an Islamic state, and early in its history defined itself in opposition to its non-Muslim neighbor, India.[69] The 1947 partition took the lives of hundreds of thousands and displaced millions.[70] For many years, the United States had a friendly relationship

Table 8.1 The Five Major Insurgent Groups in Afghanistan 2001–12

	Taliban	Al Qaeda	Haqqani Network	Hizb-i-Islami Gulbuddin	TTP
Goals	Create Sharia State	Create global Sharia	Create Sharia state	Create Sharia state	Create Sharia in Pakistan
Ethnicity	Largely Pashtun	International, but largely Arab	Multiethnic: Kashmiris, Uzbeks, Chechens, Pashtu	Many regional ethnicities	Mixed South Asian; largely Pashtun and Punjab
Level of Capabilities 2001–12	Strongest of all groups. Growing strength in Pakistan and border areas of Afghanistan.	Levels of capabilities declined substantially in South Asia. Have grown in Yemen and parts of Africa.	Moderate levels of strength in the east	Currently, the weakest of the three groups	By 2012 capabilities have declined as Pakistan forces and U.S. drones increased effectiveness of attacks.
Areas of Operations	The south and east	Global	Eastern Afghanistan	Eastern and northeastern Afghanistan	The Pashtun belt in Pakistan
Bin Laden Connection	Strong working relationship between Mullah Omar and bin Laden. Taliban provided sanctuary for Osama bin Laden		Relationship with Osama bin Laden	No known connection	Never a strong connection. Maybe no significant connection by 2012

with Pakistan, largely because of the pro-Moscow stance of India. The relationship was not without its difficulties, particularly when U.S. intelligence discovered, in 1979, that Pakistan was secretly building a uranium enrichment facility to offset India's nuclear capabilities.[71] Another concern was Pakistani dictator Gen. Mohammed Zia-ul-Haq's embrace of Islamist fundamentalist organizations, particularly Jamaat-e-Islami.

Despite these and other concerns, Pakistan became more attractive when the Soviets invaded Afghanistan in 1979. First President Carter and then President Reagan flooded the country with military and economic aid. The United States began funding the mujahedeen. Some of the more southern based-fighters would become Taliban.[72]

The main conduit for funding, logistical support, and some military training for mujahedeen became the ISI, which has powerful, sometimes autonomous, decision-making abilities. Gen. Hamid Gul (see Profile 8.3), who found Americans useful but who still loathed the United States and its culture, ran the ISI as a barony. He became and remains very popular in Afghanistan. Gul channeled foreign monies to seven warlords who made war on the Soviets. Gul favored Gulbuddin Hekmatyar, but was comfortable with other fighters, who would later become Taliban.

The often-garrulous Gul saw Pakistan as beset by Muslim-hating states intent on destroying his country and his religion. Benazir Bhutto, who became prime minister in 1988, cashiered Gul for his political indiscretions and for threatening her rule.

Profile 8.3: Hamid Gul and Imran Khan and Their Worlds

I am an Islamist. Islam is the final destiny of mankind. Islam is moderate and progressive. Islam is everything man needs. It is not necessary to become a Muslim but it is necessary to adopt the principles of Islam.[73]
—Hamid Gul to an Indian reporter, 2004

The world of retired Lt. Gen. Hamid Gul has many enemies and the United States is, off and on, one of them. By his own accounts, he determined that the United States was an enemy of Pakistan after the United States imposed sanctions, which were never effective, to prevent Islamabad from developing a nuclear arsenal.[74] He became particularly resentful when, in his analysis, the Mossad and U.S. Zionists conspired to slam airliners in the Pentagon and Twin Towers and blame it on Muslims.[75] Gul also believes that the United States blew up the plane in which Pakistani Gen. Mohammad Zia-ul-Haq was killed in 1988.[76]

Gul sees India as an enemy. He does not like Jews because he thinks they tend to conspire, particularly with Hindus, around the world to deny water, oil, and gas from Muslims.[77] "According to the clash of civilizations theory, the Jewish and Western civilizations would clash with the Muslims and Chinese."[78] As for Afghanistan, Gul emphatically sees the Western presence there as, in his words, "wrong." He stressed that the Afghans were "determined to drive out foreign occupation forces from their country . . . and meet the same fate as the Soviets."[79]

If Hamid Gul is largely a figure of the past, Imran Khan is an ascendant and charismatic politician, who will likely play a very prominent role in Pakistan's future. A retired world-class cricketer and graduate of Oxford University, the telegenic Khan describes himself as being "reborn" into Islam. He embraced Islam after the controversy of the Salman Rushdie affair.[80]

His international celebrity status, particularly in the Islamic world, and his philanthropic efforts gave him political influence after he retired from cricket, and he founded his own political party, the Pakistan Tehreek-e-Insaf (Movement for Justice).[81] Initially, the party concentrated on reducing corruption and increasing government's responsiveness. His miasma of anti-Americanism and nationalistic jingoism increased his party's popularity with the young and the religious.

He is sympathetic to the Afghan Taliban, and his position in the Pakistani Taliban is ambiguous. Afghan leaders have been very critical of his rhetorical support of the Taliban in general.[82] They allege that Khan is receiving financial support from the Taliban and that his statements have been inflammatory and subversive.[83]

Khan's affection for the Taliban is unrequited. Ironically, many Taliban dislike Khan intensely, largely because of his rakish past and his former marriage to an English woman.[84] He did, however, receive the support of an American left-wing activist, Medea Benjamin, the cofounder of Code Pink, and they held anti-U.S. rallies in Islamabad in October 2012.[85]

The ISI and the Taliban

The ISI also established contacts with bin Laden and al Qaeda leaders. A main beneficiary of American largesse was the Pakistan military and the ISI itself. In 1990, U.S. and Pakistani relations soured when President George H. W. Bush cut off military aid to Pakistan in response to Islamabad's nuclear ambitions.[86]

But relations recovered as Pakistan became an important staging ground for attacking the Taliban. As before, billions of dollars came flooding into Pakistan. Pervez Musharaf, who served as president from 1999 through 2008, diverted billions for his personal use and for his pet projects.[87]

But in November 2001, Musharaf spoke adamantly of his and his country's solidarity with the United States. But he placed Pakistan in the ranks of the Coalition and demanded economic assistance in return.[88] He got it. Musharaf denied that Pakistan created, supported, armed, or encouraged the Taliban. He dismissed the possibility of bin Laden or the Taliban placing their hands on Pakistan's nuclear weapons. He added that Pakistan's opposition to supporting the United States was "dying out," in mid-November 2001.[89]

The ISI's relationship is strong with the Taliban for several reasons. There is a common ethnicity. Many Pakistanis, nearly 12 percent of a 180 million population, are Pashtun. Vast literature has been written about the sweeping Pashtun nationalism that overarches the porous and contested borders. Pashtunwali requires that each tribesman aid each other and close ranks against a common enemy. The common enemy of some Afghan and Pakistani Pashtuns is the Coalition.

There is also a shared consuming hatred for the United States. Many Pakistani intellectuals, clerics, journalists, local politicians, and retired ISI officers loathe the United States. There is a constant screed against American hegemony, human rights abuses against Pakistanis, and American cultural degradation corrupting Pakistani youth. Above all, Islamic clerics and leaders of civil society fulminate against an American-led war against Islam. For over 30 years, Gulf States have funded Pakistani madrassas, which inculcate boys in the most narrow, puritanical, misogynistic, and religiously chauvinistic strains of Wahhabi-oriented Islam, as was discussed in earlier chapters.

Many Pakistanis believe that the United States works in concert with India and that Afghan security personnel partner with Indians to undermine Pakistani interests. Pakistani leaders can ill afford to develop the image of being controlled by Washington. They need to appear tough toward the United States.

Profile 8.4: Malala Yousafzai: Pakistan's Anne Frank

Malala Yousafzai was named after a Pashtun warrior poet of the nineteenth century.[90] Malala was born in 1997, and despite her youth, inspired many Pakistani children through her blog-diary entries. Her defiance and conviction that the world's children share a common humanity place her online diary in the canon of international children's literature. For some, she became Pakistan's Anne Frank. For this young girl's stirring diary, Malala was a finalist in the International Peace Prize, which is awarded to the child who makes a significant contribution to peace.

She became prolific by age 11, when she started writing about her sad life under the Pakistani Taliban, who prevented girls from attending school and burned boys' schools suspected of teaching girls.[91] She recorded the short life and early death of the vivacious Shabana, whom the Taliban murdered for her dancing. Her schoolmates described Malala as usually the top in her class. She wrote of her reoccurring nightmares of war and helicopters and guns and Taliban in the sylvan setting of the Swat Valley.[92] Like other Pakistani children, she would hide her books under her bed in case the Taliban searched her house. She begged other children to continue to study no matter the circumstances or consequences. Parts of the Swat Valley were almost completely under control of the Taliban. As one resident of the Swat town of Mingora said, "On the streets you only see Taliban and stray dogs."[93]

At age 13, Malala mocked Swat's regional emotional Taliban leader Mullah Fazlullah, nicknamed the "radio mullah," who "cried" for a long time on his FM radio channel.[94] Here and elsewhere in her blog, the adolescent girl ribbed the mullah about his lack of manliness.

She won Pakistan's National Peace Prize in November 2011 for her championing of girls' education.[95] The $5,800 prize is a sizable sum in Pakistan.[96] In January 2012 Malala, using her prestige as a recognized international peace advocate, announced that she would form her own political party.[97] The party would focus on children's issues. Her prestige was such that in, February 2012, the Sindh Education Ministry named a school after her.[98]

On October 9, 2012, Taliban gunmen fired at her in a bus, as she was going to school. The weepy Mullah Fazlullah had ordered her killed. But Malala did not die, despite being struck with two bullets. Unlike Anne, the Jewish-Dutch diarist to whom she is so lovingly linked, Nobel-nominated Malala lives and today receives the acclaim of the world.

Nukes for the Taliban?

Though in many ways a failed and nonunitary state, Pakistan has a thriving nuclear weapons program. Today Pakistan probably has over 100 nuclear devices, according to many open-source accounts.[99] In May 2011, Pakistan announced that it tested mobile missiles with miniaturized nuclear warheads.[100] The country's weapons production is robust and growing. Eric Edelman, undersecretary of defense in the George W. Bush administration, said in 2011, "You're talking about Pakistan even potentially passing France at some point. That's extraordinary."[101]

The Taliban's promise not to attack Pakistan's nuclear weapons has not been reassuring for U.S. decision makers. Taliban leaders pledged to Pakistan that it would not try to capture its nuclear weapons or sabotage it facilities. But the Taliban spokesman lamented that "isn't it a shame for us to have the Islamic bomb, and even then we are bowing down to the pressures of America."[102]

The Al Qaeda Connection and ISI

Pakistan's relationship with al Qaeda was, and to some extent remains, ambiguous. Pakistan has provided soldiers and some intelligence to fight the Taliban, particularly the Pakistani TTP. It has lost soldiers in battle and has handed over key al Qaeda operatives, the most notorious of whom is Khalid Sheikh Mohammed.[103]

However, it is not likely that the ISI could have been ignorant of Osama bin Laden's villa in Abbottabad, the military city where he was killed by U.S. forces who acted without the permission of Pakistani leaders.[104] Today, Abbottabad is a headquarters of a Pakistani Army division and home to many retired Pakistani officers.[105] In diplomatic language, Defense Secretary Robert Gates guardedly surmised that "someone" in Pakistan must have known that bin Laden was living in Abbotabad.[106] In the same week, U.S. Adm. Michael Mullen, chairman of the Joint Chiefs of Staff, accused the ISI of maintaining ties with Haqqani network in North Waziristan and allowing Taliban operatives to cross into Afghanistan and kill Coalition Forces.[107]

After swearing repeatedly that bin Laden was not on Pakistani soil, leaders in Islamabad were at pains trying to explain his hiding in plain sight. Quickly, Pakistan expressed surprise that bin Laden was being feted near a major military base and outrage that the U.S. force would violate Pakistani territory.[108]

The association of the ISI's external branch S Wing with the Taliban became the subject of front-page political commentary and congressional inquiry after the killing of bin Laden. Congressman Mike Rogers, chairman of the House Permanent Select Committee on Intelligence, was convinced that the S Wing "knew and looked the other way" regarding bin Laden's maneuvering in Pakistan. Saif al-Adel, the Egyptian whose military guidance to Islamic insurgents was discussed earlier, also may have had a connection to the ISI, particularly when he was an interim leader of al Qaeda.[109]

The ISI has more autonomous decision making than its Western intelligence counterparts, such as the CIA. It leaders are military, not civilian. The military influence is profound because general officers have ruled Pakistan for nearly half of its existence and the army has dominated national life in the country.[110] The ISI has also been linked to large-scale narcotics trafficking.[111]

IRAN

There is, however, clear evidence of Iranian activity—in some cases providing weaponry and training to the Taliban—that is inappropriate.[112]
                                                                              —Gen. Stanley McChrystal

Iran's leadership was never comfortable with the Taliban. During the Taliban's rise to power, Iran was wary for several reasons. The Taliban were Sunni and the Iranian leadership was Shiite, but this was not the basis of their mutual unease. The religious antagonism was aggravated by personal vendettas. Taliban troops murdered the Iranian consular staff and a large number of Afghan Shiites when they captured the northern city of Mazar-i-Sharif in 1998. Hashemi Rafsanjani, Iran's former president, promised revenge.[113] The hard-line daily newspaper *Qods* demanded that the Taliban must be "taught a lesson" because many of the victims were Hazara, who are fellow Shia.[114] The Iranian army was mobilized and deployed to the Afghan border. An invasion was averted only after the Taliban apologized for the killing.[115]

Iran has provided asylum to many of the Taliban's military opponents, and it provided weapons to the anti-Taliban Northern Alliance, if less plentiful after the conquest of Kabul. Ayatollah Khomeini, the founder of the Islamic Republic of Iran, built a security and intelligence apparatus called the Islamic Revolutionary Guard Corps (IRGC). The Quds Force, sometimes spelled Qods Force, of the IRGC has worked with many terrorist groups and murdered many Iranian dissidents and exiles around the world.[116] In December 2010, ISAF officials confirmed that they captured an IGRC[117] operative who was coordinating with the Taliban and supplying it with weapons.

In 2007, Undersecretary of State Nicholas Burns acknowledged that "Iran is now even transferring arms to the Taliban in Afghanistan." U.S. Gen. Daniel McNeill said the Iran had a role in improving the fighting capabilities of the Taliban. In April 2010, Gen. Stanley McChrystal confirmed that Iran was supplying the Taliban.[118] Tehran's support to the Taliban is consistent with its strategy of supporting many insurgent factions to keep its influence strong.[119]

There are no indications that the flow of weapons from Iran has been curtailed. According to Western sources, the Taliban were allowed to open a liaison office in the Iranian city of Zahedan in August 2012. This may be used to procure more sophisticated weapons. Further, the British Foreign Office complained to Tehran after British SAS soldiers seized a convoy carrying Iranian-produced, 122 mm rockets to be given to the Taliban.[120] In August 2012, an analyst from Jane's defense consulting called the new weapons systems a possible "game changer."[121] The Organization of Islamic Cooperation praised Iran's role in housing and proving for Afghanistan's population in its west.[122]

CHAPTER SUMMARY

In Pakistan, there are four main insurgent groups, the Afghanistan Taliban, the Pakistan Taliban, the Haqqani network, and the smallest of the groups, the Hizb-i-Islami. Two of the groups, the Afghan Taliban and the Haqqani network, have pledged fidelity to Mullah Omar. The TTP has more independence and has a different target set, which generally consists of Pakistani leaders, military, and security and intelligence personnel. Gulbuddin Hekmatyar is particularly venomous and reactionary and has enjoyed killing people for years.

The Taliban have received and continue to receive munitions, components, training, provisions, weapons, funding, shelter, and encouragement from foreign sources. Al Qaeda's aid was limited and transitory. However, two of Afghanistan's neighbors, despite assertions to the contrary, continue to provide substantial aid. Pakistan has a mixed record. As discussed in earlier chapters, the Pakistani military has arrested and killed leading Taliban operatives. But its security service, the ISI, has aided the Taliban from its creation. The ISI's external S Wing is particularly complicit in provisioning and arming the Taliban.

Iran was never comfortable with the Taliban. But because the Taliban are at war with the United States, they are seen in a more positive, if strategic, light. While not the friends of the Iranians, the Taliban are enemies of Teheran's main enemy, which is the United States.

9

‑‑‑‑

The Counterinsurgency
in Afghanistan

Previous chapters concentrated on the Taliban. The chapters pertained to their strategy, tactics, capabilities, doctrine, politics, and ambitions. This chapter moves from how and why the Taliban fight to the counterinsurgency. This chapter concentrates on how the Coalition battles the Taliban.

In April 2003, the *Baltimore Sun* ran a story with the headline "Remember Afghanistan? Anybody?"[1] Cynthia Tucker of the *Atlanta Journal Constitution* remarked, "Afghanistan is already a distant memory for the news media, for most ordinary Americans and even for foreign-policy hands in the Bush administration."[2] U.S. public attention had shifted to another war—in Iraq. At the same time, Dan Rather opened a piece with the phrase, "in the all-but-forgotten war in Afghanistan."[3] But the Afghans had not forgotten about their war, and it was not going well for government forces.

A FROST ON THE AFGHAN SPRING

The Taliban became a serious threat to the elected Afghan government by 2003–4. They did not melt away, as some Western observers predicted; they regrouped in force. The march toward Western democratic norms did not progress fast or smoothly. In the Afghan tradition, leaders fought among themselves. Some of the disputes were local and niggling, but others challenged the credibility of the post-Taliban regime.

Cultural strains began to pull at the fabric of Afghan society, and this tension has been exploited by the Taliban. The new freedoms and social license of 2002 and 2003 were never fully reconciled by all Afghans. For example, on Tolo television's *Afghan Star*, spun from *American Idol* with an Afghan flavor, a spunky 21-year-old singer named Setara let her headscarf slip while wearing Bollywood clothing and performing modern dance. She received death threats.[4] Even Afghanistan's most cosmopolitan city was held captive to Pashtun puritanism and Taliban threats.

Expectations of better lives were often not met. The country was wealthier, but not all Afghans enjoyed the new bounty. There was vast corruption and concentrated wealth in the hands of warlords and their cronies. According to a 2009 UN report, Afghans paid $2.5 billion in bribes, which was 25 percent of the gross domestic product.[5]

ILL-STARRED GENERALS

The performances of American generals in Afghanistan were mixed. Gen. David McKiernan, June 2008 to June 2009, was asked to resign a year earlier than expected because Defense Secretary Robert Gates wanted less conventional and more tailored counterinsurgency strategy.[6] He was replaced by Gen. Stanley A. McChrystal, who served from June 2009 to June 2010, and was more oriented toward special operations and counterinsurgency. But he was forced to resign over mocking comments to *Rolling Stone Magazine*.

Gen. David Petraeus, who served from July 2010 to July 2011, completed McChrystal's tour, launched a surge of forces, and retired to become director of the CIA.[7] Gen. John Allen, serving from July 2011 to early 2013, was to oversee the withdrawal of U.S. forces from Afghanistan. But like his predecessor, he was involved in a scandal with a woman. His career prospects were stymied.[8] But the shift from large-war fighting to counterinsurgency tactics was established.

Profile 9.1: "Intraspecies Predator": Calvin Gibbs and His Afghan Trophies

If some people are natural-born killers, U.S. Army S.Sgt. Calvin Gibbs would probably fit the profile. Physically imposing at six feet four, the Montana-born-and-raised soldier was convicted of leading a thrill-kill team of five U.S. soldiers in Kandahar, Afghanistan.[9] His victims were not Taliban; they were innocent civilians. Gibbs was the ringleader and relished his role. His commanding persona led other soldiers to become eager participants in assassination games. Gibbs collected body parts of his victims, such as skulls and fingers, with which he hoped to make a necklace. And he pulled teeth from corpses for unspecified purposes, perhaps more human jewelry.

He had likely been a prolific killer in Iraq too. He decorated his left shin with six tattooed skulls—three red skulls for his Iraqi quarry and three blue skulls for those he "waxed" in Afghanistan.[10] "Waxing" was a term he used frequently to refer to murdering innocent Afghans.[11]

His tour in Afghanistan had an inauspicious beginning in 2009, when he replaced a staff sergeant whose legs were blow off by a Taliban's roadside bomb. After he bonded with his new platoon, he and at least four other soldiers from the 5th Stryker Combat Brigade of the 2nd Infantry Division began to kill unarmed Afghans and stage the scenes to make them appear that the dead were Taliban. With young Afghan locals, he bartered pornography for ever-abundant AK-47s.[12] He obtained first-rate hashish from the platoon's interpreters—Yama, Crazy Kid, and Mad Max.[13]

In the first of the three thrill kills, Gibbs did not pull the trigger. He encouraged another soldier, who would turn against him in court, to toss a grenade at an arbitrarily selected Afghan target and then fire on him after the explosion. Gibbs, in a second killing, fired two rounds into a man and then staged an AK-47 at the scene. In a third killing, Gibbs threw a grenade at an Afghan and then planted a Russian-made grenade next to the corpse. In none of the three cases was there evidence that the victims were Taliban. They were likely simple villagers randomly selected for death by a man they had never met and had no reason to distrust.

The U.S. Army tried to understand how this could happen. If court testimony is accurate, Gibbs's behavior conforms to some defining traits of those suffering antisocial personality disorder (ASPD), which is sometimes called psychopathy.[14] Unlike psychosis, psychopathy is not insanity. Oxford's Kevin Dutton explains that it is a distinct cluster of traits, such as callousness, pathological lying, superficial charm, ruthlessness, a need to control and manipulate, impulsiveness, irresponsibility, and, often, criminal behavior. Levels of intelligence vary among psychopaths.[15] When blended with sadistic tendencies, the sum of these traits can produce evil.

A psychopath is an "intraspecies predator," according to a leading experimental psychologist, Robert Hare, in the field of ASPD. At trial, counsel did not claim that Gibbs was insane. There is no evidence that Gibbs suffered from visual or auditory hallucinations or was controlled by an irresistible impulse forcing him to kill. But neither is there evidence that he has a conscience. He killed men and boys, as well as elk and deer, for sport.

Some people who knew Gibbs as a youngster did not sense a dark soul or cold empathy. An elementary school employee reflected, "He was always well mannered and always a nice boy and very polite and kind, and I always remember him for that and always liked him, too."[16] A woman remembered him from high school, "He would come into the lunch room and tell us girls how nice we looked, and he was never a problem."[17]

Gibbs was sentenced to life in prison but is eligible for parole in less than 10 years.[18] His wife divorced him, and it is not likely that many people will clamor for his early release. Earlier, his wife told investigators that she noticed the skulls on his leg but did not know their significance and never asked about their meaning. This sordid slaughter became a public relations disaster for ISAF and a propaganda gift for the Taliban.

An army investigation cited a "very lax environment" in the 5th Stryker Brigade in Afghanistan that should have "raised a red flag."[19] As with psychopaths, Gibbs took no responsibility for the murders. Though he denied any illegal killings, Gibbs readily acknowledged hording teeth and other body parts as Afghan war trophies. And why not? The hunter from Montana explained, "It's like keeping the antlers off of a deer you'd shoot."[20]

COUNTERINSURGENCY

The theoretical base for fighting insurgencies is the *U.S. Army/Marine Corps Counterinsurgency Field Manual.*[21] Insurgents tap into social grievances against an existing regime. Ethnicity, tribal affiliation, religion, poverty, land occupation, and uneven income distribution are all issues that insurgents exploit to win recruits and to keep cadre. Countering the insurgency requires a mastery of all social, political, and military issues that empower the insurgents.

The United States has vast experience fighting small wars. The twentieth century—the American Century—began with a protracted, bitter, and ultimately highly divisive small war in the Philippines. Add to this the repeated interventions in Central America, most famously against Poncho Villa, and the list of "irregular wars" becomes long before the United States' accession to superpower status.[22]

The war in the Philippines has significance for the war on the Taliban. The counterinsurgency against the Muslims in Moro areas was a long, brutal, but eventually successful struggle, led by Brig. Gen. John Pershing.[23] If there is a father of U.S. counterinsurgency, it would certainly be Pershing, who pioneered many of the tactics used in Afghanistan today. He used indigenous populations in military and nonmilitary roles to defeat the insurgents.[24] Pershing stressed to his soldiers the importance of understanding local habits, customs, and religious practices. He worked with locals to foster a public administration that would build stakeholders and undercut the credibility of the insurgent Moros.[25] The focus on human development, as well as the effective and innovative military tactics, became the bedrock of success there, and many of the lessons are applied in Afghanistan today.[26]

The First World War brought the United States to major power status. In that war, the most noteworthy, certainly most illustrious, insurgency and counterinsurgency theoretician was T. E. Lawrence—Lawrence of Arabia. He stressed the necessity of understanding the insurgents' world and mind.[27] His lessons were provided in *Seven Pillars of Wisdom* and *Revolt in the Desert*, and they are still studied in U.S. Army command and staff and war colleges today. They are used to fight the Taliban.

The *Tentative Manual for Landing Operations*, published in 1934, was a standard text for small wars, as was the *U.S. Marine Corps, Small Wars Manual* of 1940, through World War II.[28] The *Small Wars Manual* was the best source for the lessons of the Corps' interventions in Central America, sometimes referred to as Banana Wars.[29] By the late 1950s and early 1960s, U.S. war planners began to look to British and French counterinsurgency doctrines.

The U.S. Army studied the British mid-century counterinsurgency in Malaya, which was very successful and which emphasized a human development strategy, as well as the unsuccessful French counterinsurgency operations in French Indo-China and Algeria, which used force and the threat of force more frequently and, ultimately, with less success. The lessons from all insurgencies were distilled and codified in U.S. professional journals and written into doctrine.[30]

This was a "golden age" of counterinsurgency literature. Several outstanding counterinsurgency theoreticians were the British officer and diplomat Sir Robert Thompson; French officer Lt. Col. David Galula,[31] called the "Clausewitz of counterinsurgency;"[32] and the American former advertising executive-turned-counterinsurgency theorist Edward Landsdale. The writings and observations of these men would serve as pillars for revisions to the U.S. counterinsurgency doctrine.[33]

The Vietnam Counterinsurgency and Human Development

Many lessons in today's counterinsurgency doctrine were learned in Vietnam. An early masterwork of the Vietnam era was Robert Taber's *War of the Flea: The Classic Study of Guerrilla Warfare*, in which he stressed the value of public relations in counterinsurgency.[34] Insurgents calculate that Western states fatigue quickly of war, particularly if the public cannot see a clear purpose for continuing military operations.[35] Taber wrote extensively about the success insurgents had when they focused on breaking the will of intervening foreign states through violence and effective propaganda. These are well-used weapons in the Taliban's arsenal today.

The most important program was the Civil Operations and Rural Development System (CORDS). Many historians agree that by 1972 it was successful. Leveraging tactics from the British in Malaya, CORDS focused on human development fundamentals, health, security, and economic fundamentals. Unfortunately, the successes of CORDS were not sufficiently written into doctrine to provide lessons for students at the academies, command and staff colleges, or war colleges.[36] But the lessons were not lost entirely.

Table 9.1 compares the legacy traits and the application to Afghanistan of counterinsurgencies in the Philippines, the Golden Age of Counterinsurgency, and Vietnam.

A New Doctrine for a New Century

After September 2001, U.S. war planners understood the need to develop a new doctrine for fighting insurgencies. Not all Third World armies had been impressed with U.S. counterinsurgency efforts in Vietnam, as evidenced by an inscription over the incinerator at the Royal Thai Army Headquarters. It reads, "Here on 26 July 1972 the Royal Thai Army burned all its American textbooks. From this dates our victory over the communists."[37]

Over 30 year later, in the early years of the twenty-first century, an eclectic band of scholars, soldiers, journalists—"an odd fraternity of experts"[38]— produced a new counterinsurgency manual, which was the *U.S. Army and Marine Corps Counterinsurgency Field Manual*, No. 3-24. In February 2006, then-Lt. Gen. David Petraeus, commanding general of the U.S. Army Combined Arms Center, directed his team to revise and reinvigorate counterinsurgency doctrine.[39] The team drew lessons from the previous insurgencies to explore new military tactics and technologies, particularly advances in surveillance and reconnaissance.[40] It fused recent approaches to human development, such as civil engineering, public health, wireless communications, and agriculture, to defeat insurgencies.[41] Many of these approaches included in 3-24 were drawn extensively by the U.S. Army in Afghanistan 2001 through 2006, as well as from the experiences in Iraq.[42]

The ratio of military-to-developmental efforts in the new counterinsurgency theory varied according to circumstance, location, and enemy strength. But the *Counterinsurgency Field Manual* set the standard of a ratio of 80 percent developmental to 20 percent lethal.[43] Because of the heavy emphasis on nonlethal measures, counterinsurgency efforts required a wide variety of skills well beyond those traditionally associated with soldiering. U.S. soldiers and Marines still needed to destroy the insurgents' bases of

Table 9.1 Legacy Traits of Three Epochs of Counterinsurgency and Their Application to Afghanistan

	Philippines	The Golden Age of Counterinsurgency	Vietnam
Legacy Traits	Pershing saw need to develop respectful relations with Muslim Filipinos and understand their culture and ceremonies; developed public administration. Pershing expanded and professionalized constabulary force and basic public administration. Survived bad publicity; highly publicized torture by the United States, particularly water-boarding; brought bad press and congressional investigations	In Malaya, the British determined that building and securing settlements and isolating the insurgent contagion is more effective than focusing almost exclusively on search-and-destroy missions. Greater emphasis on education, training, and health than ever before. This was in striking contrast to the Japanese and German counterinsurgency tactics of mass murder during World War II, which alienated those who might have been their allies. The French win the War of Algiers, but lose the war in Algeria. Golden Age writers understood the importance of public relations while prosecuting distant, complicated wars	CORDS fused development and military counterinsurgency efforts as never before, hoping to achieve unity of command. Strategic hamlets were developed on a large, systematic scale. All relevant sectors of human development were stressed in isolating the insurgents—the National Liberation Front—from the population. The success of CORDS would be replicated in Iraq and Afghanistan
Application to Afghanistan	Human development stressed over kinetic operations. Human Terrain Teams are an example of United States/ISAF attempts to understand Afghan culture. Guarding against brutality of Afghans and of Taliban when in custody. Focus on respecting Muslim beliefs and norms	Understanding the need to have long-term, sustainable development across many sectors. Reduce level of collateral killings and damage. When accidents occur, move quickly to make restitution. Keep the U.S. national will strong. Without it, military efforts will eventually fail	The strategic hamlets concept, from Vietnam and from the Golden Age, separated the population from the insurgents. The PRTs were heavily involved

support, but also needed to gain credibility and the cooperation of the populace in Afghanistan and elsewhere.[44]

The authors of the *Counterinsurgency Field Manual* found that successful practices often required engaging with the population; learning their habits, customs, and quirks; protecting and building infrastructure; tailoring information operations; engaging local politicians; and denying the insurgents sanctuary.[45] The *Counterinsurgency Field Manual* is very clear on the primacy of human development in defusing insurgencies. Counterinsurgency operators became, in effect, custodians of the populace, as long as an insurgency thrived. Killing was de-emphasized, as the doctrine underscored the nonlethal theories of T. E. Lawrence, Galula, and Thompson and the Marine Corps manual.[46]

Profile 9.2: Michael Murphy: "Happy Birthday, Baby"

The Medal of Honor is awarded to a member of the Armed Services, who distinguishes oneself conspicuously by gallantry at the risk of life above and beyond the call of duty while engaged in an action against any enemy of the United States.[47]

Lt. Michael Murphy was a Navy SEAL who won the first Medal of Honor awarded in the Afghan counterinsurgency.[48] A varsity athlete, amateur military historian, and political science major at Penn State University, he joined the navy, in his father's footsteps. His dad served in Vietnam.

He had already won the Purple Heart and the Silver Star for bravery in Afghanistan when he was tracking Taliban and al Qaeda as part of a four-man SEAL team in June 2005. The New Yorker was hunting the enemy in the Hindu Kush. When his position was betrayed, his team took fire. Leaving his secure position, he exposed himself to direct fire to signal his coordinates. While relaying his position, he was shot. He picked up his satellite phone and signed off with, "Roger that, sir. Thank you."[49] He was shot again and killed. Until his death, only 3,462 soldiers, sailors, Marines, or airmen had been awarded the Medal of Honor.[50]

His friends remember "Mikey" or "Murph" as a tough, clever, "wise-cracking" warrior. He was also a patriot.[51] In combat, the Long Island native carried a patch from the New York City Fire Department's Engine Company 53 and Ladder Company 43 and may have had it when he was killed.[52] His navy did not forget him. Maureen Murphy christened the billion-dollar navy destroyer the USS *Michael Murphy* in Bath, Maine, in May 2011. As she cracked the bottle of Champagne against the bow of her son's namesake, his mom whispered, with a soft smile and tender tone, "Happy birthday, baby." It would have been Michael's 35th.[53]

RULES FOR THE AFGHAN COUNTERINSURGENCY

Gradually, a broad set of goals emerged during the Afghan insurgency to form doctrine. They developed from doctrinal literature and evolved since the counterinsurgency began in 2002.[54]

The first rule is to sustain area ownership throughout Afghanistan. Observers of the Vietnam insurgency remarked that the U.S. troops held villages during the day, but the Viet Cong controlled them during the night. Owning territory for 12 hours of 24 is insufficient for counterinsurgency success. Rather, government forces must, in the words of Lt. Gen. Barno, head of Combined Forces Command-Afghanistan, 2003–5, "sustain area ownership" day and night. In Afghanistan, this means that military units are assigned specific battle space for extended periods. This is in contrast to "raid strategy," in which government forces were not assigned long-term control. Units operated in their own distinct territory for up to 12 months.[55]

If an area in Afghanistan is effectively controlled by government forces, it is, by definition, denied to the insurgents. As a consequence, human development can take root. This is the theory behind British Gen. David Richards's "ink spot" theory, which is based on the works of Golden Age writer Sir Robert Thompson. The metaphor refers to the slow, steady drops of ink on a white page of paper. As small drops of ink hit the page, they expand centrifugally. With enough ink drops, even if the rate of dropping is slow, the entire page will become black given enough time.[56] In Afghanistan, the growing of "ink spots" of calm and prosperity expanded, though many would be contested by the Taliban.[57]

Counterinsurgency doctrine offers a basic, three-part strategy. First, in areas of high insurgent activity, the Coalition, progovernment forces, and increasingly the ANA, engage, defeat, and clear the enemy. Second, government and Coalition forces secure and hold the area, allowing developmental specialists to begin the third stage, which is planning development projects with key economic and social value, such as bridges and roads or wells and clinics.[58]

This hands-on strategy for Afghanistan requires that Afghan and Coalition soldiers expose themselves to danger daily. Strategists remark that it is a paradox of counterinsurgency that the more "you protect your force, the less secure you are." It is vital that counterinsurgency operators mix and mingle with those whom they are required to protect. If Coalition Forces remain closeted in their compounds, they would lose the vital contact with people required to maintain credibility and friendly relations.[59]

Many Afghans, particularly those who lived in areas contiguous to Pakistan, vacillated between periods of optimism, pessimism, confusion, and fatigue, as they tried to gage the staying power of government forces in contested areas. This is common in countries in which there are extended periods of civil conflict. The longer and firmer government forces sustained the ownership of all of Afghanistan's provinces, the more these non-committed Afghans cooperated with them and actively worked against the Taliban.

Profile 9.3: Two American Women and Their Last Full Measure of Devotion

In the short amount of time that God gave her, she was able to touch thousands of people.
—A friend of the fallen Ashley White[60]

Given her cheerleader looks, winning personality and pedigreed education, Texas-born Paula Loyd could have chosen virtually any career.
—Pamela Constable[61]

In some ways they were different. One grew up in a small town in Ohio, ran track, and earned a degree in physical education at public university. The other was raised as a girl of privilege, who attended a prestigious boarding school and flourished in academically rigorous and socially challenging eastern universities. But both died young serving the U.S. Army on the Afghan battlefield.

Lt. Ashley White was raised in small-town America. Graduating from Kent State University in 2009, where she was a Chi Omega sister, she was commissioned into the North Carolina National Guard. She fell in love with Capt. Jason Stumpf and married him in the Catholic church she attended as a girl in Ohio.[62] She was deployed to Afghanistan to lead a cultural support team. She interviewed women and children about social conditions to see how they could be improved, which was a labor of love for her.

Even in the man's world of the Army Rangers she was "accepted, loved, admired and respected," said Col. Mark O'Donnell, deputy commander of the 75th Ranger Regiment.[63] In October 2011, she was traveling with fellow soldiers in Kandahar, the Taliban's homeland. She and the Rangers were killed when a roadside bomb blew up their vehicle. She became of 135th woman killed in Afghanistan and Iraq wars.

People who knew her well were not surprised that she would volunteer for a dangerous assignment, particularly if she could help girls and women. A Chi Omega sorority sister at Kent State said, "She never would turn down a challenge. She was always willing to try her hardest to do something that might be difficult or others might not be willing to do." She was 14 years old when the war in Afghanistan began, and she was 24 when her fight in that war ended. She had been married for just five months. At her funeral the bagpiper played, "Going Home." The services were held in the same church in which she was married and where she had prayed and took communion years earlier, as a small-town, Catholic girl in Ohio.[64]

Paula Loyd

By all recorded accounts, she was a first-rate field-operating social scientist. She also worked as an army grease monkey. A Texan, Paula Loyd was raised in affluence, attending the exclusive Choate Rosemary Hall, Wellesley College, and Georgetown University.[65] Like Ashley, Paula was athletic. In her Boston college days, she often rose early to row on the Charles River alongside Harvard and Radcliffe eights and fours and skulls. She was also an intellectual who read *Don Quixote* in Spanish and enjoyed herself with the Ivy set.[66] Smart, blond, and attractive, she was part of their social circle and pedigree.

A patriot, she enlisted in the army as a private and became a heavy-wheel-vehicle mechanic.[67] After her service, she became part of the Human Terrain System (HTS), as an anthropologist. In her spare time, she fed and cared for stray dogs. But while serving in Taliban-infested areas, she forgot to put on her headscarf.[68] A local man doused her with gasoline and lit her on fire. In turn, the assailant was shot by a man charged with protecting Paula.[69] The Taliban would boast of burning Ms. Lloyd to death.

A senior officer who served with her wrote on her memorial website, "She had a passion for the people of Afghanistan, and it was all we could do to keep up with her. She died doing the work of bringing peace to a people she loved and respected."[70]

In Texas, where she was born, she died from her burns, as those who loved and respected her stood at her death watch.[71] In her last days, she requested that a foundation be established to provide for Afghan women who wanted to attend her alma mater, Wellesley.[72] This young woman of privilege stipulated that the recipients be poor Hazara women, the lowest rung on the Afghan social ladder.[73]

The second rule is to seize and hold the initiative in counterinsurgency efforts in Afghanistan. Writing more than 100 years ago, C. E. Callwell, the British military historian, in his classic text *Small Wars* offered a prescription for insurgencies of the twentieth century. Part of his remedy included keeping strong the initiative against the insurgents. "It cannot be insisted upon too strongly that in a small war the only possible attitude to assume is, speaking strategically, the offensive. The regular army must force its way into the enemy's country and seek him out."[74]

These words ring true in Afghanistan today. Retired Lt. Col. David Kilcullen, of the Australian Army, reiterates the continued need to keep the insurgents on the defensive. "Whatever else you do, keep the initiative."[75] General McChrystal commented in March 2010, "We must quickly reverse the momentum of the insurgency, and build the capacity of the Afghan army and police to provide for the security of their own country."[76] General Petraeus continued the focus on raids to keep pressure on mid- and lower-level Taliban to reintegrate with Afghan society.

Rule three is to constantly apply the pressure on the enemy, which requires shifting tactics. "If a tactic works this week, it will not work next week; if it works in this province, it will not work in the next."[77] Because today's counterinsurgency is heavily developmental, maintaining the initiative often means creating new infrastructure, building new wells, repairing schools and medical clinics, and other projects. As these are being built by progovernment forces, the Taliban try to destroy them.

Rule four is to engage and promote local Afghan efforts. As long as Coalition personnel perform basic military and developmental tasks, many Afghans will see themselves in a quasi-occupational status. Pershing learned in the Philippines, and subsequent military and developmental scholars argued vehemently, that locals must be directly engaged in building their

---

Profile 9.4: Tell That to the Marine!: Than Naing's American Odyssey

The Taliban are tough, but so are Marines. Than Naing could not speak English in September 2001. He worked hard and studied math and science at night, in New York, to become an engineer. But the recent Burmese immigrant loved the United States and wanted to join the Marines in response to the Islamist attacks. He flunked the English section of the test, but studied hard, took it again, and passed. He wanted to kill Taliban. After two tours in Iraq, one of which required hospitalization after being shot by a jihadist in Fallujah in 2005, he had the chance to do so. In Marjah City, Helmand Province, he had almost daily combat with the Taliban enemy.

On June 13, 2010, Naing was checking the perimeter security near Marjah City, when he was shot in the chest and abdomen, severing his spleen and other internal organs.[78] He survived and was sent back to Bethesda, Maryland, where he had recovered from his Iraqi wounds. "In my mind, I keep thinking about being a warrior. I think tactically; that's how I am. The Marine Corps is perfect for me. I'm not a paperwork kind of guy. I just want to get back into the fight."[79]

Profile 9.5: King David: Soldier-Scholar of Afghanistan

In the twenty-first century, few Americans seemed more suited to the profession of arms than New York-born Gen. David Petraeus. His assignments, intelligence, drive, and passion for counterinsurgency operations groomed him for command of ISAF forces in Afghanistan. A graduate of West Point, he married the superintendent's daughter and excelled at a series of challenging and prestigious assignments. Like Eisenhower, he was the top graduate of his U.S. Army Command and General Staff College. A Princeton PhD, he distinguished himself by the victory in combat he brought his troops and country and by his intellectual interest in low-intensity operations in an era of large-scale wars.[80]

The soldier-scholar commanded the 101st Airborne Division, the Screaming Eagles, in the 2003 invasion of Iraq, and he led a quick and decisive victory. This cemented his reputation as a fighter. But his imperious style earned him the nickname "King David,"[81] while others referred to him as the "godfather" of counterinsurgency.

Whichever the moniker, Petraeus continued to shine. His famous surges were decisive in two wars—Iraq and Afghanistan. Commanding Fort Leavenworth's Combined Arms Center, Petraeus rewrote the military's counterinsurgency manual. After Gen. Stanley McChrystal was cashiered, King David accepted a technical demotion to command ISAF where he put his new doctrine into action.[82] He said, "There's an old saying that 'all politics are local.' Well, so are all counterinsurgency operations."[83]

But his prestige and further aspirations collapsed with revelations of a now-famous, man-grabbing catfight between the general's tongue-wagging mistress and her socialite rival. Many civilians and soldiers were stunned and saddened by the moral failings of a man often considered to be the first truly great general of the twenty-first century. The general and his mistress/biographer, Paula Broadwell, were remarkably accomplished soldiers. But Broadwell's biography of Petraeus, as well as her sobriquet for her paramour, became comedic fodder for late-night TV hosts. While others called him King David or Godfather, she called him "Peaches."[84]

---

nations. Some initial indigenous efforts will fail and others will prove, at best, marginally successful. But developmental and military efforts that succeed will give locals the necessary self-confidence to develop their states and to combat their enemies. Lawrence said of his experience leading the Arab

Revolt against the Ottoman Turkish Empire: "Do not try and do too much with your own hands. Better the Arabs do it tolerably than you do it perfectly. It is their war, and you are to help them, not win it for them." There have been significant successes in building Afghanistan's military and paramilitary capabilities. The full strength of their autonomous capabilities will be tested when ISAF begin to withdraw in 2014.[85]

Rule five is ensuring that Coalition Forces are careful about whom they target and kill. What is the right amount of offensive force to use against insurgents? In current doctrine, the ratio is 80 percent nonmilitary to 20 percent military. The ratio varies depending on the environment and

---

Profile 9.6: Michael Vinay Bhatia: "Anthropologizing" the Military

The all-but-dissertation Michael Bhatia fought his own "green hell," of sorts. His was the ivy-green hellish politics of academia. After graduating magna cum laude from the progressive and tony Brown University, he crossed the Atlantic to earn his PhD at Oxford University. He was awarded a Marshall Scholarship, and the topic of his dissertation was "The Mujahedeen: A Study of Combatant Motives in Afghanistan." To do his field research and to help the U.S. Army better understand the Afghan mind, Bhatia worked on the army's HTS, as a social scientist.

The 31-year-old was soon nicknamed "the Nutty Professor."[86] He wore red argyle socks that peeked out of his combat boots. The soldiers ribbed him about his innocuous peculiarities during their 14-hour workdays, which were frequent.[87] Mike enjoyed being a prankster, but he contended with a two-front war. In Afghanistan, he risked his life traveling with the U.S. Army as an army civilian. But his service in the HTS jeopardized his career in academia. Many prominent anthropologists loathe the HTS, which they see as militarizing anthropology. In 2007, the American Anthropological Association declared that the HTSs were "problematic" and "unacceptable."[88] It could be a career killer.

How would this feud affect the employment prospects of this tenure-track hungry and most-promising Ivy League anthropologist? He would not live to find out. While conducting research in the field, on May 7, 2009, his vehicle was hit by a roadside bomb, killing him. A man who served with him wrote, "He was a scholar, a patriot, and a brother I never had. I lost part of my soul the day he died."[89]

strength of the enemy. But the ratio leans heavily toward the developmental end of the equation. At the outset of the Vietnam War, Col. John Paul Vann explained that "The best weapon for killing is a knife. The next best is a rifle. The worst is an airplane, and after that the worst is artillery. You have to know whom you are killing."[90]

Overwhelming force may be crucial in conventional battle tactics, but it has many hazards in counterinsurgency. In counterinsurgency, indiscriminate or area attacks are often counterproductive because civilian casualties anger and alienate villagers. This outrage is exploited by the insurgents to paint counterinsurgency forces as murderers, rather than defenders. Harsh security measures based on collective guilt principles project the image of a foreign occupation. The Soviets learned this in Afghanistan.

U.S. combat forces in Afghanistan are far more selective in their killing than were the Soviets. Nonetheless, mistakes in targeting that killed or maimed have harmed non-Taliban have poisoned relations with the populace. As an example, the U.S. unintentionally killed nearly 90 civilians in a strike that was launched based on false information in 2009. The unintentional deaths brought criticism from local and national Afghan leaders. Its outcry made headlines in local, national, and international newspapers.[91]

Profile 9.7: Staff Sergeant Robert Bales: "Doom's" Anger Management Problem

He was always a happy, happy guy, full of life. I really wouldn't expect it.
—Ms. Kassie Holland, a neighbor of S.Sgt. Robert Bales

Friends, mental health professionals, and family are still trying to make sense of the middle-aged, noncommissioned officer's butchery. Robert Bales enlisted in the U.S. Army a few months after the September 2001 attacks.[92] In November 2004, he deployed to Iraq and returned to that war zone 2006 for an extended 15-month tour. Bales went back again in August 2009, which gave him three combat tours in five years.[93] He served well and bravely, being injured twice and earning multiple awards.

High school buddies remember him as an "all-American boy" who played linebacker on his Cincinnati high school football team. As he grew, so did his strength. He could bench-press 300 pounds and was nicknamed was "Doom." People found out that it was dangerous to get on his bad side.[94]

Bales had some scraps with the law earlier. Between deployments in 2008, he grabbed a woman's hand and forced it to his genitals. Then he beat up her boyfriend when he tried to intervene. He threw him against a wall. As an adolescent he had a few misdemeanors, but that did not keep him out of the army.[95] There was also a scandal involving stock fraud.[96] Above all, he was a bad drunk and got in fights. Arrested for brawling in a casino in 2002, he passed a 20-hour anger management course to avoid being charged. Doom said he learned his lesson. Only drink in moderation, and no more throwing men against walls.

But Doom could not manage his anger in March 2012, during his fourth tour of duty, and killed 16 Afghans, most of whom were women and children.[97] He shot them dead with his service assault rifle and sidearm. The Ohio-raised, 38-year-old sniper wandered off a small outpost in Kandahar to murder Afghans. In a two-part operation, Bales went to one village and killed people, went back to his post to cool off, went to another village and killed people, and was apprehended when he tried to return to post after the second killing.[98]

The United States paid compensation to the families of his victims. Usually, families of Afghans killed in accidental deaths are paid $2,000 and the wounded receive $1,000. But payment in the Bales case was many times that—$50,000 for the killed and $11,000 for the wounded.[99]

Bales faced a total of 29 charges. Some of his shooting victims lived and are crippled. Others are psychological wrecks. His defense team contended that he was shell shocked or suffering from PTSD.[100] In the course of his four deployments, he had seen some of his friends killed and maimed. A family friend said, "That's not our Bobby. Something horrible, horrible had to happen to him."[101] But his wife, Karilyn "Kari" Bales, opined that Robert seemed perfectly sane to her before he deployed to Afghanistan.[102] His fellow soldiers thought he was first rate. Capt. Chris Alexander, who commanded Bales for 15 months, said, "He's one of the best guys I ever worked with. He's not some psychopath but an outstanding soldier who gave a lot for his country."[103]

Rule six is to stress effective training. Afghan ownership can be achieved only through extensive training measures. Responsibility for civil and military affairs must be transferred to Afghan operators because those who own the country must also own responsibility for its development and protection. Without effective training, host government forces will be reliant on ISAF indefinitely.

Rule seven is to create metrics for measuring counterinsurgency in Afghanistan. Accurate metrics for measuring the status of counterinsurgency efforts are difficult. Body counts, for example, have been a traditional metric. But they can be more confusing than helpful.[104] This is because it is often difficult to know how many enemy forces were present in a combat area before and often during engagements.[105] Body counts are also easily fabricated, as evidenced by some of the reporting in Vietnam (Table 9.2).

Table 9.2   Counterinsurgency General Principles and How They Apply to Afghanistan

	General Principles of Counterinsurgency	Principles as Goals in Afghanistan
Unity of Effort	Unity means harnessing all relevant operators and decision makers in counterinsurgency into a single policy-making tool. In practice, it means smoothing issues of potential conflict and territorial rivalry in counterinsurgency. Counterinsurgency operators work in harmony	National-level agencies and international donors work in concert with ISAF, UN Coalition, and NGO partners to forge one dominant, agreed-upon plan. On the provisional level, it means cooperation among all players on the PRTs. The commander of the PRT is the final decision maker
Sustain Area Ownership	Government forces control all the territory all the time. It is insufficient for government forces to control most of the country all of the time or all of the country, but only during the day. According to doctrine, the insurgents are engaged and defeated, the area is secured, and the area is developed, assuming it is rid of insurgents	Government forces would rid Afghanistan of Taliban, other insurgent forces, and drug traffickers. Areas in Pakistan, contiguous to Afghanistan, would also be free of these elements. The "ink spots" of government control would expand to cover the entire country
Seize and Hold the Initiative	Keep the momentum against the insurgents. Keep them off balance, and do not give them the time or the space to take the offensive. Make sure the insurgents are reacting to government's initiative and military attacks	In a counterinsurgency that is overwhelmingly nonkinetic, keep the developmental pressure at many places and at all times in Afghanistan

(continued)

Table 9.2   (Continued)

	General Principles of Counterinsurgency	Principles as Goals in Afghanistan
Engage and Promote Local Efforts	Donor nations providing the capital, physical and intellectual labor, and leadership are seen as occupying forces. Effective counterinsurgency requires a transfer of skills and responsibility to the host nation	Bring Afghans into the military and developmental mix. Convince them that they are stakeholders in their country and that their generation will increasingly take leadership responsibilities
Be Careful Whom You Kill	Counterinsurgency stresses nonkinetic activity. Killing of noncombatants angers and alienates the population	The Taliban make effective use of the propaganda value of accidental combat-related deaths. They portray mistakes in targeting as intentional murders in a larger war against Islam
Stress Effective Training	If indigenous military forces and the civil service are to become effective, they must be trained. This is the production of human capital, which is necessary for effective counterinsurgency	National, provincial, and local training scheme
Create Metrics for Counterinsurgency	Metrics in counterinsurgency have been fraught with problems and outright fraud in the past. Examples of this are the inflated body counts in Vietnam	Many of the metrics are related to the military capabilities of the ANA and the abilities of the ANP. There are many developmental metrics used to determine the overall success or failure of the counterinsurgency

THEIR WORLDS HAD CHANGED

The world had changed many times for the players in the Afghan drama since Taliban remnants were scattered into Pakistan in October and November 2001. Today, the Kabul Zoo hosts up to 10,000 visitors each day. There have been at least two international artistic tributes to Marjan, the one-eyed lion. In 2004, a Texas artist donated a 300-pound bronze sculpture of Marjan to a North Carolina zoo.[106] Also, the dramatist Kenny Hunter, sponsored by Glenfiddich Whisky distillery in Scotland, scripted a play entitled *The Lion of Kabul*, ensuring that Marjan will be long remembered and perhaps even toasted.[107]

The Taliban still hate music, but many Afghans love it. Today in Kabul, Afghan children and young adults study at the National Institute of Music, where they learn folk songs and play indigenous lutes. They learn Mozart and Bach as well. An aspiring 12-year-old violinist explained, "I was selling on the streets before, so I'm very happy I came here. I want to be a good student, to learn something here, to make something of my life."[108]

It has been many years since Taliban shot and whipped men and women in Kabul's soccer stadium. In mid-September 2013, Ghazi Stadium erupted in ebullience in celebration of Afghanistan's defeating India in the South Asian soccer championship. A conga line of dancing and singing Afghans snaked through Kabul's streets, as fans hugged the trophy-clutching victorious players. The Taliban would have disapproved.

In early October 2013, Afghan sports fans rejoiced again as their country qualified for its first Cricket World Cup. Afghanistan Finance Minister Mohammad Omar Zakhilwal, also a member of the national cricket board, delightedly said that "our people have seen years and years of sadness and now we are among the best 12 cricketing nations in the world."[109]

And what became of those profiled in early chapters? In the 11 years following her abduction by the Taliban, Yvonne Ridley has held fast to her Islamic zeal, though she temporarily left journalism. Over a decade after her abduction, she remains one of the few European journalists promoting a positive image of the Taliban. Ms. Ridley entered politics on the green-red alliance of the Respect Party. In 2010, she was elected European president of the International Muslim Women's Union. She seems no more enamored of President Obama than she was of President Bush, as evidenced by her June 2010 blog entry, "Barack Obama: An Out-of-Control Psychopath with a God Complex."[110]

Ms. Ridley's daughter Daisy, who beseeched her journalist "mummy" to be more "normal" in 2001, has flowered in young womanhood. A 2011 YouTube video, "Daisy and Yvonne Ridley—Mum and Me Taster," captures some mother-daughter chit-chat. It is not likely that Daisy will soon follow in her mother's activist footsteps. An aspiring fashion model, pretty Daisy shows little passion for the dramas of international relations but much excitement about designer shoes and pink clothing.[111] By all appearances, Daisy is a very "normal" British teenager.

Nekmuhammad, the captured Soviet soldier forced to convert to Islam, finally visited his brother in Ukraine in 2012. But after a short visit, he returned to his family in Kunduz, Afghanistan, where he earlier built a tabby-colored clay house. He said with a sigh, "Afghanistan is a good place for me."[112] Lt. Gen. Boris Gromov, the last Soviet out of Afghanistan in February 1989, was awarded the highest Soviet award—the Golden Star of the Hero of the Soviet Union. He entered Russian politics after the collapse of the Soviet Union and was very successful, having been elected governor of the Moscow region in 2000.[113] Lest anyone be confused about his position on the war, he clarified, "The Soviet withdrawal from Afghanistan in 1989 was not a shameful escape accompanied by the hooting of the mujahedeen. The Soviet Army entered the country, accomplished its tasks—unlike the Americans in Vietnam—and returned to its motherland."[114]

The nine hijackers who took over an Ariana Airlines Boeing 727 in February 2000 went in different directions in Britain. Some were living rent free and on state benefits, and others adjusted more prosperously to their new lives. As of 2009, one of the hijackers was working as a cleaner—at Heathrow Airport.[115]

The five-term, conspiracy-accusing congresswoman, Cynthia McKinney, was defeated in her reelection after the 2001 attacks but ran for president of the United States on the Green Party in 2008.[116] She garnered few votes. In November 2012, she still held fast to her theory that the White House was involved in the September attacks. "My protests against Israeli interference in U.S. politics and the general events that unfolded following 9/11 ultimately resulted in me [sic] being ousted from Congress."[117]

First Lady Hillary Clinton, who used her White House prestige as a bully pulpit against Taliban misogyny in the late twentieth century, reiterated her position as secretary of state 10 years later.[118] As of late 2012, the Taliban continued to deride Secretary Clinton for slandering both the Taliban and Islam.[119] She is currently a leading prospect for her party's presidential nomination in 2016. Mavis Leno continues to voice concerns about the status of women and girls in Afghanistan.[120]

Mullah Omar remains reclusive and commanding. As of this writing, the mercurial mullah is the glue of the Afghan Taliban and is strong, capable, and threatening. Hashemi, Yale's only known Taliban, had long left New Haven and returned to Afghanistan, where he may live today.[121] "Nail Yale" is an all-but-forgotten footnote to Yale's storied history. But the long-banned Naval ROTC was welcomed back aboard campus, with a ribbon-cutting ceremony in September 2012.[122]

Nidal Hasan, still unrepentant about his Fort Hood slaughter, awaits his execution, which will probably not occur for years. Gun-control advocates cite Hasan's carnage as another example of "workplace violence" made more lethal through lax gun control laws. Others underscore the Islamic component in the shootings.

Hasan's spiritual advisor, Anwar al-Awlaki, continues to motivate jihadists around the world, though from his grave. His rhetoric still circulates in social media and print. In an aborted jihadist attack in Sheffield, England, in 2013, police found thousands of leaflets in which Awlaki called for ruthless jihad. The flyers, which the sheik wrote years earlier, were titled "Operation—'In Defence of the Prophet Muhammad.'"[123]

S.Sgt. Robert "Doom" Bales pled guilty to mass murder and was sentenced to life in prison without the possibility of parole, in late August 2013.[124] Earlier his wife, Kari, had not explained to their children why they could not see their father. Kari said, "I don't think I'm angry at anyone. I just—I want my family to be together again."[125]

Aafia Sadiqui of Brandeis and Pakistan became the subject of a biography by an American journalist, Deborah Scroggins.[126] The book was praised by some and panned by others as fawning and dishonest in its empathy-nurturing apologies for Lady al Qaeda.[127] Debbie Rodriguez, the Michigander who founded the Kabul Beauty School in 2003, wrote a best-selling account of her experience there. She was also involved in a documentary of the school.[128] There was some controversy about the academy's funding issues, but many of the Afghan graduates were deeply appreciative of the independence their new credentials gave them. Rodriguez followed up with a novel, which received some good reviews.[129]

Gary Schroen, a U.S. intelligence operative who led the initial attacks on al Qaeda and the Taliban, wrote an account of those efforts.[130] He became a regular commentator on U.S. and European talk shows. When asked years later about the government's order that he decapitate bin Laden and remit his head to headquarters as a war trophy, Schroen claimed to have retorted, without missing a beat, "I don't know what we're going to do about dry ice."[131]

Greg Mortenson, the mountain-climbing, midwestern Afghan school builder, fell off a cliff of controversy. Spending and accounting in his charity became highly questionable and, after a succession of accusations and revelations, he resigned from its board.[132] He is currently a motivational speaker.

Zardad, who ordered his man-dog accomplice Shah to bite his victims for amusement, languishes in a British prison.[133] The investigation and trial cost the British taxpayers nearly $75,000. It is not likely he will be extradited to Afghanistan soon because Britain does not extradite persons to countries that have the death penalty, barring specific guarantees.

As for Corp. Christopher Reynolds, the celebrated British sniper who earned a military cross for killing a Taliban commander at over a mile's distance, he did not adapt well to civilian life on his return to Britain. The 26-year-old Black Watch sniper was outmatched by an invisible demon who stalked him relentlessly in England; his enemy at home was depression. Reynolds went absent without official leave, his mental health deteriorated, and he viciously attacked his girlfriend. Pleading guilty to charges, he was spared a prison sentence by a sympathetic judge.

The British 617 "Dambusters," which delivered death from above to the Taliban enemy, is scheduled to disband in 2014. The nick-named "Suicide

Squadron" made history by its daring "busting" of dams in Germany's Ruhr Valley with bouncing bombs. It continued to make history in Afghanistan 70 years later with the killing power of its six-foot, supersonic Brimstone missiles, which were launched miles from the target. And it will make history, yet again, when it will re-form in 2016 as the first squadron to fly Britain's new Lightning II aircraft.[134]

On September 29, 2012, while on patrol, Army Sgt. 1st Class Daniel T. Metcalfe, 29, of Liverpool, New York, became the 2,000th American killed in Afghanistan. But he was not killed by Taliban; he was killed by an Afghan soldier in a green-on-blue attack, which continue into late 2013.[135] Theo, the springer spaniel who died on the same day as his master on the Afghan battlefield, was posthumously awarded the Dickin Award, the animal Victoria Cross, in October 2012.

The Arleigh Burke-class destroyer USS *Michael Murphy* (DDG-112) anchored in Pearl Harbor in November 2012. This is now her home.[136] An ocean and a continent away, Penn State undergraduates can chat, study, and rest in the new Lt. Michael P. Murphy Veteran's Plaza. In the center of the plaza is a bronze shield around which there is a circular walkway. On the shield is written in Greek, "With it [your shield] or on it," an allusion to the fighting spirit of the Spartans, the U.S. Navy SEALS, and the Nittany Lions' beloved fallen son, who is the university's first Medal of Honor recipient.[137]

Cpl. Mathew Bowman, the Marine who lost both legs and an arm when he stepped on an IED, was welcomed home to Indiana as a hero in summer 2011. On the interstate from Indianapolis to McCutcheon High School, in Lafayette, where he wrestled as a boy, Hoosiers of all ages waved flags and shouted their love, hope, and gratitude to the town's local champion. He was escorted in a convoy by 600 members of Legion Riders and Rolling Thunder motorcyclists. The Marine and the bikers openly wept, along with many others on the parade line.[138]

And what of Lance Cpl. William Kyle Carpenter, whose face was crisscrossed with shrapnel lacerations and blast scars when he took the impact of a grenade intended for a fellow Marine? He recovered well, after undergoing over 30 operations. The now-retired Marine became a freshman at the University of South Carolina in October 2013.[139] Today, Kyle enjoys skydiving and marathon running. An old acquaintance reminisced, "I've known Kyle since he was seven years old, and I am not surprised by his tenacity in the face of dire adversity!"[140]

Sgt. Than Naing, the Burmese-American, twice-wounded Marine, studied for his associate's degree while recuperating and was awarded "Marine of the Year," at Wounded Warrior Battalion-East, Camp Lejeune, in 2012. Maj. Paul Greenberg summed up the sentiment of leathernecks: "Sgt. Naing embodies everything that is admirable about Marines. It is people like him who make me proud to wear the Marine Corps uniform."[141]

Malala Yousafzai was released from hospital in Britain in January 2013. The month before she had been nominated for the Nobel Prize for peace by international heads of state and feted with awards from all over the world. She did not win the Nobel Peace Prize in 2013, which disappointed millions. But she said she was simply too young to deserve the award.

Malalai Kakar, the gangster policewoman of Kandahar so loved by the city's women and murdered by the Taliban, lives in memory. Other women cite her life and death as inspiration to serve as police women. The Taliban continue to try to kill them, and sometimes they succeed. But Afghan police-women are no longer rare in many parts of Afghanistan, and many have shown valor, just like Malalai.[142] The murderers of Zakia Zaki, who ran both a school and the Radio Peace station, have not been brought to justice, as of this writing. But a cultural center in her village was dedicated to her on the first anniversary of her death. "It is what she wanted, and she had begun the work before she was killed," explained her husband in 2009.[143]

In August 2012 Imran Khan, the former cricket phenomenon and current player in Pakistan's politics, tweeted to his followers to follow him on a "peace caravan" into FATA, and the Taliban threatened to kill him if he did so. One year later he embroiled himself in a legal dustup with political rivals. An opposition candidate referred to him as an agent of "Americans, Jews, Ahmadis and a person of ill character."[144] Picking up the gauntlet, Khan broadcasted, "He accused me of being a Jewish agent, and I will take him to court for it." In August 2013, Khan filed the necessary legal papers to do so.

Pakistan's ISI's retired Hamid Gul has not recanted his claim that the American Zionists and Mossad were behind the September 2001 attacks.[145] And neither did he offer any proof that they had done so. In this spirit, the Pakistani Taliban's leader Hakimullah Mehsud stands fast to his hatred of democracy. In spring 2013 he explained, "We consider democracy as unbelief. Democracy was introduced by the Jews in order to divide and create rifts among Muslims."[146]

Al Qaeda's American, Adam Gadahn, has neither softened his invectives nor increased his credibility. Azzam al-Amriki (Gadahn's al Qaeda pseudonym) delighted in July 2011 that firearms were easily available in the United States and Canada. He advised that they be purchased by Muslims to kill infidels there.[147] He is still wanted in the United States for treason.

In January 2013, John "Taliban Johnny" Walker won a suit to pray in a group with fellow Muslims in prison. He appears as committed to his faith as the day he was flushed out of a hiding hole by American soldiers over 10 years ago. Saif al-Adel, senior al Qaeda commander, had a price of $5 million in 2012 on his head.[148] He is still believed to be living in Iran.[149] On the 12th anniversary of the September 2001 attacks, Ayman al-Zawahiri, of al Qaeda, pleaded to Muslims around the world to continue to "bleed" the United States economically and to kill Americans in Afghanistan.

Paula Loyd, the well-bred anthropologist who was murdered by immolation, had her dying wish fulfilled, as a scholarship at Wellesley was established for poor Afghan women. Paula's parents traveled to Kabul as guests of the embassy. The embassy raised $2,700 from a marathon run in her honor. The scholarship's seed money was planted.[150] Paula's high-status boarding school celebrated her life and saluted her death in 2013 with the Choate Alumni Award ceremony. It was the first time Choate bestowed the award posthumously.

President George Bush had been retired for over four years by January 2013, and President Obama had just been reelected. In late April 2013, the George W. Bush Presidential Center opened with fanfare near Dallas, Texas. In addition to the five living U.S. presidents, heads of state from all over the world heard a misty-eyed George Bush salute the United States' greatness, strength, and future. The center is a 15-acre park and has the theme of a Texas prairie, with blends of native grasses and trees transplanted from the president's ranch at Crawford, Texas.[151] There is a peaceful spot to acknowledge the lost and loved who fell in Iraq and Afghanistan serving the United States.

President Obama ordered bin Laden killed, and in May 2011 U.S. Navy SEALs stormed his compound and slew him.[152] The sheik was shot, killed, and buried at sea. President Obama announced, without lament, that "this was a good day for America."[153] The killing of bin Laden would spotlight the president's successful reelection campaign. Senator McCain scoffed at Obama's taking credit for something "anybody, any president" would have done.[154] But former president Bill Clinton said, "He had to decide. And that's what you hire a president to do. You hire the president to make the calls when no one else can do it."[155]

Gen. "King David" Petraeus, considered by so many to be the 21st century's first great general, fully conquered neither the Taliban nor the sex scandal in which he was engulfed. In May 2013, the University of Southern California welcomed him to the faculty, and later in that year Wall Street employed his talents. Nonetheless, a letter to the editor in the *Washington Post* summed up the opinions of many: "How many men suffered public humiliation and career downfalls as a result of their ill-considered dalliances: Bill Clinton, John Edwards and Gary Hart, to name just three. The map is marked very clearly: Here be dragons."[156]

The general's mistress has been contrite and taciturn, but not so *Saturday Night Live*. On national television, an SNL humorist parodied Ms. Broadwell giving a deadpan reading from her biography of the general, at a swanky Washington bookstore. But the recitation had a droll and sadomasochistic twist. Delivered in monotone, the lines included, "Pull my hair, General. Pull it hard and spank me."[157]

Cat Stevens, Yusuf Islam, the reclusive and lone Western singer/songwriter whose musical artistry delighted the Taliban, made a comeback grand tour of Western cities in 2007.[158] Dropping "Islam" from his stage name, he performs as "Yusuf." He explained to his audience that the guitar, or a similar string instrument, was introduced to the world by Muslims in the seventh century, as a musical gift to all humankind.

Still the national sport, Buzkashi is played ferociously by Afghan men, and Afghan boys dream of becoming its next superstars. On that theme, the U.S. embassy in Kabul underwrote an Afghan-made movie about two poor boys who aspire to become Buzkashi's greatest players.[159] In 2013, the *Buzkashi Boys* was nominated for an Academy Award, and its two stars were flown to Hollywood for the ceremony.

Sosan Firooz, the 23-year-old Afghan spunky rapper, continues to sing publically and vivaciously despite the Taliban's ultimatum that she muzzle herself. The Taliban promised to slice off her mother's head if Sosan did not keep quiet. So Sosan responded to the threat by singing about it.[160] She continues to trumpet her generation's new freedoms, dreams, and courage.

Saad Haroon, the Pakistani pop star whose irreverent and Taliban-defiant wit connected with the Pakistani diaspora, went on tour in 2013 in Pakistan. The theme? "Don't Worry, Be Pakistani."[161] The humorist who penned and sang "Burka Woman" has also scripted a popular Pakistani children television cartoon, *Burka Avenger*. Its action hero is a modern Pakistani woman who wears a burka as a disguise when she delivers lethal karate chops to Taliban who are trying to close girl's schools or intimidate its students. Girls love the image.

Khorshid's Skateistan, the Australian creation designed to give Afghan children joy through skating, continues to do just that. In July 2013, it opened a new facility in Mazar-i-Sharif, where Pashtun, Tajik, Uzbek, and Hazara children, whose fathers and grandfathers may have fought each other in the civil wars, can skate together as friends. In early 2013, a crowd of 300 celebrated the third anniversary of the Skateistan Park in Kabul. Four girl students sang the Afghan national anthem, and there were prayers for Afghan and American children. The students held a moment of silence for the children and teachers of Sandy Hook Elementary School, in testament that other children around the world are victims of violence too (see Figure 9.1).[162]

There is no evidence that Thomas U, the German Taliban, is still linked to militant Islam. However, as of April 2013, the FBI and German security were reportedly investigating his old Sauerland Cell for linkages to the Tsarnaev brothers of Boston. The Taliban were their heroes.

Leonardo DiCaprio and the *Titanic* were no longer in vogue in Afghanistan by 2013. Bollywood movies, long popular before the Taliban, were once again the rage. As the famous Bollywood producer Kabir Khan said, "The people in Afghanistan will kill for a Hindi film. They watch nothing but Hindi films. Afghans will give their life for Hindi cinema."[163] The Afghan passion for movies still burned.

Figure 9.1   The beaming girls of Skateistan hold up a book on Skateistan's history. (© Skateistan. Reprinted with permission.)[164]

The whereabouts and status of Mohammad Ashan, the "Home Alone" simpleton; Thomas U, the German Taliban; Juma and Sameena, the boy and girl targeted unsuccessfully by the Taliban for suicide bombings; or Zarmina's children are not known to this author. If all of Zarmina's children were alive, they would range in age from approximately 16 to 33. Zarmina was 35 when she was shot by the Taliban in the soccer stadium. Beverly Giesbrecht, also known as Khadija Qahaar, is presumed dead.

By 2013, the word "Taliban" captured a place in American English as an adjective, as well as a proper noun. In May 2013, the occasionally crabby political activist Julian Bond opined that the Tea Party was the "Taliban wing" of the American right.[165] Years earlier, an angry Bond observed that the elder President Bush's cabinet was filled with "American Taliban." He did not mean it as a compliment.

But the Taliban unwittingly have enriched the vocabulary of humanity with a new term they helped create. Article 1 of the Universal Declaration of Human Rights states emphatically that "all human beings are born free and equal in dignity and rights." The bravery of demanding these rights, in the face of Taliban threats, and inspiring others to demand their basic human rights has been called "the Malala effect."[166]

AND FOR THE FUTURE . . .

As for the security of Afghanistan, the full picture will emerge as ISAF personnel withdraw from Afghanistan and prospects and details of government-Taliban talks become clear. Some observers are pessimistic and opine that stability efforts were doomed from the start.[167] Others reason that Afghanistan is far from hopeless and has achieved great strides since 2001.[168] It could be that the Taliban will become sincere in power sharing. Or it could be that like the Nazis at Munich, the Vietnamese communists in Paris, or Yasser Arafat's Palestinians in Oslo, the Taliban will sign comprehensive peace accords and then violate their terms. The Taliban do not have a strong record of diplomatic integrity.

Until most foreign forces leave Afghanistan, it is not possible to know, with any degree of certainty, how effective have been the 12-year counterinsurgency efforts. Have these efforts resulted in high national morale, a solid rule of law, and competent administrative, security and police forces? Many Afghans think so. Surveys indicate that most Afghans are more optimistic than pessimistic. Surveys conducted by the San Francisco-based Asia Foundation also found that an overwhelming majority of Afghans back the government's efforts to negotiate and reconcile with armed insurgent groups.[169]

Only 30 percent of respondents in the poll expressed sympathy for the insurgents, while nearly two-thirds said they did not support them. But when asked why the Taliban continue to fight, the most common reason cited was opposition to the presence of foreign troops in the country. Most foreign troops are scheduled to leave in the next few years.[170] Some metrics are listed in Table 9.3.

Table 9.3   Metrics of Progress[1]

Positive Metrics	Worrisome Metrics	Ambiguous Metrics
Taliban attacks against Coalition forces are down	Total Taliban attacks against Coalition forces and civilians are up	The Coalition is finding and destroying more IEDs
More Afghan villages in the South are "safe" from the Taliban	Coalition casualties (killed, maimed, and wounded) are up	Coalition night raids on Afghan homes are up
The number of Taliban commanders killed and captured is up	Afghan civilian casualties are up	Predator drone attacks inside Pakistan are up
Electricity availability and usage in Afghanistan is up	The number of IEDs being used by the Taliban is up	Coalition air strikes inside Afghanistan are up
The number of kilometers of roads in Afghanistan is up	More Afghan villages in the North and East are not "safe" from the Taliban	The number of suspected insurgents in Afghan prisons is up

(continued)

Table 9.3   (Continued)

Positive Metrics	Worrisome Metrics	Ambiguous Metrics
The number of Afghan children enrolled in school is up	Taliban rocket and other attacks originating from Pakistan are up	The number of Afghan soldiers deserting is high and unchanged
The availability of basic health care for the Afghan people is up	The number of audit reports showing mismanagement of Afghan aid funds is up	Coalition arrests of Afghan citizens are up
Overall Afghan life expectancy is up	Afghan child malnutrition has increased	The number of Afghans both returning to and fleeing from the country is up
The number of Afghan schools is up	Afghan environmental damage has increased	
Attacks on Afghan poppy eradication teams are up	Afghan drought conditions are worse	
The number of Taliban surrendering is up	The number of acres of poppies being cultivated is up	
The size of the Afghan National Army is up	Taliban assassinations of Afghan officials are up	
The size of the Afghan National and local police forces is up	Afghan child malnutrition has increased	
The number of local anti-Taliban militias is up	Afghan security force corruption rates remain high	
Areas being turned over to Afghan security forces by the Coalition are up	Taliban suicide bombings are up	
	The number of women and children suicide bombers is up	
	Coalition troop levels are falling while Taliban troop levels may be rising	
	The number of internally displaced people is up	

[1]Matthew Nasuti, "Afghan Metrics Show Taliban Winning & Losing," Kabul Press (Kabul, Afghanistan), November 16, 2011, http://www.highbeam.com/doc/1G1-272504964.html (accessed October 8, 2012).

Afterword

⸎

Salafist Dystopia

I think of it [being shot again] often and imagine the scene clearly. Even if they come to kill me, I will tell them what they are trying to do is wrong, that education is our basic right.[1]

—Malala Yousafzai, October 2012

Will all of Afghanistan be pulled into the vortex of the Taliban's dark world? Will Afghans lose their budding consensual rule of law to the Taliban's autocratic Islamism? Perhaps they will, but this not fated. Afghans can defeat the Taliban. The extent to which men and women have faith in the government of Afghanistan and see a better world for their children may determine the outcome of the insurgency. If security forces can hold Afghan territory, a very limited democracy could take root, despite the myriad challenges. The Bonn Agreement may have been pivotal in the history of Afghanistan. It solidified and codified a loose democratic form of government in Kabul. This may have fostered a sense of legitimacy in the political process and rule of law.

Sustained human development will also help determine Afghanistan's future. Incremental economic growth builds confidence in the government. Social change is particularly glacial in Afghanistan and will likely remain so. A deeply traditional and tribal society, Afghanistan is ill-prepared to absorb sudden, powerful shocks to its social fabric. But a cautioned modernity can go far to strengthen the legitimacy of the government. There is evidence that Afghans are prepared and eager for this.

As of fall 2013, there is pervasive loathing of the Taliban and the unpredictable and often unprovoked violence they deliver almost daily. This endemic despair was expressed by tribal elder Juma Gul, with admirable brevity: " 'One of my sons became a martyr. I have brought four more to fight and I will keep fighting until we are all dead. The Taliban are insulting our elders, they are killing our elders, and we decided to end this.' "[2] It is noteworthy that this simple villager, Juma, referred to his martyred son in terms of killing Taliban, not Americans. For Afghans, martyrs are those who die for Islam. For Juma, his son would go to heaven because he killed Taliban, who are turning Afghanistan into an un-Islamic hell.

Juma is not alone. Sparks of defiance against Taliban maltreatment erupted in many eastern villages in summer 2012. Some of this grit may have been led by village elders hoping to reassert their control as U.S. and other Coalition Forces leave Afghanistan. Much of this resolve is born of desperation and anger at those who showered Afghanistan with misery for years.[3] In fall 2013, many Afghans hate the Taliban.

Today, reintegration efforts may bring some Taliban into power sharing. But there will be a large cohort that will not be so easily reintegrated into the Afghan mainstream. This is the generation of young, orphaned Taliban who have known nothing but the misery and fatalism of Taliban times. For some, their home villages became killing caldrons. The political scientist Peter Singer refers to these and similarly placed children around the world as a "roving orphanage of blood and flame."[4] Traces of compassion and empathy were pounded out of boys during formative years, as they watched videos of every conceivable brutality. As boys, they were schooled in venomous and fatalistic rhetoric, intending to make killing and dying for the Taliban's Islam their highest aspiration. Can these young Taliban be reintegrated into humanity? Is it possible to rekindle the empathy in the blackened hearts of young Taliban? Today's children are the inheritors of Afghanistan's future.

BECAUSE THEY ARE TALIBAN

In his magisterial account of the Second World War, the British author Andrew Roberts considered the reasons for Hitler's loss. So decisive and menacing in 1939 and 1940, Hitler seemed unstoppable, and he was, initially. But he eventually lost the total war he created. Why? Was it because he invaded the Soviet Union? Maybe, but he came very close to capturing Moscow. His forces battered and smashed the Red Army, much of which was destroyed or was taken prisoner and murdered. Was it is his dehumanizing the Ukrainians or his monomaniacal murder of Europe's Jews? Perhaps that contributed to his failure. Was it his gratuitous declaration of war on the United States that forced the most industrialized country in the world into the European war? This certainly mattered. But finally, Roberts concludes that Hitler lost the war for the same reason he started it—"because he was a Nazi."[5]

Much of Afghanistan has become the detritus of war. The Taliban have turned orchards into wastelands and pasturelands into blood lands. Schools have become charnel houses. The Taliban may win the war and impose yet another Dark Age on the beleaguered country, but they may also lose. They could lose it for the same reason they riddle women and girls with machine-gun bullets; or fasten suicide belts onto six-year-old boys; or pump poison gas into girls' classrooms; or ban music, laughter, romance, and science; or nail amputated limbs to trees and signposts; or hoist high the severed heads of children while shouting "God is great." They will lose the insurgency for the same reason they started it—because they are Taliban.

Appendix

Coalition Military Fatalities by Year

Year	United States	United Kingdom	Other	Total
2001	12	0	0	12
2002	49	3	18	70
2003	48	0	10	58
2004	52	1	7	60
2005	99	1	31	131
2006	98	39	54	191
2007	117	42	73	232
2008	155	51	89	295
2009	317	108	96	521
2010	499	103	109	711
2011	418	46	102	566
2012	310	44	48	402
2013	118	8	22	148
Total	2292	446	659	3397

Note: Operation Enduring Freedom, iCasualties.org, http://icasualties.org/oef/ (accessed December 4, 2013).

Notes

PREFACE

1. Afghan Jokes, http://www.afghan-web.com/culture/jokes.html.

INTRODUCTION

1. Teri Whitcraft and Muriel Pearson, "Malala Yousafzai: Death Did Not Want to Kill Me," ABC News, October 5, 2013, http://gma.yahoo.com/malala-yousafzai-death-did -not-want-kill-045429952–abc-news-topstories.html?vp=1.

2. Larry P. Goodson, Contemporary Authors, Gale, 2004, October 31, 2010, http:// www.highbeam.com.

3. Anne Jones writes of the Afghans' fatalism. Source: Gareth Porter, "The General and His Afghan Labyrinth," Asia Times Online, http://www.atimes.com/atimes/South _Asia/KI24Df01.html.

4. "Taliban Statement on 10th Anniversary of 9/11 Attacks: 'Afghans Have an Endless Stamina for a Long War and . . . Will Send the Americans to the Dustbin of History,'" September 12, 2011, Special Dispatch No. 4127, http://www.memri.org/report/en/0/0/ 0/0/0/842/5632.htm.

5. Michael Forsyth, "Finesse: A Short Theory of War (Doctrine)," *Military Review*, 2004, http://www.highbeam.com/doc/1G1-121416828.html (accessed February 24, 2013).

6. "Report in Pakistani Daily: 'Next Generation of Taliban Ready to Fight'; 'Insurgents Have Recruited Hundreds of Child Soldiers'; 'This Recruitment Process Has Been Ongoing in the Waziristan Region for the Last Seven Years,'" February 16, 2011, Special Dispatch No. 3591, http://www.memri.org/report/en/0/0/0/0/0/842/5007 .htm#_edn1.

CHAPTER 1

1. "The mineral resources include copper, iron, lead, zinc, mercury, tin, chromium, lithium, tungsten, niobium, gold, and uranium (among others), as well as a variety of precious stones. Afghanistan also boasts deposits of combustible hydrocarbons, including coal, lignite, peat, and oil." Source: Globalsecurity.org, Afghanistan, Afghanistan-Environment, http://www.globalsecurity.org/military/world/afghanistan/cs-enviro.htm.

2. "Soldiers Overcome Afghanistan Terrain Challenges," U.S. Federal News Service, Including U.S. State News, 2007, http://www.highbeam.com (accessed April 17, 2011).

3. The Khyber Pass is a 53-kilometer (33 miles) passage through the Hindu Kush mountain range. Conquering armies have used the Khyber as a starting point to invade Afghanistan. It was also been a major trade route for centuries. Source: "A History of the Famous, and Infamous, Khyber Pass," Knight Ridder/Tribune News Service, September 5, 2002, http://www.highbeam.com/doc/1G1-91126212.html (accessed February 24, 2013).

4. Ibid.

5. The jezail is sometimes referred to as Afghanistan's Kentucky rifle. Source: "The Jezail, Afghanistan's Kentucky Rifle," Warlords of Afghanistan, http://www.warlordsofafghanistan.com/jezail-musket.php.

6. Mountain climbers talk about the "death zone" in mountains beginning at 26,000 feet.

7. At 14,494 feet, Mount Whitney in California is the highest mountain in the continental United States. Mount Denali in Alaska is the tallest in all of the United States.

8. Peter Jones, "Alexander in Afghanistan," *Spectator*, 2011, http://www.highbeam.com (accessed February 17, 2012).

9. Eric Glasgow, "A Short History of Buddhism," *Contemporary Review*, January 1, 1994, http://www.highbeam.com/doc/1G1-15139742.html (accessed February 24, 2013).

10. "These dates are uncertain because many of the religion's texts were destroyed. They either no longer exist or exist only in fragments. Some were destroyed by the Greek conqueror Alexander the Great (356–323 BCE) in 330 BCE; others, by Arab and Mongol invaders beginning in 650 CE. With the destruction of these texts, the religion was left with few written records." "Zoroastrianism," World Religions Reference Library, Gale, 2007, http://www.highbeam.com (accessed February 17, 2012).

11. "Sultan of Blood; He Beheaded and Raped Millions, and His Calling Card Was a Tower of Skulls. Was Emperor Tamerlane the Bloodiest Tyrant in History?" *Daily Mail* (London), 2005, http://www.highbeam.com (accessed February 17, 2012).

12. Babur was of Mongol descendant and is not considered a national hero in today's Afghanistan.

13. Sally Ann Baynard, "Afghanistan: Chapter 1A. Historical Setting," Countries of the World, 1991, http://www.highbeam.com (accessed October 31, 2010).

14. "Afghanistan: A Military History from Alexander the Great to the War on the Taliban," Targeted News Service, 2010, http://www.highbeam.com (accessed December 19, 2010).

15. "Anglo-Afghan Wars: War One (1838–1842)," *Encyclopedia of India*, 2006, http://www.highbeam.com (accessed April 17, 2011).

16. This was the Battle of Maiwand and where, out of a force of 2,476, almost 1,000 were killed, with hundreds wounded or missing.

17. Robert Nichais, "The Origins of Conflict in Afghanistan," *The Middle East Journal*, October 1, 2004.

18. Greg Myre, "In Timeless Afghanistan, a History of Turbulence," AP Worldstream, 2001, http://www.highbeam.com (accessed February 17, 2012).

19. "Newly Released Files Show Britain Once Favored Carving Up Afghanistan," AP Worldstream, January 2, 2002, http://www.highbeam.com/doc/1P1-49272408.html (accessed February 24, 2013).

20. "The US had already allied itself with Pakistan, which was Afghanistan's enemy. Pakistan and Afghanistan almost went to war in 1955. Further, Afghanistan abrogated the Durrand line treaty in 1948 before the partition. Pakistan insisted that Durrand line was sacrosanct and US backed it." Dr. Lester Grau, in e-mail correspondence with Mark Silinsky, April 1, 2013.

21. In 1955, Afghanistan signed an agreement for developmental and military assistance with Moscow. The Soviet traded petroleum products, rolled ferrous metals, and building materials in exchange for Afghan cotton, wool, and finished and unfinished leather goods. Source: Paul Robinson, "Russian Lessons: We Aren't the First to Try Nation-Building in Afghanistan," *American Conservative*, August 1, 2009, http://www.highbeam.com/doc/1G1-202626731.html (accessed February 24, 2013).

22. Sally Anne Baynard, "Afghanistan: Chapter 1F. Daoud's Republic, 1973–78," *Countries of the World*, January 1, 1991, http://www.highbeam.com/doc/1P1-28383014.html (accessed February 24, 2013).

23. Ibid.

24. Ibid.

25. Associated Press, "Ex-king Ends Exile, Heads to Afghanistan; Historic: Zaher Shah Departs from Italy," *Telegraph-Herald* (Dubuque), April 18, 2002, http://www.highbeam.com/doc/1P2-11049725.html (accessed September 16, 2012).

26. Myre, "In Timeless Afghanistan."

27. Article 10, "Afghanistan Constitution, April 9, 1923," Afghanistan Online, http://www.afghan-web.com/history/const/const1923.html.

28. Article 2, "Afghanistan Constitution, April 9, 1923," Afghanistan Online, http://www.afghan-web.com/history/const/const1923.html.

29. Articles 12, 19, and 20, "Afghanistan Constitution, April 9, 1923," Afghanistan Online, http://www.afghan-web.com/history/const/const1923.html.

30. The Constitution endorsed the Hanafi school of Sunni Islamic jurisprudence.

31. Article 21, "Afghanistan Constitution, April 9, 1923," Afghanistan Online, http://www.afghan-web.com/history/const/const1923.html.

32. Barnett R. Rubin, *The Fragmentation of Afghanistan: State Formation and Collapse in the International System*, 2nd ed. (New Haven, CT: Yale University Press, 2002), 51.

33. International Crisis Group, "Afghanistan's Flawed Constitutional Process," *ICG Asia Report*, no. 56, Kabul/Brussels, June 12, 2003.

34. Noah Tucker and Sue Sypko, "Salafist and Wahhabist Influence in Afghanistan," *Cultural Knowledge Report*, March 15, 2009, 8.

35. Joseph Fitchett, "What about the Taliban's Stingers?," *International Herald Tribune*, September 26, 2001, http://www.highbeam.com/doc/1P1-48571313.html (accessed October 13, 2012).

36. Tucker and Sypko, "Salafist and Wahhabist Influence in Afghanistan," 14.

37. Stephen D. Pomper, "Don't Follow the Bear: The Soviet Attempt to Build Afghanistan's Military," *Military Review*, September 1, 2005.

38. Scott Peterson, "Afghanistan's Lesson for Iraq," *Christian Science Monitor*, July 29, 2005.

39. Scott Doggett, "Soviets Leaving Bitter Legacy in Afghanistan—'Widespread' Torture Reported," *Chicago Sun-Times*, 1988, http://www.highbeam.com (accessed September 18, 2012).

40. " 'Systematic' Torturing of Afghans Told," *Chicago Sun-Times*, 1986, http://www.highbeam.com (accessed September 18, 2012).

41. Hannelore Sudermann, "Ex-Afghan Mourns Loss of Culture; Forced Out by Soviet Occupation, WSU Professor Unable to Return," *Spokesman-Review* (Spokane, WA), October 28, 2001, http://www.highbeam.com/doc/1P2-27323089.html (accessed February 25, 2013); and conversation with Shireen Burki, independent scholar, in e-mail correspondence with this author, October 13, 2012.

42. David Remnick, "Soviets, Afghanistan in Joint Space Mission; Trek's Purpose More Political than Scientific," *Washington Post*, August 30, 1988, http://www.highbeam.com/doc/1P2-1276098.html (accessed September 18, 2012).

43. Richard M. Weintraub, "Soviets Bolstering Afghanistan Ties; Moves Seem to Guarantee Influence after War Ends," *Washington Post*, 1987, http://www.highbeam.com (accessed September 18, 2012).

44. Jonathan Goodhand, "From War Economy to Peace Economy? Reconstruction and State Building in Afghanistan," *Journal of International Affairs* 58, no. 1 (September 22, 2004), http://www.questia.com/read/1G1-126654859/editors-foreword.

45. Phillipe Le Billon, "The Political Economy of War: What Relief Workers Need to Know," Humanitarian Practice Network Paper, no. 33, Overseas Development Institute, London, 2000.

46. A shadow economy refers to economic activities that are conducted outside state-regulated frameworks and are not audited by the state institutions. Source: Cheryl Benard and Elvira Loredo, "A Three-Pronged Approach to Confront Afghanistan's Corruption" (Viewpoint essay), *Christian Science Monitor*, June 4, 2010, http://www.highbeam.com/doc/1G1-228157931.html (accessed February 25, 2013).

47. Yu Ye Serookiy, "Psychological-Information Warfare: Lessons of Afghanistan," *Military Thought*, 2004, http://www.highbeam.com (accessed February 9, 2012).

48. Kevin Cullen, "Soviet Soldiers In Afghanistan Using More Heroin, US Officials Say," *Boston Globe*, January 31, 1987, http://www.highbeam.com/doc/1P2-7997048.html (accessed September 29, 2012).

49. "Soviet, U.S. Vets Share Horror, Pain of War," *Chicago Sun-Times*, 1988, http://www.highbeam.com (accessed September 18, 2012).

50. *The Soviet Experience in Afghanistan: Russian Documents and Memoirs*, ed. Svetlana Savranskaya, October 9, 2001, http://www.gwu.edu/~nsarchiv/NSAEBB/NSAEBB57/soviet.html.

51. Shireen K. Burki in a book review, "Edward Girardet, *Killing the Cranes: A Reporter's Journey through Three Decades of War in Afghanistan*," *Peace Review: A Journal of Social Justice* 24, no. 4 (2012): 526–30. To link to this article: http://dx.doi.org/10.1080/10402659.2012.732497.

52. John-Thor Dahlburg, "General Is Last Soviet Soldier to Quit Afghanistan," *Boston Globe*, 1989, http://www.highbeam.com (accessed September 18, 2012).

53. Other Western and Soviet military scholars saw the situation as more nuanced: "Soviets were not defeated in battle, withdrew in good order, and left behind a functioning government with a reasonable economy, improved military and improved diplomatic posture." Dr. Lester Grau, in e-mail correspondence with Mark Silinsky, April 1, 2013.

54. Some scholars, such as Dr. Lester Grau, research coordinator for the Foreign Military Studies Office at Fort Leavenworth, Kansas, see the role of the Stinger as

overrated in defeating the Soviets. Source: Dr. Lester Grau, in e-mail correspondence with Mark Silinsky, April 1, 3013.

55. Ilkhom Narziev, "When Soviet Union Withdrew from Afghanistan, Not All Its Soldiers Decided to Return Home," Knight Ridder/Tribune News Service, March 5, 2004, http://www.highbeam.com/doc/1G1-113955389.html (accessed September 29, 2012).

56. The Ukrainian government amnestied all deserters in the mid-1990s. Source: Carlotta Gall, "A Ukrainian Misses Home, but Is Afraid to Go Back; Afghanistan/Former Soviet Prisoners of War," *International Herald Tribune*, August 1, 2003, http://www.highbeam.com/doc/1P1-76614035.html (accessed September 29, 2012).

57. "When Soviet Union Withdrew from Afghanistan, Not All Its Soldiers Decided to Return Home," Knight Ridder/Tribune News Service, March 5, 2004, http://www.highbeam.com/doc/1G1-113955389.html (accessed September 29, 2012).

58. As of October 2012, the Russian government claimed that 200 troops were still missing and that 30–40 troops may be alive. Source: Slobadan Lekic, "Russia Asks Afghanistan for Help with Soviet MIAs," Associated Press, October 13, 2012.

59. Gall, "A Ukrainian Misses Home."

60. Narziev, "When Soviet Union Withdrew from Afghanistan."

61. "Afghanistan is 42 percent Pashtun, 27 percent Tajik, 9 percent Hazara, 9 percent Uzbek, 4 percent Aimak, 3 percent Turkmen, 2 percent Balochi, and 4 percent other. This gene pool has been combined with that of ancient Greeks and Macedonians, Persians, Scythians, Kushans, Sakas, Huns, Arabs, Turks, Mongols, British, and Americans." Source: "Afghanistan," *Faces: People, Places, and Cultures*, March 1, 2006, http://www.highbeam.com/doc/1G1-146497280.html (accessed February 25, 2013).

62. This book uses the term "ethnic group" as synonymous with "tribe." The Pashtuns themselves are divided in five confederations: the Durrani, Ghilzai, Karlanri, Sarbani, and Ghurghusht.

63. Gregorian Vartan, *The Emergence of Modern Afghanistan: Politics of Reform and Modernization, 1880–1946* (Stanford, CA: Stanford University Press, 1969), 29–32.

64. Ahmed Rashid, *Taliban: The Story of the Afghan Warlords* (New York: Pan Books, 2001), chap. 6, 82–94.

65. Ibid.

66. Ben Arnoldy, "Pakistan's Pashtuns, Looking for Statehood, May Look to Taliban," *Christian Science Monitor*, 2009, http://www.highbeam.com (accessed April 16, 2011).

67. The Durrani and Ghilzai are both tribal confederations and subtribes. Source: Dr. Lester Grau, in e-mail correspondence with Mark Silinsky, April 1, 2013.

68. They straddle the border areas between Pakistan and Afghanistan in Waziristan, Kurram, Peshawar, Khost, Paktia, and Paktika.

69. The larger group, located north of Peshawar, includes tribes such as the Mohmands, Yusufzais, and Shinwaris, while the smaller segment consists of Sheranis and Tarins scattered in northern Balochistan.

70. They are found mostly in northern Balochistan and include tribes such as the Kakars, Mandokhels, Panars, and Musa Khel.

71. In building the Afghan Army, Durrani versus Ghilzai commanders and cadre was an issue in the Pashtun rivalry. Source: Hayder Mili and Jacob Townsend, "Tribal Dynamics of the Afghanistan and Pakistan Insurgencies," Combating Terrorism Center, West Point, New York, August 15, 2009, 1, http://www.ctc.usma.edu/posts/tribal-dynamics-of-the-afghanistan-and-pakistan-insurgencies.

72. Vern Liebl, "Pushtuns [*sic*], Tribalism, Leadership, Islam and Taliban: A Short View," *Small Wars and Insurgencies* 18, no. 3 (2007): 492–510.

73. Maha Azzam, "The Radicalization of Muslim Communities in Europe: Local and Global Dimensions," *The Brown Journal of World Affairs*, April 1, 2007, http://www.highbeam.com/doc/1P3-1516229171.html (accessed September 16, 2012).

74. For the Taliban, Sharia is nonnegotiable. It does not evolve and cannot be refined or abrogated. As the word of God that was revealed to his Prophet, Sharia is not subject to criticism. For this reason, Muslims who criticize Sharia are subject to the death penalty because they can be labeled apostates.

75. The term "Salafist" refers to the era in which Islam was created and that many Muslims believe is a period of moral purity.

76. Juan R. I. Cole, "The Taliban, Women, and the Hegelian Private Sphere," *Social Research* 70, no. 3 (September 22, 2003).

77. MEMRI, "Urdu Magazine: 'The Prophet Muhammad Left No Legacy to the Ummah Except Weapons'; 'The Mujahideen . . . Are More Ready than Ever to Conquer Pakistan through the Path of the Prophet (Jihad and Qital in the Path of Allah),' " Special Dispatch No. 4596, March 21, 2012, http://www.memri.org/report/en/0/0/0/0/0/842/6207.htm.

78. Associated Press, "Witness Details Taliban's Demolition Tactics; Rockets, Anti-aircraft Weapons: Nation's Relics Are Destroyed," *Telegraph-Herald* (Dubuque), 2001, http://www.highbeam.com (accessed February 20, 2012).

79. Jeff Jacoby, "Taliban Achieve What They Seek: Uproar," *Boston Globe*, 2001, http://www.highbeam.com (accessed February 20, 2012).

80. Jim Shorthouse, "Unlawful Instruments and Goods: Afghanistan, Culture and the Taliban," *Capital and Class* 79 (Spring 2003).

81. Seth Jones, *Counterinsurgency in Afghanistan*, RAND Counterinsurgency Study, Vol. 4 (Santa Monica, CA: RAND Corporation, 2008), 62.

82. Farzand Ahmed, "Fatwa Factory: The Latest Religious Edict from Deoband's Dar-ul-Uloom Forbidding Women from Working in Proximity to Men Creates a Furor and Highlights Growing Intolerance," *India Today*, 2010, http://www.highbeam.com (accessed April 19, 2013).

83. Ray Takeyh, "Terror Exporter? An Experienced Journalist's Condemnation of the Saudi State and Its Relation to Wahhabi Islam Is Powerful and Insightful Despite Its Biases" (Book Review), News World Communications, 2003, http://www.highbeam.com (accessed December 3, 2013).

84. The origins of the Deobandi brand of Islam can be traced to a town, Deoband, in Uttar Pradesh state in northern India. Here can be found the second-largest Sunni seminary in the world, the Darul Uloom (House of Knowledge). Dar Uloom was officially founded on May 30, 1866, shortly after the British had destroyed the remaining fragments of the Muslim Moghul empire in 1857. Often referred to as the "University of Jihad," the madrassa has been given donations by the Saudi kingdom, most certainly because of the similarities of Deobandi and Wahhabi ideologies. Source: William Kampsen, independent scholar, in correspondence with this author, October 19, 2012.

85. "On May 10, 1857, Indian soldiers of the British Indian Army, drawn mostly from Muslim units from Bengal, mutinied to offer their services to the Mughal emperor, and soon much of north and central India was plunged into a year-long insurrection against the British." "Sepoy Mutiny, 1857–58," Global Security, http://www.globalsecurity.org/military/world/war/sepoy-mutiny.htm.

86. Tucker and Sypko, "Salafist and Wahhabist Influence in Afghanistan," 3.

87. "Deoband Power Struggle Could Change the Face of Muslim Society in India," *Tehelka*, February 5, 2011, http://www.highbeam.com/doc/1P3-2257329521.html (accessed September 16, 2012).

88. William Kampsen, in correspondence with this author, October 19, 2012.

89. The Nazis sought to forge a racial paradise in Europe, the communists saw a classless society, and Islamists dreamed of global caliphate in which non-Muslims would be forced to acknowledge their inferior status, perform self-degrading rituals acknowledging their subordination, pay taxes to Muslims, and abide by an exhaustive set of laws and injunctions designed to reinforce the degraded position of the nonbeliever.

90. Richard Phelps, "Sayyid Qutb and the Origins of Radical Islamism," *The Middle East Quarterly*, March 22, 2011, http://www.highbeam.com/doc/1G1-253626043.html (accessed September 16, 2012).

91. Tucker and Sypko, "Salafist and Wahhabist Influence in Afghanistan," 5.

92. In 1949, the year the Brotherhood's founder, Hasan al Banna, was murdered by Egyptian police, Sayyid Qutb was compiling his famous tract, "The America I Saw," a quasi-hallucinogenic account of his experiences and observations as an English-language student in Colorado in 1948/1949.

93. "Portrait of a Revolutionary: The Father of Islamic Fundamentalism (How a 20th-Century Radical Helped Create al-Qaeda) (Sayyid Qutb)," *The Economist*, July 17, 2010, http://www.highbeam.com/doc/1G1-231630541.html (accessed September 16, 2012).

94. Margot Dudkevitch, "Who was Abdullah Azzam?," *Jerusalem Post*, 2005, http://www.highbeam.com (accessed September 16, 2012).

95. Jeffrey B. Cozzens, "Victory from the Prism of Jihadi Culture," *Joint Forces Quarterly* 52 (January 2009): 86.

96. Kamran Khan and Pamela Constable, "Bomb Suspect Details Anti-U.S. Terror Force; Muslim Radical Said to Lead Thousands," *Washington Post*, August 19, 1998, http://www.highbeam.com/doc/1P2-681105.html (accessed September 16, 2012).

97. MEMRI, "#3591 – Al-Qaeda Leader Ayman Al-Zawahiri: Bin Laden Emerged from the Muslim Brotherhood," Middle East Media Research Institute, Washington, DC, September 27, 2012, http://www.memrijttm.org/clip_transcript/en/3591.htm.

98. Christina Lamb, "War on Terror: Police Butchers, Taliban's Torturer," *Mirror*, (London), October 1, 2001.

99. "The totalitarian dream or fantasy, common to both Japanese ultra-nationalism and Nazism, is that all human bodies must unite to constitute one body. Each and every human being is expected to abandon the 'will to separation' (individualism) and to embrace and to subordinate the self to the 'national will.' " Richard A. Koenigsberg, "Review of Japan's War: The Ideology of Radical Shinto Ultranationalism," Library of Social Science Review Essay, Library of Social Science, Elmhurst, New York, http://us.mg6.mail.yahoo.com/neo/launch?.rand=1bgja9b9a96ld (accessed September 16, 2012).

100. Lamb, "War on Terror."

101. Frank O'Donnell, "Afghan Escapee Tells of Life as a Torturer," *Scotsman*, October 1, 2001, http://www.highbeam.com/doc/1P2-18806438.html (accessed January 20, 2013).

102. Ian Drury and David Williams, "Body of Executed Soldier Paraded by Taliban," *Daily Mail*, July 6, 2011.

103. Joel Brown, "In 'Kite Runner,' Afghanistan on an Intimate Scale; Stages," Boston Globe, 2012, http://www.highbeam.com (accessed September 18, 2012).

104. "Afghan-Uzbek Movie Attempts to Expose Cruelty of Taliban," AP Worldstream, November 19, 2003, http://www.highbeam.com/doc/1P1-87348182.html (accessed September 17, 2012).

105. Thomas Wagner, "Anti-Taliban Movie Starring Child Beggar Is First Afghan Feature Film since Fall of Islamic Regime," AP Worldstream, December 6, 2003, http:// www.highbeam.com/doc/1P1-88092589.html (accessed September 17, 2012).

106. Siobhan McDonough, "Movie Depicting Life in Afghanistan under Taliban Shown to Washington Audience," AP Worldstream, February 20, 2004, http:// www.highbeam.com/doc/1P1-91266493.html (accessed September 17, 2012).

107. Books on the condition of women in Afghanistan include *Veiled Courage: Inside the Afghan Women's Resistance* by Cheryl Benard; *Zoya's Story: An Afghan Woman's Struggle for Freedom* by Zoya with John Follain and Rita Cristofari; *My Forbidden Face: Growing Up Under the Taliban: A Young Woman's Story*, by Latifa; and *Unveiled: Voices of Women in Afghanistan* by Harriet Logan. Source: Rob Mitchell, "Afghan Women Detail Terror under Taliban," *Boston Herald*, May 7, 2002, http://www .highbeam.com/doc/1G1-85494652.html (accessed September 18, 2012).

108. Paul Farhi, "In 'Kandahar,' a Political Movie with an Assassination Plot," *Washington Post*, 2002, http://www.highbeam.com (accessed September 17, 2012).

109. "With Taliban out, Afghan Arts Emerge," *Christian Science Monitor*, January 11, 2002, http://www.highbeam.com/doc/1G1-81584261.html (accessed September 18, 2012).

110. Constable, "Kandahar Recovers Its Pre-Taliban Personality," *Washington Post*, January 24, 2002.

111. Barbara Jones, "Kabul's Bear with No Nose: After the One-Eyed Lion of Kabul, Another Taliban Outrage in the Afghan Zoo," *Mail on Sunday*, November 25, 2001, http://www.highbeam.com/doc/1G1-80279558.html (accessed September 26, 2012).

112. "Kabul's Lion King; Kabul Zoo," *The Economist*, January 12, 2002, http:// www.highbeam.com/doc/1G1-81617665.html (accessed September 26, 2012).

113. "Kabul's Lion King," *Chicago Tribune*, January 31, 2002.

114. Jim Heintz, "Kabul's Beloved, Tormented One-Eyed Lion Dies," AP Worldstream, January 26, 2002.

115. By late 2002, animal lovers, zookeepers, and foreign governments rescued and revitalized the Kabul Zoo. China gave two lions to replace Marjan, and two deer, two bears, two pigs, and a wolf. Source: Associated Press, "China Donates Lions to Run-Down Kabul Zoo," *Record* (Bergen County, NJ), October 3, 2002, http://www.highbeam .com/doc/1P1-68243905.html (accessed October 13, 2012).

116. Professor Daniel Moran, Department of National Security Affairs, Naval Postgraduate School, in personal e-mail correspondence with Mark Silinsky, April 8, 2013.

CHAPTER 2

1. The United States would revisit some of these challenges toward modernizing Afghanistan. Source: Mark Silinsky, "Democracy, Development, and Defense: The Afghan Counterinsurgency as a Regional Model," *Washington Review of Turkish and Eurasian Affairs*, December 2010, http://www.thewashingtonreview.org/articles/democracy -development-and-defense-the-afghan-counterinsurgency-as-a-regional-model.html.

2. John F. Burns, "For Afghans, Full Circle," *New York Times*, August 13, 1998.

3. Greg Jaffe and Karen DeYoung. "Leaked Files Lay Bare War in Afghanistan; Pakistan Aid to Rebels Hinted Taliban Apparently Used Heat-Seeking Missiles." *Washington Post*, July 26, 2010 http://www.highbeam.com (accessed February 4, 2011).

4. Mark Silinsky, "The World Turned Upside Down: The Global Battle over God, Truth, and Power," (Book review), *The Middle East Quarterly*, Fall 2010, http://www.highbeam.com (accessed June 21, 2013).

5. M. Jamil Hanifi, "Reaping the Whirlwind: The Taliban Movement in Afghanistan" and "Taliban: Militant Islam, Oil and Fundamentalism in Central Asia," *The Middle East Journal*, 2002, http://www.highbeam.com (accessed November 1, 2010).

6. "The province of Punjab holds 3,153 seminaries; NWFP 1,281, Sindh 905, Balochistan 692, Azad Kashmir 151, Islamabad 94, Northern Areas 185 and FATA 300. The same report says only 22 percent of the schools were registered with the government. The NWFP has 3,795 male and 885 female teachers in 1,281 religious schools, 30 percent of whom are Afghans." Ashfaq Yusufzai, "Pakistan: Peaceful Taliban Dispute Militants' Claim to Name," Inter Press Service, September 25, 2008, http://www.highbeam.com/doc/1P1-156585741.html (accessed November 23, 2012).

7. Neamatollah Nojumi, *The Rise of the Taliban in Afghanistan: Mass Mobilization, Civil War, and the Future of the Region* (New York: Palgrave, 2002), xii.

8. Hanifi, "Reaping the Whirlwind" and "Taliban."

9. Shaun Gregory, "Pakistan: An Uncertain Ally," *Soundings* 39 (Summer 2008), http://www.highbeam.com (accessed February 17, 2012).

10. He was later killed in Kabul by a suicide bomber who had explosives in his turban. Source: "Pakistan, Afghanistan, and the Taliban," *International Journal on World Peace* 25, no. 4 (December 1, 2008), http://www.highbeam.com (accessed December 20, 2010).

11. "A Paper Peace: Afghanistan," *The Economist*, March 13, 1993, http://www.highbeam.com/doc/1G1-13569543.html (accessed September 16, 2012).

12. There are several variations to this story, some of which are undoubtedly embellished. One version has it that it was a boy who was raped.

13. Dexter Filkins, "The Legacy of the Taliban Is a Sad and Broken Land," *New York Times*, December 31, 2001.

14. Tim Cornwell, "Media Shy Mullah Who Defies the World," *Scotsman*, 2001, http://www.highbeam.com (accessed February 26, 2012).

15. William Reeves "Obituary: Dr Najibullah," *Independent* (London), September 28, 1996, http://www.highbeam.com/doc/1P2-4809400.html (accessed September 17, 2012).

16. Daniel Consolatore, "The Pashtun Factor: Is Afghanistan Next in Line for an Ethnic Civil War?," *The Humanist*, 66, no. 3 (May/June 2006).

17. "Atrocities Blamed on Taliban," *Independent* (London), November 2, 1998.

18. Ibid.

19. Filkins, "The Legacy of the Taliban."

20. The Islam of the Taliban and that found in Pakistani madrassas has its roots in the Deobandi movement, which is not mainstream Islam. The Indian-based Deobandi creed is very austere and misogynistic.

21. Filkins, "The Legacy of the Taliban."

22. "Mysterious Mullah Behind the Taliban; Jane Macartney Looks at the Events That Brought Mullah Mohammad Omar to Power in Afghanistan," *Birmingham Post* (England), 2001, http://www.highbeam.com (accessed February 26, 2012).

23. "Taliban Leader Rebounds, Vexing U.S. Forces," *Virginian-Pilot* (Norfolk, VA), October 11, 2009.

24. "In 1991, Saudi Arabia expelled bin Laden for anti-government activities. He took refuge first in Sudan, which is ruled by a militant Islamic government. In 1996, he was forced out by the Sudanese under American pressure and returned to Afghanistan, where the radical Taliban had taken control." Patricia Smith, "America's Most Wanted: The Man

Who Declared It 'the Duty' of Muslims Everywhere to Kill Americans," *New York Times Upfront*, October 15, 2001, http://www.highbeam.com (accessed February 16, 2012).

25. Linda Wertheimer, "Analysis: Saudi Arabia's Sensitivity about the Country's Ties to Osama bin Laden," *All Things Considered*, NPR, 2001, http://www.highbeam.com (accessed February 16, 2012).

26. Robert H. Reid, "CNN Tape Shows Bin Laden Call for 'Holy War' in '98 U.S. in Saudi Arabia, Israelis in Jerusalem Offend Al-Qaida Chief," *Chicago Sun-Times*, August 20, 2002, http://www.highbeam.com (accessed February 16, 2012).

27. Smith, "America's Most Wanted."

28. Kathy Gannon, "Bin Laden Rallies Muslim Youth," AP Online, 2000, http://www.highbeam.com (accessed February 16, 2012).

29. Sami Yousafzai and Ron Moreau, " 'This Mullah Omar Show,' " *Newsweek*, 2010, http://www.highbeam.com (accessed July 21, 2012).

30. "Wrath of God," *Time*, January 11, 1999.

31. *The U.S. Army/Marine Corps Counterinsurgency Field Manual* (Chicago: University of Chicago Press, 2007).

32. Some of the terminology is different. The development of the current insurgency in Afghanistan loosely follows the government's three-phase model. It does not exactly fit the model, and no single model would be appropriate for all evolutionary aspects of every insurgency.

33. For example, the Islamic Brotherhood in Egypt won the confidence of many Egyptians by presenting itself as an alternative to a failed public administration.

34. Ken Tovo, "From the Ashes of the Phoenix: Lessons for Contemporary Counterinsurgency Operations," *Special Warfare*, January 1, 2007, http://www.highbeam.com/doc/1P3-1221371071.html (accessed January 19, 2013).

35. John Malevich and Daryl C. Youngman, "The Afghan Balance of Power and the Culture of Jihad," *Military Review*, May 2, 2001.

36. David Kilcullen, *The Accidental Guerilla: Fighting Small Wars in the Midst of a Big One* (New York: Oxford University Press, 2009), 81.

37. Malevich and Youngman, "The Afghan Balance of Power."

38. William Rosenau, "Counterinsurgency: Lessons from Iraq and Afghanistan," *Harvard International Review*, March 22, 2009, http://www.highbeam.com/doc/1G1-200271859.html (accessed February 25, 2013).

39. The Taliban had been in this stage since the middle of this decade. Since about 2005, they attacked targets of opportunity, as well as those whom they considered puppets or apostates. They currently do not have the military capabilities to launch conventional warfare against the Coalition. That will occur, if it occurs at all, in phase 3.

40. Some scholars underscore that elements of Mao's model do not precisely fit the Taliban conquest because there was far weaker command and control among the Pashtuns. Dr. Lester Grau writes, "The Taliban was and is a loose coalition of Pushtun [sic] gangs of thugs who show respect to Mullah Omar, but he is certainly not directing all the Taliban activities." Dr. Lester Grau, in e-mail correspondence with Mark Silinsky, April 1, 3013.

41. Tovo, "From the Ashes of the Phoenix."

42. "Taliban Accused of Torture and Killings as Reprisals," *Seattle Post-Intelligencer*, November 1998, http://www.highbeam.com/doc/1G1-64604932.html (accessed August 26, 2012).

43. Kathy Gannon, "Afghan Women, Children Caught in Taliban Army Sweep," *Columbian* (Vancouver, Canada), September 20, 1999.

44. Filkins, "Taliban Blocking Aid to Starving Villagers," *Chicago Sun-Times*, May 31, 1998.

CHAPTER 3

1. "Rep. Adam Smith Holds a Hearing on 'Strategies for Countering Violent Extremist Ideologies,' " *Political Transcript Wire*, February 13, 2009, http://www.highbeam.com/doc/1P3-1645003381.html (accessed February 25, 2013).

2. Daniel Cooney, "Taliban Recruiting Boys to Replace Dead Fighters," *Record* (Bergen County, NJ), 2005, http://www.highbeam.com (accessed February 16, 2012).

3. Abdul Sattar, "Taliban Videos Boy Beheading Alleged Traitor—'A New Low' for Afghanistan Conflict," *Commercial Appeal* (Memphis, TN), April 21, 2007, http://www.highbeam.com (accessed February 16, 2012).

4. "Taliban Hang a Boy of 15," *Daily Mail* (London), 2007, http://www.highbeam.com (accessed February 16, 2012).

5. In the Koran, houris are mentioned or referred to as "companions" (44:54, 52:20), "restrained" (55:72), "like pearls well-guarded" (56:22–23), and "virginal" (56:35–37). Source: "Houri," *Encyclopedia of Sex and Gender: Culture Society History*, January 1, 2007, http://www.highbeam.com/doc/1G2-2896200311.html (accessed November 18, 2012).

6. A partial list of behavior and items banned included: "women working and driving, television, satellite dish, movies, photographs of people and animals, statues, stuffed toys, the internet, computer disks, non-religious music, musical instruments, cassettes, dancing, kite-flying, playing cards, chess, neckties, lipstick, nail polish, fireworks, fashion catalogues, pig-fat products, anything made with human hair." Tom Mashberg, "Taliban Ready to Fight U.S.—Afghan Extremists Abhor Western Culture," *Boston Herald*, September 19, 2001.

7. "The Agony of Afghanistan: No Music, No TV, No Dancing—and That's Just the Beginning of the Hardships of Life Under the Taliban," *New York Times Upfront*, November 12, 2001.

8. There is a current debate as to whether Mohammed ever lived. Ignaz Goldziher, a prominent historian and Arabist, argued that the hadith, the vast body of sayings and actions attributed to the Islamic prophet Mohammed, lacked historical validity. Source: "Ayoon wa Azan," *Dar Al Hayat*, International ed. (Beirut, Lebanon), May 28, 2012, http://www.highbeam.com/doc/1G1-291079217.html (accessed September 16, 2012).

9. Kathy Gannon, "Taliban Leader Bans Use of Internet," AP Online, 2001, http://www.highbeam.com (accessed February 26, 2012).

10. "TVs Outlawed in Afghanistan: Taliban Trying to Get Rid of Influences of Islam," *Charleston Daily Mail* (Charleston, WV), July 14, 1998.

11. Idira Lakshmanan, "How Omar Led Taliban to Power, Then Defeat," *Boston Globe*, December 9, 2001.

12. Ibid.

13. The Failed States Index 2007, *Foreign Policy Magazine*, July/August 2007, http://www.foreignpolicy.com/story.

14. Ibid.

15. The Watson Institute at Brown University's Global Security Matrix opines failed states are hazards to the security of the international system.

16. Olivier Roy notes that contrary to popular belief, the Taliban do not believe in a big, modernized state run under broadly Islamic rules in the manner of the

Muslim Brotherhood, but they are what he calls, neo-fundamentalists, who emphasize the rule of the Sharia, social conformity, and a small state. Source: M. E Yapp, "Fundamentalism Reborn? Afghanistan and the Taliban," *Middle Eastern Studies*, April 1, 1999.

17. "Taliban Propaganda: Winning the War of Words?," *Asia Report* 158 (July 24, 2008): 5.

18. "Afghani [sic] Religious Police Ban 'Titanic' Haircuts," *Church and State Bulletin*, March 2001, 22.

19. "Barbers Jailed by Taliban for DiCaprio-Type Haircuts," *Chicago Sun-Times*, January 26, 2001.

20. Harold H. Koh, "Overview to Country Report on Human Rights Practices for 1998," in 1998 *Human Rights Report*, U.S. Department of State, http://www.state.gov/ www/global/human_rights/drl_reports.html.

21. "Leno's Wife Sacrifices Privacy to Aid Afghan Women," *Daily News* (Los Angeles), May 23, 1999.

22. Dexter Filkins, "Afghanistan in Grip of Tyrannical Peace/Harsh Taliban Draws Dissent," *Chicago Sun Times*, October 25, 1988.

23. As a car dealer said in the early post-Taliban period, "During the Taliban time, you could walk the streets safely day and night. Now we have to sleep with guns for pillows because we can be robbed at any time." Pamela Constable, "Some in Kandahar Mourn the End of Taliban Rule: Many Residents Longingly Recall Life under Strict Islamic Code: 'We Prefer Extremism to Instability,' " *Washington Post*, January 16, 2002, http:// www.highbeam.com (accessed December 19, 2010).

24. For example, an article in *The Economist* opined, "The puritan excesses of the early days are subsiding. The Taliban leadership is moderate, essentially favouring the traditional Islam of rural Afghanistan." "Ah, Peace. (The Taliban Militia in Afghanistan Has Brought Both Peace and Efficient Administration to the Areas It Has Captured)," *The Economist*, October 28, 1995.

25. "Taliban Soldiers Reaffirm Mission, Mark Anniversary of Soviet Invasion," *Boston Globe*, December 29, 1996.

26. "Taliban Administers Public Amputation and Flogging," AP Online, April 25, 1998.

27. Filkins, "Afghanistan in Grip of Tyrannical Peace."

28. Dawna Friesen, "Slow Progress for Afghan Women," NBC News, 2013.

29. "Afghan Girl" Photo, *National Geographic*, http://photography.national geographic.com/wallpaper/photography/photos/milestones-photography/afghan-girl-portrait/ (accessed September 24, 2012).

30. Atia Abawi, "Afghan Woman Whose Nose Ears Cut Off Travels to U.S.," CNN, August 4, 2010, http://articles.cnn.com/2010-08-04/world/afghanistan.mutilated.girl .update_1_afghan-women-afghan-woman-taliban?_s=PM:WORLD.

31. Anton Antonowicz, "Face Beneath the Veil: Zarmina's Story: She Was the Afghan Woman Whose Public Execution by the Taliban Shocked the World," *Mirror* (London), June 19, 2002.

32. In an interview with ABC, Anton Antonowicz, the author of the *Mirror*'s story, believes that it was not Zarmina but her elder daughter who clubbed him, but that Zarmina drugged him. Source: "Who Was the Afghan Mom Executed by Taliban?," an interview with Anton Antonowicz, *Good Morning America*, ABC, October 2, 2000, http://abcnews.go.com/GMA/story?id=125721&page=1 (accessed September 24, 2012).

33. Antonowicz, "Face Beneath the Veil."

34. Wrekhmin Tasal, "Women Bought and Sold in Eastern Afghanistan," Institute for War and Peace Reporting, August 15, 2012, http://iwpr.net/report-news/women -bought-and-sold-eastern-afghanistan.

35. "Who Was the Afghan Mom Executed by Taliban?"

36. Antonowicz, "Face Beneath the Veil."

37. Ibid.

38. Ibid.

39. Constable, "Rural Villagers' Quiet Resistance: Taliban Abuses Were Fought with Humor, Stubbornness," *Washington Post*, December 18, 2001.

40. Ibid.

41. Gretchen Peters, "Taliban Uses Torture to Rid Afghanistan of Hashish Use," *Columbian* (Vancouver, WA), April 14, 1997.

42. Ibid.

43. Robert Spencer, "Sharia in Action in Pakistan: Angry Muslim Clerics Force Cancellation of Concert," Jihad Watch, http://www.jihadwatch.org/2012/08/sharia-in -action-in-pakistan-angry-muslim-clerics-force-cancellation-of-concert.html (accessed September 7, 2012).

44. The book is *Poetry of the Taliban* by Felix Kuehn and Alex Strick van Linschoten, Columbia Press. Source: Laura King, "Poetry of the Taliban Elicits Both Anger and Astonishment," *Los Angeles Times*, July 8, 2012.

45. "Taliban Murders Music and Merriment in Pakistan," *Al Arabiya* (Saudi Arabia), February 8, 2009.

46. "Snuffing Music, Dance and Film: The Taliban's Cultural Invasion—Local Culture in the Swat Valley Struggles to Survive the Taliban," *Yemen Times* (Sana'a, Yemen), July 29, 2009, http://www.highbeam.com (accessed September 21, 2013).

47. Dan Nelson and Emal Khan, "Taliban Underlines It Growing Power with Killing of a Dancing Girl," *Telegraph* (London), January 11, 2009, http://www.telegraph.co.uk/ news/worldnews/asia/pakistan/4217690/Taliban-underlines-its-growing-power-with -killing-of-dancing-girl-in-Pakistan.html.

48. "Taliban Murders Music and Merriment in Pakistan."

49. Charlotte Philby, "Taking on the Taliban," *Independent* (London), May 27, 2013, http://www.highbeam.com (accessed September 21, 2013).

50. Translation from the German: Lucy Powell and Toby Axelrod, "A New Layeha for the Mujahideen," *Die Weltwoche*, November 29, 2006.

51. In the first rule set, there are rules that loosely correspond to civil-military rela- tions. No lower-level commander may involve himself in disputes among the populace. Regional-level commanders may interfere, in some cases, but disputes should be handled as a first resort by religious experts (Ulema) or a council of elders (Jirga), In addition, every Taliban must be constantly vigilant, and arguments among Taliban were be adjudi- cated by Taliban leaders according to the Islamic Emirates.

52. Translation from the German: Powell and Axelrod, "A New Layeha for the Mujahideen."

53. Observers of the Taliban have confirmed the authenticity of these three sets of rules. Source: Powell and Axelrod, "A New Layeha for the Mujahideen."

54. "Taliban Flog Couple for Having Illicit Relations," *Pajhwok Afghan News* (Kabul, Afghanistan), July 28, 2010, http://www.highbeam.com (accessed July 31, 2012).

55. Renee Montagne, "Afghans Wary of Returning Virtue Police," *Morning Edition*, NPR, July 10, 2006, http://www.highbeam.com/doc/1P1-126164716.html (accessed September 17, 2012).

56. "Hijack Trial Told of 'Living Hell' under Taliban Rule," *Daily Record* (Glasgow, Scotland), November 1, 2001, http://www.highbeam.com/doc/1G1-79608091.html (accessed October 5, 2012).

57. Ibid.

58. Terri Judd, "Campaign against Terrorism: Old Bailey—Hijacker Saw Taliban Death Squads Kill Nurses," *Independent* (London), November 1, 2001, http://www.highbeam.com/doc/1P2-5198593.html (accessed October 6, 2012).

59. Ibid.

60. Stephen Wright, "Seven Afghan Hijackers Are Set Free to Fly Home: Judge's Compassion for the Young Men Who Sparked Runway Drama as They Tried to Flee the Taliban," *Daily Mail* (London), January 19, 2002, http://www.highbeam.com/doc/1G1-81928755.html (accessed October 6, 2012).

61. "Afghans Jailed for a Hijacking in England to Remain in the Country," AP Worldstream, July 13, 2004, http://www.highbeam.com/doc/1P1-96375234.html (accessed October 6, 2012).

62. "Afghans Faced Stark Choice—Seize Airliner or Die, Says Defence QC," *Birmingham Post* (England), December 7, 2001, http://www.highbeam.com/doc/1G1-80630531.html (accessed October 6, 2012).

63. The Iranians were supportive of one of the most striking military commanders in the war with the Soviets, Ahmad Shah Masood, the fabled Lion of Panjshir, who was outgunned by the Soviets and kept in a small and isolated pocket in northeast Afghanistan.

64. "Afghanistan Taliban Says It Will Eliminate Poppies and Heroin," *Seattle Post-Intelligencer*, 1997, http://www.highbeam.com (accessed November 1, 2010).

65. Yahlin Chang, "Hollywood's Latest Cause: Can a Pack of Celebrities Save Afghanistan's Women?," *Newsweek*, December 6, 1999, http://www.highbeam.com/doc/1G1-57841083.html (accessed September 24, 2012).

66. "Dear Abby," *Charleston Daily Mail* (Charleston, WV), July 23, 1999, http://www.highbeam.com/doc/1P2-18918532.html (accessed September 24, 2012).

67. "Glamour Honors Women of the Year," *Cincinnati Post* (Cincinnati, OH), November 1, 2001, http://www.highbeam.com/doc/1G1-79648911.html (accessed September 30, 2012).

68. Bill O'Reilly, "Pinheads & Patriots: Dennis Kucinich, Mavis Leno," *O'Reilly Factor* (FOX News), January 11, 2008, http://www.highbeam.com/doc/1P1-147978442.html (accessed September 30, 2012).

69. Saba Mahmood and Charles Hirschkind, "Feminism, the Taliban and the Politics of Counterinsurgency," Fathom Archive, University of Chicago Library Digital Collection, 2002, http://fathom.lib.uchicgo.edu/1/777777190136.

70. In March 2012, Secretary of State Hillary Clinton would give the International Women of Courage Award to Marym Durani, the Kandahar provincial council member and owner of a women's radio station. Source: "Afghan Woman Receives US Courage Award," *Pajhwok Afghan News* (Kabul, Afghanistan), March 9, 2012.

71. Mail Foreign Service, "Echoes of the Nazis as Taliban Forces Hindus to Wear ID tags," *Daily Mail* (London), May 23, 2001, http://www.highbeam.com/doc/1G1-74980441.html (accessed August 26, 2012).

72. U.S. Department of State, "Afghanistan: Taliban's Mullah Omar's 8/22 Contact with State Department," Cable, August 23, 1998, NODIS, 4 pp. [Excised].

73. *The 9/11 Commission Report: Final Report of the National Commission on Terrorist Attacks upon the United States,* chap. 3, sect. 3.4, p. 93, emphasis in the original.

74. "U.S. Strikes Back: Missile Strikes Ordered by President Clinton Blast Terrorist Training Camps in Afghanistan and Sudan," *Post-Tribune* (IN), 1998, http://www.highbeam.com (accessed April 24, 2013).

75. "Bin Laden Aide a Mastermind of Terror Plots," *Washington Times*, 2003, http://www.highbeam.com (accessed April 24, 2013).

76. "Taliban Leader Wants to Meet US," *Birmingham Post* (England), 2001, http://www.highbeam.com (accessed April 24, 2013).

77. Nora Boustany, "Bin Laden Now a Target in Arab Media: Criticism Emerges as Scholars Emphasize Distance from 'Distortion of Religion,'" *Washington Post*, 2001, http://www.highbeam.com (accessed April 24, 2013); and Gannon, "Taliban Says Visit by U.N. Envoy Richardson 'Significant,'" AP Online, 1998, http://www.highbeam.com (accessed April 24, 2013).

78. The organization's name was changed to the Organization of Islamic Co-operation. Source: http://www.highbeam.com (accessed April 24, 2013).

79. Sanjit Ghandi, ed., *The September 11th Sourcebooks*, vol. 7, *The Taliban File*, National Security Archive Electronic Briefing Book No. 97, September 11, 2003, http://www.gwu.edu/~nsarchiv/NSAEBB/NSAEBB358a/index.htm.

80. Constable, "New Sanctions Strain Taliban-Pakistan Ties: U.N. Action Angers Islamic Militants," *Washington Post*, 2001, http://www.highbeam.com (accessed December 18, 2010).

81. Constable, "U.N. Imposes Air, Economic Sanctions on Afghanistan: Taliban Still Refuses to Hand Over Bin Laden," *Washington Post*, 1999, http://www.highbeam.com (accessed November 1, 2010).

82. Linda Werthelmer and Noah Adams, "Profile: US Briefs NATO Defense Ministers on Status of US Military and Economic Plans after Terrorist Attacks," *All Things Considered*, NPR, September 26, 2001, http://www.highbeam.com/doc/1P1-89606971.html (accessed March 4, 2013).

83. "Musharraf Tried to Protect Taliban after 9/11," *Hindustan Times* (New Delhi, India), September 14, 2010, http://www.highbeam.com/doc/1P3-2137534191.html (accessed March 4, 2013).

84. Barry Schweid, "Taliban Better 'Think Properly,'" *Albany Times Union* (Albany, NY), September 26, 2001.

85. Ibid.

86. Schweid, "US: Bush Offer Designed in Fairness," AP Online, 2001, http://www.highbeam.com (accessed July 21, 2012).

CHAPTER 4

1. David Aaron, *In Their Own Words: Voices of Jihad* (Santa Monica, CA: RAND Corporation, 2008), 256.

2. Keith Dovkants, "Talibans in a Suicidal Fervour as They Cheer Coming Fight: Afghanistan," *Evening Standard* (London), 2001, http://www.highbeam.com (accessed February 20, 2012).

3. "Pashtunistan" is slang for the belt of Pashtun-inhabited land that straddles Afghanistan and Pakistan.

4. "Pakistan: Taliban Tightens Its Rule over Border Areas," Inter Press Service, March 13, 2007, http://www.highbeam.com/doc/1G1-161268242.html (accessed March 4, 2013).

5. Pavel Felgenhauer, "Bin Laden Best Left to Rot," *Moscow Times* (Russia), September 20, 2001, http://www.highbeam.com (accessed February 17, 2012).

6. Aaron, *In Their Own Words*, 254.

7. Ibid.

8. Noah Tucker and Sue Sypko, "Salafist and Wahhabist Influence in Afghanistan," *Cultural Knowledge Report*, March 15, 2009, 13.

9. Ashley Surdin and Patrick Paik, "War Protesters Rally at UC-Berkeley," *University Wire*, 2001, http://www.highbeam.com (accessed February 17, 2012).

10. Margot Patterson, "Experts Say Bombing Is Risky Strategy," *National Catholic Reporter*, November 2, 2001.

11. Ibid.

12. Malcolm Beith, "What a Nice Afghan! (People for the Ethical Treatment of Animals)," *Newsweek International*, October 8, 2001, http://www.highbeam.com/doc/1G1-78930265.html (accessed November 24, 2012).

13. John McCaslin, "Inside the Beltway," *Washington Times*, November 2, 2001. http://www.highbeam.com/doc/1G1-79649858.html (accessed December 13, 2012).

14. "Lawmaker Criticized on Sept. 11 Theories," *Albany Times Union* (Albany, NY), 2002, http://www.highbeam.com/doc/1G1-157567363.html (accessed December 13, 2012).

15. Gwen Tietgen, "Bush Urges America to 'Be Ready,' " *University Wire*, 2001, http://www.highbeam.com (accessed February 17, 2012).

16. On the diplomatic front, Taliban authorities asked Jesse Jackson to lead a "peace delegation" to the region. Jackson said he spoke with Secretary of State Colin Powell, who repeated the Bush administration position that it will not negotiate with the Taliban but did not urge Jackson not to go.

17. Patty Wong, "President Bush Resolute in Message to Terrorists," *University Wire*, 2001, http://www.highbeam.com (accessed February 17, 2012).

18. Bruce Berkowitz, "A Hero's Tale. (First In: An Insider's Account of How the CIA Spearheaded the War on Terror in Afghanistan)," (Book review), *Policy Review*, April 1, 2006, http://www.highbeam.com/doc/1G1-145781329.html (accessed August 26, 2012).

19. "Killer Blow in War on Terror: Inside Story of How US Caught Bin Laden, One Year on from His Death," *Daily Record* (Glasgow, Scotland), April 28, 2012, http://www.highbeam.com/doc/1G1-287911175.html (accessed December 16, 2012).

20. Tony Bridges, "Green Berets Likely Headed Back to War, Again," Knight Ridder/Tribune New Service, September 26, 2001.

21. Ibid.

22. The heavier equipment is left from the war with the Soviets: T-54 and T-62 tanks, a few armored personnel carriers, field artillery, multiple-launch rocket systems, about 15 MiG and Sukoi fighter planes, and fewer than 30 helicopters. Source: Molly Moore, "In the Taliban's Hands, an Old, Varied Arsenal," *Washington Post*, September 23, 2001, http://www.highbeam.com/doc/1P2-460129.html (accessed August 26, 2012).

23. "Afghanistan Fighters Battle-Hardened: Military Challenge: Taliban Has about 50,000 Troops Armed with AK Assault Rifles," *Telegraph-Herald* (Dubuque), September 23, 2001.

24. Joseph Fitchett. "Special Forces in Afghanistan Seek Out Targets Teams Paving Way for Strikes, Officials Report," *International Herald Tribune*, 2001, http://www.highbeam.com (accessed February 17, 2012).

25. Matthew Hickley, "Russians Join War on Taliban," *Daily Mail* (London), September 25, 2001.

26. "Short, Sharp and Devastating: Allies' Tactics to Persuade Taliban Chiefs to Hand Over Evil Bin Laden," *Daily Record* (Glasgow, Scotland), 2001, http://www.highbeam.com (accessed February 19, 2012).

27. Brian Knowlton, "U.S Targets Network of Bin Laden Tunnels Planes Begin Ammunition Airdrop for Opposition Forces on Front Line," *International Herald Tribune*, 2001, http://www.highbeam.com (accessed February 19, 2012).

28. Kim Sengupta, "Campaign against Terrorism: Weapons—'Daisy Cutter' Bombs Dropped on Taliban Caves," *Independent* (London), 2001, http://www.highbeam.com (accessed February 17, 2012).

29. Richard Norton Taylor, "Taliban Hit by Bombs Used in Vietnam," *Guardian*, November 6, 2001, http://www.theguardian.com/world/2001/nov/07/afghanistan.terrorism6.

30. Caroline Wyatt, "Dambusters Prepare for Final Tour Before Disbandment," BBC News, October 3, 2013, http://www.bbc.co.uk/news/uk-24382841.

31. Tim Bouquet, "The Dambusters in Afghanistan," Express, January 10, 2013, http://www.express.co.uk/news/uk/369747/The-Dambusters-in-Afghanistan.

32. "Army Rangers Leave Taliban Photos," AP Online, October 21, 2001.

33. "European Support for War against Terror Strongest in Britain, the Netherlands," *Chicago Tribune*, December 17, 2001, http://www.highbeam.com/doc/1G1-1206 53908.html (accessed December 6, 2012).

34. "Countries Throughout the World Share U.S. Grief," *New York Beacon*, September 26, 2001, http://www.highbeam.com/doc/1P1-79497909.html (accessed December 6, 2012).

35. "European Support for War."

36. "Don't Feel Sorry for Y Vain, Pity Daisy; Why Let Being a Mum Get in the Way of a Good Story, Ms Ridley?," *Daily Record* (Glasgow, Scotland), 2001, http://www.highbeam.com (accessed December 7, 2012).

37. "Normal Mummies Don't Get Kidnapped by the Taliban . . . ; Says the Daughter of Yvonne Ridley as They Head Off for a New Life in the Middle East," *Wales on Sunday* (Cardiff, Wales), June 29, 2003, http://www.highbeam.com/doc/1G1-105182765.html (accessed December 7, 2012).

38. "Don't Feel Sorry For Y Vain Pity Daisy; Why Let Being a Mum Get in the Way of a Good Story, Ms Ridley?," *Daily Record* (Glasgow, Scotland), 2001, http://www.highbeam.com/doc/1G1-79066920.html (accessed December 7, 2012).

39. "Normal Mummies Don't Get Kidnapped."

40. "Bush Confirms Attacks on Afghanistan," AP Online. 2001, http://www.highbeam.com (accessed February 17, 2012).

41. Juan O. Tamayo, "Taliban Surrounded in Kandahar but Pashtun Forces Remain Divided," Knight Ridder/Tribune News Service, 2001, http://www.highbeam.com (accessed February 17, 2012).

42. Tracey Eaton, "Taliban Soldiers Cross Enemy Lines to join Northern Alliance," Knight Ridder/Tribune News Service, November 19, 2001, http://www.highbeam.com/doc/1G1-80183663.html (accessed July 10, 2013).

43. Jonathan Landay and Sudarsan Raghavan, "Northern Alliance Forces Pursuing Taliban Stragglers," Knight Ridder/Tribune News Service, 2001, http://www.highbeam.com (accessed July 21, 2012).

44. "War on Terrorism: One Dead as Taliban Devotees Run Amok," *News Letter* (Belfast, Northern Ireland), October 9, 2001.

45. Ibid.

46. Nicholas Pyke, "Attack on Taliban: Raggle-Taggle Army March to Aid Taliban Setback for Coalition," *Independent* (London), October 28, 2001.

47. Noreen S. Ahmed-Ullah, "Fleeing Is Merely First Step for Thousands of Afghan Refugees," *Chicago Tribune*, October 24, 2001.

48. Many leaders on both sides of the conflict would be named as war criminals. *Conflict Mapping Afghanistan since 1978*, prepared by the Afghan Independent Human Rights Commission. Source: Roy Norland, "Top Afghans Tied to '90s Carnage, Researches Say," *New York Times*, July 23, 2012, 1.

49. Norland, "Top Afghans Tied to '90s Carnage."

50. Robin Moore, *The Hunt for Bin Laden: Task Force Dagger* (New York: Random House, 2003), 234.

51. Shamus Toomey, "Overrating the Taliban? Former Soviet Army Lieutenant Says Soldiers Will Defect to U.S. Side in Ground Attack," *Daily Herald* (Arlington Heights, IL), October 14, 2001.

52. Tom Newton Dunn, "Coward Taliban; Troops Hide in Villages," *Daily Record* (Glasgow, Scotland), October 25, 2001.

53. Ibid.

54. Paula J. Dobriansky, "Feeding Vulnerable Afghans Is a Major Part of the Strategy," *International Herald Tribune*, 2001, http://www.highbeam.com (accessed February 19, 2012).

55. Brian Murphy, "Taliban Captives Beg for Spots in US Prison," *Chicago Sun Times*, January 31, 2002.

56. Patrick Cockburn, "War on Terrorism: Defections—Taliban Execute Five of Their Own Soldiers Accused of Being Spies," *Independent* (London), October 22, 2001.

57. Robert Siegel and Noah Adams. "Profile: Taliban Reports Executing Leading Opposition Figure," *All Things Considered*, NPR, October 26, 2001, http://www.highbeam.com/doc/1P1-49646971.html (accessed September 7, 2012).

58. John J. Lumpkin, "U.S. Inserts More Special Forces, Plans Resupply of Taliban Opposition through the Winter," AP Worldstream, November 4, 2001.

59. Barbara Jones and Bob Graham, "Flowers for General Abdul and the Army Who Put the Taliban to Flight," *Mail on Sunday* (London), November 11, 2001.

60. Ibid.

61. Ibid., "Put the Taliban to Flight," *The Mail on Sunday* (London), November 11, 2001.

62. Raghavan, "Former Prisoners of Taliban Tell of Physical Abuse, Killings," Knight Ridder/Tribune News Service, December 13, 2001. http://www.highbeam.com/doc/1G1-80793004.html (accessed September 17, 2012).

63. Sometimes spelled Sare Poza or Sar Poza.

64. "By some prisoners' estimates, about 500 died in the past four years inside Sar-e-Poza, including nearly 200 from starvation." Raghavan, "Former Prisoners of Taliban."

65. Raghavan, "Taliban Prison a Nightmare of Beatings, Murder," *Albany Times Union* (Albany, NY), December 14, 2001.

66. Raghavan, "Former Prisoners of Taliban."

67. Mark Ellis, "War on Terror, Child of the Frontline: The Boy Warlord," *Mirror* (London), October 26, 2001.

68. "US Soldiers Turn on Pentagon over War Tactics," *Sunday Herald*, 2001, http://www.highbeam.com (accessed August 19, 2012).

69. "Like Rats in a Trap: Kandahar Blitz Keeps Taliban Off Balance," *Daily Record* (Glasgow, Scotland), December 3, 2001, http://www.highbeam.com/doc/1G1-80506696.html (accessed August 26, 2012).

70. In fact, bin Laden did, of course, survive. Source: Grimaldi, "Is There Humor in Afghanistan?," *Public Manager,* December 22, 2001, http://www.highbeam.com/doc/ 1G1-84343690.html (accessed December 2, 2012).

71. "Like Rats in a Trap."

72. Steve Vogel, "U.S. Forces Scour Afghan Caves for Data to Halt Future Attacks: Franks Declines to Speculate on Bin Laden," *Washington Post,* 2002, http:// www.highbeam.com (accessed July 31, 2012).

73. Ibid.

74. Ravi Nessam, "Switching Sides Pays off for Many Taliban Fighters," *Columbian* (Vancouver, WA), January 15, 2002.

75. His exact age in dispute. This author has seen different dates.

76. Mary E. O'Leary, "Ex-Taliban Apologist Surfaces at Yale," *New Haven Register* (New Haven, CT), February 28, 2006, http://www.highbeam.com/doc/1P2-125904 53.html (accessed December 1, 2012).

77. "At Yale, a Taliban Reinvents Himself: A Former Envoy for Islamic Fascists Fits in as an Undergraduate," *New Haven Register* (New Haven, CT), March 6, 2006, http:// www.highbeam.com/doc/1P2-12589036.html (accessed December 1, 2012).

78. "Roving Afghanistan Ambassador Sayyid Rahmatullah Hashemi's Speech at the University of Southern California on March 10, 2001," The Modern Religion, http://www.themodernreligion.com/jihad/afghan/speech.html (accessed December 3, 2012).

79. Ibid.

80. O'Leary, "Ex-Taliban Apologist Surfaces at Yale."

81. Cathy Young, "Educating the Taliban at Yale," *Boston Globe,* March 13, 2006, http://www.highbeam.com/doc/1P2-7945121.html (accessed December 1, 2012).

82. Jon Kouri, "Yale University: Taliban Yes; US Military No, Accuracy in Academia," March 8, 2006, http://www.academia.org/yale-university-taliban-yes-us-military-no/.

83. "A Taliban at Yale," *Manila Bulletin,* March 15, 2006, http://www.highbeam.com/ doc/1G1-143218154.html (accessed December 1, 2012).

84. "Taliban-cum-Yalie," *Washington Times,* March 14, 2006, http://www.high beam.com/doc/1G1-143210994.html (accessed December 1, 2012).

85. " 'Nail Yale' Launches Taliban Protest," *New Haven Register* (New Haven, CT), March 27, 2006, http://www.highbeam.com/doc/1P2-12588748.html (accessed February 1, 2013).

86. The running theme in Al-Adel's manuscript, "Message to Our People in Iraq and the Gulf, Specifically and to Our Islamic Ummah in General: The Islamic Resistance against the American Invasion of Qandahar and Lessons Learned," was offsetting the impressive American superiority in military capabilities, particularly its firepower, with resourcefulness, audacity, endurance, and faith in God. Source: Ben Venzke and Aimee Ibrahim, "Al-Qaeda's Advice for Mujahideen in Iraq: Lessons Learned in Afghanistan," vol. 1.0, April 14, 2003, IntelCenter, Alexandria, VA.

87. Venzke and Ibrahim, "Al-Qaeda's Advice for Mujahideen in Iraq."

88. Ibid.

89. Ibid.

90. Some scholars, notably Dr. Lester Grau, dispute the significance or even existence of Chechen troops in Afghanistan. Source: Dr. Lester Grau, in e-mail correspondence with Mark Silinsky, April 1, 2013.

91. David Williams, "Troops 'Fighting to the Last Man,' " *Daily Mail* (London), 2001, http://www.highbeam.com (accessed August 19, 2012).

92. Lisa Simeone, "Profile: Abdurrashid Dostum," *Weekend Edition Sunday*, NPR, December 2, 2001, http://www.highbeam.com/doc/1P1-115107142.html (accessed September 17, 2012).

93. Caroline Lees, "Taliban Zealots Face Might of Uzbek Warlord," *Independent* (London), October 25, 1996.

94. Ibid.

95. Joshua Partlow, "Militia Commander Campaigns for Karzai: Dostum's Record on Human Rights Is a Concern for U.S.," *Washington Post*, August 18, 2009, http://www.highbeam.com/doc/1P2-20651991.html (accessed September 17, 2012).

96. Other leaders were Mohamed Mohaqeq, leader of the Hazaras; Burhanuddin Rabbani, then recognized outside of Afghanistan as the country's president; and Karim Khalili, the leaders of eight Shia groups. Source: "Power Struggle of the Warlords: with the Taliban Vanquished Old Rivals and Enemies Come Home to Roost," *Western Mail* (Cardiff, Wales), November 15, 2001, http://www.highbeam.com/doc/1G1-80079 226.html (accessed August 26, 2012)

97. John Ydstie, "Profile: Governor of Herat, Afghanistan, Ismail Khan," *Weekend Edition Sunday*, NPR, February 3, 2002, http://www.highbeam.com/doc/1P1-499 58237.html (accessed September 17, 2012).

98. "Warlord Set His 'Human Dog' on Victims," *Western Mail* (Cardiff, Wales), October 9, 2004.

99. "Retrial of Afghan Warlord Accused of Torture Begins in London," AP Worldstream, June 8, 2005.

100. Matthew Hickley and Lech Mintowt-Czyz, "Suburban Warlord: Afghan Guerilla Chief Is Living on Benefits in a Council House," *Daily Mail* (London), July 28, 2000.

101. Ibid.

102. Pat Clarke, "Warlord Set 'Human-Dog' on His Victims: Trial Hears of Afghan Torture Horrors," *Daily Record* (Glasgow, Scotland), October 9, 2004.

103. Ibid.

104. John Simpson, "How Newsnight Found Zardad," BBC News, July 18, 2005, http://news.bbc.co.uk/2/hi/programmes/newsnight/4693783.stm.

105. Patricia Goodman, "Warlord's Conviction Bring Hope for Justice in Afghanistan," *International Herald Tribune*, July 22, 2005.

106. *Zardad's Dog* is one of three movies in the *House of Bin Laden* trilogy that was commissioned by the Imperial War Museum, London. Source: "Zardad's Dog by Langlands & Bell Goes on Show at Tate Britain," Tate Museum Press Release, July 2006, http://www.tate.org.uk/about/press-office/press-releases/zardads-dog-langlands -bell-goes-on-show-tate-britain.

107. "Zardad's Dog Is One of Three in the ...," BBC News, April 27, 2004, http://news.bbc.co.uk/2/hi/south_asia/366292935.

108. Gary Jones, "War on Terror: Delight in Kabul: Liberated: People Celebrate Fall of Taliban with Music and by Shaving Beards," *Mirror* (London), November 14, 2001.

109. Ibid.

110. Scott Peterson, "Exit the Taliban, Enter James Bond and Iranian Soap," *Christian Science Monitor*, November 23, 2001.

111. Ibid.

112. Kim Barker, "Afghanistan Belatedly Catches 'Titanic' Mania," *Sunday Gazette-Mail*, May 4, 2003.

113. Constable, "Kandahar Recovers Its Pre-Taliban Personality," *Washington Post*, January 24, 2002.

114. "Praising the Titanic," *People* (London), July 14, 2002.

115. "The Sound of Afghanistan's Revival: Music; Squelched by the Fundamentalist Taliban, a Sense of Fun Returns to Kabul, in Song, Dance, and Laughter," *Christian Science Monitor*, February 13, 2003, http://www.highbeam.com/doc/1G1-975722 43.html (accessed November 18, 2012).

116. Dexter Filkins, "Taloqan Cheers Exodus of Taliban," *Albany Times Union* (Albany, NY), November 13, 2001.

117. The American Debbie Rodriguez writes of her experience in opening Kabul's first beauty school in *Kabul Beauty School*. Source: "Kabul Beauty School: An American Woman Goes Behind the Veil," (Book review), *California Bookwatch*, August 1, 2007, http://www.highbeam.com/doc/1G1-167431751.html (accessed October 13, 2012).

118. Willis Witter, "Taliban Taboo Cast Aside as Music of Love Fills the Air," *Washington Times*, December 17, 2001.

119. "Tough Days for TV Tricksters ... MTV Captures Kabul ... the Return of Rodney Rothman," *New York Observer*, December 24, 2001, http://www.highbeam.com/doc/1G1-81473957.html (accessed November 18, 2012).

120. "The Sound of Afghanistan's Revival."

121. Zach Warren, "Searching for Comedy in the Muslim World: Reflections of a Harvard Joke Collector," *Washington Report on Middle East Affairs*, January 1, 2009, http://www.highbeam.com/doc/1P3-1644679931.html (accessed December 2, 2012).

122. Harry Kimball, "Afghans Revive Goat-Carcass Sport: Buzkashi Draws Sponsors in Post-Taliban Economy," *Newser*, posted November 18, 2009.

123. Laura King, "Afghans Resume Game: 'Goat-Grabbing' Was Banned during Taliban Regime," *Columbian* (Vancouver, WA), December 29, 2001, http://www.high beam.com/doc/1P2-23485166.html (accessed March 23, 2013).

124. Charles Moore, "Diary," *Spectator*, January 12, 2002, http://www.highbeam.com/doc/1P3-99632905.html (accessed March 23, 2013).

125. Anna Badkhen, "Many of Afghanistan's Mosques Sit Empty: Afghans Rethink Islam after Era of the Taliban's Heavy Hand," *Seattle Post-Intelligencer*, March 12, 2002.

126. Ibid.

127. Ibid.

128. "First Female Rapper Makes History in Afghanistan," Associated Press, *New York Daily News*, October 9, 2012, http://www.nydailynews.com/news/world/female -rapper-history-afghanistan-article-1.1178182.

129. Ibid.

130. Dodai Stewart, "Afghanistan's First Female Rapper Calls for the End of Abusing Women," *Jezebel*, October 9, 2012, http://jezebel.com/5950194/afghanistans-first -female-rapper-calls-for-the-end-of-abusing-women.

131. Ibid.

132. Aine Harrington, "Driven to Take Another Route: Taliban Commander Now Seeks Job as a Taxi Driver," *Herald*, November 24, 2001.

133. Brian Murphy, "Afghan Dog Fighting Back in Fashion," AP Online, February 9, 2002.

134. "A One-Eyed Lion and the Taliban ... Lifelines," *Daily Mail* (London), August 23, 2010, http://www.highbeam.com/doc/1G1-235179401.html (accessed November 24, 2012).

135. Malcom Garcia, "As Taliban Leave, Prostitution, Alcohol, Other Vices Return to Kabul," Knight/Ridder/Tribune New Service, January 30, 2002.

136. Sonja Barisic, "Rights Group to Send Furs to Afghanis," AP Online, January 29, 2002, http://www.highbeam.com/doc/1P1-49865012.html (accessed November 24, 2012).

137. David Usborne, "Fur Special Issue: Fur and Loathing," *Independent* (London), November 21, 2002, http://www.highbeam.com/doc/1P2-1719550.html (accessed November 24, 2012).

138. Ravi Nessman, "Starving Afghans Seek Out Food," AP Online, January 10, 2002.

139. Brian Murphy, "A Cruel Reality for Agree to Surrender: Front-Line Fighting Continues," *Charleston Gazette* (Charleston, WV), 2001, http://www.highbeam.com (accessed July 21, 2012).

140. Paisley Dodds, "AP: Gitmo Teens Say Taliban Stole Youth," AP Online, June 7, 2005.

141. Daniel Williams, "Afghan King's Role in Nation's Future Remains Clouded," *Washington Post*, 2001, http://www.highbeam.com (accessed July 30, 2012).

142. "Storms and Tea Cups: Charity and Truthfulness (Greg Mortenson's Book 'Three Cups of Tea')," *The Economist*, April 23, 2011, http://www.highbeam.com/doc/1G1-254503604.html (accessed December 14, 2012).

143. Schweid, "Food Aid to Afghanistan Doubles," AP Online, January 2, 2002, http://www.highbeam.com/doc/1P1-49270115.html (accessed January 19, 2013).

144. U.S. Institute for Peace, "Five Years after the Fall of the Taliban: Afghanistan Beyond the Bonn Agreement," a public meeting of the Afghanistan Working Group, http://www.usip.org/events/2006/1206_afghanistan_bonn.html.

145. The factions were the Northern Alliance; the Shura of Rome, representing the exiled former Afghan King Zaher Shah; the Shura of Cyprus, with three representatives from the Shia' Hazara community; and a Peshawar group led by Pir Said Gaylani. Source: "Afghanistan Post 11 September," War on Terrorism Special Report, BBC Monitoring, October 1, 2002.

146. Thomas Johnson, "Afghanistan's Post-Taliban Transition: The State of State-Building after War," *Central Asian Survey* 25, nos. 1–2 (March–June 2006): 3.

147. Schweid, "Food Aid to Afghanistan Doubles."

148. Johnson, "Afghanistan's Post-Taliban Transition," 4.

149. Lucian Kim, "Young Leaders Take Afghan Helm," *Christian Science Monitor*, December 6, 2001.

150. "Suddenly in Bonn," *The Economist*, December 12, 2001, 18.

151. "Afghanistan's Bonn Agreement One Year Later: A Catalog of Missed Opportunities," *Human Rights News*, December 5, 2002.

152. Vincent Curtis, "Sapping Insurgent Strength," *Esprit de Corps*, April 1, 2011.

153. Sonia Kolesnikov, "Economic Reconstruction for Afghanistan," United Press International, November 19, 2001.

154. Spc. Anna K. Perry, "Reconstruction Efforts Spawn Hope in Southern Afghanistan," Combined Joint Special Operations Task Force.

155. "Iraq and Afghanistan Reconstruction: Bobby Wilkes," congressional testimony, 2007, http://www.highbeam.com/doc/1p1-144593929.html (accessed March 25, 2013).

156. Ibid.

157. "Afghanistan Provincial Reconstruction Teams," 455th Air Expeditionary Wing Public Affairs, Bagram Air Base, http://www.bagram.afcent.af.mil/library/factsheets/factsheet.asp?id=4652.

158. "Schultheis, Rob 1943–," *Contemporary Authors, New Revision Series*, January 1, 2006, http://www.highbeam.com/doc/1G2-3483100129.html (accessed January 19, 2013).

159. Robert Border, "Provincial Reconstruction Teams in Afghanistan: A Model for Post-Conflict Reconstruction and Development," *Journal of Development and Social Transformation,* http://www.maxwell.syr.edu/uploadedFiles/moynihan/dst/borders1.pdf ?n=8411.

160. Beth Cole, director, Office of Civil-Military Cooperation, the U.S. Agency for International Development, said this at the Civil Affairs Engagement Roundtable XVII, George Mason University, Arlington Campus, on March 22, 2013. Mr. Silinsky was in attendance.

161. Web Relief Site, Center for Humanitarian Cooperation, May 31, 2003.

162. Samuel Chan, "Sentinels of Afghan Democracy: The Afghan National Army," Working Paper 128 of S. Rajaratnam School of International Studies, Singapore, June, 1, 2007.

163. Creating the police was also important, but this service is in the Department of Interior.

164. This author was in attendance at the Afghanistan Counterinsurgency School in July 2008 when a Pashtun prince said to the audience, "Afghans love their guns. When an Afghan man comes home in the evening, he will kiss his rifle before he kisses his wife."

165. Amin Tarzi, "Disarmament in Afghanistan—Which Militias and What Weapons?," Radio Free Europe/Radio Liberty, April 20, 2005.

166. Another reason why the desertion rate was high was because some recruits felt swindled. They claimed that they were promised extravagant benefits such as a $200 bonus and training in the United States. When it became apparent that they would receive neither, some deserted their posts and returned to their villages. Others claimed to have been impressed into the army by local commanders. Source: "Hopes for Rapidly Building Army Fade; Afghanistan: Low Wages Cause Some Soldiers to Quit So Training Takes Longer," *Telegraph-Herald* (Dubuque), August 15, 2002.

167. U.S. Lt. Gen. William Caldwell, the commander of NATO's training mission in Afghanistan, put the loss at 32 percent of its personnel each year and said that nearly 23 percent of police desert. Source: Slobodan Lekic, "AP Exclusive: Afghan Forces to Start Taking Over," AP Online, 2011, http://www.highbeam.com/doc/1A1-8cb35e2e8c894 f16a21504e52688ed78 (accessed September 17, 2012).

168. Antonio Giustozzi, "Afghanistan's National Army: The Ambiguous Prospects of Afghanization," Global Terrorism Analysis/The Jamestown Foundation, May 1, 2008.

169. Tom Niblock, U.S. Embassy, Kabul, embassy blog, April 2, 2008.

170. Michael Phillips, "Betrayal, and Death, in the Barracks," *Wall Street Journal,* April 14, 2012, 9.

171. "Afghan National Security Forces," *The Nation* (Karachi, Pakistan), October 18, 2010, http://www.highbeam.com/doc/1G1-239869310.html (accessed March 25, 2013).

172. Dina Temple-Raston, "Her Best Shot: The Taliban Leave Death Threats on Her Door at Night," *Marie Claire,* April 1, 2007

173. Kim Barker, "Afghan Female Cop Sheds Burqua, Acts Like One of the Guys," *Chicago Tribune,* July 12, 2006.

174. Ibid.

175. Emma Cowing, "Dying for the Job," *Scotsman,* September 30, 2008.

176. "Afghanistan's Senior-Most Policewoman Assassinated," *Hindustan Times* (New Delhi, India), September 29, 2008.

177. "Women's Police Training Centre Inaugurated," *Palhwok Afghan News* (Kabul, Afghanistan), December 8, 2009.

178. Mahbubul Haq, *Reflections on Human Development* (New York: Oxford University Press, 1995).

179. Peter Middlebrook and Mark Sedra, "Lessons in State Building in the Post 9.11 Era (Afghanistan's Problematic Path to Peace)," *Foreign Policy in Focus*, March 1, 2004.

180. "Broadcasting for Better Health in Afghanistan Radio Plays Promote Improved Health Practices," USAID News Release, Kabul, September 1, 2004.

181. "Afghan Radio Station Begins to Find Voice of Its Own," *China Daily*, July 5, 2002.

182. "Struggling Afghan Community Radio Station Continues Broadcast Efforts," *WE!*, February 1, 2004.

183. Ibid.

184. "Afghan Radio Station Begins to Find Voice of Its Own."

185. "Women Journalists Targeted for Murder in Afghanistan," *Telegraph-Herald* (Dubuque), June 27, 2007.

186. Ibid.

187. Bruce McPhail, "Afghan Journalist Rewarded for Her Bravery in the Face of Madness," *Middle East*, January 1, 2009.

188. "Afghanistan: Education," EIU ViewsWire New York, August 24, 2007.

189. Ibid.

190. "Afghanistan's Education System Assessed in Special Report by ADB and Partners," M2 Presswire, July 30, 2002.

191. Lt. Gen. William Caldwell stressed importance of education in the Afghan services. Source: Lt. Gen. William B. Caldwell and Capt. Nathan K. Finney, "Security, Capacity, and Literacy," *Military Review*, January–February 2001, 23.

192. "Illiteracy Undermines Effectiveness of Afghan Army," *Daily Star* (Beirut, Lebanon), September 15, 2009, http://www.highbeam.com/doc/1G1-207812294.html (accessed September 17, 2012).

193. The foundations of Afghanistan's new and relatively progressive educational system were laid. Teachers were hired and paid more frequently than in the past; school facilities were built and many of the children who had studied in open-air schools are able to study indoors; and girls flooded into a new school system eager to embrace them.

194. Mark Magnier, "Scouting in Afghanistan Gives New Meaning to Motto 'Be Prepared,' " *Sunday Gazette-Mail*, June 23, 2013, http://www.highbeam.com/doc/1P2 -34815904.html (accessed July 1, 2013).

195. Ibid.

196. Lt. Gen. William Caldwell Bolland, a preventative medicine physician, stressed that nearly two-thirds of all Soviet troops who served in Afghanistan were hospitalized for disease. Source: Mike Eckel, "Preventing Disease Tough in Afghanistan," Associated Press, December 2, 2002.

197. Eckel, "Fighting Diseases while Fighting a War on Terror: Preventative Military Medicine in Afghanistan," AP Worldstream, December 1, 2002, http://www.highbeam .com/doc/1P1-70024899.html (accessed March 4, 2013).

198. The plan was to develop a Basic Package of Health Services (BPHS) that would reduce infant and maternal mortality ratios, control communicable diseases, manage malnutrition and disabilities, and be developed by international agencies, particularly the World Health Organization. Source: U.S. Army Sgt. Nina J. Ramon, 345th Mobile Public Affairs Detachment, "Afghan Villagers Get Medical Care."

199. "Doctors without Borders Close Projects in Afghanistan," *Community Action,* August 16, 2004, http://www.highbeam.com/doc/1G1-122619687.html (accessed November 24, 2012).

200. Duncan Buck, "A Tragic Loss of Skateistan Youth," Skateistan, September 10, 2012, http://www.skateistan.org/blog/tragic-loss.

201. Steve Inskeep, "Afghanistan's First Skateboarding Park Opens," *Morning Edition,* NPR, December 31, 2009, http://www.highbeam.com/doc/1P1-174658583.html (accessed September 26, 2012).

202. "Afghan Kids Get on Their Skateboards for a Better Future," *Irish Times,* July 25, 2009, http://www.highbeam.com/doc/1P2-20571142.html (accessed September 26, 2012).

203. Richard Leiby, "Young Skaters Lost to Afghan Violence," *Washington Post,* September 14, 2012, http://www.highbeam.com/doc/1P2-33648191.html (accessed September 26, 2012).

204. Gianluca Mezzofiore, "Afghanistan: Kabul Suicide Bomber Kills Skateboard Kids in NATO Attack," *International Business Times,* September 11, 2012.

205. Laura King, "Young Skateboarders Killed in Kabul Suicide Bombing," *Seattle Times,* September 12, 2012.

206. Rhianon Bader, development and communications director, Skateistan, in e-mail correspondence with this author, responded to Mark Silinsky's e-mail, "I am writing a book about the Taliban and I mentioned Khorshid," January 2, 2013.

207. Afghans were requested not to be "offended if you see a NATO member blowing his/her nose in front of you," and "Sometimes Coalition members will pat each other on the back when they get excited. They may even do this to you if they are proud of the job you've done. Once again, they don't mean to offend you." The pamphlet further explains to Afghans that winking is usually innocuous, as are questions about their daughters and wife/wives.

208. Joel Brown, " 'Frontline' Examines Afghan 'Boy Play' Underworld," *Boston Globe,* April 20, 2010, http://www.highbeam.com/doc/1P2-21559961.html (accessed September 17, 2012).

209. "Dancing boys dressed in women's clothing are becoming increasingly common at Kabul weddings. They wear makeup, wigs, and bells on their feet." Source: "Boys Dancing Tradition Increases in Wedding Functions," *Pajhwok Afghan News* (Kabul, Afghanistan), July 7, 2011, http://www.highbeam.com/doc/1G1-261034060.html (accessed September 17, 2012).

210. Diana West, "Dying Over the Truth: Why the Afghan Army Is Killing Our Soldiers," Stop Radical Islam.Org, August 30, 2012, http://www.radicalislam.org/blog/dying-over-truth-why-afghan-army-killing-our-soldiers/#fm.

211. "Afghan Cops at Massacre High on Dope: Inquest of 5 Brit Troops Reveals Drug Use," *Mirror* (London), February 8, 2011. http://www.highbeam.com/doc/1G1-24854 0785.html (accessed September 17, 2012).

212. Opium is used to pacify children is some homes. It quiets babies and relieves pain. Source: Aunohita Mojumdar, "In Afghanistan, Drug Rehab for Children," *Christian Science Monitor,* July 14, 2010.

213. Hamid Shalizi, "Afghan Clerics Demand Punishment for Koran Burners," Reuters, March 2, 2012.

214. Yochi J. Dreazen, "Koran Burning in Afghanistan Fuels Bloody New Attacks on U.S. Forces," *National Journal,* 2012, http://www.highbeam.com/doc/1P3-25941 48151.html (accessed October 3, 2012).

215. "Fury at Koran Burning Fuels Violence Across Afghanistan," *Independent* (London), April 4, 2011, http://www.highbeam.com/doc/1P2-28344125.html (accessed October 3, 2012).

216. "Jihad Is Becoming as American as Apple Pie and as British as Afternoon Tea," Jihad Watch, March 20, 2010, http://www.jihadwatch.org/2010/03/jihad-is-becoming-as-american-as-apple-pie-and-as-british-as-afternoon-tea.html.

217. "Nidal Hasan, Terrorist—aka 'Alien Unlawful Belligerent,' " States News Service., November 17, 2009, http://www.highbeam.com/doc/1G1-216011623.html (accessed November 16, 2012).

218. Brad Knickerbocker, "Alleged Fort Hood Shooter Maj. Nidal Hasan Faces March 2012 Trial," *Christian Science Monitor*, July 20, 2011, http://www.highbeam.com/doc/1G1-261921784.html (accessed November 16, 2012).

219. Patrik Jonsson, "Fort Hood Shooting: Al Qaeda Now Portrays Nidal Hasan as Terrorism Star," *Christian Science Monitor*, October 19, 2010, http://www.highbeam.com/doc/1G1-239929996.html (accessed November 16, 2012).

220. "Wolf Again Asks Administration Not to Send Guantanamo Detainees Back to Yemen," States News Service, November 12, 2009, http://www.highbeam.com/doc/1G1-216047776.html (accessed November 16, 2012).

221. Jason Burke, "Anwar al-Awlaki Obituary," *Guardian*, October 2, 2011, http://www.guardian.co.uk/world/2011/oct/02/anwar-al-awlaki.

222. Gordon Lubold, "Why Is Anwar Al-Awlaki Terrorist 'No. 1?,' " *Christian Science Monitor*, May 19, 2010, http://www.highbeam.com/doc/1G1-226781505.html (accessed November 17, 2012).

223. "Isolated Incidents . . .," *Jerusalem Post*, November 11, 2009, http://www.highbeam.com/doc/1P1-173133526.html (accessed November 16, 2012).

224. Tim Lister and Paul Cruickshank, "Anwar Al-Awlaki: Al Qaeda's Rock Star No More," *St. Joseph News-Press*, September 30, 2011, http://www.highbeam.com/doc/1P2-29770255.html (accessed November 16, 2012).

225. Alastair Beach, "Family Hits Out at US in Fury at Fate of Awlaki's Slain Son," *Independent* (London), October 19, 2011, http://www.highbeam.com/doc/1P2-29887887.html (accessed November 17, 2012).

226. Ahmed Al-Haj and Brian Murphy, "Al-Awlaki: from Voice for Jihad to Al-Qaida Figure," AP Worldstream, September 30, 2011, http://www.highbeam.com/doc/1A1-3784f3f02ed4440db11259845c1bdc8d.html (accessed July 3, 2013).

227. "In Kabul, the Taliban Sank but the Movie 'Titanic' Goes On," *Chicago Tribune* 2003, http://www.highbeam.com (accessed September 17, 2012).

CHAPTER 5

1. "Report Says Taliban Raised $400 Million Last Year," Radio Free Europe, States New Service, September 11, 2012.

2. Grant R. Highland, Essay 2003, "New Century, Old Problems: The Global Insurgency with Islam and the Nature of War on Terrorism," in *Chairman of the Joint Chiefs of Staff Strategy Essay Competition*, Washington, DC: National Defense University Press, 2003, 29. http://oai.dtic.mil/oai/oai?verb=getRecord&metadataPrefix=html&identifier=ADA415486.

3. Bakhtiyorjon U. Hammidov, "The Fall of the Taliban Regime and Its Recovery as an Insurgent Movement in Afghanistan," master's of military art and science thesis, U.S. Army Command and General Staff College, 2004, 44.

4. Muhammad Amir Rana, "The Taliban Consolidate Control in Pakistan's Tribal Regions," Combating Terrorism Center at West Point, June 15, 2008.

5. Ibid.

6. Ibid.

7. Zofeen Ebrahim, "Pakistan: Displaced by War, Thousands Depend on Charities," Inter Press Service, 2010, http://www.highbeam.com (accessed March 26, 2013).

8. Paul Haven, "Taliban Orchestrating Deadly Attacks in Afghanistan from Safe Haven in Pakistan, Afghan Intelligence Says," Associated Press Worldstream, September 23, 2003.

9. Jan McGirk, "In Foreign Parts: Forces of Conservatism Meet Their Match in a Middle-Class Mother and Froth Cappuccino," *Independent* (London), October 19, 2002.

10. "Afghanistan's Deposed Clerics Enjoy an Unbothered Exile," *The Economist*, January 15, 2005.

11. "Taliban Outlines Efforts to Regroup," *Albany Times Union* (Albany, NY), 2003, http://www.highbeam.com/doc/1G1-157685051.html (accessed August 26, 2012).

12. M. H. Khatana, "Descent into Chaos: The U.S. and the Failure of Nation Building in Pakistan, Afghanistan, and Central Asia," *Journal of Third World Studies*, April 1, 2011, http://www.highbeam.com/doc/1P3-2428787361.html (accessed March 26, 2013).

13. Dr. Salem Javed, "A Rebuttal of Surat Khan Marri on the Hazaras," *Lahore Daily Times Online in English*, July 1, 2012.

14. Mahvish Ahmad, "Pakistan Bombing Hints at Free Rein for Radicals in Quetta," *Christian Science Monitor*, June 19, 2012.

15. "Varsity Woman Prof Shot Dead in Quetta," *The Nation* (Karachi, Pakistan), April 27, 2010.

16. "Former Olympian Boxer Killed in Quetta," *Financial Post* (Karachi, Pakistan), June 17, 2011.

17. "Boy Found Dead in Quetta," *Daily Post* (Lahore, Pakistan), June 21, 2011.

18. "Former Olympian Boxer Killed in Quetta" and "Financial Three Dead in Quetta Tribal Clash," *Daily Post* (Lahore, Pakistan), February 5, 2011.

19. "Balch Scholar Shot Dead in Quetta," *Hindustan Times* (New Delhi, India), June 2, 2011.

20. "Taliban Backed Supporters Forbid Women from Eating out in Quetta," *Hindustan Times* (New Delhi, India), January 25, 2009.

21. "Pakistan: Few Women Health Workers in Balochistan," IRIN Asia English Service, July 7, 2010.

22. Eric Schmitt and Mark Mazzetti, "New Taliban Haven Raises Alarms for U.S. Pakistan Border City a Militant Pipeline," *International Herald Tribune*, February 11, 2009.

23. "Pakistan Allowing Taliban Territory Use: British Officer," *Hindustan Times* (New Delhi, India), May 19, 2006.

24. Schmitt and Mazzetti, "New Taliban Haven Raises Alarms."

25. David E. Sanger and Eric Schmitt, "U.S. Weights Expanding Covert War in Pakistan Attacks Considered on Taliban in Quetta," *International Herald Tribune*, March 19, 2009.

26. Constable, "U.S. Says Taliban Has a New Haven in Pakistan," *Washington Post*, 2009, http://www.highbeam.com (accessed July 21, 2012).

27. Associated Press, "Taliban Launches New Afghan Operation," May 28, 2007; "Deputy Emir of the Believers Declares Beginning of the Series of Spring Operations (Admonition)," SITE Intel Group, March 24, 2008.

28. " 'Kidnapping, Bombings and Vendettas Have Long Been a Way of Life in Quetta,' " *Herald*, 2012, http://www.highbeam.com (accessed July 21, 2012).

29. Declan Walsh, "Afghan Drugs Barons Flaunt Their Wealth and Power," *Guardian*, April 7, 2006; "Four Suspected Militants Detained," *Pajhwok Afghan News*, May 31, 2009; "Taliban Leader Killed in Helmand," *Pajhwok Afghan News*, October 22, 2008.

30. Anand Gopal, "Can Afghanistan Taliban Absorb Blow to Quetta Shura?," *Christian Science Monitor*, 2010, http://www.highbeam.com (accessed July 30, 2012).

31. "Quetta-Based Taliban Move to Karachi," *The Nation* (Karachi, Pakistan), April 29, 2009, http://www.highbeam.com/doc/1G1-198820365.html (accessed August 22, 2012).

32. Burka Woman Saad Haroon, YouTube, http://www.youtube.com/watch?v=-LzOU6ETxI8.

33. "Pakistan Comics Deflect Taliban with Ridicule," *Daily News Egypt*, October 12, 2011, http://www.highbeam.com/doc/1G1-269932884.html (accessed October 7, 2012).

34. Ibid.

35. Hani Taha, "Saad Haroon: Comic Relief," *Express Tribune* with the *International Herald Tribune*, February 21, 2001, http://tribune.com.pk/story/121725/saad-haroon-comic-relief/.

36. "Saad Haroon: Pakistan as a Bad Bollywood Comedy," Radio Open Source, comment section, August 11, 2011, http://www.radioopensource.org/saad-haroon-pakistan-as-a-bad-bollywood-comedy/.

37. "Taliban's Top Man Baradar Captured," APS Diplomat News Service, February 22, 2010, http://www.highbeam.com/doc/1G1-219459749.html (accessed September 19, 2012).

38. Ben Arnoldy and Issam Ahmed, "Mullah Abdul Ghani Baradar Capture: Triumph of Pakistan-US Cooperation?," *Christian Science Monitor*, February 16, 2010, http://www.highbeam.com/doc/1G1-219051675.html (accessed September 19, 2012).

39. Sajjad Tarakzai, "Pakistan to Release Senior Taliban Commander on Saturday," Yahoo News, http://news.yahoo.com/pakistan-release-senior-taliban-commander-saturday-161006722.html (accessed September 20, 2013).

40. Gopal, "Afghanistan War: Who's Who in the Taliban Leadership," *Christian Science Monitor*, February 25, 2010, http://www.highbeam.com/doc/1G1-219808170.html (accessed September 23, 2012).

41. Gopal, "Qayyum Zakir: The Afghanistan Taliban's Rising Mastermind," *Christian Science Monitor*, April 30, 2010, http://www.highbeam.com/doc/1G1-225299098.html (accessed March 26, 2013).

42. Ibid.

43. Karin Brulliard and Joshua Partlow, "Taliban Commander Captured; in String of Arrests, Pakistan Has Gone After Afghan Militants," *Washington Post*, February 23, 2010, http://www.highbeam.com/doc/1P2-21308182.html (accessed September 19, 2012).

44. Mir Zia, "Taliban Agrees to Stop Training," AP Online, May 19, 2000, http://www.highbeam.com/doc/1P1-26701829.html (accessed September 19, 2012).

45. Gopal, "Afghanistan War."

46. Ron Moreau, "The Taliban's New Dirty Dozen," *Newsweek International*, 2012, http://www.highbeam.com (accessed September 19, 2012).

47. A police inspector summed up the Taliban's presence: "Taliban militants have established a world record of savagery. They have slaughtered soldiers and common

people with knives and displayed their heads in public places to send a message across the forces that they must not chase them at the behest of government." Ashfaq Yusufzai, "Taliban Militants Have Established a World Record of Savagery," Jihad Watch, December 7, 2012, http://www.jihadwatch.org/2012/12/taliban-militants-have-established -a-world-record-of-savagery.html.

48. Yusufzai, "Taliban Militants Have Established."

49. "Haqqani Founder's Son Reportedly Killed; Afghanistan; Taliban Denies Operative Died in Pakistan Airstrike," *Seattle Times*, August 27, 2012, http://www.highbeam.com/doc/1G1-301110275.html (accessed September 23, 2012).

50. Secretary of State Hillary Rodham Clinton formally designated the militant Haqqani network on September 8, 2012. Source: Steven Lee Myers and Eric Schmitt, " U.S. Adds Haqqani Network to Terror List," *International Herald Tribune*, September 8, 2012, http://www.highbeam.com/doc/1P1-208670506.html (accessed September 23, 2012).

51. "Haqqani Network Makes Peace-Talks Overture; Member: Taliban Leader Must OK Sitting Down with U.S.," *Washington Times*, November 14, 2012, http://www.highbeam.com/doc/1G1-308433124.html (accessed November 15, 2012).

52. "Haqqani Network Commander Killed Near Islamabad," *Nation*, Karachi, Pakistan, 2013, http://www.highbeam.com/doc/1G1-348841223.html (accessed November 14, 2013).

53. "Terrorist Organizational Models," in *A Military Guide to Terrorism in the Twenty-First Century*, August 15, 2007, http://www.au.af.mil/au/awc/awcgate/army/guidterr/ch03.pdf.

54. Bill Roggio, "The Afghan Taliban Top Leaders," February 23, 2010, http://www.longwarjournal.org/archives/2010/02/the_talibans_top_lea.php

55. "Islamic 'Charities' That Are 'Misinterpreting Islam' Giving Taliban $200 Million a Year," *Frontpage Magazine*, December 12, 2012, http://www.jihadwatch.org/2012/12/islamic-charities-that-are-misinterpreting-islam-giving-taliban-200-million-a-year .html.

56. Shahid Afsar, Chris Samples, and Thomas Wood, "The Taliban: An Organizational Analysis," *Military Review*, May–June 2008.

57. Dexter Filkins, "Karzai Is Said to Doubt West Can Defeat Taliban," *New York Times*, June 11, 2010; "Taliban Member Responsible for Selecting Suicide-Bomb Sites Targeted," ISAF, December 29, 2010.

58. Ron Moreau, "Do the Taliban Get PTSD?," *Newsweek*, December 6, 2010; Yousafzai and Moreau, "How the Taliban Lost Its Swagger," *Newsweek*, February 27, 2011.

59. Borzou Daragahi, "Afghan Taliban Intelligence Network Embraces the New," *Los Angeles Times*, April 13, 2011.

60. Gretchen Peters, *Crime and Insurgency* (West Point, NY: Combating Terrorism Center, 2010).

61. Ruhullah Khapalwak and Carlotta Gall, "Taliban Kill Afghan Interpreters Working for U.S. and Its Allies," *New York Times*, July 4, 2006; C. J. Chivers, "Afghanistan's Hidden Taliban Government," *New York Times*, February 6, 2011.

62. Impersonating or pretending to agree with the enemy is religiously sanctioned and embedded in Islam's history. Mohammed, himself, gave practical guidance for lying and deceiving the non-Muslim enemy. The Suras that advocate deception, lying, confabulating, and prevaricating to advance the cause of Islam or to protect the Islamic community include Suras 3:28, 4:139, 4:144, 5:57, 9:23, 9: 29, 60:1, 60:2., 60:3, and 60:13.19.

63. There are other parallels, though inexact, to highly authoritarian and regimented states. In Nazi Germany and postwar communist countries, the intelligence and security services were not encumbered by any set of Western-based civil rights or laws. Neither are the Taliban today.

64. Antonio Giustozzi, *Decoding the New Taliban* (New York: Columbia University Press, 2009).

65. As Salafists, the Taliban look to the biographies, traditions, and references to the lives of first-generation Muslims, particularly Mohammed. Source: According to Ibn Ishaq, Mohammed suspected that a captive Jew was hiding some of his personal property from him. To obtain necessary information, Mohammed lit a campfire on the Jew's chest until he revealed the location, which he did. Ibn Ishaq, Tabari, vol. 8, 122–23.

66. Jacki Lyden, "Barnett Rubin on the Taliban and Its Relationship to Al-Qaida and Osama bin Laden," *Weekend Edition Sunday*, NPR, September 23, 2001.

67. Gabriela Perdomo, "The Afghanistan Question, Citizens of Western Nations Engaged in the War on Terror Are Growing Impatient with the Lack of Results," *Global Monitor*, May 1, 2008, http://www.angus-reid.com/analysis/40012/the_afghanistan _question/.

68. In late 2007 President Bush said, "My biggest concern is that people say, 'Well, we're kind of tired of Afghanistan and, therefore, we think we're going to leave.' That would be my biggest concern." Source: Mathew Lee, "Bush, Rice Fret over Afghanistan Fatigue," Associated Press, December 21, 2007.

69. Robert Fisk, "Thousands Massacred by Taliban," *Independent* (London), 1998, http://www.highbeam.com (accessed February 20, 2012).

70. In "On Killing: The Psychological Cost of Learning to Kill in War and Society," Lt. Col. Dave Grossman notes the use of atrocity works well "when institutionalized as policy by revolutionary organization, armies and governments." He cites the example of the Viet Cong in the early phases of the war in Vietnam. See also Giustozzi, *Decoding the New Taliban*.

71. "Lash and Burn: Taliban Vice Squads Returning to the Fray," *London Sunday Times*, June 24, 2012, 24.

72. Aryn Baker, "The Girl Gap," *Time*, January 21, 2008.

73. Amir Shah, "Afghanistan Elementary School Set on Fire," AP Online, September 3, 2003.

74. Usatoday.com (U.S.), August 5, 2012.

75. Ibid.

76. Kevin Sieff, "Afghan Girls' Education Back in Shadows," *Washington Post*, April 25, 2012, 1.

77. "Effective Public Administration Vital to Deliver Services to Afghan Citizens, Says World Bank Report." U.S. Federal News Service, Including U.S. State News, June 10, 2008.

78. "District Police Chief Wounded by Mine Blast in Afghan West," *Peshawar Afghan Islamic Press* (in Pashto), August 6, 2012.

79. "Taliban Claim Responsibility for Police Battalion Attack in Afghan South," *Peshawar Afghan Islamic Press* (in Pashto), June 19, 2012.

80. Yusufzai, "Taliban Face Sick Police," Inter Press Service, December 9, 2012, http://www.ipsnews.net/2012/12/taliban-face-sick-police/.

81. "VOA News: U.N.'S Ban Condemns Taliban Attack on Afghan U.N. Physicians," U.S. Federal News Service, Including U.S. State News, September 14, 2008, http://www.highbeam.com/doc/1P3-1554523771.html (accessed August 26, 2012).

82. "Taliban Propaganda: Winning the War of Words?," *Asia Report* 158 (July 24, 2008): 12.

83. David Tarrant, "Psychological Warfare May Be a Key Weapon for Outgunned Taliban," Knight Ridder/Tribune News Service, 2001, http://www.highbeam.com (accessed July 21, 2012).

84. Yousafzai and Moreau, "The Very Picture of Propaganda," *Newsweek*, March 8, 2004.

85. "Taliban Propaganda," 13.

86. Ibid., 14.

87. Often these themes are presented in different artistic genre, particularly poetry. One poem published on El Emarah is "Death Is Gift," in which the poet promises to the Afghan nation that he will never "bow to Bush . . . not kiss the hand of Laura Bush, nor will I bow to Rice." Source: Raphael Satter, "UK Publisher to Release Taliban Poetry Anthology," AP Worldstream, May 5, 2012, http://www.highbeam.com/doc/1A1-2f47ca11eac243dfac853068655c54c0.html (accessed March 26, 2013).

88. "Taliban Propaganda," 18.

89. Sarah Lyall, "Bold Tactics for Islam's Converts: Radical Groups Target the Impressionable," *International Herald Tribune*, August 18, 2006, http://www.highbeam.com/doc/1P1-127555121.html (accessed December 9, 2012).

90. "How Afghanistan Stole Yvonne Ridley's Heart," *South Wales Echo* (Cardiff, Wales), February 27, 2002, http://www.highbeam.com/doc/1G1-83415248.html (accessed December 9, 2012).

91. "Wilders Causes Another Row: Pre-Captivity Stockholm Syndrome," *Brussels Journal*, June 1, 2009, http://www.brusselsjournal.com/node/3946.

92. James Dobbins, "Moral Clarity and the Middle East," speech delivered to the New America Foundation, August 24, 2006.

93. The Pakistani Taliban, or Tehrik el Taliban, are more focused on the Pakistani government.

CHAPTER 6

1. Edward Cody, "Taliban Strategy: Prolong Conflict," *Washington Post*, October 21, 2001.

2. Ibid.

3. Ibid.

4. Tim McGirk, "Army of God Runs into the Afghan Sands," *The Independent* (London), 1996, http://www.highbeam.com (accessed February 20, 2012).

5. Sabrina Tavernise, "Taliban's Popularity Begins to Wither among Pakistanis' Strict Laws and Violence Drive Citizens Back to the Government for Help," *International Herald Tribune*, 2009, http://www.highbeam.com (accessed December 19, 2010).

6. Sudarsan Raghavan, "One American Wounded in Two-Hour Battle al-Qaida, Taliban fighters," Knight Ridder/Tribune News Service, 2002, http://www.highbeam.com/doc/1G1-84040728.html (accessed December 3, 2013).

7. Matt Kelley, "Taliban Pouring into Afghanistan: U.S. General Says Top U.S. Commander Says Fighters Trained by Al-Qaida Entering Country from Pakistan," *Oakland Tribune*, 2003, http://www.highbeam.com (accessed November 1, 2010).

8. Ben Venzke and Aimee Ibrahim, "Al-Qaeda's Advice for Mujahideen in Iraq: Lessons Learned in Afghanistan," vol. 1.0, April 14, 2003, 12, IntelCenter, Alexandria, VA.

9. Al Adel did not specify the proposed number of fighters in the smaller band. Based on other passages in the literature, the number would probably be around 10 men.

10. The wording of al Adel's 2003 manuscript is not clear, but his use of the word "trench" probably refers to defensive berms, shelters, as well as temporary trenches.

11. Venzke and Ibrahim, "Al-Qaeda's Advice for Mujahideen in Iraq," 12.

12. Ibid.

13. "Taliban's Notorious 'Hit-and-Run' Strategy Frustrated Soviets, U.S. Alike," *Chicago Tribune*, 2001, http://www.highbeam.com (accessed February 20, 2012).

14. Kevin Sieff, "Taliban Commander Turns Self In ... for Reward on 'Wanted' Poster," *Washington Post Online*, April 17, 2012, http://www.washingtonpost.com/blogs/blogpost/post/taliban-commander-turns-self-in-for-reward-on-wanted-poster/2012/04/17/gIQAbVjqNT_blog.html.

15. "Taliban Commander Tries to Claim Reward for His Own Capture," *Telegraph*, April 18, 2012, http://www.telegraph.co.uk/news/worldnews/asia/afghanistan/9210567/Taliban-commander-tries-to-claim-reward-for-his-own-capture.html.

16. This author heard an Afghan prince explain this at the Afghanistan Counterinsurgency Academy, 2008.

17. This was certainly the case against the Soviets, when mujahideen used horses in raids against Soviet soldiers. Sources: Associated Press, "Ancient Warfare Persists as Rebels Use Horse Power; Afghanistan: The Horse Is Better than 4-Wheel Drive in the Mountains," *Telegraph-Herald* (Dubuque), 2001, http://www.highbeam.com (accessed February 20, 2012).

18. Wally Santana, "U.S. Sweep in Afghanistan Yields Weapons, Not Enemy: Troops Raise Possibility Taliban, Al Qaeda Were Tipped Off," *Washington Post*, April 27, 2002, http://www.highbeam.com/doc/1P2-367804.html (accessed September 7, 2012).

19. Chris Hawley, "Troops Destroy Biggest Cache Found in Afghanistan—Hundreds of 500-Pound Bombs Buried in Dry Riverbed," AP Worldstream, October 4, 2002, http://www.highbeam.com/doc/1P1-68395072.html (accessed August 25, 2012).

20. "US Blows Up Booby-Trapped Buildings in Southern Afghanistan," Philippines News Agency, November 17, 2010, http://www.highbeam.com/doc/1G1-242336847.html (accessed August 25, 2012).

21. There are an estimated 90 million AKs in the world today. U.S. soldiers in Vietnam openly admired the weapon, particularly when it stood in contrast to early versions of the M 16. It never jammed, even in wet, muddy, or sandy conditions.

22. The AK-47 weighs seven pounds and comes with a 30-round magazine. It is accurate to 330 yards and fires at a rate of 600 rounds a minute.

23. Mark McDonald, "Kalashnikov Reflects on AK-47 Assault Rifle," *Sunday Gazette-Mail*, 2003, http://www.highbeam.com (accessed July 21, 2012).

24. There is a precedent with al Qaeda, which was captured in the movie *Blackhawk Down*.

25. Venzke and Ibrahim, "Al-Qaeda's Advice for Mujahideen in Iraq."

26. Ustad Basir Arifi, secretary for the Disarmament of Illegal Armed Groups program in northern Afghanistan, said weapons left there by the Soviet Union are now being moved by professional smugglers to the southern provinces where the Taliban Islamist movement has its stronghold. Source: "Afghanistan: Taliban Smuggles Soviet-Era Weapons from North," Inter Press Service, June 27, 2007, http://www.highbeam.com/doc/1G1-165748516.html (accessed August 26, 2012).

27. "Taliban Uses Weapons Made in China, Iran," *Washington Times*, June 5, 2007, http://www.highbeam.com/doc/1G1-164527683.html (accessed September 7, 2012).

28. "Taliban Have Rocket-Propelled Grenades Strong Enough to Kill Anyone in 30-Ft Radius," *Hindustan Times* (New Delhi, India), August 22, 2008, http://www.highbeam .com/doc/1P3-1537909301.html (accessed August 26, 2012).

29. "Taliban Army Battle-Hardened Guerrillas," *Cincinnati Post*, October 2, 2001, http://www.highbeam.com/doc/1G1-78861687.html (accessed August 26, 2012).

30. "Mad Max Tactics of Taliban's Cavalry," *Mail on Sunday* (London),2001, http:// www.highbeam.com (accessed December 21, 2011).

31. Venzke and Ibrahim, "Al-Qaeda's Advice for Mujahideen in Iraq,"10.

32. Ibid., 13.

33. Martin Finucane, "Muslim Woman Who's Sought by FBI Lived Uneventfully," *Deseret News* (Salt Lake City), April 5, 2003, http://www.highbeam.com/doc/1P2 -7085930.html (accessed March 26, 2013).

34. "Aafia Siddiqui," *New York Times*, September 24, 2010, http://topics.nytimes.com/ top/reference/timestopics/people/s/aafia_siddiqui/index.html.

35. Dina Temple-Raston, "The FBI's Most Wanted Woman: Is Aafia Siddiqui a Vicious Terrorist or the Victim of Extreme Identity Theft?," *Marie Claire*, January 1, 2009, http://www.highbeam.com/doc/1G1-191999115.html (accessed November 7, 2012).

36. James Bone, "Aafia Siddiqui Demands No Jewish Jurors at Attempted Murder Trial," *Times* (London), January 15, 2010, http://www.timesonline.co.uk/tol/news/ world/us_and_americas/article6988777.ece (accessed May 2010).

37. Temple-Raston, "The FBI's Most Wanted Woman."

38. Amy Sahba, "Trial of Al Qaeda-Linked Scientist Starts in New York," CNN, January 19, 2010.

39. "Jury Selection for Aafia's Jan. 19 Trial Finalized," Philippines News Agency, January 15, 2010, http://www.highbeam.com/doc/1g1-216728361.html (accessed November 7, 2012).

40. Tom Hays and Larry Neumeister, "Outburst Gets Terror Suspect Pulled from Courtroom," *Deseret News* (Salt Lake City), January 20, 2010, http://www.highbeam .com/doc/1P2-21146081.html (accessed March 26, 2013).

41. "Haqqani's 'Dubious Role' in Dr Aafia's Trial Exposed," *The Nation* (Karachi, Pakistan), September 25, 2010, http://www.highbeam.com/doc/1G1-238297485.html (accessed December 9, 2012).

42. "Aafia Siddiqui Term 'Political Sentence,' " *The Nation* (Karachi, Pakistan), December 9, 2012, http://www.highbeam.com/doc/1G1-311400397.html (accessed December 13, 2012).

43. Katherine Ozment, "Who's Afraid of Aafia Siddiqui?," *Boston Magazine*, October 2004, archived from the original on January 25, 2009, http://www.bostonmagazine.com/ articles/whos_afraid_of_aafia_siddiqui (accessed February 3, 2009).

44. Dan Edge, "Children of the Taliban," *Frontline*, PBS, August 14, 2009.

45. Arwa Damon, "Taliban Brainwashes Kids with Visions of Virgins," CNN, January 6, 2010.

46. While the Afghan intelligence service National Directorate of Security (NDS) says that the Taliban are isolating "lazy and low-profile students" in Pakistani madrassas to send them on suicide missions.

47. Jayshree Bajoria, "Pakistan's Education System and Links to Extremism," Council on Foreign Relations, June 1, 2009.

48. Tahir Andrabi, Jishnudas Das, C. Christine Fair, and Asim Ijaz Khwaja, "The Madrasa Myth," *Foreign Policy*, June 1, 2009.

49. "Taliban Suicide Bomber Dressed as Schoolboy Kills 31 Army Cadets," *Independent* (London), February 11, 2011.

50. "Police Arrest Two Afghan Boys for Suicide Bomb Plan," AFP, February 12, 2012.

51. "Taliban Extremist Targets Funeral: Afghan, Coalition Forces Capture Terrorists," U.S. Federal News Service, Including U.S. State News, September 11, 2006, http://www.highbeam.com/doc/1P3-1125829951.html (accessed August 26, 2012).

52. Heidi Vogt and Faiez Rahim, "Afghan Army Says Ministry Attacker Was Outsider." AP Worldstream, 2011, http://www.highbeam.com (accessed December 23, 2011).

53. "Afghan President Condemns Wedding Attack, Orders Probe," *Peshawar Afghan Islamic Press* (in Pashto), July 14, 2012.

54. "Taliban Is Top Suspect in Bombing at Wedding," *USA Today*, July 16, 2012, 5.

55. The girl said, "I was buying toffees from a roadside vendor on my way to school. When I opened my eyes, I found myself in a room. They fed me biscuits and I fell unconscious ... Then they tried to put a suicide belt on me." Source: Owais Tohid, "Are Pakistan's Taliban Using Children as Weapons?," *Christian Science Monitor*, June 22, 2011, http://www.highbeam.com/doc/1G1-259557913.html (accessed August 26, 2012).

56. "Ex-Taliban Girl Trainee Warns of Army of Female Suicide Bombers," *Hindustan Times* (New Delhi, India), January 2, 2011.

57. "Female Bomber Kills 12 in Kabul to Avenge Film," *Times of Oman* (Muscat, Oman), September 18, 2012.

58. "Taliban Suicide Bomber Dressed as Schoolboy."

59. Ibid.

60. "Boy: Taliban Recruited Me to Bomb Troops," AP Online, June 25, 2007, http://www.highbeam.com/doc/1Y1-107772255.html (accessed September 29, 2012).

61. "Taliban Puts Afghan Boy in Suicide Vest," AP Online, June 25, 2007, http://www.highbeam.com/doc/1Y1-107772203.html (accessed September 29, 2012).

62. "The Six-Year-Old Tricked into Being a Suicide Bomber; Juma Gul: 'I Felt the Bomb,' " *Daily Mail* (London), June 27, 2007, http://www.highbeam.com/doc/1G1-16 6053776.html (accessed September 29, 2012).

63. Ashfaq Yusufzai, "Pakistan: Taliban Increasingly Trains Girls as Suicide Bombers," Inter Press Service, July 18, 2008, http://www.highbeam.com/doc/1P1-15 4385253.html (accessed September 29, 2012).

64. Ibid.

65. Ibid.

66. William S. Lind, "Our Illiterate Infantry," *American Conservative*, 2011, http://www.highbeam.com (accessed August 19, 2012).

67. "Taliban's New Tactic Come Out, Fire and Disappear," *Hindustan Times* (New Delhi, India), May 31, 2009.

68. Ian Bruce, "Details Emerge of Deadly Taliban Ambush," *Herald*, June 13, 2006, http://www.highbeam.com/doc/1P2-23631299.html (accessed August 25, 2012).

69. "Window World Backs Mission for Veterans Airlift Command," *Manufacturing Close-Up*, February 26, 2012, http://www.highbeam.com/doc/1P2-30795148.html (accessed July 13, 2013).

70. C. J. Chivers, "Marines Push through Sniper Fire; Despite Taliban Tactic, US Gains in Marja Battle," *Boston Globe*, 2010, http://www.highbeam.com (accessed August 16, 2012).

71. "Afghan Militants Kill 10 French, Hit U.S. Base," *Southtown Star*, August 20, 2008, http://www.highbeam.com/doc/1N1-12308A06D13A7238.html (accessed December 3, 2013).

72. Dion Nissenbaum, "Taliban Attacks Gain Sophistication," *Charleston Gazette* (Charleston, WV), July 16, 2010.

73. "NATO Says Taliban Use Hezbollah Tactics," AP Online, 2006, (accessed August 19, 2012).

74. "Sniper Wars Taliban's New Terror; Taliban's New Terror Tactic Targets Scots," *Sunday Mail* (Glasgow, Scotland), 2009, http://www.highbeam.com (accessed December 21, 2011).

75. Andrew Gregory, "Hunt for Taliban 'Killing Machine,' " *Mirror* (London), April 12, 2010.

76. Ibid.

77. "Brigade Artist Prepares for Fourth Tour of Duty in Afghanistan," *Sevenoaks Chronicle*, 2013, http://www.highbeam.com (accessed July 3, 2013).

78. "Two Soldiers Killed with One Bullet Fired by Taliban Sniper," *Daily Mail* (London), July 9, 2011, http://www.highbeam.com/doc/1G1-260924083.html (accessed September 30, 2012).

79. Nancy A. Youssef, "Taliban Turns to Snipers: Tactic Change Shows Militia 'Suffering Heavy Losses,' General Says," *Sunday Gazette-Mail*, 2009, http://www.high beam.com (accessed December 21, 2011).

80. "Sniper Wars."

81. "Crackshot Christopher Kills Taliban Warlord: from One Mile Away, Amazing Shot by Hero Scot in Afghanistan War Zone," *Daily Record* (Glasgow, Scotland), August 8, 2009, http://www.highbeam.com/doc/1G1-205311035.html (accessed September 26, 2012).

82. Colin Nickerson, "Mines Take Bloody Toll in Afghanistan Explosive Devices, Reportedly Left as Soviets Withdrew, Threaten Returning Refugees," *Boston Globe*, August 29, 1988, http://www.highbeam.com/doc/1P2-8076765.html (accessed August 25, 2012).

83. Raymond Whitaker, "Cycle of Violence," New Statesman (1996), May 11, 2009, http://www.highbeam.com/doc/1P3-1712399041.html (accessed November 24, 2012).

84. Bruce, "Taliban 'Using Weapons Made in China,' " *Herald*, September 5, 2007, http://www.highbeam.com/doc/1P2-23666810.html (accessed September 17, 2012).

85. "Army's Vehicles Not Tough Enough: Taliban Just Build Bigger Bombs," *Washington Times*, 2012, http://www.highbeam.com (accessed August 19, 2012).

86. Though ammonium nitrate is illegal in Afghanistan, farmers can use urea-based fertilizers on crops. The ammonium nitrate fertilizer in Afghanistan is usually imported from Pakistan. Ammonium nitrate has long been used as both a fertilizer and an explo sive. Source: "Blumenthal Urges Crackdown of Explosive Devices in Afghanistan," States News Service, November 17, 2011, http://www.highbeam.com/doc/1G1-27 4319377.html (accessed August 25, 2012).

87. Dexter Filkins, "Raids Uncover Huge Fertilizer Bomb Stashes in Afghanistan; Afghan Bomb Cache Found; Huge Stash of Fertilizer Had Potential to Create Thousands of Explosives," *International Herald Tribune*, November 12, 2009, http:// www.highbeam.com/doc/1P1-173001205.html (accessed August 25, 2012).

88. Figures provided to the *Washington Post* show that U.S. and Afghan troops have seized about 480 tons of ammonium nitrate fertilizer this year, enough explosive material to manufacture 30,000 to 50,000 IEDs. During the same period U.S. and Afghan troops have either triggered or discovered 16,600 of the bombs, a slight increase over 2011. In June alone, U.S. and Afghan forces encountered 1,900 IEDs, a record amount in a single month for the 11-year war. Source: "Fertilizer for Roadside Bombs Being Smuggled into

Afghanistan," *Seattle Times*, August 19, 2012, http://www.highbeam.com/doc/1G1 -300271122.html (accessed August 25, 2012).

89. Jeffery T. Burroughs, " 'Bulldogs' Hunt IEDS in Afghanistan," *Army Reserve Magazine*, July 1, 2006, http://www.highbeam.com/doc/1P3-1094469231.html (accessed August 25, 2012).

90. Stew Magnuson, "Mini-Flail Robots Readied for Afghanistan Bomb Clearing Operations," *National Defense*, January 1, 2012, http://www.highbeam.com/doc/1G1-27 7620994.html (accessed August 25, 2012).

91. Tiffanie Dismor, "Laf. Marine to Receive Purple Heart," wlff.com 18 News, March 16, 2011, http://www.wlfi.com/dpp/news/local/lafayette-marine-bowman-will-receive -the-purple-heart.

92. Martyn McLaughlin, "He Died a Hero: 'Victoria Cross' for Life-Saver Theo," *Scotsman*, October 26, 2012, http://www.highbeam.com/doc/1P2-33811497.html (accessed January 5, 2013).

93. "Tears for Hero and His Faithful Friend; Afghan Life-Savers Come Home; Dogs Join Tributes to Liam and Theo," *Daily Record* (Glasgow, Scotland), March 11, 2011, http://www.highbeam.com/doc/1G1-251133079.html (accessed January 5, 2013).

94. "One Exceptional Man and His Dog; Soldier and His Faithful Dog Nominated for a Great Scot Award After Frontline Tragedy Courage of Lost Hero Liam and Devoted Theo Moves Nation," *Sunday Mail* (Glasgow, Scotland), August 7, 2011, http:// www.highbeam.com/doc/1G1-263589000.html (accessed January 5, 2013).

95. "Lance Corporal Liam Richard Tasker Killed in Afghanistan," States News Service, March 2, 2011, http://www.highbeam.com/doc/1G1-250353783.html (accessed January 5, 2013).

96. "Medal for Theo," *Daily Record* (Glasgow, Scotland), September 7, 2012, http:// www.highbeam.com/doc/1G1-301798327.html (accessed January 5, 2013).

97. "Tears for Hero and His Faithful Friend."

98. "Lance Corporal Liam Richard Tasker Killed in Afghanistan."

99. "Hero's Salute; Awards Show Special Fallen Liam Tasker and Sniffer Dog Theo Are Our Great Scots 2011; Ovation for Dead Soldier at Ceremony," *Sunday Mail* (Glasgow, Scotland), September 11, 2011, http://www.highbeam.com/doc/1G1-266 661796.html (accessed February 2, 2013).

100. Jill Lawless, "Theo, War Dog Who Died in Afghanistan, Honored with British Dickin Medal," *Huffington Post*, October 25, 2011.

101. Theo, the Springer Spaniel, also received the Dickin Medal.

102. "Military Dog to Be Honoured for Saving Countless Human Lives," U.S. Federal News Service, Including U.S. State News, February 25, 2010, http://www.highbeam.com/ doc/1P3-1970095631.html (accessed December 19, 2012).

103. "U.S. Troops Winning War Against IEDs of Taliban; Dogs and Devices Sniff out Top Killer," *Washington Times*, May 25, 2012, http://www.highbeam.com/doc/1G1-290 704837.html (accessed December 19, 2012).

104. "Finding Taliban IEDS Is a Game for Military Dogs," States News Service, July 22, 2011, http://www.highbeam.com/doc/1G1-262050741.html (accessed December 19, 2012).

105. " 'Houn Dawgs' Finding IEDs in Afghanistan," States News Service, January 26, 2010, http://www.highbeam.com/doc/1G1-217557465.html (accessed December 19, 2012).

106. Nonetheless, there is a strong lyrical canine connection. The "Houn Dawg" Battalion's official song is, "You Gotta Quit Kicking My Dog Around." Source: Maj.

Vance Holland, Executive Officer, 203D EN BN, to Mark Silinsky in e-mail correspondence, July 16, 2013. Subject: Response to inquiry about the 203D's mission.

107. R. J. Pasant's Testimonial for Collin J. Bowen at http://www.collinbowen.com/apage4.html.

108. Mark Berman, "Soldier's Burial Wish Is Fulfilled; Maryland Guardsman Had Helped Train Afghan Soldiers," *Washington Post*, March 26, 2008.

109. Katherine Shaver, "Md. Guardsman Dies After Attack in January," *Washington Post*, March 16, 2008.

110. Ibid.

111. E-mail correspondence between Ursula B. Bowen Palmer and Mark Silinsky, "Re: SFC Collin J Bowen," April 2, 2013.

112. Collin Bowen homepage, http://www.collinbowen.com/index.html (accessed January 17, 2013).

113. The killing took place in the Gereskh district of Helmand. Vogt and Khan, "Afghanistan: Taliban Level Food Warehouse for US," Associated Press, Yahoo News, October 20, 2012, http://news.yahoo.com/afghanistan-taliban-level-food-warehouse-us-090532218.html.

114. "Morbidity and Mortality Weekly Report," Thallium Poisoning Center for Disease Control from Eating Contaminated Cake—Iraq 2008, vol. 57, no. 37, 10015–18.

115. "Afghan Schoolgirls Poisoned by the Taliban," Al Jazeera Online (in English), May 24, 2012.

116. Alison Gendar and James Gordon Meek, "Al Qaida Has Had Persistent Interest in Cyanide," *New York Daily News*, June 19, 2006.

117. "Al Qa'ida, Taliban Stooges Provide Poisoned Biscuits to Schoolchildren," Kabul Radio Afghanistan in Pashto, May 1, 2004.

118. Ibid.

119. "Afghan Schoolgirls Poisoned the Taliban."

120. Kay Johnson, "U.S. Analyzes Turncoat Attacks in Afghanistan; Afghan Recruit Kills Two Military Trainers Soon as Rifle Issued," *Charleston Gazette* (Charleston, WV), August 18, 2012, http://www.highbeam.com/doc/1P2-33494692.html (accessed September 8, 2012).

121. Hamid Shalizi, "Afghan Army Says Taliban Infiltration Very Successful," Reuters.com, March 3, 2012.

122. Thomas Harding, "Afghans Face New Vetting Over, 'Green on Blue' Killings," *London Daily Telegraph*, August 17, 2012.

123. " 'Green on Blue' Attacks Not an Indicator of Taliban Infiltration: Allen," *Kabul Daily Outlook* (in English), May 23, 2012.

124. "U.S. General Says Ramadan a Factor in Murders of U.S. Troops by Their Afghan Partners," *Washington Post*, August 23, 2012.

125. "US Sending Agents to Afghanistan to Crop Taliban Infiltration in Local Forces," *Hindustan Times*, 2011, http://www.highbeam.com (accessed December 23, 2011).

126. "US Army Distributed Guide to Troops: 'Avoid Arrogance' and 'Respect Islam' in Order to Avoid Attack by Afghan Soldiers," Jihad Watch, August 24, 2012, http://www.jihadwatch.org/2012/08/us-army-distributes-guide-to-troops-avoid-arrogance-and.html.

127. "Taliban Fighters Killed while Posing as Afghan National Police Officer," U.S. Federal News Service, Including U.S. State News, 2007, http://www.highbeam.com (accessed December 21, 2011).

128. Patrick Quinn and Faiez Rahim, "Taliban's New Tactic: High-Profile Inside Jobs," AP Online, 2011, http://www.highbeam.com (accessed December 20, 2011).

129. Matthew Rosenberg, "Taliban Attacks Kill Nine Afghan Police Officers," *New York Times*, April 4, 2012.

130. "Taliban 'Has Spies in Brit Army Bases': Col Richard Kemp, Ex Commander in Afghanistan," *Mirror* (London), August 28, 2010, http://www.highbeam.com/doc/1G1-2 35818142.html (accessed March 26, 2013).

131. Seth G. Jones, "Afghan Training Violence: Repairing the Vetting Process Is Key," RAND Corporation, September 6, 2012, http://www.rand.org/blog/2012/09/afghan -training-violence-repairing-the-vetting-process.html.

132. Anna Edwards, "Pictured with the Man Who Shot Him Dead Moments Later: RAF Policeman Grins Alongside Rogue Afghan Policeman Who Opened Fire on Him and Comrade," Mail Online, November 5, 2013, http: www.dailymail.co.uk/news/article -2487867/RAF-policeman-grins-alongside-rogue-Afghan-policeman-opened-comrade -moments-later.html.

133. Patrick Cockburn, "Taliban: We Recruited Bodyguard Who Murdered Karzai's Brother," *Belfast Telegraph*, July 13, 2011.

134. Vogt and Mirwais, "Taliban Tunnel More than 480 Out of Afghan Prison," AP Worldstream, April 24, 2011, http://www.highbeam.com/doc/1a1-2d05d5198ed54e298 d0ae0967e491554.html (accessed August 22, 2012).

135. Kevin Sieff, "US Delays Transfer of Major Prison to Afghans from 2012 to 2014," *Buffalo News* (Buffalo, NY), August 13, 2011.

136. "Dadullah Killing a Major Gain for Kabul, NATO-led Campaign," *Hindustan Times* (New Delhi, India), May 13, 2007.

137. Peter Popham, "Mullah Dadullah, Ruthless Taliban Commander," *Independent* (London), May 14, 2007.

138. "A Look at Mullah Dadullah's Life," AP Online, May 13, 2007.

139. "Death of a Talib; Afghanistan (the Implications of Mullah Dadullah's Killing)," *The Economist*, May 19, 2007, http://www.highbeam.com/doc/1G1-163484927.html (accessed September 21, 2012).

140. Popham, "Mullah Dadullah."

141. "One-Legged Mullah Dadullah—America's New Frankenstein in Afghanistan," *Hindustan Times* (New Delhi, India), September 27, 2006.

142. An Indian scholar B. Raman said he was key in advocating suicide attacks. Source: "Dadullah Killing a Major Gain for Kabul, NATO-Led Campaign," *Hindustan Times* (New Delhi, India), May 13, 2007.

143. "Afghanistan-May 12: High-Ranking Taliban Commander Killed," *APS Diplomat Recorder*, May 19, 2007.

144. "Secret Army of Taliban Fighters—Claim," *Birmingham Evening Mail* (England), February 1, 2002.

145. "Tartan Taliban Held in Swoop by MI5 Agents: Tartan Taliban Arrested; Scot Held During Swoops by Anti-terror Squads," *Sunday Mail* (Glasgow, Scotland), November 30, 2003, http://www.highbeam.com/doc/1G1-110661108.html (accessed December 5, 2012).

146. Alan MacDermind, "Adventures of the Tipton Taliban; Five Unlikely Terrorists on Way Home from US Detention," *Herald*, February 20, 2004, http://www.highbeam .com/doc/1P2-23559601.html (accessed December 5, 2012).

147. Lindh was named after a Beatle, John Lennon, and a chief justice, John Marshall. He was the middle child of a middle-class California family. Source: Ellen Goodman, "John Walker to Abdul Hamid: Tolerance Can't Be Blamed for Yielding a

Taliban-American," *Charleston Daily Mail* (Charleston, WV), December 15, 2001, http://www.highbeam.com/doc/1P2-18953463.html (accessed September 7, 2012).

148. "A Long, Strange Trip to the Taliban: He Was a Bright, Quiet Kid from the Heart of Hot-Tub Country. How Did John Walker Lindh Go from Hip-Hop to Holy War? The Story of a Spiritual Journey Gone Awry—and What Lies Ahead for the United States' Most Controversial POW," *Newsweek*, December 17, 2001, http://www.highbeam.com/doc/1G1-80784801.html (accessed October 7, 2012).

149. Tom Mashberg, "Prisoner of His Beliefs—Passion for Islam Turns Walker Taliban," *Boston Herald*, December 9, 2001, http://www.highbeam.com/doc/1G1-80666692.html (accessed September 7, 2012).

150. Ibid.

151. "Lindh Sues for 'Religious Right' to Group Prayer," *Sun Newspaper*, September 2, 2012.

152. "American's Journey to Extremism: How Adam Gadahn Became Tied to Terror," *Chicago Tribune*, October 30, 2006. http://www.highbeam.com/doc/1G1-153524387.html (accessed September 7, 2012).

153. Ibid.

154. "Publicity Campaign Launched in Afghanistan to Publicize $1 Million Reward for Adam Gadahn, American Fugitive Born in California, Charged with Treason," U.S. Federal News Service, Including U.S. State News, May 30, 2008, http://www.highbeam.com/doc/1P3-1488672661.html (accessed September 7, 2012).

155. Paul Kamolnick, a sociology professor at East Tennessee State University, wrote, "It is inadvisable that one use Gadahn's public persona to draw inferences to either his private intellectual acumen or public utility as a senior communications analyst and propagandist for Al Qaeda. A careful reading of Gadahn's Abbottabad letter indicates the working a very shrewd analytic mind, deeply immersed in the contemporary information landscape, and also deeply concerned about Al Qaeda's loss of operational control to murderous franchises acting and speaking in its name." Source: Paul Kamolnick's correspondence with Mark Silinsky, e-mail, November 26, 2013.

CHAPTER 7

1. Sabrina Tavernise. "Organized Crime in Pakistan Feeds Taliban; Criminal Groups in Pakistan Help Taliban; Kidnappings, Bank Heists and Extortion Generating Millions for Insurgency," *International Herald Tribune*, April 31, 2009, http://www.highbeam.com/doc/1P1-170215570.html (accessed March 26, 2013).

2. This is a rough estimate as of 2005. As the number of U.S. troops in Afghanistan declines, the figure declines. Source: Mark K. Blanchfield, "Transportation Challenges in Afghanistan," *Army Logistician*, 2005, http://www.highbeam.com (accessed December 15, 2010). Afghanistan has a road network of only 21,000 kilometers, 18,207 kilometers of which are unpaved (compared to approximately 123,000 kilometers of state-maintained roads in Texas).

3. Nearly 80 percent of this is routed through Pakistan, amounting to nearly 500 trucks per day. Source: "Warlord Inc. Extortion and Corruption Along the US Supply Chain in Afghanistan," Report of the Minority Staff, U.S. House of Representatives, June 22, 2010.

4. Figure accurate as of 2010.

5. Blanchfield, "Transportation Challenges in Afghanistan."

6. Ibid.

7. Aram Roston, "How the US Army Protects Its Trucks by Paying the Taliban: Insurance, Security, or Extortion?," *Guardian*, November 13, 2009.

8. Ibid.

9. "Supply Chain in Afghanistan," *The Nation* (Karachi, Pakistan), 2010, http://www.highbeam.com (accessed December 15, 2010).

10. Ibid. "If it exceeds 20 percent, the transporters find it cheaper to divert the cargo through Iran. The central Asian route is being availed, but is two or three times the cost and adds about 20 days of transport time. The system works quite well since the cost of payments for the bureaucracy and tribes is known in advance and factored into the final price."

11. This was a 79-page report, titled "Warlord, Inc., Extortion and Corruption Along the U.S. Supply Chain in Afghanistan."

12. Karen DeYoung, "U.S. Indirectly Paying Warlords; Security Deal in Afghanistan Military Objectives Being Undermined, Report Says," *Washington Post*, 2010, http://www.highbeam.com (accessed December 15, 2010).

13. Douglas Farah and Pamela Constable, "Drug Business Flourishes in Afghanistan; Taliban Denies Involvement but Is Said to Reap Profit From Taxes, Transport," *Washington Post*, 1998, http://www.highbeam.com (accessed November 1, 2010).

14. Ghulam Dastageer, "Forced Donations," *Karachi Herald* (in English), April 12–30, 2012, 65.

15. Ibid.

16. Tavernise, "Organized Crime in Pakistan Feeds Taliban."

17. "Rs9.7m Bank Heists in Karachi," *The Nation* (Karachi, Pakistan), 2010, http://www.highbeam.com (accessed December 9, 2010).

18. Blanchfield, "Transportation Challenges in Afghanistan."

19. "Three Suspected Taliban Bank Attackers Killed in Kabul Encounter," *Asian News International*, 2009, http://www.highbeam.com (accessed December 31, 2010).

20. "Theft Under the Taliban? Perish the Thought," *New York Times*, 2000, http://www.highbeam.com (accessed December 31, 2010).

21. "Taliban Kidnapping VIPs to Raise Funds for Terror Activities," Press Trust of India, 2010, http://www.highbeam.com (accessed December 9, 2010).

22. Tavernise, "Organized Crime in Pakistan Feeds Taliban."

23. Griff Witte and Haq Nawaz Khan, "Dozens Rescued in Taliban Kidnapping of Pakistani Students," *Washington Post*, 2009, http://www.highbeam.com (accessed December 9, 2010).

24. David Rohde and Choe Sang-Hun, "Taliban Release 12 Korean Hostages; Release of 7 Others Is Expected Soon," *International Herald Tribune*, 2007, http://www.highbeam.com (accessed December 31, 2010).

25. Dina Temple-Raston, "Taliban Showing New Willingness on Prisoner Swap," *Morning Edition*, NPR, August 15, 2012.

26. Ian Fisher, "Taliban Are Released for Italian's Freedom; Ransom Draws International Criticism," *International Herald Tribune*, March 23, 2007, http://www.highbeam.com/doc/1P1-136749707.html (accessed October 7, 2012).

27. Scott Simon, "Murdered Afghan Interpreter Worked with Journalists," *Weekend Edition Saturday*, NPR, April 14, 2007, http://www.highbeam.com/doc/1P1-139507761.html (accessed October 7, 2012).

28. "Upon hearing of Dadullah's death, the translator's brother exclaimed, 'Congratulations! Congratulations!' I was so happy I started crying." Source: "Taliban Chief's Death a Big U.S. Victory," AP Online, May 13, 2007, http://www.highbeam.com/doc/1Y1-106294939.html (accessed October 7, 2012).

29. Charmaine Noronha, "Canadian Woman Kidnapped in Pakistan," AP Worldstream, November 14, 2008, http://www.highbeam.com/doc/1A1-D94EV8B03.html (accessed September 28, 2012).

30. "Convert to Islam, Founder of Pro-jihad Website, Dies in Taliban Captivity," Jihad Watch, http://www.jihadwatch.org/2010/11/convert-to-islam-founder-of-pro-jihad-website -dies-in-taliban-captivity.html.

31. Cheetah, Global Moderator, "Re-Poor Beverly Giesbrecht," CEMB Forum, http://www.councilofexmuslims.com/index.php?topic=4726.0.

32. "Taliban: French Journalists Traded for Insurgents," AP Online, June 30, 2011.

33. "Taliban Murder Top Afghan Policewoman," *Independent* (London), 2008, http://www.highbeam.com (accessed December 10, 2010).

34. Dusan Stojanovic, "Afghan Assassination Probe Stalled," AP Online, 2002, http://www.highbeam.com (accessed December 10, 2010).

35. Rod Nordland, "Taliban Aim at Officials in a Wave of Killings," *New York Times*, June 9, 2010, http://www.nytimes.com/2010/06/10/world/asia/10taliban.html.

36. Stojanovic, "Afghan Assassination Probe Stalled."

37. Dawood Azami, "The 'Dissenting' Clerics Killed in Afghanistan," BBC World Service, November 18, 2013, http://www.bbc.co.uk/news/world-asia-22885170.

38. The figure 800 is assumed to refer to those killed during the Taliban's force from power in 2001. But the article is not entirely clear on this point. Source: Azami, "The 'Dissenting' Clerics."

39. "Taliban Kills Afghan Angel; Executed After Delivering Aid Doc Quit Top Job to Help Poor Were Found on Friday," *People* (London), April 8, 2010, http://www.highbeam.com/doc/1G1-233884196.html (accessed September 18, 2012).

40. "Taliban Assassinations Now Weapon of Choice; 'Nowhere Is Safe'; Kandahar Killings Persuade Government Workers to Give Up," *Seattle Times*, 2010, http://www.highbeam.com (accessed December 16, 2010).

41. "Taliban Fighters Murder Female Nurse in W. Afghanistan," Xinhua News Agency, 2009, http://www.highbeam.com (accessed December 10, 2010).

42. "Taliban Kill Miners in Afghan North," *Peshawar Afghan Islamic Press* (in Pashto), August 4, 2012.

43. "Taliban Kill Miners in Afghan North," Peshawar Afghan Islamic Press (in Pashto), August 4, 2012.

CHAPTER 8

1. Michael Cohen, "Casus Pax," *Foreign Policy*, May 2, 2011.

2. Vanda Felbab-Brown, "Implications of Osama Bin Laden's Death," Brookings Institution item, May 2, 2011.

3. This comment was made by the al Qaeda leader Abu Mosab al-Suri in 1999. Source: David Aaron, *In Their Own Words: Voices of Jihad* (Santa Monica, CA: RAND Corporation, 2008), 254.

4. In three sentences he referred to himself three times in a style very distinct from that of his host Mullah Omar. Source: Aaron, *In Their Own Words*, 254.

5. Cohen, "Casus Pax."

6. Robert D. Lamb, "Bin Laden Is Dead: Is It Time to Leave Afghanistan?," Center for Strategic and International Studies, May 2, 2011.

7. Ali K. Chishti, "The Future of Al Qaeda," *Friday Times* Online, (Lahore, Pakistan), May 17, 2012.

8. Brian Fishman, terrorism research fellow at the New American Foundation, remarked in June 2011. Anna Mulrine, "New Al Qaeda Leader Ayman al-Zawahiri: Do His Flaws Diminish Group's Threat?," *Christian Science Monitor*, June 20, 2011, http://www.highbeam.com/doc/1G1-259345967.html (accessed September 18, 2012).

9. Raymond Ibrahim, "Ayman Zawahiri and Egypt: A Trip through Time," Middle East Forum, http://us-mg6.mail.yahoo.com/neo/launch?.rand=4kvp8f7aems7l (accessed December 9, 2012).

10. Jarret Brachman, an analyst, commented on his strong verbal as well as military skills. Source: Chishti, "The Future of Al Qaeda."

11. "Rep. Jackson Lee Addresses the Death of Al Qaeda Leader Abu Yahya Al-Libi," U.S. Federal News Service, Including U.S. State News, June 7, 2012, http://www.highbeam.com/doc/1P3-2679881841.html (accessed September 18, 2012).

12. "Al-Libi Dead, Pak Case against Drones Weakens," *Hindustan Times* (New Delhi, India), June 13, 2012, http://www.highbeam.com/doc/1P3-2685131681.html (accessed September 18, 2012).

13. "Egyptian Saif Al-Adel Chosen as Al Qaeda Acting Chief," *Hindustan Times* (New Delhi, India), May 18, 2011, http://www.highbeam.com/doc/1P3-2350360251.html (accessed September 18, 2012).

14. Ibid.

15. "Top Al-Qaeda Ranks Are Keeping Footholds in Iran," *Daily News Egypt*, 2011, http://www.highbeam.com (accessed October 8, 2012).

16. Abdel Bari Atwan, *The Secret History of Al Qaeda* (Berkeley: University of California Press, 2006), 221–23.

17. "Al Qaeda's Hand in Tipping Iraq toward Civil War; Creating Chaos in Iraq Serves Al Qaeda's Goal of Uniting the Muslim World Under One Caliph," *Christian Science Monitor*, March 20, 2006, http://www.highbeam.com/doc/1G1-143416288.html (accessed October 8, 2012).

18. "Top Al-Qaeda Ranks Are Keeping Footholds in Iran."

19. Brian Murphy, "Iran May Have Loosened Reins on Al-Qaida Figures," *Sunday Gazette-Mail*, July 20, 2011, http://www.highbeam.com/doc/1P2-29115170.html (accessed October 8, 2012).

20. Yassin Musharbash, "A Top Terrorist Returns to Al-Qaida Fold," Spiegel Online, October 25, 2010, http://www.spiegel.de/international/world/saif-al-adel-back-in-waziristan-a-top-terrorist-returns-to-al-qaida-fold-a-725181.html.

21. George Michael, "Adam Gadahn and Al-Qaeda's Internet Strategy," *Middle East Policy*, September 22, 2009, http://www.highbeam.com/doc/1G1-210368259.html (accessed September 18, 2012).

22. "Al Qaeda: Resilient and Organized: Fierce Fighting by Holdouts Displays Terror Group's Cohesion, Local Support," *Christian Science Monitor*, 2002, http://www.highbeam.com (accessed February 20, 2012).

23. Eric Schmitt, "U.S. Intelligence Chief Sees Cracks in Qaeda," *International Herald Tribune*, February 1, 2012, http://www.highbeam.com/doc/1P1-202222074.html (accessed September 18, 2012).

24. George Crile, *Charlie Wilson's War* (New York: Grove Press, 2003), 473.

25. Heidi Vogt and Rahim Faiez, "Afghans Say Airstrike Killed Haqqani Leader; Afghans: Haqqani Leader Killed," *Washington Post*, August 27, 2012, http://www.highbeam.com/doc/1P2-33531250.html (accessed October 7, 2012).

26. There is a large dispute among Western observers of the Haqqani network about its affiliation with the Taliban. This author sees the Haqqani network as a quasi-independent arm of the Taliban.

27. Marc W. Herold, "The Failing Campaign," *Frontline* 19, no. 3 (2002).

28. Steve Coll, *Frontline*, PBS, October 3, 2006; Anand Gopal, "The Most Deadly US Foe in Afghanistan," *Christian Science Monitor*, May 31, 2009.

29. Einar Wigen, *Islamic Jihad Union: Al-Qaida's Key to the Turkic World?* (Kjeller, Norway: Norwegian Defence Research Establishment, 2009).

30. Ari Shapiro, "Haqqani Network's Reign of Terror on Afghanistan," *Morning Edition*, NPR, 2009, http://www.highbeam.com (accessed December 17, 2010).

31. "Germany's First Suicide Bomber in Afghanistan?," *Der Spiegel*, March 15, 2008.

32. Petter Nesser, "Lessons Learned from the September 2007 German Terrorist Plot," *CTC Sentinel* 1, no. 4 (2008).

33. This author is not convinced that the Haqqani suicide bombers are still more lethal or sophisticated than the Taliban. Both groups have improved their techniques, tactics, and procedures regarding suicide bombings.

34. "ISI maintains link with militant commanders, says Musharraf," Press Trust of India, 2009, http://www.highbeam.com (accessed December 17, 2010).

35. "Siraj Haqqani Shares Name of Father Only: Differs in Philosophy, Tactics," U.S. Federal News Service, Including U.S. State News, 2007, http://www.highbeam.com (accessed December 17, 2010).

36. "Pakistan: Haqqani 'Most Ominous Threat to US Pak Ties,' " *Pakistan Today Online*, July 31, 2012.

37. "There Are Considerable Distances between Nawaz Sharif and the United States," *Islamabad Jinnah* (in Urdu), July 27, 2012.

38. "Haqqani Network Is Afghanistan and US's Most Deadliest Foe: CSM," *Asian News International*, 2009, http://www.highbeam.com (accessed December 17, 2010).

39. Shapiro, "Haqqani Network's Reign of Terror on Afghanistan."

40. "Haqqani Network Getting Desperate: Campbell," *Pajhwok*, 2010, http://www.highbeam.com (accessed December 17, 2010).

41. Shapiro, "Haqqani Network's Reign of Terror on Afghanistan."

42. Jonathan Schanzer, "Hitler's 'Grossmufti von Jerusalem,' " *Jerusalem Post*, September 5, 2008, http://www.highbeam.com/doc/1P1-156174758.html (accessed November 4, 2012).

43. Matthew Kaminsiki, "The German Connection, How the Muslim Brotherhood Found a Haven in Europe," (Book review), *Wall Street Journal*, May 6, 2010, http://online.wsj.com/article/SB10001424052748703961104575226372646226094.html.

44. Yassin Musharbash, "Terror Investigation: German Islamist Resurfaces by Video from Afghanistan," Spiegel Online, October 22, 2008, http://www.spiegel.de/international/germany/terror-investigation-german-islamist-resurfaces-by-video-from-afghanistan-a-585730.html.

45. Nicholas Kulish and Souad Mekhennet, "German Police Seize Terror Suspects on Jet," *International Herald Tribune*, September 27, 2008, http://www.highbeam.com/doc/1P1-156689258.html (accessed November 4, 2012).

46. "German 'Taliban' killed by U.S.," *Daily Mail* (London), October 5, 2010, http://www.highbeam.com/doc/1G1-238616363.html (accessed November 4, 2012).

47. Sam Webb, "German Neo-Nazi Turned Jihadist Who Went to Fight in Afghanistan Admits He Made a 'Big Mistake' After Wife Misses Supermarkets and Her Mobile Phone," *Daily Mail*, November 2, 2012.

48. Ibid.

49. "German Taliban 'Put Off by Dirt and Violence,' " *Searchlight Germany*, November 2, 2012, http://searchlight-germany.blogspot.com/2012/11/german-taliban-put-off-by-dirt-and.html.

50. John Ydstie, "Profile: Radical Afghan Warlord Gulbuddin Hekmatyar a Wanted Man by Afghan and US Forces for His Past Crimes and Possible Threat to Peace in the Country," *All Things Considered*, NPR, 2002, http://www.highbeam.com (accessed December 18, 2010).

51. Ibid.

52. Kathy Gannon, "Renegade Hekmatyar Vows in Videotaped Message to Fight Afghan President, Foreign Troops," AP Worldstream, 2003, http://www.highbeam.com (accessed February 21, 2012).

53. Shapiro, "Haqqani Network's Reign of Terror on Afghanistan."

54. "Tribal Areas under Centralized Control," *Daily Times*, December 16, 2007.

55. "Taliban Rename Their Group," *The Nation* (Karachi, Pakistan), 2009, http://www.highbeam.com/doc/1G1-194301565.html (accessed December 3, 2013).

56. *Dawn Magazine*, vol. 1, issue 7, February 22, 2005.

57. "In a Message on Eid Al-Adha, Pakistani Taliban Chief Hakimullah Mehsud Warns of 'Well-Orchestrated' Attacks in Coming Days, Pledges to Fight Until 'There Is No More … (Kufr) on the Earth,' " MEMRI's Jihad and Terrorism Threat Monitor, November 9, 2011, http://www.memrijttm.org/content/en/report.htm?report=5794&m=UPP.

58. "The $120,000 Farmhouse Where Pakistan Taliban Chief Died," AFP (Pakistan), November 3, 2013, http://news.yahoo.com/120-000-farmhouse-where-pakistan-taliban-chief-died-214050981.html.

59. "Pakistan: New Government Struggles to Control Taliban," Inter Press Service, 2008, http://www.highbeam.com (accessed December 18, 2010).

60. "Second Editorial: Tribal Areas under Centralized Control," *Daily Times*, December 16, 2007.

61. Arabinda Acharya, Syed Adnan Ali Shah, and Sadia Sulaiman, "Making Money in the Mayhem: Funding Taliban Insurrection in the Tribal Areas of Pakistan," *Studies in Conflict and Terrorism* 32, no. 2 (February 2009): 95–108.

62. Laura King, "Taliban Blamed for Attack on Bhutto," *Los Angeles Times*, December 28, 2007.

63. "The Taliban Are Reborn, and They Have Pakistan to Thank," *Daily Star* (Beirut, Lebanon), 2010, http://www.highbeam.com (accessed December 17, 2010).

64. "TTP Can Use Bank Robberies & Kidnapping Route in Future," *Pakistan Press International*, 2009, http://www.highbeam.com (accessed December 17, 2010).

65. Qandeel Siddique, *Tehrik-E-Taliban Pakistan—an Attempt to Deconstruct the Umbrella Organization and the Reasons for Its Growth in Pakistan's North-West*, DIIS Report, 2010, no. 12, p. 11, Danish Institute for International Studies, Copenhagen, Denmark.

66. "Pakistan Taliban Threats to West Limited, Analysts Say; Capability to Attack U.S., Europe Seen Tied to Homegrown Terrorists," *Washington Times*, 2010, http://www.highbeam.com (accessed December 17, 2010).

67. "Pakistani Leaders: Hakimullah Mehsud Is A Martyr; Maulana Fazlullah: 'Even a Dog' Killed by the U.S. 'Is a Martyr,' " MEMRI Special Dispatch 5516, November 10, 2013, http://us-mg6.mail.yahoo.com/neo/launch?.rand=aosg7k2iu7kdf#.

68. "Hiding in Plain Sight: The Problem with Pakistani Intelligence," Stratfor, May 4, 2011.

69. India has one of the world's largest Muslim communities at an estimated 100 million. However, it is largely Hindu and there have been centuries of warfare between Hindus and Muslims.

70. "Pakistan and India: A Rivalry That Threatens the World," *The Economist*, May 19, 2011.

71. Lawrence Wright, "The Double Game," *The New Yorker*, May 16, 2011. Taken from James Arnold Miller, "The Witches' Brew: Pakistan, India, Afghanistan, the Taliban, Al-Qaeda, and Other Violent Islamic Extremist Groups," Interaction Systems Incorporated Papers (ISIPs), no. 12, May 27, 2011.

72. Ibid.

73. Sheela Bhatt, "Hamid Gul," *India Abroad*, February 13, 2004, http://www.highbeam.com/doc/1P1-93041280.html (accessed September 29, 2012).

74. "Gulled by Hamid Gul; Ex-intelligence Chief a Taliban Mouthpiece," *Washington Times*, December 4, 2009, http://www.highbeam.com/doc/1G1-213534105.html (accessed September 29, 2012).

75. Ibid.

76. "I am Favourite Whipping Boy of US: Hamid Gul," *Financial Post* (Karachi, Pakistan), 2010, http://www.highbeam.com/doc/1P3-2203897211.html (accessed September 29, 2012).

77. "Water Issue Matter of Life and Death for Pak: Nizami," *The Nation* (Karachi, Pakistan), March 22, 2010, http://www.highbeam.com/doc/1G1-221941578.html (accessed September 29, 2012).

78. Abdul Mohi Shah, "A War in Afghanistan Will Spread to Pakistan, Warn Experts," *India Abroad*, October 5, 2001, http://www.highbeam.com/doc/1P1-79281072.html (accessed September 29, 2012).

79. "Afghans Will Defeat US, Says Ex-ISI Chief Hamid Gul," *Hindustan Times* (New Delhi, India), November 6, 2006, http://www.highbeam.com/doc/1P3-1202739551.html (accessed September 29, 2012).

80. MEMRI, http://www.memri.org/report/en/0/0/0/0/0/0/5790.htm, November 8, 2011.

81. Alison Kervin, "Imran Khan: 'What I Do Now Fulfills Me Like Never Before,' " *Sunday Times* (London), August 6, 2005 (accessed November 5, 2007).

82. Khaama.com (Afghanistan), October 13, 2012.

83. Ibid.

84. " 'Liberal' Imran Khan a 'Slave' of US, Europe: Pakistan Taliban," *Hindustan Times* (New Delhi, India), November 12, 2011, http://www.highbeam.com/doc/1P3-2509136841.html (accessed October 28, 2012).

85. Andrew Buncombe, "Imran Khan Braves March into Pakistan's Taliban Heartland," *Independent* (London), October 5, 2012, http://www.highbeam.com/doc/1P2-33722460.html (accessed October 28, 2012).

86. Wright, "The Double Game."

87. For years, U.S. leaders have accused the Pakistanis of support for the Taliban and have offered, what they see, as irrefutable proof of strong, existing ties. Bruce Riedel, a former intelligence officer and an advisor to President Obama, stated that Pakistan depends

on the Taliban to maintain influence in Afghanistan, a necessary precondition to having security with India. Pakistan is concerned that the United States would betray Pakistani interests in Afghanistan, making them more vulnerable to India. Source: Karen DeYoung and Karin Brulliard, "Change Overdue in U.S.-Pakistan Relationship, Key Officials Say," *Washington Post*, May 15, 2011.

88. Lally Weymouth, "This Is Not a War, Pakistan's President on the Price of His Cooperation and the Taliban's Future," *Newsweek*, November 19, 2001.

89. Ibid.

90. Mera Passion Pakistan, "Talking Back," March 1, 2012, http://merpassionpakistan.com/english/talking-back.

91. "Pakistan Teen Nominated for International Peace Award," *Times of India* (Pakistan), November 21, 2011, http://timesofindia.indiatimes.com/world/pakistan/Pakistan-teen-nominated-for-international-peace-award/articleshow/10814218.

92. "Malala Yousafzai, Pakistani Teen, Nominated for International Children's Peace Prize," *Huffington Post*, November 21, 2011, http://www.huffingtonpost.com/2011/11/21/malala-yousufzai-pakistan_n_1105528.html.

93. Saeed Shah and Nancy A. Youssef, "Taliban Adopting Conventional Tactics," *Charleston Gazette* (Charleston, WV), May 16, 2009, http://www.highbeam.com/doc/1P2-20277337.html (accessed November 24, 2012).

94. Mariam Magsi, "Malala Yousufzai: A Child Hero," *Smart Local News*, November 30. 2011, http://smartlocalnews.blogspot.com/2011/11/malala-yousufzai-child-hero.html.

95. "Swat Girl Gets Peach Prize, Rs500,000," *Nation* (Karachi, Pakistan), November 25, 2011.

96. Nasir Habib, "14-Year-Old Girl Wins Pakistan's First Peace Prize," *St. Joseph News-Press*, November 24, 2011.

97. "I Will Form My Own Political Party: Malala," *Financial Post* (Karachi, Pakistan), January 4, 2012.

98. "School Named After Malala Yousufzai," *Financial Post* (Karachi, Pakistan), April 23, 2012.

99. "Pakistan and India: A Rivalry That Threatens the World."

100. "India and Pakistan: The World's Most Dangerous Border," *The Economist*, May 19, 2011.

101. Andrew Bast, "Pakistan's Nuclear Surge," *Newsweek*, May 15, 2011.

102. Matthew Rosenberg and Owais Tohid, "Taliban Say They Won't Hit Nuclear Arsenal," *Wall Street Journal*, May 26, 2011.

103. Banyan, "The Insanity Clause," *The Economist*, May 5, 2011.

104. Bruce Riedel, "After Bin Laden," *Washington Post*, May 6, 2011.

105. Mike McPhate, "Abbottabad: Pakistan Town Where Osama Bin Laden Was Killed," *Washington Post*, May 2, 2011.

106. Elisabeth Bumiller, "Gates Says No Sign That Top Pakistanis Knew of Bin Laden," *New York Times*, May 19, 2011.

107. European Strategic Intelligence and Security Center, "Hints at Mistrust between U.S. and Pakistan," May 2, 2011.

108. "After Osama Bin Laden: They Got Him," *The Economist*, May 4, 2011.

109. Asra Q. Nomani, "Saif al-Adel and the Death of Daniel Pearl," *Foreign Policy*, May 19, 2011.

110. Sadanad Dhume, "Pakistan as Terror Sanctuary," *Wall Street Journal*, May 4, 2011.

111. Bill Gertz, "Directorate S Probed," *Washington Times*, May 12, 2011.

112. Vogt and Faiez, "Taliban Train in Iran, NATO General Says," *Deseret News* (Salt Lake City), May 31, 2010.

113. Anwar Faruqi, "Iran-Taliban Differences Come to a Head over Dead Diplomats," AP Online, 1998, http://www.highbeam.com (accessed February 21, 2012).

114. "Iran Prepares to Fight Afghanistan," *Chicago Sun-Times*, 1998, http://www.highbeam.com (accessed February 21, 2012).

115. "Pakistan-Iran: Turf-Battle over Afghan Rubble," Inter Press Service, 1995, http://www.highbeam.co (accessed February 21, 2012).

116. Some of the significant terrorist activities of the IRGC include the 1983 U.S. Embassy bombing in Beirut, the 1988 Kuwait Airlines hijacking, and the two attacks on Jewish and Israeli sites in Argentina.

117. Jonathan Spyer, "The Revolutionary Guardsman That Wasn't, or Was He? Capture of a Quads Force Operative on Afghan Soil Would Have Been Highly Sensitive for Afghanistan's Government," *Jerusalem Post*, December 29, 2010.

118. Sara A. Carter, "Iran Training Taliban Fighters to Use Surface-to-Air Missiles," *Washington Examiner*, October 26, 2010.

119. Kenneth R. Timmerman, "Iran's Ties to Al Qaeda; Evidence Mounts of Regime's Support for Terror," *Washington Times*, May 5, 2010.

120. Ben Farmer, "Taliban Opens Office in Iran," *London Telegraph*, August 1, 2012.

121. Ibid.

122. "OIC Envoy Hails Iran's Constructive Role in Afghanistan," FARS News Agency (Tehran), March 8, 2011.

CHAPTER 9

1. Lori Robertson, "Whatever Happened to Afghanistan?," *American Journalism Review*, June 1, 2003, http://www.highbeam.com/doc/1G1-102904045.html (accessed December 6, 2012).

2. Ibid.

3. Ibid.

4. Peter Rainer, "Afghan Star," *Christian Science Monitor*, July 31, 2009.

5. A family will have to pay $160 in a year when the average Afghan makes barely $425 a year. Source: "A Decade of War—and Less Optimism; Life in Afghanistan; Corruption, Violence Grow, and a Lack of Security Becomes Pressing Problem," *Seattle Times*, October 5, 2011, http://www.highbeam.com/doc/1G1-268830486.html (accessed November 29, 2012).

6. "A Look at US Generals in Afghan War," AP Online, 2012, http://www.highbeam.com/doc/1A1-ce19b6c67a494a46b2ccc283607886d3 (accessed November 21, 2012).

7. Ibid.

8. Ibid.

9. Others indicted for thrill killing were Spc. Adam Winfield, Spc. Michael Wagnon II, Pvt. Andrew Holmes, and Cpl. Jeremy Morlock. There was an assortment of charges.

10. "Afghans Killed for Sport, Says Report," *Irish Times*, March 29, 2011, http://www.highbeam.com/doc/1P2-28293340.html (accessed November 22, 2012).

11. Andrew Purcell, "Porn, Hashish and Killing for Kicks . . . What Fuelled a GI Death Squad in Afghanistan," *Sunday Herald*, October 3, 2010, http://www.highbeam.com/doc/1P2-26018890.html (accessed November 22, 2012).

12. Ibid.

13. Craig Whitlock, "Grisly Allegations against U.S. Soldier," *Washington Post*, September 30, 2010, http://www.highbeam.com/doc/1P2-26000574.html (accessed November 22, 2012).

14. Only a trained mental health professional can make a valid diagnosis. This author is not trained or qualified to determine conclusively whether SGT Gibbs is a psychopath. However, his behavioral characteristics strongly indicate that he has psychopathic traits. Dr. Kevin Dutton offers an unscientific but interesting self-test at http://wisdomofpsychopaths.com/kevin-dutton.html.

15. Kevin Dutton, interviewed by Neil Shubin, *Science Weekly*, the *Guardian* podcast, http://www.theguardian.com/science/series/science (accessed August 13, 2013).

16. "US Soldier Sentenced to Life in Prison for Afghan Atrocities," States News Service, November 11, 2011, http://www.highbeam.com/doc/1G1-272259105.html (accessed November 22, 2012).

17. "Don't Prejudge Staff Sgt. Calvin Gibbs," Letter to the editor from Mary Mattheis, *Billings Gazette* (Billings, MT), October 26, 2010, http://billingsgazette.com/news/opinion/mailbag/article_e39a5766-e098-11df-a5b3-001cc4c03286.html.

18. Brad Knickerbocker, "Sergeant Seen as 'Kill Team' Leader Found Guilty in Afghanistan Atrocities," *Christian Science Monitor*, November 10, 2011, http://www.highbeam.com/doc/1G1-272137332.html (accessed November 22, 2012).

19. "Army Reviews Leadership in Alleged Thrill Kills; Brigadier General Appointed; Could Lead to More Training for Troops," *Seattle Times*, November 23, 2010, http://www.highbeam.com/doc/1G1-242923077.html (accessed November 22, 2012).

20. Knickerbocker, "Sergeant Seen as 'Kill Team' Leader."

21. *U.S. Army/Marine Corps Counterinsurgency Field Manual*, No. 3-24, Marine Corps Warfighting Publication No. 3-33.5 (Chicago: University of Chicago Press, 2007).

22. Kyle Teamey and Brian Gellman, "Counterinsurgency 101," *Military Intelligence Professional Bulletin*, April 1, 2005

23. One of the more remarkable figures in U.S. military history, Pershing began the counterinsurgency as a captain and was promoted over many senior officers to brigadier general during the war in large part because of his counterinsurgency success.

24. Thomas S. Bundt, "An Unconventional War: The Philippine Insurrection 1899," *Military Review*, May 1, 2004.

25. "From 1899 to 1902, the United States used over 500 small garrisons (increased from 53 in 1900) throughout the Philippines." Source: Timothy K. Deady, "Lessons from a Successful Counterinsurgency: The Philippines, 1899–1902," *Parameters* 35 (Spring 2005): 57.

26. "The US military, with a field strength of 24,000 to 42,000 plus a large number of Philippine auxiliaries, defeated an insurgent force estimated at 80,000 to 100,000." Source: Glenn A. May, *A Past Recovered* (Manila: New Day, 1987), 152, quoted in Brian McAllister Linn, *The Philippine War: 1899–1902* (Lawrence: University of Kansas Press, 2000), 325.

27. Rod Propst, "Insurgency and the Role of the 21st Century Foreign Area Officer: An Introductory Guide," *FAO Journal*, March 2008.

28. "We Wrote the Book on Counterinsurgency, Literally," U.S. Federal News Service, Including U.S. State News, June 28, 2006.

29. Robert M. Cassidy, "Back to the Street without Joy: Counterinsurgency Lessons from Vietnam and Other Small Wars," *Parameters* (Summer 2004).

30. Cassidy, "US Army Counterinsurgency and Contingency Operations Doctrine 1942–1976," *RUSI Journal* (August 1, 2007).

31. Galula is cited and praised often in 3-24. His masterwork, *Counterinsurgency Warfare: Theory and Practice*, written in 1964, became an instant COIN classic and reflected his experience fighting against the Germans in World War II and later devising COIN doctrine while serving in China, Greece, Indo-China, and Algeria.

32. Terence J. Daly, "Classical Principles of Counterinsurgency," *Marine Corps Gazette* 90 (December 2006): 53–57.

33. Ibid.

34. Propst, "Insurgency and the Role."

35. Ibid.

36. Shawn Brimley and Vikram Singh, "Averting the System Reboot: Innovations and Critical Lessons from Iraq Must Be Preserved," *Armed Forces Journal* (December 2007): 34–37, 47.

37. Remy M. Mauduit, "Counterinsurgency Is Dead" (editorial), *ASPJ Africa and Francophonie, Air and Space Power Journal* 4, no. 2 (Spring 2013), http://www.au.af.mil/au/cadre/aspj/apjinternational/af/Index.asp.

38. "An Interview with LTC John Nagl," CHIPS, April 1, 2007.

39. Sarah Sewall, "Modernizing US Counterinsurgency Practice: Rethinking Risk and Developing a National Strategy," *Military Review*, September 1, 2007.

40. Daly, "Classical Principles of Counterinsurgency."

41. Jacob Kramer, "The Two Sides of COIN: Applying FM 3-24 to the Brigade and Below Counterinsurgency Fight," *Infantry Magazine*, 2007, http://www.highbeam.com/doc/1G1-172905321.html (accessed December 3, 2013).

42. Though the manual was published after the period of this study's analysis, beta versions were distributed and many of the doctrinal issues were in practice from other sources. To some extent, the manual confirmed and made doctrinal the successful strategies in play during the post-Taliban, five-year period.

43. The manual uses the terms "lethal" and "non-nonlethal" tactics.

44. Robert Tomes, "Relearning Counterinsurgency Warfare," *Parameters* 34 (Spring 2004).

45. The new doctrine was controversial from the beginning and the authors fought a two-front ideologically battle. One set of antagonists was the more conventionally oriented military planners within the Army and Marines. The other set was the increasingly alienated and hostile academia, some of whom began to campaign angrily against association with the DoD.

46. Kramer, "The Two Sides of COIN."

47. "Rep. Peterson Lauds Congressional Medal of Honor Announcement for PSU Grad Lt. Murphy," U.S. Federal News Service, Including U.S. State News, October 17, 2007, http://www.highbeam.com/doc/1P3-1367390571.html (accessed September 30, 2012).

47. Janie Blankenship, " 'Iron-Souled Warrior' Awarded First Medal of Honor for Afghanistan Service," *VFW Magazine*, January 1, 2008, http://www.highbeam.com/doc/1P3-1417377651.html.

49. "Fallen Navy SEAL Honored with Warship," *USA Today*, June 8, 2011, http://usatoday30.usatoday.com/news/military/2011-05-08-seal-hero-warship_n.htm.

50. "Rep. Peterson Lauds Congressional Medal of Honor Announcement."

51. President George W. Bush, "Official Presentation of Medal of Honor to the Family of Navy SEAL Lieutenant Michael P. Murphy," http://www.usa-patriotism.com/heroes/fallen/michael_murphy.htm.

52. Blankenship, " 'Iron-Souled Warrior' Awarded."

53. "Fallen Navy SEAL Honored with Warship."

54. These rules are the author's and were distilled from many doctrinal standardized texts, particularly the *Counterinsurgency Handbook*, U.S. commanders, and literature he received at the Afghanistan Counterinsurgency Academy in 2008. The rules have not changed substantially from 2008 through fall 2012.

55. These rules are the author's and were distilled from many doctrinal standardized texts, particularly the *Counterinsurgency Handbook*, 2007, p. 32, http://usacac.army.mil/CAC2/MilitaryReview/Archives/English/MilitaryReview_2008CRII0831_art014.pdf.

56. Greg Mills, Terence McNamee, and Denny Lane, "Security Vortex: Warlords and Nation Building," *National Interest*, September 1, 2006.

57. Mills, McNamee, and Lane, "Finding the 'Right Stuff' in Afghanistan: Reducing Violence and Bringing the US Military Under NATO Command Won't Be Easy," *Christian Science Monitor*, July 10, 2006.

58. Mills, McNamee, and Lane, "Security Vortex."

59. Associated Press, "U.S. Beefs Up Forces on Afghan Border; the Change in Tactics Is Part of a New Strategy," *Telegraph-Herald* (Dubuque), March 3, 2004, http://www.highbeam.com/doc/1P2-11119456.html (accessed September 8, 2012).

60. Brian Albrecht, "A Community Salutes 1st Lt. Ashley White Stumpf, Who Died in Afghanistan," Cleveland.com, November 1, 2011, http://blog.cleveland.com/metro/2011/11/a_community_salutes_1st_lt_ash.html.

61. Pamela Constable, "A Terrain's Tragic Shift: Researcher's Death Intensifies Scrutiny of U.S. Cultural Program in Afghanistan," *Washington Post*, February 18, 2009, http://www.highbeam.com/doc/1P2-19903623.html (accessed November 20, 2012).

62. *Plain Dealer* Staff, "1st Lt. Ashley White Stumpf Laid to Rest in Mogadore," *Cleveland Plain Dealer*, October 31, 2011, http://blog.cleveland.com/metro/2011/10/1st_lt_ashley_white_stumpf_lai.html.

63. Albrecht, "A Community Salutes."

64. Ibid.

65. Farah Stockman, "Anthropologist's War Death Reverberates," *Boston Globe*, February 12, 2009, http://www.highbeam.com/doc/1P2-19873620.html (accessed November 20, 2012).

66. Ibid.

67. Constable, "A Terrain's Tragic Shift."

68. Constable, "Bomb Kills 3 U.S. Soldiers in Afghanistan; Attack Comes on Heels of Another and as U.S. Vice President-Elect Arrives in Region," *Washington Post*, January 10, 2009, http://www.highbeam.com/doc/1P2-19731244.html (accessed November 20, 2012).

69. Don M. Ayala was the contractor who placed his 9 mm pistol against the assailant's head and blasted a bullet through it. In May 2009, he was sentenced to five years' probation and a fine. Source: Josh White, "No Jail Time in Retribution Killing Overseas," *Washington Post*, May 9, 2009, http://www.highbeam.com/doc/1P2-20243338.html (accessed November 21, 2012).

70. Maximilian Forte, "The Unreported Death of Staff Sgt. Paula Loyd of the Human Terrain System: Third Researcher to Die," *Zero Anthropology*, January 8, 2009.

71. Stockman, "Anthropologist's War Death Reverberates."

72. Donors can contribute to the Paula Loyd Foundation at 1521 Sedwick Road, Durham, North Carolina, 27713, or http://www.paulaloydfoundation.org.

73. "Parents Honor Daughter's Last Wishes with College Aid for Afghan Women," *Daily News*, May 20, 2010, http://www.highbeam.com/doc/1P2-27464727.html (accessed November 21, 2012).

74. David Kilcullen, "Twenty-Eight Articles: Fundamentals of Company-Level Counterinsurgency," Joint Information Operations Center (IO Sphere Publication), 35.

75. Ibid.

76. "McChrystal Bans Night Raids without Afghan Troops," *Times of Oman* (Muscat, Oman), March 6, 2010.

77. Eliot Cohen, Conrad Crane, Jan Horvath, and John Nagl, "Principles, Imperatives, and Paradoxes of Counterinsurgency," *Military Review*, April 1, 2007.

78. E-mail correspondence between Robert Bates, combat artist and Marine, and Mark Silinsky, September 2, 2013.

79. Paul Greenberg, "Wounded Warrior Shows True Grit to Stay in the Fight," Wounded Warrior Project, March 18, 2011, http://www.usa-patriotism.com/articles/tv/wounded_warrior02.htm.

80. "How Petraeus Commands," *Washington Times*, March 1, 2012, http://www.highbeam.com/doc/1G1-281694392.html (accessed November 24, 2012).

81. "X-Rated Emails and the Very Toxic Love Tangle That Brought Down the CIA Boss; as a Second General Is Dragged into the Sex Scandal Gripping America," *Daily Mail* (London), November 4, 2012, http://www.highbeam.com/doc/1G1-308384593 .html (accessed November 25, 2012).

82. Trudy Rubin, "Obama, Petraeus Need to Bond," *Buffalo News* (Buffalo, NY), June 30, 2010, http://www.highbeam.com/doc/1P2-25279863.html (accessed November 25, 2012).

83. Ken Dilanian, "From General to CIA Director: Petraeus Moving to Insular Agency," *Sunday Gazette-Mail*, May 1, 2011, http://www.highbeam.com/doc/1P2 -28582706.html (accessed November 24, 2012).

84. Olga Khazan, "Petraeus Resignation: Who Is Paula Broadwell," *Washington Post*, November 11, 2012, http://www.highbeam.com/doc/1P2-33972913.html (accessed January 20, 2013).

85. Graham Bowley, "As Foreigners Depart, Afghan Warlords; in a Challenge to Karzai, Former Mujahedeen Chief Tells Followers to Mobilize," *International Herald Tribune*, November 14, 2012.

86. " 'Nutty Professor' Pays a Heavy Price," *Southtown Star* (Chicago), March 9, 2009, http://www.highbeam.com/doc/1N1-1272C7FCEFC1A5A0.html (accessed October 1, 2012).

87. Ibid.

88. Bill Stamets, "Anthropologists at War," *In These Times*, June 19, 2008, https://www.inthesetimes.com/article/3749/anthropologists_at_war/.

89. Tom Garcia, "A Story from the Field," October 21, 2009, Michael Vinay Bhatai Tribute, http://wwwrespectance.com/micahel_bhatia.

90. Peter Maas, "Professor John Nagl's War," *New York Times*, January 11, 2004.

91. Jason Straziuso, "Afghanistan Blames Vendetta for Civilian Deaths," Associated Press, September 15, 2008.

92. Anna Mulrine, "Sgt. Robert Bales: Details Emerge on Soldier Charged with Killing Afghan Villagers," *Christian Science Monitor*, March 17, 2012, http://www.highbeam .com/doc/1G1-283309888.html (accessed September 29, 2012).

93. Ibid.

94. James Dao, "At Home, Asking How 'Our Bobby' Became War Crime Suspect," *New York Times*, March 18, 2012, http://www.nytimes.com/2012/03/19/us/sgt-robert-bales-from-small-town-ohio-to-afghanistan.html?pagewanted=all&_r=0.

95. Manuel Valdes and Mike Baker, "Second Prior Assault Cases Surfaces against Robert Bales," *Christian Science Monitor*, March 22, 2012, http://www.highbeam.com/doc/1G1-284111789.html (accessed September 29, 2012).

96. Ibid.

97. Knickerbocker, "Sgt. Robert Bales: Defense Team Begins Building Case on PTSD," *Christian Science Monitor*, March 18, 2012, http://www.highbeam.com/doc/1G1-28 3437040.html (accessed September 29, 2012).

98. "U.S.: A 2-Part Rampage," *Chicago Sun-Times*, March 25, 2012, http://www.high beam.com/doc/1N1-13DBB442C8748918.html (accessed September 29, 2012).

99. Heidi Vogt and Mirwais Khan, "Afghans: U.S. Paid $50,000 per Victim in Shooting Spree," Associated Press, March 25, 2012, http://www.washingtontimes.com/news/2012/mar/25/afghans-us-paid-50000-victim-shooting-spree/.

100. Knickerbocker, "Sgt. Robert Bales."

101. Dao, "At Home, Asking How."

102. "Sarg on Kill Rap 'Is Sane,' " *Mirror* (London), March 27, 2012, http://www.highbeam.com/doc/1G1-284273638.html (accessed September 29, 2012).

103. "Afghan Kill Suspect a Good Soldier," *Mirror* (London), March 19, 2012, http://www.highbeam.com/doc/1G1-283433675.html (accessed September 29, 2012).

104. A glaring example of the national leadership misusing body counts and similar statistics to advance its political agenda is the misrepresentation of the battle situation in Vietnam. Body counts of the enemy dead were proven to be cavalier in approach, intentionally exaggerated, sometimes irrelevant, and often misleading. They gave the false impression to the American public that victory was near and that U.S. force levels could be reduced soon as part of a comprehensive de-escalation.

105. Kilcullen, "Twenty-Eight Articles Fundamentals of Company-Level Counter-insurgency," *Military Review*, May 1, 2006.

106. "Artist Creates Bronze Sculpture of Marjan, the One-Eyed Lion, for Donation to Kabul Zoo," AP Worldstream, March 28, 2004, http://www.highbeam.com/doc/1P1-92768929.html (accessed January 12, 2013).

107. Susan Mansfield, "Arts Review: Reflecting Glenfiddich: Spey's Programme," *Scotsman*, February 22, 2011, http://www.highbeam.com/doc/1P2-28018210.html (accessed January 12, 2013).

108. Jerry Harmer, "New School Tries to Revive Music in Afghanistan," AP Online, May 15, 2010, http://www.highbeam.com/doc/1A1-D9FNCPH00.html (accessed January 20, 2013).

109. Rizwan Ali, "Rousing Cricket Triumph for War-Weary Afghanistan," Associated Press, October 5, 2013, http://news.yahoo.com/rousing-cricket-triumph-war-weary-afghanistan-150312843-spt.html.

110. Yvonne Ridley, "Barack Obama: An Out Of Control Psychopath with a God Complex," Yvonne Ridley website, June 1, 2012, http://yvonneridley.org/.

111. "Daisy and Yvonne Ridley—Mum and Me Taster," http://www.youtube.com/watch?v=xd1HfGI6ffU.

112. Russia Today produced a documentary on Nekmuhammad entitled "The Last Soviet in Afghanistan." As of September 2013, it could be viewed at http://www.youtube.com/watch?v=TveNjPw5H5Q&list=PL5TVYC3MLdhBdQBFsa_tkmikvHCN-TWG7.

113. Jim Heintz, "Last Russian General Warns US on Afghanistan," AP Worldstream, February 13, 2009, http://www.highbeam.com/doc/1A1-D96AP0A01.html (accessed December 17, 2012).

114. Boris Gromov and Dmitry Rogozin, "Russian Advice on Afghanistan," *International Herald Tribune*, January 12, 2010, http://www.highbeam.com/doc/1P1 -174943922.html (accessed December 17, 2012).

115. "Hijacker Is Working as a Cleaner at Heathrow; Armed: One of the Hijackers During the Stansted Siege Terminal 5: Mohammidy," *Daily Mail* (London), May 16, 2008, http://www.highbeam.com/doc/1G1-179086894.html (accessed December 13, 2012).

116. Scott Simon, "Green Party's Cynthia McKinney Runs for President," *Weekend Edition Saturday*, NPR, October 25, 2008, http://www.highbeam.com/doc/1P1-1575 13980.html (accessed December 13, 2012).

117. V. Shuman, " '9/11 Not Work of Terrorists,' " *New Straits Times*, November 20, 2012, http://www.highbeam.com/doc/1P1-210650336.html (accessed December 13, 2012).

118. "Clinton: Ex-Taliban Must Respect Women's Rights," AP Worldstream, May 13, 2010., http://www.highbeam.com/doc/1A1-D9FM5LP04.html (accessed December 16, 2012).

119. "Taliban: We Get Bad Press," *Republican & Herald* (Pottsville, PA), October 20, 2012, http://www.highbeam.com/doc/1P2-33787414.html (accessed December 16, 2012).

120. "If the Taliban Regains Power," *Virginian-Pilot* (Norfolk, VA), September 28, 2010, http://www.highbeam.com/doc/1G1-238141413.html (accessed December 16, 2012).

121. Verbal conversation between Flagg Youngblood and this author in Washington, DC, December 12, 2012.

122. "Naval ROTC Returns to Yale," States News Service, 2011, http://www .highbeam.com (accessed December 11, 2012).

123. "Lethal Haul of Weapons Found After Car Seized," *Birmingham Mail* (England), June 11, 2013, http://www.highbeam.com/doc/1G1-333376159.html (accessed July 3, 2013).

124. "Karzai: Afghan Sentence Won't Bring Back Victims," AP Online, 2013, http:// www.highbeam.com (accessed August 25, 2013).

125. Erica Hill, Jeff Glor, and John Miller, "Interview with Robert Bales' Wife; Terror Alert!," *CBS This Morning*, July 2, 2012, http://www.highbeam.com/doc/1P1-20 6677383.html (accessed December 13, 2012).

126. "God-Daughters," (review of *Wanted Women: Faith, Lies, and the War on Terror: The Lives of Ayaan Hirsi Ali and Aafia Siddiqui*), *The Economist*, January 7, 2012, http://www.highbeam.com/doc/1G1-276371078.html (accessed December 13, 2012).

127. Diana West, "Ayaan Hirsi Ali Biographer Flouts Facts," *Washington Examiner*, January 29, 2012, http://www.highbeam.com/doc/1P2-30608559.html (accessed December 13, 2012).

128. "VOA News: Kabul Beauty School Book—How Close to Reality?," U.S. Federal News Service, Including U.S. State News, June 11, 2007, http://www.highbeam.com/ doc/1P3-1286618631.html (accessed December 14, 2012).

129. Chetna Keer, "Afghanistan: On the Right Pitch, Rukhsana's Taliban Cricket Club," Women's Feature Service, 2012, http://www.highbeam.com (accessed December 14, 2012).

130. Rick Baillergeon, "First In: An Insider's Account of How the CIA Spearheaded the War on Terror in Afghanistan," *Infantry Magazine*, May 1, 2006, http://www.highbeam.com/doc/1G1-153517321.html (accessed December 16, 2012).

131. Tom Sutcliffe, "Last Night's Viewing," *Independent* (London), May 2, 2012, http://www.highbeam.com/doc/1P2-31264780.html (accessed December 16, 2012).

132. "Greg Mortenson Would Know: WSU Research Shows Charitable Donors Expect Their Money to Be Used Exactly as They Specify," States News Service, July 5, 2011, http://www.highbeam.com/doc/1G1-260597242.html (accessed December 14, 2012).

133. The last account known to this author is dated 2005. Had Zardad been released, it would likely have commanded headlines in the British press. See "After [Pounds Sterling] 3M and a 2-Year Police Probe, This Afghan Warlord Was Found Guilty of Crimes in his Homeland. Now He'll Cost Us [Pounds Sterling] 30,000 a Year to Keep in Prison," *Daily Mail* (London), 2005, http://www.highbeam.com (accessed December 30, 2012).

134. Caroline Wyatt, "Dambusters Prepare for Final Tour Before Disbandment," BBC News, October 3, 2013, http://www.bbc.co.uk/news/uk-24382841.

135. "U.S. Suspects Haqqani Tie to Afghan Insider Attacks," *Daily Herald* (Arlington Heights, IL), October 6, 2012, http://www.highbeam.com/doc/1G1-304953350.html (accessed December 12, 2012).

136. "USS *Michael Murphy*, Navy's Newest Destroyer Arrives in Pearl Harbor," States News Service, November 22, 2012, http://www.highbeam.com/doc/1G1-309599 678.html (accessed December 13, 2012).

137. Chris Rosenblum, *Centre Daily Times* (State College, PA), September 15, 2012, http://www.centredaily.com/2012/09/15/3336707/psu-memorial-honors-hero-vet.html.

138. Posted by Laughing Wolf, "Welcome Home CPL. Bowman," July 7, 2011, BlackFivehttp://www.blackfive.net/main/2011/07/welcome-home-cpl-bowman.html.

139. Dan Lamothe, "Cpl. Kyle Carpenter, Wounded Warrior Marine and Grenade Blast Survivor, to Retire," July 29, 2013, http://blogs.militarytimes.com/battle-rattle/2013/07/29/cpl-kyle-carpenter-wounded-warrior-marine-and-grenade-blast-survivor-to-retire/.

140. Commentary by Cindy Reese, *Marine Times*, "Cpl Kyle Carpenter, Wounded Warrior and Grenade Blast Survivor, to Retire." http://blogs.militarytimes.com/battle-rattle/2013/07/29/cpl-kyle-carpenter-wounded-warrior-marine-and-grenade-blast-survivor-to-retire/

141. Perry Chiaramonte and Mike Jaccarino, "How 9/11 Turned a New Immigrant into a Proud Marine," Fox News.com, May 25, 2012, http://www.foxnews.com/us/2012/05/25/marine-tale-how-one-man-served-his-adopted-country/.

142. "Afghan Women Overcoming Barriers," *Daily Herald* (Arlington Heights, IL), December 27, 2009, http://www.highbeam.com/doc/1G1-215326368.html (accessed December 16, 2012).

143. "Afghanistan: Radio Station Director's Murder Still Unpunished Two Years Later," Reporters Without Borders, June 5, 2009, http://www.rawa.org/temp/runews/2009/06/05/afghanistan-radio-station-directorand-8217-s-murder-still-unpunished-two-years-later.html.

144. "Will Take Fazlur Rehman to Court for Calling Me Jewish Agent: Imran Khan," *Express Tribune* (Pakistan), August 4 2013, http://youknowfirst.blogspot.com/2013/08/will-take-fazlur-rehman-to-court-for.html.

145. Arnaud de Borchgrave, "Pakistan's Heavyweights," *Pittsburgh Tribune-Review*, November 7, 2012, http://www.highbeam.com/doc/1P2-33861977.html (accessed December 13, 2012).

146. "Zarb-e-Momin 5," Middle East Media Research Institute (MEMRI), Jihad—South Asia Studies Project, April 11, 2013, Special Dispatch No. 5269, http://www.memri.org/report/en/0/0/0/0/0/0/7127.htm (accessed April 10, 2013).

147. Anonymous, "Different Gun Laws, but Both Can Be Silly," *Winnipeg Free Press*, July 2, 2011, http://www.highbeam.com/doc/1P3-2392106001.html (accessed December 11, 2012).

148. Andrew Buncombe and David Usborne, "US Claims Al-Qa'ida Scalp as Drone Attack Kills Terror Network's No 2," *Independent* (London), June 6, 2012, http://www.highbeam.com/doc/1P2-31499326.html (accessed December 13, 2012).

149. Brian Murphy, "Al-Qaida Papers Highlight Tense Dealings with Iran," AP Online, May 4, 2012, http://www.highbeam.com/doc/1A1-9fc9da5946384af58960fee53aefc4d0.html (accessed December 13, 2012).

150. Donors can contribute to the Paula Loyd Foundation at 1521 Sedwick Road, Durham, North Carolina, 27713, or http://www.paulaloydfoundation.org. Source: Constance Cooper, "Parents Honor Daughter's Last Wishes with College Aid for Afghan Woman," *Virgin Islands Daily News*, May 20, 2010, http://www.highbeam.com/doc/1P2-27464727.html (accessed December 13, 2012).

151. Jamie Stengle, "Bush Library to Feature Park Recreating Prairie," AP Online, October 30, 2012, http://www.highbeam.com/doc/1A1-537c621af3ae456c9530ab37e3a2dc20.html (accessed December 13, 2012).

152. David Espo and Dozier Kimberly, "Obama: Bin Laden's Death a 'Good Day' for America," AP Online, May 1, 2011, http://www.highbeam.com/doc/1A1-2cfbb4c4bff047c98842abbbf7053cdc.html (accessed December 13, 2012).

153. Ibid.

154. Bill O'Reilly, "Obama Ad Politicizes Bin Laden Raid," *O'Reilly Factor*, FOX News, April 30, 2012, http://www.highbeam.com/doc/1P1-204893249.html (accessed December 13, 2012).

155. Ibid.

156. "Why Infidelity Matters," *Washington Post*, November 25, 2012, http://www.highbeam.com/doc/1P2-33928010.html (accessed December 13, 2012).

157. The Reliable, " 'Saturday Night Live' Spoofs Paula Broadwell's Reading at Politics & Prose" (video), *Washington Post*, November 19, 2012, http://www.highbeam.com/doc/1P2-34001807.html (accessed January 26, 2013).

158. "Comeback of Yusuf Islam (Cat Stevens)," AP Online, April 27, 2007, http://www.highbeam.com/doc/1Y1-105723003.html (accessed December 16, 2012).

159. "Afghan Boys from Nominated Film to Walk Red Carpet," AP Online, February 7, 2013, http://www.highbeam.com/doc/1A1-0708760aa4f64f468cb4ce728c6d702d.html (accessed March 23, 2013).

160. Kelly Coiella, "Afghan Woman Challenges Convention through Rap," CBS News, December 1, 2012, http://www.cbsnews.com/video/watch/?id=50136236n.

161. "Don't Worry Be Pakistani," Saad Haroon.com, http://wsaadharoon.com/events/dont-worry-be-pakistani-stand-up-comedy%e2%80%8f/ (accessed August 10, 2013).

162. "Skateistan Kabul's 3 Year Anniversary," Skateistan, http://www.skateistan.org/blog/skateistan-kabuls-3-year-anniversary (accessed December 31, 2012).

163. "Afghanistan Crazy about Bollywood, but Lacks Official Market," *Hindustan Times* (New Delhi, India), April 18, 2010, http://www.highbeam.com/doc/1P3-2013 014871.html (accessed December 11, 2012).

164. "Skateistan Kabul's 3 Year Anniversary," Skateistan.

165. In verbal communication with this author, Mr. Bond claims that he did not coin the term "Taliban wing," but that he heard a Republican use it in reference to the more conservative wing of that political party. Date of conversation, October 7, 2013.

166. "The Malala Effect," States News Service, November 23, 2012, http://www.highbeam.com/doc/1G1-309690900.html (accessed October 16, 2013).

167. Jeffrey Zhao, "Doomed from the Start: Looking Back on Afghanistan, 2001," Harvard *International Review*, Fall 2013, http://www.questia.com/read/1G1-3469 28491/doomed-from-the-start-looking-back-on-afghanistan.

168. Peter Bergen, "Afghanistan Is Not Hopeless," *Winnipeg Free Press*, March 16, 2013, http://www.questia.com/library/1P3-2918610651/afghanistan-is-not-hopeless#articleDetails.

169. International Development and other foreign agencies had a margin of error of plus or minus 5.1 percent. Source: Slobodan Lekic, "Poll: Most Afghans Optimistic about Future," AP Online, November 14, 2012, http://www.highbeam.com/doc/1A1-3eaa2d7 1693d43359d0dcabfe64ae952.html (accessed November 15, 2012).

170. Lekic, "Poll: Most Afghans Optimistic about Future."

AFTERWORD

1. Basharat Peer, "The Girl Who Wanted to Go to School," *The New Yorker*, October 10, 2012 (accessed October 15, 2012).

2. Dawn.com (Pakistan), July 20, 2012.

3. Wassem Nikzad and Sardar Ahmad, "Tribesmen Rise Up Against Afghan Taliban," Agence France-Presse, Yahoo.com, July 20, 2012.

4. Peter Singer, "Children at War: The Lost Generation," *Globalist*, March 16, 2005. http://www.theglobalist.com/StoryId.aspx?StoryId=4455.

5. Wording and context confirmed in an e-mail from Andrew Roberts to this author. Reply to "Subject: I would like to paraphrase your good words in my book"; To: andrew @roberts-london.fsnet.co.uk, January 6, 2013.

Bibliography

Aaron, David. *In Their Own Words: Voices of Jihad.* Santa Monica, CA: RAND Corporation, 2008.

Acharya, Arabinda, Syed Adnan Ali Shah, and Sadia Sulaiman. "Making Money in the Mayhem: Funding Taliban Insurrection in the Tribal Areas of Pakistan." *Studies in Conflict and Terrorism* 32, no. 2 (February 2009): 95–108.

"Afghanistan: A Military History from Alexander the Great to the War on the Taliban." Targeted News Service. 2010. Accessed December 19, 2010. http://www.high beam.com.

Afsar, Shahid, Chris Samples, and Thomas Wood. "The Taliban: An Organizational Analysis." *Military Review*, May–June 2008.

Andrabi, Tahir, Jishnudas Das, C. Christine Fair, and Asim Ijaz Khwaja. "The Madrasa Myth," *Foreign Policy*, June 1, 2009.

"Anglo-Afghan Wars: War One (1838–1842)." *Encyclopedia of India.* 2006. Accessed April 17, 2011. http://www.highbeam.com.

Antonowicz, Anton. "Face Beneath the Veil: Zarmina's Story: She Was the Afghan Woman Whose Public Execution by the Taliban Shocked the World." *Mirror* (London, England), June 19, 2002.

Baillergeon, Rick. "First In: An Insider's Account of How the CIA Spearheaded the War on Terror in Afghanistan." *Infantry Magazine*, May 1, 2006. Accessed December 16, 2012. http://www.highbeam.com/doc/1G1-153517321.html.

Barfield, Thomas. *Afghanistan a Cultural and Political History.* Princeton, NJ: Princeton University Press, 2010.

Berkowitz, Bruce. "A Hero's Tale. (*First In: An Insider's Account of How the CIA Spearheaded the War on Terror in Afghanistan*)," (Book review), *Policy Review*, April 1, 2006. Accessed August 26, 2012. http://www.highbeam.com/doc/1G1 -145781329.html.

Blanchfield, Mark K. "Transportation Challenges in Afghanistan." Army Logistician, March 1, 2005. Accessed December 15, 2010. http://www.highbeam.com/doc/1G1-131050553.html.

Blankenship, Janie. "'Iron-Souled Warrior' Awarded First Medal of Honor for Afghanistan Service." VFW Magazine, January 1, 2008. http://www.highbeam.com/doc/1P3-1417377651.html.

Buck, Duncan. "A Tragic Loss of Skateistan Youth." Skateistan, September 10, 2012. http://www.skateistan.org/blog/tragic-loss.

Cassidy, Robert M. "Back to the Street without Joy: Counterinsurgency Lessons from Vietnam and Other Small Wars." Parameters (Summer 2004).

Cigar, Norman. Al-Qa'ida's Doctrine for Insurgency: Abd al-Aziz al-Muqrin's "A Practical Course for Guerrilla War." Washington, DC: Potomac Books, 2009.

Clarke, Richard. Senate Committee on Banking, Housing and Urban Affairs. The Financing of Terror Organizations, 108th Cong.1st sess., October 22, 2003.

Cohen, Eliot, Conrad Crane, Jan Horvath, and John Nagl. "Principles, Imperatives, and Paradoxes of Counterinsurgency." Military Review, April 1, 2007.

Cohen, Michael. "Casus Pax." Foreign Policy, May 2, 2011.

Cole, Juan R. I. "The Taliban, Women, and the Hegelian Private Sphere." Social Research 80, no. 3 (September 22, 2003).

Coll, Steve. "The Return of the Taliban," Frontline, PBS, October 3, 2006, http://www.pbs.org/wgbh/pages/frontline/taliban/.

Coll, Steve. Ghost Wars: The Secret History of the CIA, Afghanistan, and Bin Laden, from the Soviet Invasion to September 10, 2001. New York: Penguin Books, 2004.

Crews, Robert, D., and Amin Tarzi. The Taliban and The Crisis of Afghanistan. Cambridge, MA: Harvard University Press, 2009.

Crile, George. Charlie Wilson's War. New York: Grove Press, 2003.

Daly, Terence J. "Classical Principles of Counterinsurgency," Marine Corps Gazette, 90 (December 2006), 53–57.

Dobbins, James. After the Taliban: Nation-Building in Afghanistan. Washington, DC: Potomac Books, 2008.

Felbab-Brown, Vanda. "Implications of Osama bin Laden's Death." Brookings Institution item, May 2, 2011.

Fergusson, James. The Taliban: The Unknown Enemy. Cambridge, MA: De Capo Press, 2011.

Filkins, Dexter. "The Legacy of the Taliban Is a Sad and Broken Land." New York Times, December 31, 2001.

Galula, David. Counterinsurgency Warfare: Theory and Practice. Westport, CT: Praeger Security International, 1964.

Gentile, Gian. Wrong Turn: America's Deadly Embrace of Counterinsurgency. New York: The New Press, 2013.

Giustozzi, Antonio. Decoding the New Taliban. New York: Columbia University Press, 2009.

Giustozzi, Antonio. Koran, Kalashnikov, and Laptop: The Neo-Taliban Insurgency in Afghanistan 2002–2007. New York: Columbia University Press, 2008.

Goodhand, Jonathan, "From War Economy to Peace Economy? Reconstruction and State Building in Afghanistan." Journal of International Affairs 58, no. 1 (September 22, 2004).

Gopal, Anand. "Afghanistan War: Who's Who in the Taliban Leadership." Christian Science Monitor, February 25, 2010. Accessed September 23, 2012. http://www.highbeam.com/doc/1G1-219808170.html.

Gopal, Anand. "The Most Deadly U.S. Foe in Afghanistan." *Christian Science Monitor*, May 31, 2009.

Gregory, Shaun. "Pakistan: An Uncertain Ally." *Soundings*. 2008. http://www.highbeam.com. Accessed February 17, 2012.

Hanifi, M. Jamil. "Reaping the Whirlwind: The Taliban Movement in Afghanistan/ Taliban: Militant Islam, Oil & Fundamentalism in Central Asia." *The Middle East Journal*. 2002. http://www.highbeam.com. Accessed November 1, 2010.

Highland, Grant R. "New Century, Old Problems: The Global Insurgency within Islam and the Nature of the War on Terror." In *Chairman of the Joint Chiefs of Staff Strategy Essay Competition*, 17–30. Washington, DC: National Defense University Press, 2003.

Hopkirk, Peter. *The Great Game: The Struggle for Empire in Central Asia*. New York: Kondansha International, 1994.

Jaffe, Greg, and Karen DeYoung. "Leaked Files Lay Bare War in Afghanistan; Pakistan Aid to Rebels Hinted Taliban Apparently Used Heat-Seeking Missiles." *Washington Post*. Accessed February 4, 2011. http://www.highbeam.com.

Jones, Seth. *Graveyard of Empires: America's War in Afghanistan*. New York: Norton, 2009.

Kaplan, Fred. *The Insurgents: David Petraeus and the Plot to Change the American Way of War*. New York: Simon and Schuster, 2013.

Kilcullen, David. *The Accidental Guerilla: Fighting Small Wars in the Midst of a Big One*. New York: Oxford University Press, 2009.

King, Laura. "Poetry of the Taliban Elicits Both Anger and Astonishment." *Los Angeles Times*, July 8, 2012.

Koh, Harold H. "Overview to Country Report on Human Rights Practices for 1998." U.S. Department of State. In 1998 *Human Rights Report*, http://www.state.gov/www/global/human_rights/drl_reports.html.

Komer, R. W. *The Malayan Emergency in Retrospect*. Novato, CA: RAND Corporation, 1972.

Lamb, Robert D. "Bin Laden Is Dead: Is It Time to Leave Afghanistan?" Center for Strategic and International Studies, May 2, 2011.

Le Billon, Phillipe. "The Political Economy of War: What Relief Workers Need to Know." Humanitarian Practice Network Paper, no. 33. London: Overseas Development Institute, 2000.

Mahmood, Saba, and Charles Hirschkind. "Feminism, the Taliban and the Politics of Counterinsurgency." Fathom Archive. University of Chicago Library Digital Collection, 2002. http://fathom.lib.uchicgo.edu/1/777777190136.

Malevich, John, and Daryl C. Youngman. "The Afghan Balance of Power and the Culture of Jihad." *Military Review*, May 2, 2001.

McFate, Montgomery, and Andrea V. Jackson. "The Object Beyond War: Counterinsurgency and the Four Tools of Political Competition." *Military Review*, November 1, 2006.

Michael, George. "Adam and Al-Qaeda's Internet Strategy." *Middle East Policy*, September 22, 2009. http://www.highbeam.com/doc/1G1-210368259.html. Accessed September 18, 2012.

Mills, Greg, Terence McNamee, and Denny Lane. "Security Vortex: Warlords and Nation Building." *National Interest*, September 1, 2006.

Moore, Robin. *The Hunt for Bin Laden: Task Force Dagger*. New York: Random House, 2003.

"Morbidity and Mortality Weekly Report." Thallium Poisoning Center for Disease Control from Eating Contaminated Cake—Iraq. 2008, vol. 57. no. 37, 10015–18.

Moyar, Mark. "A Question of Command: Counterinsurgency from the Civil War to Iraq." New Haven, CT: Yale University Press, 2009.

Nagl, John. *Learning to Eat Soup with a Knife: Counterinsurgency Lessons from Malaya and Vietnam*. Westport, CT: Greenwood, 2002.

Nojumi, Neamatollah. *The Rise of the Taliban in Afghanistan: Mass Mobilization, Civil War, and the Future of the Region*. New York: Palgrave, 2002.

Perry, Walter L., and John Gordon IV. *Analytic Support to Intelligence in Counterinsurgencies*. Santa Monica, CA: RAND Corporation, 2008.

Peters, Gretchen. *Crime and Insurgency*. West Point, NY: Combating Terrorism Center, 2010.

Phelps, Richard. "Sayyid Qutb and the Origins of Radical Islamism." *The Middle East Quarterly*, 2011. http://www.highbeam.com. Accessed September 16, 2012.

Pomper, Stephen D. "Don't Follow the Bear: The Soviet Attempt to Build Afghanistan's Military." *Military Review*, September 1, 2005.

Rana, Muhammad Amir. "The Taliban Consolidate Control in Pakistan's Tribal Regions." Combating Terrorism Center at West Point, June 15, 2008

Rashid, Ahmed. *Descent into Chaos: The United States and the Failure of Nation Building in Pakistan, Afghanistan, and Central Asia*. New York: Viking, 2008.

Rashid, Ahmed. *Taliban: The Story of the Afghan Warlords*. New York: Pan Books, 2001.

Ridley, Yvonne. *In the Hands of the Taliban: Her Extraordinary Story*. London: Robson Books, 2001.

Roggio, Bill. "The Afghan Taliban Top Leaders," February 23, 2010. http://www.longwarjournal.org/archives/2010/02/the_talibans_top_lea.php.

Rubin, Barnett R. *The Fragmentation of Afghanistan: State Formation and Collapse in the International System*. 2nd ed. New Haven, CT: Yale University Press, 2002.

Sewall, Sarah. "Modernizing U.S. Counterinsurgency Practice: Rethinking Risk and Developing a National Strategy," *Military Review*, September 1, 2007.

Summers, Harry G., Jr. "Tet's 30th Anniversary Presents a Good Opportunity to Cut through the Bodyguard of Lies That Distort That Battle's Real Significance." http://www.vwam.com/vets/tet/tet2.html.

"Taliban Propaganda: Winning the War of Words?" International Crisis Group. *Asia Report* 158 (July 24 2008).

Tanner, Stephen. *Afghanistan: A Military History from Alexander the Great to the War against the Taliban*. Philadelphia: De Capo Press, 2009.

Tasal, Wrekhmin. "Women Bought and Sold in Eastern Afghanistan." Institute for War and Peace Reporting. August 12, 2012. http://iwpr.net/report-news/women-bought-and-sold-eastern-afghanistan.

Tovo, Ken. "From the Ashes of the Phoenix: Lessons for Contemporary Counter-insurgency Operations." *Special Warfare*, January 1, 2007. Accessed January 19, 2013. http://www.highbeam.com/doc/1P3-1221371071.html.

Tucker, Noah, and Sue Sypko. "Salafist and Wahhabist Influence in Afghanistan." *Cultural Knowledge Report*, March 15, 2009.

"The United States Army in Afghanistan, Operation Enduring Freedom." Center for Military History Online. http://www.history.army.mil/brochures/Afghanistan/Operation%20Enduring%20Freedom.htm.

U.S. Army/Marine Corps, *Counterinsurgency Field Manual*, No. 3-24. Marine Corps Warfighting Publication No. 3-33.5. Chicago: University of Chicago Press, 2007.

U.S. Department of State. *Counterinsurgency for U.S. Government Policy Makers—A Work in Progress.* United States Government Interagency Counterinsurgency Initiative, October 2007.

Vartan, Gregorian. *The Emergence of Modern Afghanistan: Politics of Reform and Modernization, 1880–1946.* Stanford, CA: Stanford University Press, 1969.

Venzke, Ben, and Aimee Ibrahim. "Al-Qaeda's Advice for Mujahideen in Iraq: Lessons Learned in Afghanistan." Vol. 1.0. IntelCenter/Tempest, April 14, 2003.

Wright, Lawrence. *The Looming Tower, Al-Qaeda and the Road to 9/11.* New York: First Vintage Books, 2006.

Index

Addiction, 37
Affiliated insurgent groups. *See* Insurgent groups
Afghan counterinsurgency: effective training, 172; engaging and promoting local efforts, 168, 169–70; legacy traits and epochs applicable to, 163t; metrics for measuring status, 172–73; pressure tactics, 168; rules, 165–73; seize and hold initiative, 167–68; sustain area ownership, 165–66. *See also* Coalition Forces; U.S. military action, in Afghanistan
Afghan government forces, 91
Afghan hurt locker, 115–16
Afghan Interim Authority (AIA), 65
Afghanistan: Bollywood movies in, 181; British invasion of, 3–4; constitution of, 5; corruption in, 7; as failed state, 32, 33t; foreign aid to, 4; foreign fighters in, 20; futuristic action, 182–83; globalization and, 30, 31; history, 2–5; landscape of, 1–2; life in, 30; map of, 3f; mines in, 114; mountains in, 2; people of, 9–11; post-Taliban regime, 174–82, 185–86; reaction to the fall of the Taliban, 60–65; reintegration efforts, 186; religious schools, 29; roads, 128;

Soviet invasion of, 5–8; taxation, 129. *See also* Bonn Agreement; Insurgency; Insurgent groups; Taliban; U.S. military action, in Afghanistan; *Specific cities*
Afghan National Army (ANA), 68
Afghan National Police (ANP), 69
Afghan National Security Forces (ANSF), 68
Afghan noncombatants, 91
Afghans: Arab, 20; civil service, Taliban and, 32; Coalition Army forces, 104, 120; constitution, 5; conversion to Sunni Islam, 2; counterinsurgency, 165–73; culture, 26; economy, communication and, 71; fighters/warriors, 101–2; Hindi cinema, 181; insurgency, 26; intermarriage with Arab women, 84; military training of, 75; music, 175; non-Pashtun, 10; refugee camps, 6; refugee women, 41; religion and, 62; spring, 157–58; view of martyrs, 186; weapons, 103–5. *See also* Pashtuns
Afghan Star, 158
Agha, Sayyid Tayyab, 87
Agricultural production, 32
Ahmed, Wakil, 12
Ahu, 105

AIA (Afghan Interim Authority), 65
AID (U.S. Agency for International
  Development), 67
AK-47, 103, 104, 105. *See also* Weapons
AK-47M, 104
AK-74, 104
Akhund, Mullah Dadullah, 121–22
al-Adel, Saif: as al Qaeda "caretaker,"
  138–39; articles by, 57; evaluation of
  war in Afghanistan, 57–58;
  prize money on, 179; tactical
  recommendations of, 102; on Taliban,
  57–58, 105, 106
al-Amriki, Azzam. *See* Gadahn, Adam
al-Awlaki, Anwar, 176–77
Albright, Madeleine, 41
Alexander, Chris, 172
Alexander the Great, 2
Alexandra, Princess, 117
al-Hamzi, Nawaf, 77
Al Jazeera, 49, 132
"Allahu Akbar," 30
Allen, John, 75, 119–20, 158
al-Libi, Abu Yahya, 138
al Qaeda: Arabs affiliated with, 26; goals/
  agenda, 140; as an insurgent group,
  137–40, 148t; ISI and, 153; lady, 106–7;
  leaders, 138–39; mujahedeen and, 8;
  Muslim Brotherhood and, 13;
  Northern Alliance and, 51; operational
  base, 139; poisoning expertise, 118;
  raiding operations, 102;
  reconnaissance, 102; status, 140;
  strength, 139; Taliban and, 51, 102;
  temporary dirt shelters, 102; traps, 102;
  "trenches," 102, 111. *See also* Taliban;
  U.S. military action, in Afghanistan
"Al-Zarqawi" of Afghanistan. *See*
  Akhund, Mullah Dadullah
al-Zawahiri, Ayman, 14–15, 45, 138, 179.
  See also Al Qaeda
Ambush attacks, 110–12
American Anthropological
  Association, 170
American Friends Committee, 64
Ammonium nitrate, 114, 225n.86
Amnesty International, 6
Amputations, 34
ANA (Afghan National Army), 68

Animals, torturing of, 16–17
ANP (Afghan National Police), 69
ANSF (Afghan National Security
  Forces), 68
Antiair weapons, 102
Antisocial personality disorder
  (ASPD), 164
Anxiety, 33
Apostasy, 133
Arab Afghans, 20
Arab jihadis, 26
Ariana Airlines Boeing 727, 176
Armored pickup trucks, 105
Arms. *See* Weapons
Army, of Afghanistan, 68, 69
Army of Retribution, 4
Arsenic poison, 119
Art, 37
Article 1 of the Universal Declaration
  of Human Rights, 182
Ashan, Mohammad, 103
ASPD (antisocial personality
  disorder), 164
Autobiography of Malcolm X, 123
Azizulah, 108
Azzam, Sheikh Abdullah, 14
Azzam the American. *See* Gadahn, Adam

Babur, 3, 192n.12
Bales, Karilyn "Kari," 172, 177
Bales, Robert "Doom," 171–72, 177
Baltimore Sun, 157
Baluchistan, 82, 83–85
Bamiyan Province, 67
Banana Wars, 161
Bank robbery, 129–30
Baradar, Mullah Abdul Ghani, 86
Barbers, 33
Barno, David, 85
Barter economy, 4
Basic Package of Health Services (BPHS),
  214n.198
Bates, Robert, 112, 115
Beards, 34
Bergdahl, Bowe, 131
Betrayal, 119–21
Bhatia, Michael, 170
Bhutto, Benazir, 146, 149
Bidar, Mubariz, 62

bin Laden, Osama: Abbotabad, Pakistan, 153; Haqqani and, 141; ISI and, 21; Islamism and, 13, 30; killing/death of, 137, 138, 180; Muslim Brotherhood and, 13, 14–15; Omar and, 23, 24, 41; Qutb's influence on, 13, 14; Saudi expulsion of, 23, 199n.24; Taliban and, 21, 41–42, 137–38; United States and, 41–43
Black Tulips, 114
Blitzkrieg warfare, 105–6
Blowback from Crime, 133–35
Blumenthal, Richard, 114
Bollywood movies. *See* Films
Bombing, Suicide, 108–9
Bond, Julian, 182
Bonn Agreement: army, 68–69; civil service, 70–71; communications, 71; economy, 66–67; education, 72–73; health care, 73; police force, 69; significance, 185; villages and provinces, 67–68
Booby traps, 104, 108
Bowen, Collin J., 117–18
Bowman, Ken, 115
Bowman, Mathew, 115, 178
Boys: suicide attacks, 107–8; as Taliban recruits, 29–30
BPHS (Basic Package of Health Services), 214n.198
Breininger, Eric, 143
Britain: Indian Mutiny, 13, 196n.85; invasion of Afghanistan, xvii, 3–4
British Tipton Taliban, 122
Brydon, William, 3
Buddhas of Bamiyan, 12
Buddhism, 2
Burka Avenger, 181
Burns, Nicholas, 154
Burrows, George, 4
Bush, George H. W., 150
Bush, George W., 92, 180
Businesses/businessmen, violence against, 93. *See also* Violent tactics
Butterfly bomb, 114
Buzkashi, 62, 181
Buzkashi Boys, 181

A Call from Hindu Kush, 143
Callwell, C. E., 167

Cameron, David, 120
Cannabis, 75
Carpenter, William Kyle, 111–12, 178
Cat Stevens. *See* Yusuf Islam
Celestial harems, 30
Chamberlin, Wendy, 43
Chemical poisons, 119
Chess, 61
Child abuse, 75
Child suicide bombing, 108
Civilizations, 75
Civil Operations and Rural Development System (CORDS), 162
Civil servants, attacks on, 95
Civil service, 70–71
Clapper, James, 140
Clerics, 25
Clinton, Bill, 41, 180
Clinton, Hillary, 33, 41, 176
Clouds, 15
Coalition Forces: air forces, 57; ambush attacks on, 110–11; counterintelligence specialists, 119; cultural mishaps, 75; drug abuse, 75; ethical and logistical dilemma, 128; hostility toward, 104; intelligence and counterintelligence, 90, 91, 91t; Northern Alliance soldiers, 53; roadside bombs, 114–15; selective in killings and targets, 170, 171; Stinger missiles, 51; Taliban functioning as, 53; villagers, 103; violent tactics against, 85, 102
Coalition Humanitarian Liaison Cells, 67
Coalition snipers, 113
Coll, Steven, 141
Comedians, 37
Committees, 83, 89, 89t
Communications, 32, 72; violent attacks on, 94–95
Communist Party, 19
Conventional warfare, 26. *See also* Insurgency
CORDS (Civil Operations and Rural Development System), 162
Corolla vehicles, 105
Corruption, 7
Counterinsurgency: golden age, 161, 163t; manuals, 162, 164; new doctrine, 162, 164; Philippines, 6, 69, 160–61, 163t;

theoreticians, 161; Vietnam, 161–62, 163t. *See also* Afghan counterinsurgency

Counterintelligence, 90–91, 91t

"Crackshot Christopher," 113

Cricket, 175

Culture and Information committees, 89

Cyanide poison, 119

Dahtyari, Saba, 84

"Daisy and Yvonne Ridley—Mum and Me Taster," 175

Dance and dancing, 37

Darul Uloom, 13, 196n.84

Dasht-e-Archi, 58

Davis, Geena, 41

Death zones, in mountains, 2, 192n.6

Deoband, India, 13

Deobandism, 13, 196n.84

Department of State, U.S., 41, 42

Depression, 33

De Rijke, Joanie, 97

Derluguian, Georgi, 51

DiCaprio, Leonardo, 33, 61, 181

Disloyalty, 30

Doctors Without Borders, 73, 96

Donatello (bear), 16–17

Dostum, Abdul Rashid, 58, 122

Durrand Line, 146

Durranis, 10–11, 12t

Dutton, Kevin, 159

Earthquakes, 1

Economy: Bonn Agreement, 66–67; communication and, 71; decline, 31–34; incremental growth, 185; Taliban's strategy, 92. *See also* Failed states

Edgar, David, 114

Education, 32, 72–73; human capital and, 73; literacy, 73; violent attacks on, 94

Education committees, 89

Egyptian Muslim Brotherhood, 5

Eichmann, Adolf, 143

Electrical grids, 31

Electric shocks, 6

Electronic media, 97

Elizabeth II, 49

Entrepreneurs, violence against, 93. *See also* Violent tactics

Escape from the Taliban, 16

Extortion, through taxation, 129

Fahim, Mohammed Qasim, 58

Failed states, 32, 33t

Falk, Richard, 46

Fatwas, 13

Fazlullah, Mullah, 146, 152

Fear, 30, 96

Female suicide bomber, Haqqanis and, 142

Feminist Majority, 41

Ferguson, Richard, 40

Fighting skills, 101–2

Films, 181

Finance committees, 89

Firearms. *See* Weapons

Firooz, Sosan, 62–63, 181

First World War, 4

Folk songs, 31

Foreign noncombatants, 91

Four-legged warfare, 101–2

Fox, Liam, 116

Franks, Tommy, 55

Fulford, Alex "Sketch," 55

Funding, 89–90. *See also* Hawala

Gadahn, Adam, 77, 123, 124t, 139, 179

Galula, David, 69, 95, 161

Gates, Robert, 105, 153, 158

Gerdi Jangal Shura, 88

German Taliban, 143–44

Germany, Haqqanis' connection to, 142

Ghilzais, 11, 12t

Ghurghusht, 11, 12t

Gibbs, Calvin, 158–60

Giesbrecht, Beverly, 131–32

Girardet, Edward, 8

Globalization, 30, 31

Grand Mufti of Jerusalem, 143

Greenburg, Paul, 178

Green hell, 110–12

Green-on-blue attacks, 90, 118–20

Green-on-green attacks, 118

Gromov, Boris, 8, 176

Guerilla legend, 104

Gul, Ghazi, 97

Gul, Hamid, 20, 149–50, 179

Gul, Juma, 110, 186

Hanjour, Hani, 77
Haq, Abdul, 53
Haqqani, Jalaluddin, 20, 87, 101, 140–42
Haqqani, Sirajuddin, 87, 140, 141–42
Haqqani network, 87–88, 140–42,
    148t, 153
Hare, Robert, 159
Harems. *See* Celestial harems
Haroon, Saad, 85–86, 181
Hasan, Nidal Malik, 76–78, 176
Hashemi, Rahmatullah, 55–56
Hashish, 37
Hawala, 89–90. *See also* Funding
Hazara Democratic Party, 83
Hazarajat, 27
Hazaras, 6, 22, 83, 101
Health care, 33, 73, 96
Hearst, Patty, 129
Hekmatyar, Gulbuddin, 5, 6, 20, 99, 109,
    144–45. *See also* Hezb-i-Islami
Helmand River, 3
Herat Province (2007), 120
Hezb-i-Islami, 109, 140, 144–45, 148t
Highway robbery, 128–29
Hindi films. *See* Films
Hindu Kush (mountain ranges), 2
Hindus, in Afghanistan, 30, 41
Hitler, Adolf, 143
Hizb el Islami-Gulbuddin (HiG). *See*
    Hezb-i-Islami
Horses, 103, 105–6
Houn Dawg, 117
Human development, 185
Human rights, 5
Human Rights Report (1998), 33
Human Rights Watch, 23
Human Terrain System (HTS), 167
Humor, 61–62
Hunter, Kenny, 175

Ikwan. *See* Muslim Brotherhood
Impersonation, 119
IMU (Islamic Movement
    of Uzbekistan), 48
India: Bollywood movies, 181; Deobandi
    Islam, 13; Mughal Empire, 3; partition,
    147; Sepoy revolt, 13, 196n.85
Indian Mutiny, 13, 196n.85
Individual weapons, 104–5

Infiltration, 119–21
Information operations, 96–98
Innocence of the Muslims, 109
Insurgency: defined, 24–25; elements, 24;
    first phase of, 25–26; general template,
    24–27, 27t; landscape and, 1–2;
    second phase of, 26; third phase
    of, 26
Insurgent groups: al Qaeda, 137–40, 148t.
    See also al Qaeda; Haqqani network,
    140–42, 148t; Hezb-i-Islami, 144–45,
    148t; Taliban. *See* Taliban; TTP,
    145–47, 148t
Intelligence, 90–91, 91t
Interior Affairs committees, 89
Interior Ministry Forces, 69
International Muslim
    Women's Union, 175
International Red Cross, 52
International Security Assistance Force
    (ISAF), 66, 114
Internet, ban on, 30, 31
Interservices Intelligence Directorate
    (ISI) of Pakistan, 20–21; al Qaeda and,
    153; military leaders, 153; S Wing, 153;
    Taliban and, 150–51, 153
In the Hands of the Taliban (Ridley), 97
Investment, 32
Iran, 153–54; Afghan refugee camps in, 6;
    aiding insurgents in Afghanistan, 147;
    bomb components in Afghanistan
    from, 114; flow of weapons to Taliban,
    59, 105, 154; leadership, 40, 154; Shia
    Muslims, 154; Taliban and, 40, 154;
    Taliban's relation with, 40, 154
Iranian diplomats, killing of, 40
Iron horses. *See* Motorcycles
ISAF (International Security Assistance
    Force), 66, 114
Islam, 2, 13. *See also* Deobandism
Islamic Emirate of Afghanistan, 21
Islamic Movement of
    Uzbekistan (IMU), 48
Islamic Revolutionary Guard Corps
    (IRGC), 154
Islamism, defined, 13

Jama'a Islami party, 20
Jamiat Ulema-e Islam in Quetta, 50

Jawbreaker, 47. *See also* U.S. military action, in Afghanistan
Jezails, 2, 192n.5
Jirga, 5. *See also* Loya Jirga
Jokes. *See* Humor

Kabir, Maulavi Abdul, 87
Kabul: Babur and, 3; beauty school, 61; bombing of Indian Embassy in, 141; British capture of, 3, 4; civil servants, 71; Defense Ministry attack, 120; high-profile attacks, 133; post-Taliban, 64, 174–75; Serena, 108; Skateistan Park, 181; Taliban's conquest of, 21, 26, 31; U.S. embassy in, 181; woman suicide bomber, 109. *See also* Bonn Agreement
Kabul Beauty School, 177
Kabul Sports Stadium, 34
Kabul University, 7, 72
Kabul Zoo, 174
Kahn, Imran, 179
Kakar, Malalai, 69–70, 179
Kalashnikov. *See* AK-47
Kandahar: Kakar, Malalai, 70, 179; as murder capital, 133; Northern Alliance's march to, 54; Omar, 21, 22, 24; post-Taliban, 60; Sar-e-Poza prison in, 53–54; theatrical escapes of Taliban, 121; U.S. Army Rangers, 49; zone defense of Taliban, 57
Kandahar, 16
Karlanris, 11
Karzai, Hamid, 11, 60, 65, 66
Khan, Ayub, 4
Khan, Farooq, 133
Khan, Genghis, 2
Khan, Imran, 150
Khan, Ismail, 58–59
Khan, Kabir, 181
Khan, Mohammad Daoud, 4, 5
Khomeini, Ayatollah, 154
Khorshid, 74–75
Khost Province, 119
Khwazak, 35
Khyber Pakhtunkhwa, 82, 87
Khyber Pass, 2, 192n.3
Kidnapping, 130–31
Kilcullen, David, 168

Kim (Kipling), 4
Kipling, Rudyard, 4
Kite flying, 13, 61
The Kite Runner, 15
Koran, burning of, 75
Kunduz: Nekmuhammad, 8–9, 175; Northern Alliance, 53, 58; Taliban poisoned girls, 119

Laden, Osama bin, 102, 123
Landscape, of Afghanistan, 1–2
Landsdale, Edward, 161
La Republica (newspaper), 131
Lashkar-e-Tabya (LET), 146
Laughing, 61–62
Lawrence, T. E., 161, 169–70
Leaders/leadership: al Qaeda, 138–39; Haqqani network, 142; Hezb-i-Islami, 145; Iran, 154; ISI, 153; Quetta Shura, 86–87; Taliban, 21, 85; TTP, 146–47
Lee, Barbara, 138
Leno, Mavis, 41, 176
LET (Lashkar-e-Tabya), 146
Liam and Theo, 115–16
Lindh, John Phillip Walker, 122–23, 124t, 179, 228n.147
The Lion of Kabul (Hunter), 175
Literacy, 73. *See also* Education
Lothian, Graeme, 113
Loya Jirga, 5, 66
Loyd, Paula, 167
Lunge, 104
Lute, Douglas E., 85

Mad Max style, 105
Madrassas, 20, 107–8, 199n.6
Mafioso, 129
Malik, Rehman, 147
Mao Tse Tung, 25, 82
Marjan (lion), 16–17, 174–75
Martyrs committees, 89
Massoud, Ahmed Shah, 22, 51
Mastrogiacomo, Danielle, 131
Mazar-e-Sharif, 21–22, 26, 53, 154
McCarthy, Brent, 121
McChrystal, Stanley, 85, 153, 154, 158, 168
McKiernan, David, 158
McKinney, Cynthia, 46–47, 107, 176

McNeill, Daniel, 154
Medical services, 33
Medicins Sans Fontieres (MSF). *See*
    Doctors Without Borders
Mehsud, Baitullah, 82, 130, 145–46
Mehsud, Hakimullah, 146, 179
Mehsud, Latif, 147
Mental health, 33
Mercury compounds poison, 119
Metcalfe, Daniel T., 178
MI-8, 105
MI-24, 105
Military council committees, 89
Military prisons, 65
Mines, 114
Ministry of Defence of the United
    Kingdom, 116
Mir, Haroun, 90
Miram Shah, Pakistan, 141
Miramshah Shura, 87–88
Mohammed (Prophet), 12, 30
Mohammed, Atta, 53
Mohammed, Khaled Sheik,
    106–7, 153
Mongols, 2–3
Mortenson, Greg, 65, 177
Motorcycles, 105
Mountains, 1, 2. *See also* specific
    mountains
Mount Nowshak, 2
Mount Whitney, 2, 192n.7
Mughal Empire, 3
Mujahedeen: antipersonnel mine, 114;
    differences among parties, 8; German,
    143; ISI, 149; Pakistani leaders and, 20;
    Saudis aid to, 19; Soviet Army and, 2;
    U.S. aid to, 6, 19, 149
Mullah Dadullah. *See* Akhund, Mullah
    Dadullah
Mullahs, 26
Mullen, Michael, 153
Multitactical attacks, 120
Murder, 132–33
Murder holes, 112–13. *See also* Snipers
Murphy, Michael, 164, 178
Musharaf, Pervez, 150–51
Music, 175
Muslim Brotherhood, 13
Muslims, life of, 30

Muslim Youth Organization of
    Afghanistan, 5
Muttaqi, Amir Khan, 87
Myers, Richard, 53

Naing, Than, 168, 178
Najibullah, Mohammad, 8, 21, 68
Narco-terrorism, 129
Narcotics trafficking, 127, 129, 133, 134t
National Institute of Music, Kabul, 175
NATO, 119
Navy SEALS, 178
Nazis, 6, 143, 197n.89
Nekmuhammad, 8–9, 175–76
Nonviolent intimidation tactics, 96
Northern Alliance, xviii; cluster bombs,
    51–52; Jawbreaker and, 47; march of,
    51–53; mountain fighters, 50;
    Operation Anaconda, 51; Tajiks and
    Uzbeks, 101–2
Northwest Frontier Provinces (NWFP).
    See Khyber Pakhtunkhwa
Nuclear weapons, Pakistan, 152–53

Obama, Barack, 75, 180
O'Donnell, Mark, 166
Omar, Mullah, 11, 176; Baluchistan, 82;
    bin Laden and, 23, 24, 41; Haqqani,
    Sirajuddin and, 141–42; Internet, ban
    on, 30, 31; killing of local warlords, 21;
    Mehsud, Baitullah and, 82; missiles,
    108; mullahs and, 26; political charisma
    of, 22; profile of, 22–24; spokesman of,
    30; TTP and, 145, 146; United States
    and, 41, 42. *See also* Shuras; Taliban
Operation Anaconda, 51
Opium, 75, 215n.212
Orakzai, Misri Khan, 132
Organization of Islamic Cooperation, 154
Osama, 15–16

Pace, Peter, 48–49
Pakistan, 147, 149–53; Afghan refugees,
    51; al Qaeda, 153; ammonium nitrate,
    114; Dadullah and, 122; mujahedeen
    and, 20; munitions, 114; nuclear
    weapons program, 152–53; Pashtun
    belt, 10, 205n.3; religious schools, 29;
    Shuras, 83–88; suicide bombings in,

109; TTP, 146; U.S. relations with, 147, 149. *See also* Interservices Intelligence Directorate (ISI) of Pakistan; Taliban
Pakol, 104
Panzerfaust, 104
Parwan Detention Facility, 75
Pashtun belt, 10
Pashtunistan, 205n.3
Pashtuns, 9–11, 11t, 12t. *See also* Afghans
Pashtunwali, 10, 11t
People for the Ethical Treatment of Animals (PETA), 47, 64
Percovich, Oliver, 74
Pershing, John, 69, 160–61
Peshawar Shura, 87
PETA (People for the Ethical Treatment of Animals), 47, 64
Petraeus, David, 85, 158, 162, 168, 169, 180
Philippines, counterinsurgency in, 6, 69, 160–61, 163t
Pickup trucks, 105
Pink mist, 113–18
Poison, 118–19
Poitier, Sidney, 41
Police force, 69, 95
Political Affairs committees, 89
Pomper, Stephen, 6, 193n.37
Posttraumatic stress disorder (PTSD), 7
Powell, Colin, 43
Print media, 97
Prisoners and Refugees committees, 89
Prophet, re-creating time of, 30
Prostitution, 64
Provincial reconstruction team (PRT), 67–68
Psychopath, 159
Psychopathy, 159
PTSD (posttraumatic stress disorder), 7
Public gatherings, suicide attacks on, 108
Public revenge killings, 34
Punjabis, 84

Quds Force, 154
Quetta Shura, 83–87. *See also* Shuras
Qutb, Sayyid, 13–14, 197n.92

Rabbani, Burhanuddin, 5, 21, 66
Radio, 32, 71, 94

Radio Mullah. *See* Fazlullah, Mullah
Radio Peace station, 179
Rafsanjani, Hashemi, 154
Rahman, Abdul, 132
Rahmani, Muhammad Hassan, 86
Raiding operations, 102
Rather, Dan, 157
Razzak, Mullah Abdul, 87
Reagan, Ronald, 6
Reconnaissance, 102
Recruitment committees, 89
Recruits, of Taliban, 29–30
Regional Military Shura. *See* Shuras
Rehman, Waliur, 146
Reintegration efforts, 186
Religions, 2, 192n.10
Religious council committees, 89
Religious schools, 29
Repatriation committees, 89
Reynolds, Christopher, 113, 177
Rezayee, Shaim, 73
Ridley, Yvonne, 49, 97, 132, 175
Rings, of support, 88
Road network, 1
Roadside bombs, 113–18
Robberies, 128–30
Rodriguez, Debbie, 61, 177
Rogers, Mike, 153
Royal Thai Army Headquarters, 162
RPG-7 Soviet rocket launcher, 104, 111
Rules, for Afghan counterinsurgency: effective training, 172; engaging and promoting local efforts, 168, 169–70; metrics for measuring status, 172–73; pressure tactics, 168; seize and hold initiative, 167–68; sustain area ownership, 165–66
Rumsfeld, Donald, 42, 47, 97
Rushdie, Salman, 150

Sadiqui, Aafia, 106–7, 177
Safi, Ali, 39–40
Salafism, 12–13, 31t
Salafists: defined, 196n.75; Deobandi movement, 13; ideology, 12; Muslim Brotherhood and, 13
Sameena, 110
Sanctions, on Taliban, 42–43
Sanctuary, 82

Sarbanis, 11, 12t
Sar-e-Poza prison, 53–54
Saudi Arabia, 6, 19, 23, 34
Sawyer, Diane, 61
Schoolgirls, poisoning of, 118–19
Schroen, Gary, 47, 177
Scroggins, Deborah, 177
Security, 34
Sendero Luminoso, 129
Sepoy revolt. *See* Indian Mutiny
September 11, 2001, terrorist
    attacks, 43, 49, 77
Shabana, 37
Shadow economy, 194n.46
Shah, Abdullah, 59, 60
Shah, Mohammed Zahir, 4–5, 65
Sharia, 5, 34, 132
Shells, 103
Shia Islam, 6, 40
Shuras: committees, 83; constitution and,
    5; Gerdi Jangal, 88; Miramshah, 87–88;
    Peshawar, 87; Quetta, 83–87
Sick, Gary, 46
Singing, 31
Skateistan Park, Kabul, 181
Slavery, abolition of, 5
Snipers, 112–13
Soccer, 30, 175
Social services, 32
Soviet Union: atheism, 19, 62; collapse of,
    8; international prestige projects,
    engaging Afghans in, 7; invasion of
    Afghanistan, xvii, 5–9, 66, 149; jihad
    against the, 141; military and economic
    aid to Afghanistan, 4; mujahedeen
    campaign against, 144; munitions for
    Afghans, 8, 114; treaty of friendship, 4;
    withdrawal from Afghanistan, 8, 176
Stalin, Joseph, 129
Starvation, 64–65
Stinger missiles, 8, 51
Strategy(ies), 92–93. *See also* Tactics
Streep, Meryl, 41
Stumpf, Jason, 166
Substance abusers, 37
Sufi Muslims, 61
Suicide attacks, 107–10, 141. *See also*
    Tactics
Sunni Islam, 2, 13, 23, 40

Sustained human development, 185
Swat Valley, 37, 152

Taber, Robert, 161–62
Tactics: ambush attacks, 110–12;
    betrayal, 119–21; blitzkrieg warfare,
    105–6; four-legged warfare, 101–2;
    impersonation, 119–21; infiltration,
    119–21; information operations,
    96–98; murder holes and snipers,
    112–13; nonviolent intimidation
    tactics, 96; pink mist, 113–18; poison,
    118–19; purpose, type, and examples
    of, 98t; roadside bombs, 113–18;
    suicide attacks, 107–9; tough fighters,
    101–2; violent, 93–96; weapons, 103–5.
    See also Strategy(ies)
Tajik: mountain fighting skills, 101–2;
    Northern Alliance and, 50, 51, 101–2;
    Taliban and, 63–64
Taliban: al Qaeda's tactical
    recommendations, 102; apostasy, 133;
    bank robbery, 129–30; blowback from
    crime, 133–35; boys and young men,
    29–30, 107–8; Buddhas of Bamiyan
    and, 12; committee, 89;
    counterintelligence, 90–91, 91t; crime
    matrix, 134t; criminal activities, 127;
    criminal operations, 127; cruelty,
    15–16, 30; Deobandi Islam and, 13;
    destructing non-Islamic culture,
    12–13; diaspora, 81–83; fall, 53–55;
    fighting skills, 101–2; foreign relations,
    40–42; four-legged warfare, 101–2;
    funding, 89–90; goals and implications
    of agenda on daily life, 31t;
    governmental structure, 81; highway
    robbery, 128–29; insurgency template,
    24–27, 27t; intelligence, 90–91;
    interrogation, 90–91; introduction to,
    19–21; kidnapping, 130–31; leaders,
    21; life under, 31–34; local appearance,
    104; modernity and, 30–31; murder,
    132–33; Najibullah and, 21; narcotics
    trafficking, 127, 129, 133, 134t; NATO
    soldiers, attack, 119; Pashtunwali and,
    10; phases of warfare and, 27t; poison,
    118–19; political and social codes,
    38–39; reaction to defeat of, 60–65;

recruits, 29–30; resistance to, 36–38; retreat of, 50–51; rings of support, 88; robberies, 128–30; RPG-7, 104; Salafism and, 12–13; sanctions on, 42–43; sanctuary, 82; security functions, 90–91; settling tribal scores, 21–22; snipers, 112–13; sources of weapons, 105; strategies, 92; suicide attack, 107–9; taxation, 129; temporary end of fighting, 58–59; tough fighters, 101–2; traits of, 31t; use of camouflage, 112–13; vehicles, 105–6; weapons, 103–5. *See also* Afghans; al Qaeda; Tactics

Tasker, Liam, 116

Taxation, 129

Tehrik i-Taliban Pakistan (TTP), 145–47, 148t

Television, ban on, 31

Temporary dirt shelters, 102

Tentative Manual for Landing Operations, 161

Terrorizing, as strategy, 92

Thallium poison, 119

Theo. *See* Liam and Theo

Third Reich, 143

Thomas U, 143–44. *See also* German Taliban

Thompson, Robert, 161

Three Cups of Tea (Mortenson), 65

Timur, 3, 192n.11

Tipton Five. *See* British Tipton Taliban

Titanic, 60

Tora Bora, 51

Tough fighters, 101–2

Tourism, 82

Traps, 102

"Trenches," 102, 111

Tsarist Russia. *See* Soviet Union

Tsevam, Gennady. *See* Nekmuhammad

Tucker, Cynthia, 157

Ukraine, 9

Ulema council committees, 89

United States: financial aid, 4; First World War and, 161; military prisons, 65; Qutb on, 14; Taliban's relation with, 41–42; war in Afghanistan. *See* U.S. military action, in Afghanistan

Universal Declaration of Human Rights, 182

UN Office for Refugees in Quetta, 50

U.S. Agency for International Development (AID), 67

U.S. Air Force, 47

U.S. Army and Marine Corps Counterinsurgency Field Manual, 162, 164

U.S. Army Rangers, 49

U.S. Centers for Disease Control and Prevention, 33

U.S. Green Berets, 47

U.S. Mafia, 127

U.S. Marine Corps, Small Wars Manual, 161

U.S. military action, in Afghanistan, xvii–xviii; air base, 48; American generals, 158–60; British soldiers in, 48; divided opinion on, in United States, 46–47; early fighting, 48–49; end of, 58–59; fall of Taliban, 53–55; Global Hawk, 49; preparation, 45–48; protests against, in Pakistan, 46; Taliban's response to, 50–51. *See also* Counterinsurgency; Northern Alliance

USS *Michael Murphy* (DDG-112), 178

U.S. Special Forces, 45. *See also* Coalition Forces

Uzbekistan, 49

Uzbeks, 22, 58, 101

Valleys, 1

Values, 75

Vann, John Paul, 171

Vehicles, 105–6

Vernon, Chris, 84

Viet Cong, 25, 104, 165

Vietnam: counterinsurgency, 7, 25, 26, 161–62, 163t

Villagers: bullying, 25; cluster bombs and, 52; Coalition Forces and, 103; communications and, 71; counterinsurgency and, 171; insurgency and, 27; nonphysical resistance of, 36, 94; post-Taliban concern, 64; secret police and, 30; self-defense efforts, 94. *See also* Afghans

Violent tactics: civil servants and police, 95; communications, 94–95; economic and entrepreneurial enterprises, 93; education, 94. *See also* Tactics

Wahhabi, 6
War of the Flea: The Classic Study of Guerrilla Warfare (Taber), 161
"Waxing," 159
Waziristan, 82, 87, 112
Weapons, 103–5
Weeping Mullah. *See* Fazlullah, Mullah
White, Ashley, 166–67
Wilson, Charlie, 141
Winslet, Kate, 61
Women: abduction of, 109; Afghan refugee, 41; *Burka Avenger*, depiction in, of, 181; civil and criminal protections for, 5; education of, 36, 72–73, 94, 182; health care and, 33; illiteracy rate, 72; intermarriage of, 84; Islam and, 97; Islamists and, 14; leftists and, 14, mental health of, 33; murder of, 132; poisoning of, 118–19; police officers in Afghanistan, 132, 179
Woo, Karen, 133
World Trade Center, 49, 106. *See also* September 11, 2001, terrorist attacks

Young Intellectuals of Afghanistan, 39
Young men, as Taliban recruits, 29–30. *See also* Suicide attacks
Yousafzai, Malala, 37–38, 151–52, 179
Yusuf Islam, 33, 180–81

Zadrans, 141
Zakat, 129
Zakhilwal, Mohammad Omar, 175
Zaki, Zakia, 71–72, 179
Zakir, Mullah Abdul Qayoum, 86
Zardad, 177
Zardad, Faryadi Sarwar, 59–60
Zardad's Dog, 60
Zarmina, 35–36, 182
Zia-ul-Haq, Mohammad, 149
Zoroastrianism, 2

About the Author

MARK SILINSKY is a 31-year veteran of the defense intelligence community. He has served as a senior analyst in U.S. Army intelligence; an Army civilian foreign area officer (FAO) for Eurasia, Russian language; an Africa analyst for the Defense Intelligence Agency; an action officer for the Joint Staff, J5; and a research fellow as part of the Exceptional Analyst Program. He was graduated Phi Beta Kappa from the University of Southern California; received an MPhil in international relations from Oxford University, under the supervision of Sir Michael Howard; and took an MS in international development from Tulane University. He was graduated from the National Intelligence University, the Naval War College, and the National Defense University. He is also a 2008 graduate of the Afghanistan Counterinsurgency Academy, located near Kabul.